HOMEMAKERS TREASURED COOKBOOK

COMPILED BY

Madison County (Alabama) Extension Homemakers

Printed by
HICKLIN PRINTING CO.
713 Arcadia Circle, NW
Huntsville, Alabama 35801

DEDICATION

The Madison County Extension Homemakers wish to dedicate our cookbook to our county agents who have contributed so much to our organization, in memory of our deceased agents, and in honor of those living and still contributing.

Miss May I. Curaton—1920	Deceased
Miss Evelyn Payton	Deceased
Miss Elizabeth Deloney	Deceased
Mrs. Lillie Maude Alexander	
Mrs. Oenone Cook	Deceased
Miss Christine Huber	
Mrs. Jacquelyn B. Outlaw Ifill	
Ms. Victoria Coffee	

National Organization Colors—Purple And Gold

Copyright 1988
By Madison County Extension Homemakers
All Rights In This Book
Reserved Including The Right
To Reproduce This Book Or Parts
Thereof In Any Form—Printed In U.S.A.
Library Of Congress Catalog Number 81-50802
Standard Book Number 87397-192-2

HISTORY

Extension homemakers clubs began in the very early 1900s when they were known as tomato clubs. Mothers and daughters went to learn to can tomatoes and other homemaking skills, sort of a "Country Woman's College." The idea then, as now, is to spread teachings to neighborhood women, not just club members. Toward a goal of better homes and communities, we learn about citizenship, leadership, workmanship, and friendship.

In 1914 the United States Congress passed an act making the Extension Service available in all states, supported by the United States and county governments. Dr. J. F. Duggar, head of the agriculture department at Auburn University, began training students as farm agents and home demonstration agents to go into the fields and homes of rural Alabama and teach new ideas by demonstration. Our first agent came to teach the women how to can tomatoes. She wanted a large open place to work and selected the Monrovia Blacksmith Shop. It had a continuous fire, a hot water vat, and plenty of running water from the mill race. They canned tomatoes and they kept. Once-a-month all-day demonstrations followed.

Under the guidance of these agents, home demonstration clubs were formed. They gave the demonstrations and directed the clubs' activities. As the agents' responsibilities increased, they could no longer give the demonstrations to each club. Club representatives now went to the courthouse for the demonstration and presented the program to their club members. This presented opportunities for leadership development as we assumed more responsibility for our activities. Clubs were organized in town as all homemakers were anxious to improve.

In 1965 we became Extension Homemakers Clubs, and in the early seventies, independent of the Extension Service. Since the demonstrations given by the home agents are open to everyone, we continue to get many of our programs from them and participate in the workshops they provide.

We have a strong county organization of 27 clubs, urban and rural, members of the state, national, and international Homemakers organization, the largest educational organization in the world. Our county has sent many leaders to serve on the state board. In recent years Madison County has provided a state president, vice-presidents, health and safety chairman, public relations and newsletter editor, international and citizenship chairman, and district director.

Through the years we have had a wide variety of programs and projects from the first countywide reception held upstairs over the county feed store—quite a nice affair after the party dresses managed to pass the cotton seed meal and feed sacks down below—to this year's cultural arts show and tea held at the Steamboat Gothic House. Everyone wore party dresses to these two occasions, but dress for most other occasions really has changed. We used to look forward to a new dress and hat, gloves, etc., for the spring dress review and fall achievement luncheon. Now gone are the days of hats and gloves. You know how it is so warm in late October, especially when you have a new winter outfit. Well, after one of our luncheons, the hat of one of our members blew off and sailed away; maybe that was the end of the hat era.

To produce better beds and increase the use of cotton, 300 mattresses were the goal in 1935, that is, making the mattresses from "scratch."

In 1947 the Madison County Safety Council was organized by a home agent to encourage farm, home, and highway safety. In cooperation with the health department, a rural survey was conducted to determine how many homes were wired and had wells or cisterns. Other safety activities included first-aid kits in every member's home; encouraged safety habits among schoolchildren; studied water supplies and ways to keep them safe; community clean-up; how members could help in civil defense; and advocated necessary legislation.

Making quilts, showing them, and selling them always has been popular. Some of the early money-making projects were picking cotton, $4.66 for 930 pounds; presenting plays; selling articles at curb markets; and providing meals for a Jersey sale at $.50 a plate. A March 1939 order of business included acquiring pigs and each member's raising one for a barbecue in July.

Now a typical year includes a monthly meeting with educational programs presented by club members and sometimes by guest experts. In the spring, home-sewn fashions are shown; and during National Homemakers Week, a tea and cultural arts display are held. June is state meeting time at Auburn University. A wide variety of workshops and learning sessions are presented. We like to think of it as "battery-charging" time. Most plan a family outing during the summer months, and in October the achievement luncheon is awards time.

We have come a long way and look forward to the challenges the 1980s present to us. We are better homemakers, citizens, and leaders because of our membership and the Extension Home Agents' support and the programs they present.

UPDATE TO HISTORY SECTION FOR COOKBOOK

The 1980s have brought a change in image. In answer to the growing need for volunteers, homemakers are responding. Nationally, homemakers is one of the world's largest volunteer educational organizations. With successful educational projects such as promoting seat belt use and the ABC's of nursery safety, we are also supporters of Child Life at Huntsville Hospital, goats for the people of Haiti, and many other causes. In 1988 we hosted the Alabama Extension Homemakers Council Meeting here in Huntsville and one of our own was installed as president of the state organization.

We have met the challenge of the 1980s by changing to meet the needs of our membership and our communities. The future is bright with our involvement in a nation-wide project, Family Community Leadership. It is a leadership training program, offered to women, teaching them the skills to affect public policy. We want to make a "difference" in Madison County.

Mary Anne Riley
South Parkway

RECIPE FOR A SUCCESSFUL YEAR FOR MADISON COUNTY HOMEMAKERS

1 spoonful of enthusiasm
¼ cup of helpful members
2 ozs. of easy mix preparation
3 drops of heart and soul
Sugar to taste

4 cups of all-purpose effort
⅔ cup of smiles
1 T. unclouded vision
5 ozs. self-rising prayer
Dash of spice

Forget the bitterness

Put all ingredients into 1 club—any size. Double-check everything. Never permit ingredients to become lumpy or separated. Club should be of right temperature—never lukewarm. Time is of the greatest importance while ingredients are being used. After several tries, everything will come naturally. Tears over first efforts are perfectly natural. The results are well worth the endeavor. The recipe will produce only enough to serve the purpose. Anything extra can be shared but cannot be stored. This is only to be used with the people who care about the club. Serve your recipe topped with love, decorated with trust. And after all the work and time and toil, sit back and say, "Father, thank you for loving us."

Mrs. L. M. Taylor
President, Madison County Extension Homemakers
1980-1981

HOMEMAKER'S CREED

As a Homemaker Club Member:

I BELIEVE that through working together in a group, we can enlarge our vision and enrich the lives of all people.

I BELIEVE that the greatest force which molds character comes from the home and I pledge myself to create a home which is morally wholesome, spiritually inspiring, mentally stimulating, and physically healthful and convenient.

I BELIEVE in my work, as a homemaker, and accept the responsibilities it offers to be helpful to others and to create a more contented family and community life, so that in the end life will be more satisfying.

I BELIEVE in God as the ruling factor in all life, a God who inspires in us strength, endurance, tolerance, and faith for our careers as mothers, homemakers and community leaders.

CONTENTS

History
Appetizers 9
Beverages 13
Breads 27
Cakes and Frostings 66
Desserts 116
Pies and Pastries 139
Candies and Cookies 174
Cooking Lite 201
Eggs 222
Meats 228
Poultry and Game 278
Salads and Salad Dressing 304
Seafood 341
Canning and Freezing 351
Miscellaneous 365
Vegetables 422
Helpful Hints 460
Index 466

WELCOME SOMEONE HOME
The Alabama Reunion '89

Cookbook Revised during the Celebration of
"Welcome Someone Home —
The Alabama Reunion '89"

SAUSAGE BALLS

BALLS:

1 lb. ground chuck beef
½ lb. good pork sausage
1 tsp. Worcestershire Sauce
¼ cup onion
celery salt, garlic powder to taste
1 cup bread or cracker crumbs
2 tbsp. tomato catsup

Mix and roll into balls. Fry or bake until brown on both sides. Remove from pan.

SAUCE:

1 bottle Heinz Chili Sauce
10 oz. jar grape jelly
juice of 1 lemon
powdered ginger to taste

Cook until thick and jelly is well dissolved.

Add sausage balls to sauce when ready to serve and reheat both in heavy stoneware covered pot. Serve with assorted crackers and colorful toothpicks.

Rachel Sturdivant, University

PARTY RYE SQUARES

½ lb. medium-sharp cheddar cheese, grated
1 cup mayonnaise
1 onion, grated
2 tsp. Worcestershire Sauce
6 slices bacon, fried crisp and crumbled
2 5/8 oz. slivered almonds
salt and pepper to taste
1 loaf sliced party rye bread

Mix all ingredients and spread on party rye slices. Bake in 400° oven for 10 minutes. Can be made ahead and frozen.

Susan Bullington, South Parkway

SHRIMP SANDWICHES

8 oz. cream cheese
juice of one lemon
1 small onion, chopped
1 stalk celery chopped
1 lb. cooked shrimp, chopped
1 tbsp. bell pepper, chopped
¼ cup chopped fresh parsley
salt and pepper to taste

Mix cream cheese and lemon juice. Add other ingredients. Spread on buttered bread. Can also be used to stuff cucumbers. Makes 25 sandwiches.

Libby Livingston, Big Cove

CHILI CHEESE DIP

1 can chili without beans
8 oz. cream cheese
chopped onion to top

Mix together cream cheese and chili. Heat to simmer. Take off heat and add chopped onion. Serve in chafing dish with Fritoes.

Libby Livingston, Big Cove

RHONDA'S ORANGE-COCONUT BALLS

1 6 oz. can frozen orange juice
1 16 oz. box vanilla wafers (crushed)
1 stick margarine (melted)
1 16 oz. box confectioners sugar
½ to 1 cup chopped nuts
1⅓ cups shredded coconut

Mix first five ingredients thoroughly. Form into small balls and roll in coconut. More flavorful when made at least one day before serving.

Mildred Fanning, Monrovia

CHOCOLATE COATED PRETZELS

1 lb. white chocolate
1 med. size bag of pretzels (round or stick)

Place chocolate in top of a double boiler. Place over hot water and stir until melted. DO NOT place double boiler on the stove (this will thicken and not melt thin enough to dip your pretzels in). The hot water from your faucet will be hot enough. When chocolate has melted use a fork or ice pick to dip the pretzels in the chocolate (the ice pick fits nicely in holes of pretzels for dipping).

Mildred Fanning, Monrovia

RICE KRISPIE CHEESE BALLS

2 cups flour
½ lb. extra sharp cheese (grated)
2 cups Rice Krispies
2 cups grated cheddar cheese
2 sticks soft oleo
pinch of salt
¼ tsp. cayenne pepper

Have cheese and oleo at room temperature. Mix oleo and cheese with hands. Add salt and flour, work together. Add Rice Krispies and mix well. Make into small balls. Place on baking sheet. Press lightly with fork. Bake at 375° for 10 minutes. Place on paper towels. Makes about 45.

Mildred Fanning, Monrovia

WADIS CHEESE BALL

2 small pks. cream cheese or 1 large package
2 pks. thin sliced corn beef
1 bunch fresh green onion
1 tbsp. soy sauce
1 tsp. Accent
1 cup pecans

Chop corn beef and onions. Mix together with soy sauce, Accent, and ½ cup pecans. Knead in cream cheese, form into ball and roll in remainder of pecans. Better if made a day before and stored in refrigerator.

Mildred Fanning, Monrovia

TACO DIP

(Layers)
1st—1 16 oz. can refried beans
2nd—2 mashed avocados (lemon juice added for color)
3rd—1 16 oz. carton sour cream
4th—1 8 oz. jar Pace Picante Sauce or Old El Paso Taco Sauce
5th—½ to ¾ cup chopped black olives
6th—½ to ¾ cup chopped green onion
7th—2 tomatoes chopped
8th—1 cup grated cheddar cheese

Use a shallow nine or ten inch (round or square) dish. Serve with Tortilla Chips. Chill 2 to 4 hours before serving.

Patty Shepard, South Parkway

GREAT CRACKERS

1 16 oz. oyster crackers
2 6 oz. Pepperidge Farms Plain Fish Crackers
⅔ cup vegetable oil
1 1 oz. Hidden Valley Ranch Salad Dressing Mix

In large bowl put oil and salad dressing mix, mix well. Add crackers and mix until oil disappears. Empty on to a 9X10 pan. Bake in oven for 10 minutes at 170º. Let cool and store in a covered container. Serves a large group.

Myrtle Briethaupt, Westbury

HOT HAM SANDWICHES

1 stick butter
4 tbsp. chopped onion
4 tbsp. horseradish mustard
4 tsp. poppy seed

Swiss cheese slices
Ham slices (from leftover baked ham)

Make paste of first four ingredients, spread on sandwich buns. Place ham and swiss cheese on buns. Wrap sandwiches in foil. Bake at 350° for 20 minutes.

Joan Shady, Athens Pike

COTTAGE CHEESE-SPINACH CUPS

1½ cups low-fat cottage cheese
2 (10 oz.) pkg. frozen chopped spinach, thawed
4 eggs, beaten

1 tsp. salt
¼ tsp. pepper
¼ tsp. ground nutmeg
miniature cream cheese pastry shell

Drain cottage cheese well using a strainer; set aside. Drain chopped spinach well, and press between layers of paper towels to remove excess moisture. Combine cottage cheese, spinach, and next 4 ingredients; stir well. Spoon 2 tsp. mixture into each pastry shell; bake at 350° for 25 to 30 minutes or until set. Yield: about 6 dozen.

Sue Vanhoozen, Madison Cross

MINIATURE CREAM CHEESE PASTRY SHELLS

3 cups all-purpose flour
¼ tsp. salt

1 (8 oz.) pkg. cream cheese, softened
1 cup butter or margarine

Combine flour and salt. Cut in cream cheese and butter until mixture resembles coarse crumbs. Press mixture together with hands until it forms a dough. Shape dough into 72 (1-inch) balls. Place each into an ungreased 1¾-inch muffin pan; press dough onto bottom and sides to form shells. Yield: 6 dozen.

Sue Vanhogzen, Madison Cross Roads

BEVERAGES

APRICOT MILK DRINK

2 cups milk
1 pt. vanilla ice cream
12 apricot halves, drained
1 T. lemon juice
¼ tsp. almond extract

In blender, blend 1 cup milk, ice cream, apricots, and lemon juice until smooth. Add remaining cup milk and almond extract. Serve immediately. Yield: 4½ cups.

Glenn Sanderson, Harvest

BANANA SLUSH FRUIT PUNCH

4 cups sugar
6 cups water
5 bananas, mashed
1 46-oz. can pineapple juice
1 12-oz. can frozen orange juice, thawed
1 12-oz. can frozen lemonade, thawed
Ginger ale

Dissolve sugar completely in water. Add bananas and juices. Place in ½-gallon container and freeze. Set slush out 20-25 minutes before serving. When ready to serve, place in punch bowl and pour ginger ale over slush.

Barbara Stluka, Davis Hills

BLENDER DRINK
(225 calories)

½ banana or ½ cup any fruit in season
¾ cup skim milk
1 egg
1 level T. frozen orange juice
Add sweetner to taste if desired

Winnie Linney, South Huntsville

CHOCOLATE MOCHA PUNCH

7 cups water
¼ cup instant coffee
2 cups nonfat dry milk
½ cup sugar
Dash of salt
1 qt. chocolate ice cream, softened
1 cup chilled whipping cream
Ground nutmeg

Heat 1 cup of water to boiling; dissolve instant coffee in water. Stir in remaining water, the dry milk, sugar, and salt. Refrigerate until chilled, 3 or 4 hours. Place ice cream in punch bowl. Pour chilled coffee mixture on ice cream; swirl ice cream throughout coffee mixture. Beat whipping cream in chilled small mixer bowl until very soft peaks form. Top punch with mounds of whipped cream. Sprinkle whipped cream with nutmeg. Serves 16 (about ¾ cup each).

Dorothy Mellette, Central

ECONOMY PUNCH

1 pkg. (2-qt size) presweetened Kool-Aid
1 tall can pineapple juice
1 lg. btl. ginger ale

Combine Kool-Aid and juice in gallon jar. Fill with water and mix well. Pour into punch bowl and add ginger ale.

Sandy Hughey, New Sharon

EGG NOG

2 eggs
1 can Eagle Brand milk
1 tsp. vanilla
¼ tsp. salt
1 qt. milk
½ pt. heavy cream, whipped
Nutmeg to taste

Combine well-beaten eggs, Eagle Brand milk, vanilla, and salt. Gradually beat in milk until well blended. Gently fold in whipped cream. Sprinkle with nutmeg.

Margaret Birchfield, Central

FROSTY GOLDEN PUNCH

1 6-oz. can frozen lemonade concentrate
1 6-oz. can frozen orange juice concentrate
1 6-oz. can frozen pineapple juice concentrate
2 lg. btls. (7 to 8 cups) ginger ale, chilled
1 12-oz. can apricot nectar, chilled
½ cup lemon juice
1 qt. lemon sherbet

Add water to frozen concentrates according to directions. Add chilled apricot nectar and lemon juice. Just before serving spoon in sherbet. Pour ginger ale down side of bowl. Makes 20-25 ½-cup servings.

Susie Hoffmeyer, Hillwood

FRUIT CRUSH

3 cups water
2 cups sugar
1 46-oz. can pineapple juice
1½ cups orange juice
¼ cup lemon juice
3 ripe bananas, mashed
3 qts. ginger ale, chilled

Mix water and sugar in saucepan; bring to boil. Remove from heat and stir in fruit juices and bananas. Pour into ice trays and freeze. Serve frozen cubes with ginger ale. May keep this in the freezer and serve a few at a time or place all in a punch bowl to serve.

Jesse Little, Harvest

GRAPE WINE

Use enough fully ripe grapes to fill ¾ full a 5-gallon crock, (about a bushel). Place washed grapes into crock and mash well with dasher. Cover with clean cloth and put crock top in place. Let stand 2 days then mash again; repeat 2 more times (6 days in all). Strain juice off mashed fruit and put juice into 5-gallon jug. A plastic jug can be used, but glass is better. The juice will not fill the jug. Add 10 pounds of sugar, enough warm water to fill jug up to where it starts to taper into neck. Place air lock or water seal on bottle and let set until all bubbles are gone from around top of juice. This may be 6 weeks or longer. You can either bottle at this point or add about a quart of warm water with as much sugar added to it as water will completely dissolve, about a cup. When bubbles stop again you may bottle.

Jeanie Marsh, Harvest

HOT APPLE CIDER PUNCH

½ gal. apple cider
1 cup lemon juice, lemon Jello, or lemon Kool-Aid
2 cups frozen orange juice
2 cinnamon sticks
1 tsp. whole cloves
1 cup sugar

Mix together and simmer 10 minutes.

Ruth Whitt, Madison Cross Roads

Beverages

HOT CHOCOLATE MIX I

4 cups powdered milk
1½ cups coffee creamer
2½ cups powdered sugar
¾ cup cocoa

Mix all ingredients together and store in closed container. Mix 4 tablespoons of mix with 1 cup of boiling water.

Carolyn Underwood, Hazel Green

HOT CHOCOLATE MIX II

1 8-qt. box Carnation instant nonfat dried milk
1 1-lb. box powdered sugar
1 1-lb. box Nestle's Quik
1 8-11 oz. jar Creamora

Mix entire contents of each item together in large container and mix well. Store tightly covered. To use: Fill cup about ¼ full of mix and add boiling water and stir well.

Pat Zurasky, Rainbow Mountain-South Parkway

HOT CIDER PUNCH I

2 cups water
1 T. ground nutmeg
1 T. ground ginger
6 whole cloves
6 whole allspice
2 2-in. cinnamon sticks
1 gal. apple cider
1 cup sugar
1½ cups firmly packed brown sugar

Combine water and spices in a large saucepan; cover and bring to a boil. Boil 10 minutes. Add apple cider and sugars. Simmer over low heat 10 minutes, stirring frequently. Serve hot. Yield: about 5 quarts.

Dorothy Mellette, Central

HOT CIDER PUNCH II

4 cups water
4 cups apple cider
⅔ cup orange-flavor Tang
¼ tsp. cinnamon
⅛ tsp. nutmeg
⅛ tsp. ground cloves

Combine all ingredients in a saucepan; blend well. Heat to boiling. Serve hot in punch cups or mugs. Makes about 2 quarts or 16 servings using mugs.

Roberta Freidman, Harvest

HOT DR PEPPER

Heat Dr Pepper to boiling point; do not boil. Serve as you would hot tea. Delicious!

Louise McGehee, Hurricane

HOT MOCHA MIX

1 cup cocoa
2 cups sugar
2 cups nonfat dry milk
2 cups nondairy coffee creamer
½ cup instant coffee

Mix well. To serve: Add 3 tablespoons mix to 1 cup of boiling water. Add ¼ teaspoon vanilla. Top with marshmallows or whipped cream.

Nancy Teasdale, South Huntsville

HOT PUNCH

Put in perk coffee pot:
4 cups cranberry juice
⅔ cup sugar
1 12-oz. can frozen lemonade, thawed
2 T. honey

Put in basket:
6 cloves
2 cinnamon sticks
1 lemon, sliced

Perk several minutes. Makes 10 cups hot punch.

Ethel Huse, Davis Hills

HOT SPICE TEA

2 cups sugar
1 tsp. nutmeg
1 tsp. cinnamon
1 tsp. allspice
4 cups cold water

4 tea bags
12 cups boiling water
1 cup orange juice
1 cup lemon juice
1 cup pineapple juice

Boil sugar, spices, and cold water 10 minutes. Put in tea bags; add boiling water, orange, lemon, and pineapple juices. Let steep 5 minutes. Let spices settle before serving. May be refrigerated and warmed over. Yield: 20 cups.

Mrs. Carl Vaughn (Helen); Submitted by daughter,
Mrs. Bob Irwin (Virginia), Monrovia

HOT TEA MIX

1 lg. jar Tang
1 cup instant tea, with sugar and lemon

1½ cups sugar
2 tsp. cinnamon
1 tsp. ground cloves
1 tsp. ground allspice

Mix all together, place in airtight container. To serve add 1 tablespoon mix to 1 cup boiling water.

Glenda Beard, Harvest

INSTANT RUSSIAN TEA I

2 cups sugar
2 cups Tang

½ cup instant tea
1 tsp. cinnamon
½ tsp. ground cloves

Mix together. Use 1 to 2 teaspoons per cup of water.

Dorothy Moore, New Sharon

INSTANT RUSSIAN TEA II

1 cup instant tea
2 cups Tang
2 pkgs. Wyler's lemonade mix

1¼ cup sugar
1 tsp. cinnamon
½ tsp. cloves

Mix all of above together. To serve use 3 or 4 teaspoons with water in a mug or glass. May be served cold or hot.

Mrs. O. V. Mitchell, Central

LIME ICE PUNCH

1 sm. pkg. lime gelatin dessert
1 cup sugar
1 qt. boiling water
Juice of 3 lemons
1 qt. cold water
46 oz. unsweetened pineapple juice
Green food coloring
1 qt. ginger ale

Dissolve gelatin and sugar in boiling water. Add juices, cold water, and enough food coloring to make it a pleasing color. Freeze in milk cartons. Remove from freezer 4 hours before serving. Add ginger ale and serve. Will be slushy. Serves 25.

Doris B. Sells, South Parkway

LIME JELLO PUNCH

2 pkgs. lime Jello
1½ cups sugar
2 no. 2 cans pineapple juice
1 sm. can frozen lemonade
1 sm. can frozen limeade
1 qt. ginger ale

Dissolve Jello as directed on package. Add sugar while Jello is hot. Add pineapple juice and frozen lemonade diluted to make 1 quart. Add limeade diluted as directed. Add ginger ale immediately before serving.

Martha Sparks, Rainbow Mountain

MILK PUNCH

1½ qts. vanilla ice cream, softened
3 cups chilled pineapple juice
⅓ cup orange juice or apricot juice
1 T. lemon juice
4 cups cold milk

In mixing bowl while beating softened ice cream, gradually add fruit juices, then milk. Pour into chilled cups and serve.

Glenn Sanderson, Harvest

MILKSHAKE

3 scoops vanilla (or favorite flavor) ice cream
1 egg
1 T. chocolate (or any flavor) syrup
Milk

Put ice cream in blender with egg and flavoring. Pour milk over ice cream until about ½ of the ice cream is covered. Blend on mix for about 30 seconds. May add fresh fruit, bananas, peaches, strawberries, etc., instead of flavoring. Yield: 2 6-ounce servings.

Roberta Friedman, Harvest

ORANGE AND PINEAPPLE PUNCH

½ gal. unsweetened orange juice
½ gal. unsweetened pineapple juice
½ gal. unsweetened pineapple sherbet

Mix together. Scoop sherbet on top.

Mrs. R. D. Sibley, Big Cove

PARTY PUNCH I

2 qts. water
1 cup sugar
1 lg. can pineapple juice
1 sm. frozen lemonade
2 tsp. almond extract
1 tsp. vanilla

Boil water and sugar until dissolved. Cool. Add juice, lemonade, almond extract, and vanilla. Better if made ahead and frozen to a slush. Stir and serve while partly frozen.

Ila Wilkinson, Central

PARTY PUNCH II

6 pkgs. cherry or lime Jello
1½ gal. water
1 qt. strong tea (omit tea if lime is used)
Juice of 12 lemons
1 qt. pineapple juice
2 qts. orange juice
3-4 cups sugar
Red or green food coloring (optional)

Dissolve Jello in 2 quarts boiling water. Add tea and sugar; stir and let cool. Add juices and rest of water and food coloring, if desired. Some of punch frozen in gelatin mold or ice cube trays looks very pretty floating in punch instead of ice cubes. Serves 100.

Mrs. O. V. Mitchell, Central

PINK PARTY PUNCH

2 cups boiling water
2 pkgs. fruit-flavored Jello
6 cups cold water
½ cup sugar

1 sm. can frozen orange juice
1 sm. can frozen lime or lemonade
1 lg. can pineapple juice
1 qt. ginger ale

Add boiling water to Jello. Strawberry or cherry flavor is good. Dissolve. Add cold water, sugar, and fruit juices. Add the ginger ale when ready to serve. Make the day before and freeze. Let thaw a few hours before serving and add ginger ale. Then you do not have to use ice in the drink. Frozen cherries, strawberries, raspberries, or mashed bananas may be added. Serves 50.

Bettye Richardson, South Parkway
Pat Zurasky, Rainbow Mountain-South Parkway

PUNCH

1 qt. 7-Up
1 32-oz. can pineapple juice
1 32-oz. can orange juice
1 32-oz. can grapefruit juice

1 jar cherries
3 oranges, sliced
3 lemons, sliced
1 fifth vodka (optional)

Mix in large container. Put in bowl and float the sliced fruit on top.

Jeanette Schlernitzauer, Athens Pike

"RECITAL" PUNCH

2 qts. water
8 cups sugar
2 lg. cans fruit punch
12 lg. oranges, juiced
12 lg. lemons, juiced

3 qts. strawberries, sliced or quartered
8 bananas, sliced
2 cups crushed pineapple
6 cups ice

4 btls. club soda

Boil water and sugar 5 minutes; then cool. Add fruit punch and fruits. At serving time, add 6 cups ice and 4 bottles club soda. Makes 12 quarts or more.

Mary Anne Riley, South Parkway

ROSY PUNCH

1½ cups sugar
2 cups boiling water
4 cups cranberry juice
⅓ cup lime juice
2 cups orange juice
6 cups ginger ale, chilled
Lime slices

Dissolve sugar in boiling water; cool. Stir in cranberry juice, lime juice, and orange juice; chill thoroughly. Add ginger ale at serving time. Garnish with lime slices. Yield: 3½ quarts.

Dorothy Mellette, Central

RUBY FRUIT PUNCH

1 lg. ginger ale
1 T. lemon juice
1 orange, sliced
1 qt. cranberry cocktail juice
1 cup apple juice

Mix, chill, and serve.

Roberta Friedman, Harvest

RUSSIAN TEA I

1 gal. boiling water
3 tea bags
1 sm. can frozen orange juice
½ cup lemon juice
2 cups sugar
1 tsp. cloves
1 stick cinnamon

Boil water; add tea bags (then remove); add remaining ingredients and let simmer.

Margaret Mann, Owens Cross Roads

RUSSIAN TEA II

3 tsp. tea (tie in bag)
2 tsp. cloves
16 cups water
2 cups sugar
Juice of 4 oranges
3 lemons
1 lime

Put tea and cloves in water, steep 4 minutes, strain, and pour over sugar. Stir until dissolved; keep hot. Add orange juice and thin slices of lemon and lime, with lime on lemon, and serve. Serve hot, not boiled.

Alta Newman, Central

RUSSIAN TEA PUNCH

1 pkg. Jello (strawberry or lime depending upon color desired)
2 pt. hot water
2 T. tea leaves
2 cups sugar
Juice of 12 lemons
1 lg. can pineapple juice
1 btl. ginger ale
1 pt. sherbet
Food coloring (optional)

Dissolve Jello in 1 pint hot water. Add enough water to make 1 gallon. To 1 pint of hot water, add 2 tablespoons of tea leaves and let stand for 20 minutes and strain. Add to above mixture. Add sugar, juice of 12 lemons or lemon juice equal to 12 lemons, and pineapple juice. Refrigerate overnight. Stir well. When ready to serve, add ginger ale and sherbet. You can add red or green food coloring if desired. Yield: approximately 2 gallons.

Wanda Ailor, Blossomwood

7-UP SURPRISE PUNCH

1 46-oz. can pineapple punch
10 7-oz. btls. 7-Up
2 6-oz. cans frozen orange juice concentrate, thawed
½ tsp. peppermint extract

Combine pineapple juice, 7-Up, and thawed orange juice in large punch bowl. Add peppermint extract and ice cubes. Serves 32.

Mrs. O. V. Mitchell, Central

SUMMERTIME ICED TEA

6 tea bags
4 cups boiling water
1 6-oz. can frozen lemonade concentrate, thawed, undiluted
1 6-oz. frozen orange juice or limeade concentrate, thawed, undiluted
1½ cups sugar
10 cups water

Steep tea bags in boiling water about 5 minutes; discard tea bags. Add remaining ingredients. Serve over ice. Yield: 1 gallon.

Bettye Richardson, South Parkway

INSTANT COFFEE MIXES

MOCHA FLAVORED
½ cup instant coffee
½ cup sugar
1 cup coffee creamer
2 tbsp. cocoa

VIENNA FLAVORED
½ cup instant coffee
⅔ cup sugar
⅔ cup coffee creamer
1 tsp. cinnamon

ORANGE FLAVORED
½ cup instant coffee
¾ cup sugar
1 cup coffee creamer
½ tsp. dried orange peel

Blend flavors individually in food processor. Store in air tight containers. To serve use 2 heaping tsp. in cup of boiling water.

Eva Stiles Brown, Monrovia

MARY KATHERINE'S PUNCH

Frozen Ring:
1 carton Mayfield pineapple sherbet and whole strawberries — freeze in jello mold

Dissolve:
1 small pkg. strawberry jello (use wild strawberry for Christmas)
1 cup sugar
1 cup hot water

Let cool and add in the following:
1 pkg. strawberry Kool-aid
2 qts. cold water
1 large can unsweetened pineapple juice

In punch bowl add the above mixture along with the frozen ring until it begins to melt, and add 12 oz lemon/lime soda or wink.

Mary Katherine Roark, Madina Cross Roads

TOMATO JUICE COCKTAIL

¼ cup chopped carrots
¼ cup chopped onions
¼ cup chopped sweet pepper
1 sm. bay leaf

Tomatoes to make 3 pts. of juice
¼ cup lemon juice
1 T. sugar
Salt to taste
1 T. Worcestershire sauce

Combine first 5 ingredients and simmer 30 to 40 minutes. Put through sieve and add to all other ingredients. Simmer 5 to 10 minutes. Chill before serving. If canning, bring to a boil and seal.

Mary Sanders, Central

BREADS

ANGEL BISCUITS

1 pkg. yeast
3 T. sugar
½ cup lukewarm water
¾ cup shortening
5 cups self-rising flour
2 cups buttermilk
1 tsp. soda
½-1 tsp. salt

Dissolve yeast with 1 tablespoon of sugar in water. Cut shortening into flour. Combine buttermilk, soda, and salt. Add buttermilk and yeast mixtures and remaining sugar to flour. Place in airtight container and refrigerate. Mixture will keep until ready to bake. 425 degrees for 15 minutes.

Roberta Friedman, Harvest

LEONA'S HOT BISCUITS

2 cups self-rising flour
2 T. Crisco
½-⅔ cup buttermilk

Mix well to the softness or stiffness of marshmallow. Roll out ½-inch thick. Bake in buttered pan. When done, brush top with margarine for shine and taste. Serve hot.

Leona Mills, Big Cove

MAYONNAISE BISCUITS

1½ cups self-rising flour
½ cup mayonnaise
½ cup sweet milk

Mix together and roll out on floured board. Cut into biscuits and bake at 450 degrees until brown.

Mrs. Eugene Smith (Nina), Monrovia

SOURDOUGH BISCUITS

1 cup flour
⅓ cup shortening
2 tsp. baking powder
¼ tsp. salt
¼ tsp. soda
1 cup sourdough starter

Mix ingredients and roll out ¼ to 1-inch thick. Cut with a biscuit cutter. Place biscuits on a greased pan. Let rise 30 minutes. Bake for 12 minutes in a 450-degree oven.

Ira Maples Hughes, Owens Cross Roads

Breads

SOURDOUGH STARTER

1 pkg. yeast	2 cups all-purpose flour
2 cups warm water or milk	1 T. sugar

Combine all ingredients in large glass or ceramic bowl. Cover with cheesecloth and let stand at room temperature 24 to 48 hours, stirring occasionally. Cover loosely with plastic wrap and store in refrigerator. Allow to come to room temperature before using. Use or replenish every 7 to 10 days. To replenish: Add equal amounts of warm water or milk and flour. Let stand at room temperature until mixture begins to bubble then cover and refrigerate. Starter can be frozen if you do not plan to use for several weeks. Allow to come to room temperature before using.

Ira M. Hughes, Owens Cross Roads

BREAD STICKS

Biscuit Dough: Add ⅓ cup milk all at once to 1 cup Bisquick. Stir with fork into a soft dough. Beat dough 20 strokes; dough will be soft and sticky. Knead 8 to 10 times on lightly floured cloth-covered board. Roll into 6x4-inch rectangle. Cut into 12 strips. Melt ¼ cup butter; pour half of it into a 9-inch square pan. Pour remaining butter over tops of sticks which have been arranged in pan. Sprinkle lightly with salt. Bake in 450-degree oven for 10 to 15 minutes, until golden brown. Makes 12 sticks.

Donna Brannan, Owens Cross Roads

GARLIC TOAST

1 pkg. dry yeast	1 T. melted oleo
1 cup lukewarm water	1 tsp. salt
1 T. sugar	3 cups sifted enriched flour
	Garlic butter

Soften yeast in water. Add remaining ingredients, except garlic butter. Put in greased bowl and let rise till doubled; fold over and over; do not punch down. Knead and make into rolls, putting garlic butter in center, place in pan, let rise 30 mintues. Then bake at 400 degrees for 20 minutes or until golden brown. Yield: 18 to 20 rolls.

Garlic Butter

½ stick oleo   ¼ tsp. garlic

Melt oleo and mix with garlic.

Mrs. Eugene Smith (Nina), Monrovia

GRAHAM CRACKERS

1 cup graham flour   ½ cup shortening
1 cup whole wheat flour   ¾ cup packed brown sugar
1 cup all-purpose flour   ⅓ cup honey
1 tsp. baking powder   1 tsp. vanilla
½ tsp. baking soda   ½ cup milk
¼ tsp. salt   3 T. granulated sugar
                 1 tsp. cinnamon

In large pitcher stir together flours, baking powder, soda, and salt. In large mixing bowl cream together shortening, and brown sugar till light. Beat in honey and vanilla till fluffy. Add flour mixture alternately with milk, ending with dry ingredients. Beat well after each addition. Seal tightly and chill for several hours or overnight. Divide dough into quarters, place one quarter on well-floured pastry sheet, roll out to a 15x5-inch rectangle. Cut lightly into 6 small rectangles, approximately 5x2½ inches. Place on ungreased baking sheet, repeat with remainder of dough. With tines of fork mark a line across the center of each rectangle and score holes. Combine granulated sugar and cinnamon, sprinkle over crackers. Bake at 350 degrees for 13 to 15 minutes. Remove from baking sheet promptly. Yield: 24.

Brenda Williams, Harvest

HOT HERB BREAD ITALIAN STYLE

1 loaf Italian bread (about   ¼ tsp. oregano
   14 inches)   ½ tsp. dried dillweed
½ cup soft butter or margarine   1 garlic clove, minced
1 tsp. parsley flakes   Parmesan cheese, grated
                 Aluminum foil

Cut bread diagonally in one-inch slices. Blend butter and all spices. Put mixture between bread slices and shape foil around loaf, leaving top open and twisting ends. Sprinkle top with cheese. Heat in hot oven (400 degrees) for 10 to 15 minutes.

Carolyn Griner, Rainbow Mountain

HUSHPUPPIES

2 cups self-rising cornmeal
1 T. self-rising flour
1 T. salt (approximately)

1 egg
1 med. onion, chopped
1 cup milk

Mix and sift dry ingredients. Add egg, chopped onion, and milk, and mix well with dry ingredients. Drop by tablespoonfuls into hot oil. Will rise to top and float when done. May add chopped fresh green onion or cheese. Yield: 3 to 4 dozen.

Patsy Brazelton, Owens Cross Roads

2-GRAIN WAFERS

2 cups whole wheat flour
1 cup quick oats
½ tsp. salt

½ tsp. garlic salt (if used with meat salad)
⅓ cup oil
1 cup apple juice or water

Combine ingredients and form into roll. Wrap in wax paper and refrigerate for 3 hours. Cut as thin as possible; dip a fork in water and press each slice flat. Bake on a greased cookie sheet in a 350-degree preheated oven for 25 to 30 minutes or until crisp. Cool and store in air tight container. Freezes well.

Barbara Hoover, Monrovia

CHILI CORN BREAD

1 lb. ground beef
½ onion
½ green pepper
1 tsp. black pepper
1 tsp. chili powder
1 tsp. salt
1 can tomatoes

1 can whole kernel corn
1 cup self-rising cornmeal or Jiffy cornmeal
1½ tsp. sugar
¾ cup boiling water
1 egg
¾ cup buttermilk
1 T. oil

Brown meat and drain. Saute onion and green pepper. Add to meat; add pepper, chili powder, and salt. Add tomatoes. Drain corn and layer over the above. Combine cornmeal, sugar, and oil. Stir in boiling water. Beat egg and stir in buttermilk. Add to cornmeal mixture. Pour the cornmeal over the meat mixture. Bake at 375 degrees until golden brown on top.

Mary Kantor, Westbury

CORN BREAD SUPREME

1 cup self-rising meal
½ cup Wesson oil
1 sm. can cream-style corn
1 cup sour cream
3 eggs, beaten

Combine all ingredients; place in baking pan. Bake in 415-degree oven until done, approximately 25 minutes.

Billie Creel, Big Cove

CORNMEAL DUMPLINGS
(This recipe is more than 100 years old.)

1 cup cornmeal
1½ cups boiling water
1 tsp. sugar
½ tsp. salt
1 egg

Add cornmeal gradually to the boiling water, stir vigorously, and cook until a thick mush is formed. Add sugar and salt and cool. Add egg and beat well, drop by rounded tablespoons onto a floured board, roll into small balls and dredge lightly with flour. Drop into boiling liquid and cook very slowly for about 15 minutes. Dumplings can be made in broth in which a ham bone has been cooked, beef broth, chicken broth, and turnip green "pot-licker" (especially good in pot-licker).

Mrs. Allen Drake (Wilma), Monrovia

MEXICAN CORN BREAD I

½ cup cooking oil
3 eggs, lightly beaten
1 cup buttermilk
1½ cups self-rising cornmeal
½ tsp. salt
¼ tsp. cayenne pepper
1 cup grated sharp Cheddar cheese
1 cup finely chopped green peppers
1 med. onion, chopped
1 8-oz. can cream-style corn

Combine oil, eggs, and buttermilk. With large wooden spoon, combine cornmeal mix, salt, cayenne, cheese, green pepper, and onion. Mix well then stir in buttermilk mixture and corn, drained 5 minutes before using. Transfer to a lightly greased 9x13-inch baking pan and bake in preheated 375-degree oven for 45 minutes.

Dorothy Mellette, Central

MEXICAN CORN BREAD II

1 cup self-rising cornmeal
½ cup cooking oil
2 eggs
⅓ cup chopped onion
½ lb. grated cheese
2 hot peppers, chopped
1 sm. can creamed corn

Cook as any other corn bread.

Elaine Story, Pulaski Pike

APPLE MUFFINS

1 cup honey
1 cup oil
4 eggs
¾ tsp. salt
1 tsp. allspice
1 tsp. nutmeg
2½ cups whole wheat flour
2 tsp. baking powder
1 tsp. cinnamon
½ cup powdered milk
1¾ cups grated apple, including peel (2 lg. apples)
1 tsp. vanilla

Beat honey, oil, and eggs. Mix dry ingredients. Add to honey mixture. Stir well. Add and fold together the apple and vanilla. Fill muffin tins half full and bake at 400 degrees for 12 to 15 minutes. Remove from tins to cool. Yield: 24 large or 40 small.

Donna Butler, Poplar Ridge

BANANA MUFFINS

½ cup margarine, softened
½ cup sugar
2 eggs, beaten
1 tsp. vanilla
3 ripe bananas, mashed (about 1 cup)
1¼ cups flour
½ tsp. soda

Combine margarine and sugar; beat until light and fluffy. Add eggs and vanilla and beat well. Stir in bananas. Combine flour and soda; add to creamed mixture, stirring just enough to moisten dry ingredients. Fill muffin pans ⅔ full. Bake at 350 degrees for 25 minutes or until done. Serve hot. Yield: about 15.

Jeannette Broad, Big Cove

BRAN MUFFINS I

1 cup whole wheat flour	1 egg, beaten
1 tsp. baking soda	½ cup honey
1½ cups bran	¾ cup milk
½ cup dates	2 T. oil

Mix together dry ingredients. Moisten with remaining ingredients, stirring only enough to blend. Bake in cupcake paper liners at 350 degrees for 15 to 20 minutes. Cool, remove paper liners, and store leftover muffins in airtight bag or tin. Variations: May add ½ cup chopped nuts, granola, sunflower seeds, crushed pineapple, blueberries, raisins, chocolate chips, etc.

Diane McFarland, Harvest

BRAN MUFFINS II

1 cup self-rising flour	1¼ cups bran cereal
½ cup granulated sugar	1 cup milk
½ tsp. salt	1 egg
	¼ cup vegetable oil

Blend first 3 ingredients together. Set aside. Stir cereal and milk until moist. Let stand 5 minutes. Add flour mixture and egg and oil. Stir until just mixed. Bake at 400 degrees for 20 minutes.

Gail Hutcheson, Rainbow Mountain

BRER RABBIT MUFFINS

2 cups enriched self-rising flour	¾ cup milk
½ tsp. cinnamon	3 T. oil
¼ tsp. ground cloves	½ cup chunky peanut butter
¼ tsp. nutmeg	¼ cup dark molasses
1 egg	2 T. brown sugar
Chopped peanuts	

Stir together first 4 ingredients. Combine egg, milk, oil, peanut butter, molasses, and brown sugar. Add liquid all at once to flour mixture, stirring only until flour is moistened. Fill greased muffin cups ⅔ full. Sprinkle each muffin with chopped peanuts. Bake in preheated 425-degree oven 20 to 25 minutes, or until golden brown. Yield: 12.

Debbie Maples, Owens Cross Roads

COUNTRY SAUSAGE MUFFINS

½ lb. sausage
1 cup all-purpose flour
1 cup self-rising cornmeal
1 2-oz. jar pimiento

1 egg
½ tsp. soda
1 8-oz. French onion dip
¾ cup milk

Brown sausage, stirring to crumble. Drain well, reserving 2 tablespoons drippings. Combine flour, meal, sausage, pimiento, egg, and soda. Add reserved drippings, onion dip, and milk. Stir just enough to moisten dry ingredients. Fill greased muffin tins ⅔ full. Bake at 425 degrees for 20 to 25 minutes or until golden brown. Yield: 1 dozen.

Barbara Webster, Owens Cross Roads

CREAM OF WHEAT MUFFINS

1 cup uncooked cream of wheat
1 cup self-rising flour
1 cup milk

¼ cup oil
1 egg
10 drops yellow food coloring

Stir gently and do not overbeat. Grease pan and bake at 425 degrees. Yield: 12.

Mrs. Claude Bridges (Lara), Monrovia

YEAST MUFFINS

2 cups lukewarm water
1 pkg. dry yeast
4 cups self-rising flour, sifted
¼ cup sugar

1 egg
Pinch salt
¾ cup Wesson oil

Beat or stir well all ingredients. Cover and place in refrigerator overnight. Grease muffin tins and fill ⅔ full. Bake in 425 degree oven about 20 minutes. Yield: about 18.

Mrs. Bob Erwin (Virginia), Monrovia

BRAN PANCAKES

1½ cups flour
½ cup bran
Pinch of salt
3 T. baking powder
¼ cup wheat germ (optional)
2 eggs, slightly beaten
2 T. honey
1 cup yogurt (optional)
1-1½ cups milk

Combine dry ingredients. Blend in eggs, honey, yogurt, and enough milk to make batter the consistency of cream. Cook on hot griddle. Serves 4.

Marianne Mullen, Westbury

PANCAKE HAWAIIAN

2 T. butter or margarine
3 eggs
⅛ tsp. salt
⅓ cup sifted all-purpose flour
½ cup pineapple juice
Grated rind of ½ lemon
2 tsp. lemon juice
1 cup crushed pineapple
¼ pound Cheddar cheese, grated (about 1 cup)

Place the butter in a 10 to 12-inch skillet, and set in preheated very hot oven (450 degrees) while pancake ingredients are being mixed. Beat eggs and salt until light and foamy in large mixing bowl. Add flour to eggs and beat until smooth. Add pineapple juice and blend. Remove skillet from oven and tip back and forth to distribute melted fat over bottom surface. Pour in all of the batter and bake at 450 degrees for 12 minutes or until pancake is delicately browned and edges draw away from pan sides. As pancake is cooking, place lemon rind, lemon juice, and crushed pineapple in saucepan to warm over medium heat. When pancake is done, remove from oven and distribute half the grated cheese over it; roll pancake, using 2 forks. Turn out on heat-proof platter or leave in skillet for the next cooking step, transferring to warm serving dish when completed. Pour pineapple sauce over pancake and sprinkle remaining cheese on top. Place under broiler and broil until cheese melts and just begins to brown. Serve while hot. Serves 2 to 4. Adaptable as either entree or dessert. Pancake Hawaiian plus beverage makes a perfect luncheon for two.

Gloria Radke, South Huntsville

PANCAKES
(Fun ways to start the day with pancakes)

1. Prepare pancake batter. Trickle batter from teaspoon to form smiley face on hot griddle. Allow to brown. Pour batter over and finish pancake as usual.
2. Butterflies: Cut pancakes in half; place curved sides together with cooked sausage link for body.

Linda Warren, South Huntsville

PEANUT-BUTTER HOTCAKES
(Children love these. Make the batter several hours before using.)

⅓ cup melted butter
⅓ cup peanut butter
2 med. eggs
¼ tsp. salt
1¼ tsp. baking powder

1 tsp. sugar
1¼ cups milk
1¼ cups flour
6 slices bacon, cooked crisp, crumbled

Beat the melted butter, peanut butter, and eggs thoroughly. Add the rest of ingredients, stirring in the bacon last. Bake as usual and serve with melted butter.

Lila M. Brown, Harvest

POTATO PANCAKES

4 lg. potatoes, pared
¼ cup grated onion
2 eggs, slightly beaten
2 T. flour

¾ tsp. salt
Dash of nutmeg
Dash of pepper
Shortening for frying

Grate potatoes; drain well; pat dry with dish towel; measure 3 cups. In large bowl combine grated potatoes with onion, eggs, flour, salt, nutmeg, and pepper. In large heavy skillet, slowly heat oil, ⅛-inch deep until very hot but not smoking. For each pancake, drop 3 tablespoons potato mixture at a time. Fry until golden brown. Drain on paper towels.

Margaret West, Big Cove

PUFFY GERMAN PANCAKE

3 eggs
¾ cup flour
¼ tsp. salt
½ cup milk

2 T. butter
Powdered sugar
Butter
Lemon juice

Beat eggs with fork. Add ½ cup flour and salt then ¼ cup flour. Beat well; add ¼ cup milk, beat, and add ¼ cup milk. Put cold butter on souffle dish. Pour ingredients into dish. Put in oven at 450 degrees for 20 minutes then turn heat to 375 degrees for 10 minutes. Serve sprinkled with powdered sugar, butter, and lemon juice. Makes 1 large puffy thing that could serve 2. Eat immediately.

Gayle Tindol, Rainbow Mountain

QUICK BREADS

BANANA BREAD

1 ¾ cups flour
⅔ cup sugar
1 tsp. baking powder
½ tsp. salt

¼ tsp. soda
½ cup oil
1 cup mashed bananas
2 eggs, slightly beaten

¼ cup pecans

Preheat oven to 350 degrees. Grease 1 loaf pan. In a bowl use a fork to mix the first 5 ingredients. Cut in oil; stir in bananas and eggs until blended. Add pecans. Bake for 1 hour. Cool in pan on wire rack for 10 minutes. Makes 1 loaf.

Mrs. W. L. Hoover (Barbara), Monrovia

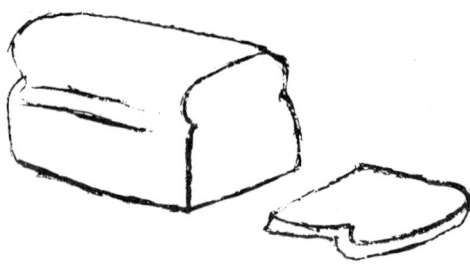

BANANA NUT BREAD I

1 egg
1 tsp. vanilla
1 cup sugar
¼ cup salad oil
1¼ cups mashed banana (2-3)

½ cup milk
2½ cups all-purpose flour
3 tsp. double-acting baking powder
½ tsp. salt
1 cup walnuts

Combine egg, vanilla, sugar, and oil in large bowl and beat with wooden spoon until well blended. Add enough milk to bananas to measure 1¾ cups. Then add bananas and milk to egg mixture. Sift flour, baking powder, and salt together and add all at once to batter. Then add walnuts last. Pour into greased 9x5x3-inch loaf pan or several smaller pans. Heat oven to 350 degrees. Bake 60 to 65 minutes or until cake tester in center comes out clean. When completely cool wrap in plastic or foil and store at least 12 hours before serving.

Irma Long, University

BANANA NUT BREAD II

½ cup Wesson oil
1½ cups sugar
1 cup mashed bananas
1 tsp. soda
2 eggs

4 T. buttermilk
1½ cups sifted flour
1 tsp. vanilla
1 cup nuts (black walnuts preferred)

Bake at 325 degrees for 45 minutes in tube pan.

Icing

5 T. brown sugar
3 T. butter
2 T. cream

Pour over cake after you remove it from oven. Sprinkle with coconut and return to oven and brown lightly.

Elaine Story, Pulaski Pike

BLUEBERRY TEA BREAD

2 cups flour
1 cup sugar
1½ cups blueberries

2 eggs
1 cup milk
3 T. salad oil
1 tsp. grated fresh orange rind

In a large bowl mix flour and sugar. Stir in blueberries. In small bowl beat together eggs, milk, oil, and orange rind. Add all at once to flour mixture. Stir until dry ingredients are moistened. Turn into greased 9x5-inch loaf pan. Bake in 350 degrees oven 1 hour or 70 minutes or until cake tester inserted comes out clean. Remove and cool 10 minutes; remove from pan and cool completely. Sprinkle with powdered sugar before cutting to serve. Yield: 1 loaf.

Jeannette Broad, Big Cove

BOSTON BROWN BREAD

2 cups rolled graham cracker crumbs
1¾ cups unsifted flour
2 tsp. soda
½ tsp. salt
½ tsp. ground mace
½ cup vegetable shortening
1 egg
1⅔ cups buttermilk
⅔ cup molasses
1⅓ cups dark seedless raisins

Thoroughly mix first five ingredients; set aside. In the large bowl of electric mixer beat shortening until light and fluffy; add egg and beat until blended. Add buttermilk and molasses, blending well. Add dry ingredients and beat at medium speed for two minutes. Fold in raisins. Turn batter into four well-greased 16-ounce cans with paper in the bottoms. Bake in preheated oven at 350 degrees for about 45 minutes or until tester in center comes out clean. Cool on wire rack for 30 minutes before removing from cans. Makes 4 5-inch loaves.

Mary Frances Mitchell, Madison Cross Roads

She measured out the butter with a very solemn air,
The milk and sugar also, she took the greatest care
To count the eggs correctly and to add a little bit
Of baking powder, which you know beginners oft omit.
Then she stirred it all together and baked it for an hour,
But she never quite forgave herself for leaving out the flour.

CRANBERRY BREAD

1½ cups white or brown sugar
½ cup soft or melted butter
1¾ cups orange juice
2 lg. eggs, beaten
1 tsp. salt

5 cups flour
1 T. baking powder
1 tsp. baking soda
2 cups chopped nuts
3-4 cups chopped fresh cranberries

2 T. grated orange rind

Combine sugar, butter, orange juice, and eggs. Stir until well blended. Sift salt, flour, baking powder, and soda. Add nuts and stir them through the flour so they are well coated. Stir the dry ingredients into the liquid ingredients until dry ingredients are thoroughly moistened. Last, fold in the cranberries blended with the grated orange rind. Pour the batter into 2 well-buttered loaf pans and let stand for 20 minutes. Bake in a 350-degree oven until browned and done, about 1 hour. A toothpick thrust into the center should come out clean.

Lila M. Brown, Harvest

CRANBERRY-NUT BREAD

2 cups all-purpose flour
1 tsp. soda
½ tsp. salt
¼ cup sugar

½ cup buttermilk
1 egg, well beaten
1 cup whole-berry cranberry sauce
1 cup chopped pecans or walnuts

Combine dry ingredients, except nuts, in a mixing bowl. Add buttermilk, egg, and cranberry sauce; stir well (do not beat). Stir in nuts. Spoon batter into a well-greased 8½x4½x2⅝-inch loaf pan. Bake at 300 degrees for 1 hour or until bread tests done. Yield: 1 loaf.

Eloise Pittman, Blossomwood

GOOD DATE LOAF

1 btl. maraschino cherries
1 lb. dates
2 cups boiling water
2 level tsp. soda
2 cups sugar
2 eggs

2 rounded T. butter, softened
2 cups chopped nut meats
2 tsp. vanilla
3 cups flour
Pinch of salt
¼ cup cherry wine (optional)

Drain cherries and save juice. Cut dates in small pieces. Dissolve soda in boiling water. Pour over dates. Combine sugar, eggs, butter, nuts, and vanilla. Add flour, salt, and date mixture. Mix well. Add cherries and ⅓ cup of cherry juice and cherry wine. Mix well. Bake in greased and floured tube pan or 2 small loaf pans at 350 degrees for approximately 1 hour.

Be what your friends think you are; avoid what your enemies say you are.

LEMON BREAD

½ cup milk
2 eggs (room temperature)
½ cup oil
Grated peel of 1 lemon
1 cup sugar

½ cup chopped nuts
1⅔ cups flour
½ tsp. salt
¼ cup sugar, mixed with juice of 1 lemon

1 tsp. baking powder

Grease and flour 1 loaf pan. In the blender mix milk, eggs, oil, lemon peel, sugar, and nuts. Add to dry ingredients. Bake at 350 degrees for 60 or 70 minutes. While still hot, pour sugar and lemon juice mixture over loaf.

Norma Colbath, South Parkway

Do as well as you can today and perhaps tomorrow you can do better.

PINEAPPLE BREAD

¾ cup packed brown sugar
¼ cup shortening
1 egg
2 cups flour
1 tsp. baking soda

½ tsp. salt
⅓ cup orange juice
1 8¼-oz. can crushed pineapple in heavy syrup
½ cup chopped pecans

Beat brown sugar and shortening until light; beat in egg. Stir in flour, baking soda, salt, and orange juice. Stir in pineapple with juice and pecans. Spread in loaf pan that has been greased on the bottom only. Bake in a 350-degree oven for 55 minutes. Cool completely before slicing.

Mrs. Marshall Byrd, Jr., Madison Cross Roads

POPPY SEED BREAD

1 box yellow cake mix
1 box instant lemon pudding
4 eggs

½ cup oil
1 cup hot water
¼ cup poppy seed

Mix ingredients in order. Place in 2 greased bread pans. Bake at 350 degrees for 30 minutes.

Darlene Reichmann, Rainbow Mountain

PUMPKIN BREAD I

4 eggs
3 cups sugar
1 can pumpkin
3½ cups sifted plain flour
1½ tsp. salt
1 tsp. nutmeg

2 tsp. cinnamon
2 tsp. baking soda
⅔ cup water or orange juice
  (orange juice best)
1 cup cooking oil
½ cup nuts (pecans or walnuts)
½ cup raisins

Mix in this order: Beat eggs, add sugar (beat), add pumpkin (beat), add flour with spices and soda (beat), and add juice and oil and beat well, finally adding nuts and raisins. Pour into 4 1-pound well-greased and floured coffee cans leaving at least 2 inches at the top for rising. Place in preheated oven and bake at 350 degrees for 1 hour. Delicious toasted then topped with butter and/or favorite jam or jelly.

Julie Linderman, Vestavia

PUMPKIN BREAD II

⅔ cup shortening
2⅔ cups sugar
4 eggs, slightly beaten
2 cups pumpkin or 1 16-oz. can
⅔ cup water

3½ cups self-rising flour
1 tsp. cinnamon
¼ tsp. cloves
½ cup nuts, coarsely chopped
⅔ cup dates
1½ tsp. salt

Heat oven to 350 degrees; grease and flour two 9x5x3-inch loaf pans or 4 small foil loaf pans. In a large bowl, cream shortening and sugar until fluffy. Stir in eggs, pumpkin, and water. Blend in all flour (except ¼ cup); toss cinnamon, cloves, nuts, dates, and salt in the ¼ cup flour and stir into mixture; Pour into pans. Bake until a tester will come out clean, about 1 hour at 350 degrees.

Mary Moore, Central

PUMPKIN BREAD III

3½ cups sifted flour
1½ tsp. salt
3 cups sugar
2 tsp. soda
1 tsp. nutmeg

4 eggs
⅔ cup water
1 cup oil or shortening
2 cups canned pumpkin
Nuts and/or candied cherries

Mix all dry ingredients together. Add the rest. Grease and flour 2 loaf pans. Bake at 350 degrees for 1 hour.

Lanita Presson, Owens Cross Roads

RAISIN BREAD

3 T. margarine
½-1 cup sugar
3 eggs
1 cup raisins
1 T. grated lemon rind

3 cups self-rising flour
1 tsp. cinnamon
1 tsp. lemon extract
½ tsp. vanilla
1 cup milk

Cream margarine and sugar; add eggs 1 at a time, beating well after each addition; stir in raisins and lemon rind. Mix flour and cinnamon. Combine lemon extract, vanilla, and milk; alternating with dry ingredients, add to raisin mixture. Pour into greased and floured 9x5x3-inch pan. Bake at 350 degrees for 45 to 50 minutes. Yield: 1 loaf.

Jeannette Broad, Big Cove

SPICED ZUCCHINI BREAD

3 cups flour
2 tsp. soda
1 tsp. salt
½ tsp. baking powder
1½ tsp. cinnamon
¾ cup chopped pecans or walnuts

3 eggs
2 cups sugar
1 cup oil
2 tsp. vanilla
1 8-oz. can crushed pineapple, drained

2 cups shredded zucchini

Combine flour, soda, salt, baking powder, cinnamon, and nuts; set aside. Beat eggs lightly in a large mixing bowl, add sugar, oil, and vanilla; beat until creamy. Stir in pineapple and zucchini. Add dry ingredients, stirring only until dry ingredients are moistened. Spoon batter into 2 well-greased and floured 9x5x3-inch loaf pans. Bake at 350 degrees for 1 hour. Cool 10 minutes before removing from pan; turn out on rack and cool completely.

Mrs. L. M. Taylor, Big Cove

SPOON BREAD

2 cups water
1 cup white cornmeal
1 cup milk

1 T. shortening
1 tsp. salt
2 eggs

Mix water and meal and bring slowly to boiling point; cook for 5 minutes. Add milk, shortening, salt, and well-beaten eggs. Beat thoroughly and bake in well-greased pan for 25 minutes at 425 degrees. Serve from the same dish with a spoon.

Ruth Chambers, Darwin Downs

STRAWBERRY BREAD

3 cups flour
2 cups sugar
3 tsp. cinnamon
1 tsp. soda

1 tsp. salt
4 eggs, well beaten
1¼ cups oil
1 cup chopped nuts

2 10-oz. pkgs. frozen strawberries, undrained

Sift dry ingredients together. Add remaining ingredients, stirring carefully, just enough to mix all ingredients. Pour into 2 greased and floured loaf pans. Bake at 350 degrees for 1 hour. Cool 10 minutes in pans. (For nice little gifts at Christmas time, use 4 small-size disposable loaf pans and bake at 325 degrees for 50 minutes.)

Maude Taylor, Central
Ruth W. Chambers, Darwin Downs

ZUCCHINI BREAD I

3 eggs
1 cup oil
2 cups sugar
2 cups grated unpeeled zucchini
3 tsp. vanilla

1 tsp. salt
1 tsp. soda
3 cups flour
3 tsp. cinnamon
¼ tsp. baking powder

½ cup chopped nuts

Beat eggs until fluffy. Add oil, sugar, zucchini, and vanilla. Mix well. Add dry ingredients and nuts. Pour into 2 greased and floured loaf pans. Bake 1 hour at 325 degrees.

Norma Colbath, South Parkway

ZUCCHINI BREAD II

(Moist and marvelous: The flavor combination of chocolate, vanilla, and almonds spiced with cinnamon is superb.)

3 eggs
2 cups sugar
1 cup vegetable oil
2 1-oz. bars unsweetened baking chocolate
1 tsp. vanilla

2 cups grated zucchini
3 cups flour
1 tsp. salt
1 tsp. cinnamon
¼ tsp. baking powder
1 tsp. baking soda

1 cup coarsely chopped nuts

Beat eggs until lemon colored. Beat in sugar and oil. Melt chocolate over hot water and stir into egg mixture along with vanilla and zucchini. Sift flour, salt, cinnamon, baking powder, and soda. With large spoon, stir into zucchini mixture along with nuts. When thoroughly mixed, spoon into 2 well-oiled 9x5-inch loaf pans. Bake at 350 degrees 1 hour and 20 minutes or until done. Let cool in pans for 15 to 20 minutes; turn out on rack. Serve when thoroughly cooled or chilled; cut into thin slices. Yield: 2 large loaves.

Mrs. Erle P. Douglass (Evelyn), Monrovia

ROLLS

BATTER BUNS

⅔ cup warm water (not hot, 110-115 degrees)
1 pkg. active dry yeast
2 T. sugar

½ tsp. salt
¼ cup soft shortening
1 egg
1⅔ cups Gold Medal Flour

Measure water into mixer bowl. Add yeast, stirring to dissolve. Measure flour by dipping method or by sifting. Add sugar, salt, shortening, egg, and 1 cup of the flour. Combine, using mixer on low speed and guiding batter into beaters with rubber scraper. Add the remaining flour. Beat with scraper until smooth. Spoon into greased muffin cups, filling each a scant ½ full. Let rise in warm place (85 degrees) until batter reaches top of muffin cups, 30 to 40 minutes. Heat oven to 375 degrees and bake 18 to 20 minutes, until golden brown. Serve warm. Yield: about 12 buns.

Donna Brannan, Owens Cross Roads

Breads

BEER ROLLS I

4 cups Bisquick　　　　　1 12-oz. can of beer, cold
　　　　　　　　2 T. sugar

Mix all ingredients. Pour into greased muffin pan, filling cups ½ full. Bake at 375 degrees until golden brown.

Connie Wagner, Rainbow Mountain

BEER ROLLS II

3 cups Bisquick　　　　　1 T. sugar
　　　　　　　　1 13-oz. can beer

Mix; spoon into greased muffin tins. Bake at 400 degrees for 12 to 15 minutes. Yield: 12.

Brenda Williams, Harvest

BUTTERMILK ROLLS

1 pkg. yeast
½ cup warm water
2 cups buttermilk, warmed
1 tsp. salt
3 T. sugar

5 T. melted shortening
½ tsp. baking soda
½ tsp. baking powder
Flour
Margarine, melted

Put yeast in warm water and let stand while you place buttermilk in a large bowl with salt, sugar, shortening, soda, and baking powder. Stir well. Add dissolved yeast and enough flour to make a good biscuit dough. Knead about 5 minutes, roll and cut or place in a greased bowl. Cover with cloth and let stand in refrigerator overnight. Two hours before needed take dough out of refrigerator. Punch down and roll out on a floured board or cloth to about ¼-inch thick; cut and shape as you like. Dip in melted margarine and put in slightly greased pan. Let rise to double in bulk in a warm place. Bake in preheated oven 15 to 20 minutes at 425 degrees.

Mrs. O. V. Mitchell, Central

CLOVER TEA ROLLS

2 cups sifted flour
¼ cup sugar
¾ tsp. baking powder

½ tsp. salt
⅓ cup shortening
½ cup milk
3 T. lemon juice

Sift dry ingredients into bowl. Cut in shortening until it resembles coarse meal. *Combine milk and lemon juice.* Quickly stir into flour mixture to form a soft dough. Knead on floured board. Form into small balls about the size of marbles. Put 3 in each cup of a greased muffin pan. Bake at 450 degrees for 15 minutes.

Carol Paschal, Blossomwood

ICEBOX YEAST ROLLS

½ lb. margarine, softened
¼ cup sugar
3 eggs, beaten slightly
    1 heaping tsp. salt
    1 pkg. yeast
    1 cup lukewarm water
        4 cups plain flour

Cream margarine and sugar. Add eggs and salt. Dissolve yeast in lukewarm water. Add flour and water-yeast mixture, alternately. Cover bowl and put in refrigerator overnight. Roll out and cut into rounds. Dip in butter and fold over. Let rise 1 hour before cooking. Cook at 400 to 425 degrees until done.

Bonnie Nelson, Heritage

INSTANT YEAST ROLLS

1 pkg. dry yeast
¼ cup warm water
½ cup sugar
    1 cup buttermilk
    ¼ cup cooking oil, shortening, or oleo
        2 cups self-rising flour

Dissolve yeast in warm water. Combine the ingredients. Knead as though making biscuits. Roll to about ½-inch thickness and cut with biscuit cutter. Place a pat of margarine on each and fold in half. Place on a greased baking sheet and let stand at least ½ hour and not more than 3 hours. Bake at 400 degrees until brown.

Mrs. Bob Freeman, Poplar Ridge
Mrs. Marvin Sharp, Central

NO-KNEAD REFRIGERATOR ROLLS

2 pkgs. dry yeast
2 cups warm water
6½ - 7 cups sifted flour
½ cup sugar
2 tsp. salt
1 egg
¼ cup soft shortening

Dissolve yeast and water in mixing bowl and add sugar, salt, and half the flour. Beat thoroughly for 2 minutes. Add eggs and shortening. Gradually beat in the rest of flour until smooth. Cover with damp cloth. Place in refrigerator and punch down occasionally as dough rises. About 2 hours before baking cut off amount needed and return rest of dough to refrigerator. Shape while cold into rolls and place on greased baking sheet. Brush tops with melted butter. Let rise until light, 1½ to 2 hours. Heat oven to 400 degrees and bake for 12 to 15 minutes.

Jeanette Schlernitzauer, Athens Pike

REFRIGERATOR ROLLS

1 tsp. sugar
2 yeast cakes
2¼ cups lukewarm water
½ cup sugar
1 T. salt
2 T. melted shortening
2 eggs, beaten
8 plus cups flour

Add 1 teaspoon sugar to yeast and stir until liquefied. Add ¼ cup lukewarm water. Mix 2 cups water, sugar, salt, and shortening. Add eggs and 4 cups of flour. Beat. Stir in 4 plus cups flour. Mix well (do not beat). Cover and refrigerate. When ready to bake, remove from refrigerator and let rise. Bake at 400 degrees for 20 to 25 minutes.

Gail Hutcheson, Rainbow Mountain

ROLLS

6 T. Crisco
1 tsp. salt
¼ cup sugar
1 egg
1 cup hot water
1 pkg. yeast
¼ cup warm water
3½ - 4 cups sifted flour

Put Crisco, salt, sugar, and egg into mixer bowl. Add hot water. Allow mixture to cool to lukewarm. Dissolve yeast in warm water and add to mixture. Add half of flour and beat until glossy. Add remaining flour; refrigerate. Remove amount needed about 2 hours before serving. Knead and shape; let rise; and bake at 400 degrees. Delicious and easy.

Mrs. L. L. Tuck, Harvest

SPOON ROLLS

1 pkg. dry yeast
2 cups lukewarm water
4 cups self-rising flour

¼ cup sugar
¾ cup melted shortening
1 egg, beaten

Dissolve yeast in water. Mix all ingredients; store covered in refrigerator overnight. Pour in greased muffin tins ½ full and bake in preheated oven at 400 degrees for 20 minutes.
      Mary Frances Mitchell, Madison Cross Roads

SUSAN'S REFRIGERATOR ROLLS

1 cup mashed Irish potatoes,
 cooked
⅔ cup shortening or oil
½ cup sugar
1 tsp. salt

2 eggs
1 pkg. yeast
½ cup lukewarm water
1 cup warm milk
6 - 8 cups sifted flour

Mash potatoes; add shortening, sugar, salt, and beaten eggs. Cream well. Dissolve yeast in lukewarm water and add lukewarm milk; add to potato mixture. Add sifted flour to make soft dough. Toss on floured board and knead well. Put into large bowl and let rise until double in bulk. Knead slightly. Place in covered bowl and rub top with butter. Put in refrigerator until ready to bake. About 1 hour before baking pinch off dough, shape into rolls, and let rise until light, for about 1 hour. Bake 15 to 20 minutes at 400 degrees.
      Mrs. Hugh Tipton (Bessie Mae), Monrovia

WHOLE WHEAT YEAST ROLLS I

1 pkg. dry yeast
1 cup warm water
1 tsp. salt
¼ cup sugar

6 T. oil
3½ cups flour (½ plain and ½
 whole wheat)
1 egg, beaten

Sprinkle yeast in ¼ cup warm water. Combine all the above then add yeast. Put in large bowl and cover; oil the top of dough. Store in refrigerator (can be kept a week). When ready to use, roll out and shape into rolls. Let rise about 1 hour. Bake at 400 degrees for 10 to 12 minutes.
      Mrs. W. L. Hoover (Barbara), Monrovia

WHOLE WHEAT YEAST ROLLS II

1 tsp. salt
¼ cup honey
6 T. shortening
1 cup scalded milk
1 pkg. dry yeast

2 T. lukewarm water
1 egg, beaten
3 cups flour (½ plain and ½ whole wheat)
¼ cup bran
¼ cup wheat germ

Combine salt, honey, shortening, and scalded milk cooled to lukewarm. Add yeast that has been dissolved in 2 tablespoons lukewarm water. Add beaten egg. Beat in 2 cups flour, bran, and wheat germ and beat until smooth. Add remaining flour and enough more (if needed) to make dough easy to handle. Store in refrigerator. When ready to use punch down and make into rolls. Let rise to double in bulk. Bake at 400 degrees for 12 to 15 minutes.

Mary Sanders, Central

YEAST ROLL

1 pkg. active dry yeast
¼ cup water
½ cup scalded milk
2 T. sugar

¾ tsp. salt
2 T. butter, melted
1 egg
2 cups plain flour

Dissolve yeast in water, add cooled milk, sugar, and salt. Let stand for 5 minutes. Add butter, egg, and mix well. Stir in flour. Cover and let rise. Knead 1 to 2 minutes. Shape into rolls. Bake at 400 degrees for 10 to 15 minutes.

Kay Bass, Big Cove

YEAST BREADS

BROWN YEAST BREAD

3 T. yeast
2 T. sugar
1 cup warm water
7 cups whole wheat flour
2 tsp. salt

½ cup honey
2 eggs
1 lg. can evap. milk
½ cup oil
2 cups warm water

Approx. 4 cups white flour

Mix yeast, sugar, and warm water and let get bubbly. Mix remaining ingredients, except white flour, then add yeast mixture; blend till smooth and thin. Add white flour a little at a time while mixing, till dough starts to pull away from sides of bowl. Blend 5 minutes. Place dough onto well-oiled surface; roll out till about ¼ to ½-inch thick; shape into 4 loaves and place in well-oiled loaf pans. Let rise for 1½ hours in warm place, or place in an oven preheated to 250 degrees then turned off. Keep dough covered with a damp cloth while rising in oven for 25 to 30 minutes. Also place pan of water under loaves to help keep moist. Bake at 325 degrees for 25 minutes on bottom rack. Cool on rack.

Roberta Friedman, Harvest

CHEESE BREAD

1 pkg. yeast
1 cup warm water
1 egg
¼ cup sugar

½ cup Wesson oil
1 tsp. salt
3 cups flour, unsifted
1 cup cheese, grated

Dissolve yeast in water. Beat egg, sugar, and oil together. Add salt to flour. Add flour mixture to egg mixture gradually. Add yeast and water. Stir in grated cheese. Grease and flour small loaf pans. Place dough in small pans. Let dough rise 1 hour. Bake at 300 degrees for 1 hour.

Sue Price, Westbury

CRACKED WHEAT BREAD

3 T. sugar
2 tsp. salt
⅓ cup shortening

2 cups warm milk (not hot)
1 cup cracked wheat
2 pkgs. yeast

2 cups all-purpose flour

Mix sugar, salt, shortening, milk, cracked wheat, and yeast. Add flour until dough is very stiff. Knead for 10 minutes. Let rise in a bowl, covered until double in bulk (1 to 3 hours). Punch down and divide into two loaves. Let rise for 1 to 2 hours. Bake at 375 degrees for 30 to 40 minutes.

Darlene Reichman, Rainbow Mountain

DILLY BREAD

1 pkg. yeast
¼ cup warm water
1 cup creamed cottage cheese, heated until lukewarm
2 T. sugar
1 egg, unbeaten

1 T. instant minced onion
1 T. butter
2 T. dill seed
1 tsp. salt
¼ tsp. soda
2¼-2½ cups flour

Soften yeast in water. Heat cottage cheese until lukewarm. Combine with rest of ingredients in mixing bowl except flour. Add flour to form stiff dough, beating well after each addition. Cover and let rise in warm place (85 to 90 degrees) until light and double in size, 50 to 60 minutes. Stir down. Turn into well-greased 8-inch round 1½-2-quart casserole. Let rise in warm place till light, 30 to 40 minutes. Bake at 350 degrees for 40 to 50 minutes or until light brown. Brush with soft butter and salt.

Stella Miller, Fleming Hills

IRISH BREAD

½ cup dry milk
2 cups water
¾ cup sugar
2 pkgs. yeast

1 cup *lard* (melted and cooled)
2 T. salt
3 eggs (double is 5 eggs)
Flour

Dissolve milk in warm water. Add ¼ cup sugar and yeast. When yeast starts to bubble add lard, salt, sugar, and eggs. Beat well. Add flour and beat until blended. Beat in enough flour to make dough thick and sticky. Let rise in pan until double. Turn out on floured board. Knead dough so you can handle it; cut into pieces with floured hands. Grease pans. Let rise and bake in 350-degree oven for 45 minutes or until done.

Rita Pratte, South Parkway

RAISIN CASSEROLE BREAD

4¼-4¾ cups unsifted flour
½ cup sugar
1 tsp. salt
2 pkgs. dry yeast

1 cup milk
½ cup water
¼ cup margarine
1 cup seedless raisins

1 egg (at room temperature)

In a large bowl thoroughly mix 1½ cups flour, sugar, salt, and undissolved yeast. Combine milk, water, and margarine in a saucepan. Heat over low heat until liquids are warm. (Margarine does not need to melt.) Gradually add to dry ingredients and beat 2 minutes at medium speed of electric mixer, scraping bowl occasionally. Stir in enough additional flour to make a stiff batter. Cover; let rise in a warm place, free of draft, until doubled in bulk, about 1 hour. Stir batter down, beat in raisins for about ½ minute. Turn into 2 greased 1-quart casseroles. Brush on egg. Bake in moderate oven (350 degrees) about 40 to 45 minutes or until done. Remove from casseroles and cool on wire racks. Honey can be substituted for sugar. (Stirring down: When a batter bread recipe calls for stirring down it means to stir raised dough until it is reduced to almost its original size.) *Janice Coombe, Hurricane*

SOY NUT BREAD

2 cups soaked (overnight) soybeans
2 pkgs. dry yeast
½ cup lukewarm water
3½ cups hot water

½ cup honey
1 T. oil
4 tsp. salt
¾ cup soy flour
White flour, unbleached

Soak soybeans overnight. Next day dissolve yeast in lukewarm water. Blend soybeans in hot water. Add honey, oil, salt, and yeast. Add soy flour and enough unbleached flour to make dough. Let rise at least once until doubled. Shape into 4 loaves and let rise again until doubled. Bake at 350 degrees for ½ hour; reduce heat to 325 degrees and continue baking for ½ hour more. Brush tops with oil and cool on racks.

Gloria Radke, South Huntsville

STAFF OF LIFE BREAD

2 pkgs. dry yeast
2 tsp. salt
3 T. sugar

2 cups warm water
¼ cup cooking oil
Flour*

Mix all ingredients. Knead about 10 minutes, with hooks or by hand, until satiny and with small surface blisters. Place in a greased bowl, turning to grease all surfaces (I like bacon drippings best). Cover with foil and folded cloth. Let rise in cool oven, placing a large pan (big enough to hold about a gallon) of boiling water on bottom rack. When dough doubles in size, punch down, divide into two balls and let rest on a floured surface, covered with inverted bowl, for about 15 minutes. Roll out to a roughly triangle shape, then roll tightly, pushing out any remaining air bubbles and sealing by pinching together at seams and ends. Place in well-greased loaf pans and repeat rising procedure. When doubled in bulk turn oven on to 350 degrees and bake until well browned, about 25 minutes. Turn out on rack and cool. Variations: Divide dough into 3 portions, roll into cylinders and bake on meal-sprinkled cookie sheet. Use brown sugar and 1½ cups rye or whole wheat flour.
*Enough flour to make a soft dough if you use dough hooks. If kneading by hand, use enough to make a dough firm enough to handle, approximately 7 to 10 cups.

Evelyn Ryan, Harvest

Twixt optimist and pessimist
The difference is droll;
The optimist sees the doughnut,
The pessimist sees the hole.

TWO-TONE RYE TWIST

4 cups sifted all-purpose flour
4 cups whole rye flour
2 env. yeast
2½ cups warm water
¼ cup melted butter
⅓ cup dark molasses
3 tsp. salt

2 tsp. caraway seeds, crushed
1 cup whole-bran cereal
¼ cup cocoa
2 tsp. instant coffee
Cornmeal
1 tsp. cornstarch
½ cup cold water

Combine 3 cups all-purpose flour with rye flour. Blend well and reserve. Sprinkle yeast into warm water. Stir till dissolved; add butter, molasses, salt, and caraway. Pour ½ mixture into second large bowl. To ½ of mixture add bran, cocoa, and coffee; mix well. Stir in enough flour mix to make soft dough (about 3 cups). Turn onto floured surface. Knead for about 5 minutes. (Use some all-purpose flour to keep from sticking). Place dough in greased bowl. Cover. Let rise approximately 45 minutes. To remaining ½ of yeast mixture stir in approximately 3½ cups flour mix. Turn onto floured board; knead 5 minutes. Put in greased bowl and let rise for 45 minutes. Grease 2 cookie sheets and dust with cornmeal. When finished rising, punch down. Knead a few times. Divide each type in half. Roll into 18-inch ropes. Twist together 1 dark and 1 light rope. Pinch ends together. Put on cookie sheet. Let rise 45 minutes. Brush tops with butter; bake 45 minutes at 350 degrees. Mix cornstarch and water in saucepan. Bring to boil; boil 1 minute. Brush on top of loaves after the 45-minute period. Bake additional 3 minutes. Let cool before cutting.

Carolyn Griner, Rainbow Mountain

WHOLE WHEAT BREAD I

1 pkg. yeast
½ cup warm water
1 cup brown sugar
⅓ cup shortening
4½ cups all-purpose flour

2 tsp. salt
1 cup scalded milk
1 cup cool water
2 cups whole wheat flour

Dissolve yeast in warm water. Dissolve sugar, shortening, and salt in the hot milk. Add cool water. Cool mixture to lukewarm. Add yeast. Stir in whole wheat flour. Add enough of the all-purpose flour to make a moderately stiff dough. Turn out on floured bread board and knead until dough is smooth (8 to 10 minutes). Place dough in greased bowl. Turn so greased dough is on top. Cover with damp cloth. Let rise until doubles (about 2 hours). Punch down. Turn out on bread board. Divide into 3 parts. Let rise 10 minutes. Shape into loaves; put into greased bread pans. Let rise again. Bake at 375 degrees until it starts to brown (10 to 15 minutes). Reduce heat to 350 degrees and bake until done, about 20 to 30 minutes. Yield: 3 small loaves.

Margaret West, Big Cove

WHOLE WHEAT BREAD II
(Very good)

¼ cup sugar
1 cup warm water
1 pkg. yeast
2⅔ cup heated milk

½ cup honey or molasses
1 T. salt
⅓ cup oil
7 cups whole wheat flour

Stir sugar into warm water in small bowl and sprinkle yeast over it. Dissolve. In large mixing bowl stir together milk, honey or molasses, salt, and oil. When lukewarm add yeast mixture. Sift in whole wheat flour, stir until well mixed. If dough is sticky add more flour. Turn out on board and knead well. Place dough in clean bowl, cover with damp cloth, and let rise until double in bulk. Turn out on board and knead. Shape into 2 loaves and place in greased 9x5x3-inch loaf pans. Cover with damp cloth and let rise until double in bulk. Preheat oven to 450 degrees and bake. Cool on wire rack. This bread is dark, moist, slightly coarse in texture and the flavor is unusually good.

Mrs. Hugh Tipton (Bessie S.), Monrovia

SWEET ROLLS AND DOUGHNUTS

CINDY'S SALLY LUNNS

1 cup cold coffee, strong
1½ cups brown sugar
1 cup soft butter
1 tsp. nutmeg

1 tsp. cinnamon
1 tsp. baking powder
1 tsp. soda
3¾ cups plain flour

Mix all ingredients. Drop by tablespoons on greased sheet. Bake at 350 degrees 10 or 15 minutes. If batter is not pretty stiff, add more flour. When cool, frost with powdered sugar frosting or glaze.

Opaline West, Madison Cross Roads

CREAM CHEESE DANISH

1 cup sour cream
½ cup sugar
1 tsp. salt
½ cup melted butter

2 pkgs. dry yeast
½ cup warm water (105-115 degrees)
2 eggs, beaten
4 cups all-purpose flour

Heat sour cream over low heat; stir in sugar, salt, and butter. Cool until lukewarm. Sprinkle yeast over ½ cup warm water in large mixing bowl stirring until yeast dissolves. Add sour cream mixture, eggs, and flour. Mix well. Cover tightly and refrigerate overnight. Next day: Divide dough into 4 equal parts. Roll out each part on well-floured board into (4) 12x8 rectangles. Spread ¼ of cheese filling down one side of rectangle. Roll up like jelly roll (longways). Pinch edges together and fold ends under. Place seam side down on greased baking sheet. Slit. Cover and let rise 1 hour. Bake at 375 degrees for 12 to 15 minutes. Spread with glaze while warm.

Cheese Filling

2 8-oz. pkgs. cream cheese, softened
¾ cup sugar
1 egg, beaten
⅛ tsp. salt
2 tsp. vanilla

Combine cream cheese, sugar, egg, salt, and vanilla. Mix well.

Glaze

2 cups powdered sugar
4 T. milk
1 tsp. vanilla

Pam Hudson, Fleming Hills

ENGLISH (HARLEQUIN) SCONES

2 cups plain flour
2 tsp. double-acting baking powder
½ tsp. salt
4 T. butter
2 eggs
½ cup half-and-half

Sift flour, baking powder, and salt into mixing bowl. Use fork and knife to cut butter into mixture, as with pastry. Break eggs into another bowl, reserving a little white to brush on scone tops. Beat eggs with half-and-half and beat into flour mixture. Then roll out dough and cut. Brush with egg white and sprinkle with sugar. Bake at 450 degrees for 15 minutes.

Gloria Radke, South Huntsville

FRENCH TOAST

3 T. sugar
1 - 1¼ tsp. cinnamon
3 med. - lg. eggs

White bread
1 stick of butter
Bacon
Orange slices

Set frypan at 250 to 275 degrees. Lightly butter pan. Dip both sides of white bread in sugar, cinnamon, and egg mixture and cook on each side until lightly browned. Rub the top lightly with a stick of butter. Serve with bacon and orange slices. Really special topped with whipped cream and strawberries or other fresh fruit. This is my daughters' favorite breakfast.

Linda Warren, South Huntsville

GLENDA'S BEIGNETS
(French Doughnuts)

2 cups all-purpose flour
¾ cup sugar
Dash of salt
1 tsp. baking powder
1 T. light corn syrup

1 egg white
1 T. cooking oil
⅓ cup milk
1 tsp. vanilla
Powdered sugar

Mix together all ingredients except powdered sugar until dough is stiff. Roll on floured surface to pie crust thickness, about ⅛ inch. Cut into about 1-inch squares. Place in deep fat fryer with oil at 375 to 400 degrees. Cook until golden brown, turning as needed. Drain and sprinkle with powdered sugar while hot. Serve hot.

Glenda Beard, Harvest

QUICKIE DOUGHNUTS

1 can biscuits
Oil

Powdered sugar
Jelly

Open the can of biscuits. Set electric skillet to 375 degrees. Add oil as if for pan frying. Make 5 slits in biscuits from outer edge not quite to center. Make deep indentation with thumb in center. Pan fry on each side until delicate brown. Shake in powdered sugar or sprinkle on both sides. Put a dab of jelly in center. This comes in handy when the kids drop in unexpectedly. They love 'em!

Connie Kramer, Darwin Downs

YEAST ROLLS

1 cup margarine
2 cups sifted flour
Dash of salt
1 pkg. yeast
½ cup plus 1 T. sugar

3 T. warm water
½ tsp. salt
3 eggs, separated
Cinnamon
½ cup chopped nuts

Mix margarine, flour, and dash of salt as for pie crust. Dissolve yeast and 1 tablespoon sugar in water; add salt. Beat egg yolks and add to yeast; combine with flour mixture. Divide into 4 pieces; roll out round as for pie crusts. Cut rounds into 8 wedges. Beat egg whites until stiff, adding ½ cup sugar. Spread onto dough. Sprinkle with cinnamon and nuts. Roll each wedge into horn shapes. Bake at 350 degrees for 15 to 20 minutes. When cool frost with a butter icing. Yield: 32.

Darlene Reichman, Rainbow Mountain

CORN AND SOUR CREAM CORNBREAD

1 cup self-rising meal
½ tsp. salt
2 eggs-slightly beaten
½ cup oil

1 small carton of sour cream (8 oz.)
1 small can creamed corn (8½ oz.)

Preheat oven to 400°. Grease pan and heat. Add corn and cornbread mixture, bake for 25 to 30 minutes. This won't brown until the very last minute, so watch it. Serve warm.

Margaret Hornsby, Hurrican

RAISIN SPICE ROLLS

4½ to 5½ cups bread flour
1 cup mashed potato flakes
¼ cup sugar
1 tsp. salt
¾ tsp. cinnamon
¼ tsp. nutmeg

2 pkg. active dry yeast
2 cups milk
½ cup butter
2 eggs
1 cup raisins

Topping:
1 tbsp. butter, melted
1 tbsp. sugar

¾ tsp. nutmeg

Grease 13x9-inch pan or two 9-inch round cake pans. Lightly spoon flour into measuring cup; level off. In large bowl, combine 1½ cups flour, potato flakes, sugar, salt cinnamon, nutmeg and yeast; blend well. In medium sauce pan, heat mild and margarine until very warm (120-130°F). Add warm liquid and eggs to flour mixture. Blend at low speed until moistened; beat 3 minutes at medium speed. Stir in raisins and an additional 2½ to 3 cups flour until dough pulls cleanly away from sides of bowl. On floured surface, knead in ½ to 1 cup flour until dough is smooth and elastic, about 10 minutes. Place dough in greased bowl: cover loosely, with cloth towel. Let rise in warm place (80 to 85°F) until light and doubled in size, about 45-60 minutes. Punch down dough to remove all air bubbles. Divide dough into 24 pieces; shape into balls. Place in prepared pan. Cover; let rise in warm place until light and doubled in size, about 30-45 minutes. Heat over to 400°F. Bake 15 to 20 minutes or until golden brown. Immediately remove from pan; brush with melted margarine. Combine 1 tbsp. sugar and ¾ tsp. nutmeg; sprinkle over rolls. Cool. 24 rolls.

Ruth Ann Stalnaker, Hillwood

BISQUICK BANANA BREAD

⅓ cup vegetable oil
1½ cups mashed ripe banana
  (3 large)
½ tsp. vanilla

3 eggs
2⅓ cups bisquick
1 cup sugar
½ cup chopped nuts

Heat oven to 350°. Grease bottom of loaf pan. 9x5x3 generously. Beat all ingredients with a spoon 30 seconds. Pour batter into a pan. Bake 55 to 65 min. until wooden toothpick comes out clean, cool 5 min. Loosen sides of loaf; remove from pan, Yields 1 loaf.

Patsy A. Vaughn, South Parkway

CINNAMON ROLLS

2 pkg. active dry yeast
½ cup warm water (110°-115°)
1½ cups milk
½ cup shortening

½ cup sugar
2 tsp. salt
2 eggs (room temperature)
6½-7 cups flour

1. Stir yeast into warm water in large bowl.
2. Heat mild, shortening, sugar and salt together to about 110°. Add to yeast.
3. Beat in 2 cups of flour and add eggs.
4. Beat in as much remaining flour as possible and then continue to add remainder gradually, kneading 8-10 min.
5. Place dough in large greased bowl, cover and let rise in warm place (85°F) until doubled (about 1-1½ hours).
6. Punch down and turn out on a lightly floured surface. Divide in two and let the dough rest 10 min.
7. Roll out dough in a 20" x 10" rectangle. Spread on softened butter or margarine. Sprinkle with sugar and cinnamon.
8. Roll up like jelly roll, starting at long side. Pinch edges to seal. Cut in 1" slices with knife and place in greased 8" or 9" layer or square pans. Brush with butter or margarine.
9. Let rise until double (30-45 min). Bake at 375° for 25 min. May be frosted when cooled.

Yields: 4 coffee cakes (8" or 9" square or round)

Variation: Caramel Nut Rolls

Same as cinnamon rolls except a caramel but syrup is placed in the pan before the rolls. For syrup boil 3 tbsp. butter or margarine. ½ cup brown sugar, ⅓ cup corn syrup and 2 tbsp. water for 1 min. Sprinkle chopped nuts on top of syrup in pan. After baking, quickly turn pans over to cool on a wire rack.

HELOISE WAFFLES — VERY CRISP

2 cups Bisquick
1 egg

1⅓ (club soda) soda water (10 oz.)
½ cup oil

Mix in blender or processor only till smooth. Bake in hot iron. Bake remaining batter as it doesn't keep. Freeze waffles left over.

Barcie Buist, Westbury

CHEESE BREAD

1 slightly beaten egg
1 cup carnation milk
½ cup water
¼ tsp. salt
3¾ cups bisquick
1½ cups sharp shredded cheese

Combine everything vigorously! Spoon into loaf pan. Bake at 350° for 55 minutes.

Nancy O. Kramer, University

BLUEBERRY MUFFINS

Cream:
½ cup margarine
2 eggs

1 cup sugar

Add:
2 cups plain flour
½ cup milk

2 tsp. baking powder
1½ cup blueberries (15 oz. can, drained)

Bake at 375° for 25-30 minutes. Sprinkle with sugar.

Kelly S. Brewer, Monrovia II

BRAN-NUT BREAD

1 cup Golden Harvest Price Bran
2½ cups Golden Harvest Whole Wheat Flour
2 tsp. baking powder
½ tsp. baking soda
½ tsp. seasoning salt
¼ cup vegetable oil
¾ cup corn syrup
1 egg
1 cup milk
1 cup walnuts chopped or chopped fine sunflower seeds

Mix dry ingredients and liquid ingredients separately. Pour liquid into dry ingredients and mix. Pour into loaf pan. Bake at 375° for 45 min.

*1 cup buttermilk and ⅓ cup water may be used in place of milk

Evelyn Lorenza, University

MASTER'S MUFFINS
(Master's Golf Tournament)

1½ sticks butter
1 cup sour cream
2 cups self-rising flour

Mix butter, sour cream and flour. Bake in ungreased small muffin tins at 350° for 20-25 min. Makes 24

Marie Buist, Westbury

PAULINE'S ROLLS

Grease well muffin pans for 18 rolls, Sift then measure 3½ cups flour. Mix in large bowl.

¼ cup shortening
1 tsp. salt
2 tbsp. sugar

1¼ cups lukewarm water
1 egg well beaten
1 cake fresh yeast (crumbled)

Add flour all at once, beat with fork to make a soft dough. Spoon dough into muffin pans, filling half full. Cover with damp cloth, let rise in warm place. 1 hour until light. Turn on oven to 425° or 450°. Bake rolls 15 min. or until lightly browned. Dough may be covered with damp cloth and stored in refrigerator 1-1½ hrs. before ready to use. The spoon into pan and let rise for an hour before cooking.

Marie Buist, Wesbury

EASY CHEESE BREAD   1 loaf

2½ cups biscuit mix
2 tsp. poppy seeds
1 cup milk

1 cup (4 oz.) shredded sharp cheese
1 egg, beaten

Combine biscuit mix cheese, and poppy seeds in a large bowl. Combine egg and milk, add to biscuit mixture. Mix vigorously for one (1) minute. Spread into a lightly greased 8½ X 4½ X 3-inch loaf pan. Bake at 350° F. for 35 min. or until golden brown.

Virginia Cornelison, Hurrican Club

HONEY NUT BREAD

⅓ cup honey
⅓ cup sugar
½ tsp. salt
2 cups flour
¾ tsp. baking powders
1 tbsp. lemon juice

1 egg
⅔ cup buttermilk
3 tbsp. melted butter or margarine
½ tsp. soda
1 tbsp. lemon rind

Mix well and spoon batter into greased and floured pan. Bake at 350° for 50 to 55 minutes.

Virginia Cornelison, Hurrican Club

PLAIN CORN BREAD

1 tbsp. oil
1 cup buttermilk
1 egg (beaten)
1 cup corn meal (plain)

½ tsp. salt
¼ tsp. soda
2 tsp. baking powder

Mix all ingredients together. Mix well. Pour in hot greased pan. Cook in oven 500° for 8-10 min. depending on oven, how it heats.

Bessie Mae Tipton, Monrovia

CAKES, FROSTINGS, DESSERTS, PIES AND PASTRIES

APPLE CAKES

APPLE CAKE I

1¾ cups sugar
3 eggs
1 cup cooking oil
2 cups sifted flour
1 tsp. baking soda
1 tsp. cinnamon
1 tsp. salt
2 cups sliced apples
1 cup chopped nuts

Beat sugar and eggs well. Add oil and mix until creamy. Sift flour, soda, cinnamon, and salt together. Mix well with first mixture. Fold in apples and chopped nuts. Pour into a greased 9x13-inch pan and bake at 350 degrees for 45 minutes to 1 hour.

Filling

1 cup sugar
1 T. white syrup
½ cup buttermilk
½ stick margarine
½ tsp. soda
½ tsp. vanilla

Mix and boil to soft ball stage. Pour over the cake while both are hot. Leave cake in pan. Punch holes in cake with a toothpick before pouring the filling over it. Delicious served right from the pan or may be stored in refrigerator covered and is even better several days later.

Alta Neely, New Sharon

APPLE CAKE II

1 cup sugar
½ cup butter
1 egg
1 tsp. soda
2 cups diced apples
½ cup coffee (liq.)
1½ tsp. vanilla
1½ cup flour
1 tsp. cinnamon
Dash of salt

Mix ingredients all together and put in a 9-inch square pan. Sprinkle top with brown sugar and nuts. Bake at 375 degrees for 45 minutes or until done.

Mabel Albright, Darwin Downs

APPLE DATE CAKE
(Apple pie filling makes this easy)

2 cups sifted all-purpose flour
1 cup sugar
1½ tsp. baking soda
1 tsp. salt
1 tsp. ground cinnamon
½ tsp. ground allspice
2 eggs, slightly beaten
1 21-oz. can apple pie filling
½ cup cooking oil
1 tsp. vanilla
1 cup chopped dates
¼ cup chopped walnuts
Whipping cream (optional)

Sift together flour, sugar, soda, salt, cinnamon, and allspice. Combine eggs, pie filling, oil, and vanilla; stir into flour mixture and mix well. Stir in dates and nuts. Pour into greased and floured 13½x8¾x1¾-inch baking dish. Bake in 350-degree oven for 40 to 45 minutes. Cut in squares; serve with a dollop of whipped cream, if desired. Serves 12.

Vicki Coffee, Extension Agent

FRESH APPLE CAKE

2 cups diced apples
1 cup granulated sugar
1 egg
1 cup flour, sifted
1½ tsp. soda
1 tsp. cinnamon
1 tsp. cloves
½ cup chopped pecans

Mix apples and sugar; let stand until sugar is dissolved. Add the egg and beat well. Stir dry ingredients together and combine with apple mixture. Add nuts. Pour into 8x8-inch greased pan and bake for 40 minutes at 375 degrees. Immediately cover with sauce.

Sauce

⅓ cup brown sugar
⅓ cup granulated sugar
2 T. flour
¼ cup butter
1 cup water
1 tsp. vanilla
¼ cup chopped pecans

Mix together the sugars and flour; add to melted butter and water. Add vanilla. Bring to a boil and pour over cake. Sprinkle with nuts.

Linda Clark, Owens Cross Roads

VERMONT APPLE CAKE

2 cups sifted flour
1 tsp. baking powder
1 tsp. soda
1 tsp. salt
1 tsp. cinnamon
¾ cup butter
1⅓ cups sugar

1 cup maple syrup
2 eggs
1 tsp. vanilla
⅓ cup sweet milk
3 cups finely chopped apples
1 cup chopped pecans
Apple slices for garnish

Sift first 5 ingredients together. Cream butter and sugar; blend in syrup. Beat in eggs and vanilla. Gradually add dry ingredients and milk. Beat. Stir in apples and pecans. Pour into two 9-inch pans or one 9x13x2-inch buttered and floured pan. Bake at 350 degrees for 40 to 45 minutes. Cool for 5 minutes before removing from pan.

Vermont Apple Cake Topping

¾ cup brown sugar
½ cup maple syrup
1 stick butter

1 T. all-purpose flour
¼ cup evap. milk
1 tsp. vanilla
½ cup coconut

Cook together (all except vanilla and coconut) for 8 minutes. Stir while cooking. Remove from heat and stir in vanilla and coconut. Beat for 2 or 3 minutes. Spread on warm cake.

Mrs. Herman Johnston (Mildred), Monrovia

CHOCOLATE CAKES

AUNT ANN'S WACKY CAKE

1½ cups flour
½ tsp. salt
3 T. cocoa
1 tsp. soda

1 cup sugar
2 tsp. vinegar
1 tsp. vanilla
5 T. oil

1 cup water

Sift the dry ingredients together right in a 9x13-inch cake pan. Make 3 holes in the dry ingredients. Put vinegar in the first hole. Put vanilla in the second hole. Put oil in the third hole. Pour the cup of water over the whole thing and mix well. Bake for 25 to 30 minutes at 350 degrees.

Linda De Haye, Vestavia
Betty Cothran, Athens Pike

CHOCO-DOT PUMPKIN CAKE

2 cups flour
2 tsp. baking powder
1 tsp. baking soda
½ tsp. salt
1½ tsp. cinnamon
½ tsp. ground cloves
¼ tsp. allspice
¼ tsp. ginger

2 cups sugar
4 eggs
2 cups pumpkin
1 cup vegetable oil
1 cup All-Bran (½ Bran Flakes)
1 cup semi-sweet chocolate morsels
1 cup chopped nuts
Powdered sugar glaze (optional)

Sift together flour, baking powder, soda, salt, spices, and sugar. Set aside. In large mixing bowl, beat eggs until foamy. Add pumpkin, oil, and All-Bran; mix well. Add sifted dry ingredients, mixing only until combined. Stir in chocolate morsels and nuts. Spread evenly in ungreased 10x4-inch tube pan. Bake at 350 degrees for about 1 hour and 10 minutes. Cool completely before removing from pan. Place on cake plate; drizzle with glaze if desired. Yield: 16 servings or 2 loaves.

Betty Johnson, Hurricane

CHOCOLATE ECLAIR CAKE
(No Baking)

1 box honey graham crackers
2 reg. pkgs. French vanilla pudding, instant

3 cups milk
1 9-oz. container Cool Whip

Butter 9x13-inch pan and line bottom with honey grahams. Beat pudding with milk. Fold in Cool Whip. Pour half of mixture over crackers. Add another layer of crackers then rest of pudding. Finish with another layer of crackers. Top with frosting.

Frosting

2 1-oz. squares unsweetened chocolate, melted
1½ cups powdered sugar

3 T. milk
2 T. white Karo syrup
1 tsp. vanilla
2 T. soft butter

Whip all ingredients with spoon. Spread over top layer of crackers. Refrigerate for 24 hours. This cake tastes just like chocolate eclairs.

Nancy Teasdale, South Huntsville

CHOCOLATE FUDGE CAKE

2 cups flour
2 cups sugar
½ tsp. salt
2 sticks oleo

1 cup water
3 T. cocoa
1 tsp. baking soda
½ cup buttermilk

1 tsp. vanilla

Sift flour, sugar, and salt together in large bowl. Put oleo, water, and cocoa in a saucepan. Bring to a boil and pour over flour mixture. Add soda, buttermilk, and vanilla. Pour over other mixture and mix well. Bake at 350 degrees for 25 minutes. Make icing 5 minutes before cake is done. Bake in a 9x13-inch pan.

Icing

1 stick oleo
6 T. milk
3 T. cocoa

1 box powdered sugar
½ cup chopped nuts
1 tsp. vanilla

Melt oleo with other ingredients in a pan. Bring to boil. Pour over cake when taken from oven.

Faye C. Gwin, Madison Cross Roads

CHOCOLATE-NUT ZUCCHINI CAKE

3 sq. unsweetened chocolate
3 cups unsifted flour
1½ tsp. baking powder
1 tsp. baking soda
1 tsp. salt

4 eggs
3 cups sugar
1½ cups salad oil
1 cup nuts
3 cups grated zucchini

Melt chocolate over hot water. Cool. Preheat oven to 350 degrees. Grease and flour 10-inch tube pan. Sift flour, baking powder, soda, and salt. Set aside. Beat eggs until thick. Add sugar 1 cup at a time. Beat well. Add oil and chocolate; mix well. At low speed add dry ingredients. Mix until smooth. Add nuts and zucchini. Stir well. Bake for 1 hour and 15 minutes or until done.

Jeanette Schlernitzauer, Athens Pike

CHOCOLATE YEAST CAKE

2 ozs. unsweetened chocolate
1 pkg. yeast
¼ cup warm water
1 cup shortening
3 cups flour
1 tsp. baking soda
½ tsp. salt
3 eggs
2 cups sugar
1 cup milk
½ cup chopped pecans

Melt chocolate and set aside. Grease and flour 10-inch tube pan. Combine all ingredients; pour batter into pan; cover with aluminum foil and refrigerate for 6 hours or overnight. Remove foil and bake at once at 350 degrees for 45 minutes, then 300 degrees for 45 minutes longer.

Margaret West, Big Cove

MISSISSIPPI MUD CAKE

2 cups sugar
1 cup shortening
3 eggs
⅓ cup cocoa
¼ tsp. salt
1½ cups plain flour
3 tsp. vanilla
1 cup chopped pecans
Marshmallows or marshmallow creme

Cream sugar, shortening, and eggs and beat well. Sift cocoa, salt, and flour. Add to sugar mixture. Add vanilla and nuts. Pour in a greased and floured oblong pan. Bake at 300 degrees for 30 minutes. Remove from oven. Spread top with marshmallows or marshmallow creme. Return to oven for 3 mintues.

Icing

⅓ cup cocoa
1 box powdered sugar
1 stick margarine
1 tsp. vanilla
1 cup pecans
½ cup evap. milk

Sift cocoa and powdered sugar; add margarine, vanilla, nuts, and milk. Spread on cake while cake is hot. Let stand for 2 hours before cutting.

Joyce Tullis, Poplar Ridge

MOCHA CAKE

8 ozs. semi-sweet chocolate chips
¼ cup water
½ cup sugar
5 eggs, separated
2 tsp. (dry) instant coffee
1 tsp. vanilla
1 pkg. Nabisco chocolate wafers

Mix chocolate chips, water, and sugar in double boiler and stir over hot water. Add beaten egg yolks, coffee, and vanilla. Cool and fold in egg whites beaten until stiff. In 9x13-inch pan alternate crushed wafers and mix, beginning and ending with wafer crumbs. Chill 2 hours or freeze.

Gina Guess, Hazel Green

PETER PAUL MOUND CAKE

1 box German chocolate cake mix

Mix and bake cake as directed on box. Let cool completely. Split layers after cooling.

Filling

1 cup sugar
1 cup whipping cream (save ¼ cup for frosting)
1 tsp. vanilla
12 lg. marshmallows
½ lg. can or pkg. angel flake coconut

Mix sugar and whipping cream together. Cook 5 minutes. Remove from heat. Stir in vanilla and marshmallows. Add coconut. Beat well. Spread between layers.

Frosting

1 stick margarine, melted
1 cup firmly packed brown sugar
¼ cup cocoa
Vanilla
¼ cup sifted powdered sugar

Cook the melted margarine, brown sugar, and cocoa together for 2 minutes. Add cream and let mixture come to a boil. Remove from heat. Add vanilla and powdered sugar; cream thoroughly and frost cake.

Annelle Blackwell, New Sharon

QUICK CHOCOLATE SYRUP CAKE

1 stick oleo
1 cup sugar
4 eggs

1 16-oz. can chocolate syrup
2 tsp. vanilla
1 cup self-rising flour

Mix all above ingredients and bake in a 9x13-inch pan for 25 to 30 minutes at 350 degrees.

Frosting

1 stick oleo
¼ cup cocoa
⅓ cup milk

12 lg. marshmallows
1 box powdered sugar
1 cup pecans (optional)

Melt first 4 ingredients together. Add sugar and pecans. Beat until of spreading consistency.

Gina Guess, Hazel Green

RANDY'S CHOCOLATE COOKIE SHEET CAKE

2 cups flour
2 cups sugar
1 tsp. baking soda
2 tsp. cinnamon
2 sticks margarine

4 T. cocoa
1 cup water
2 eggs
½ cup buttermilk
1 tsp. vanilla

Mix flour, sugar, soda, and cinnamon in large bowl. Mix margarine, cocoa, and water in a saucepan and bring to a boil; pour over dry ingredients. Add eggs, buttermilk, and vanilla. Mix well and pour in greased and floured jelly-roll pan (cookie sheet with edges). Bake at 350 degrees for 15 minutes.

Icing

1 stick margarine
4 T. cocoa

6 T. buttermilk
1 lb. box powdered sugar
1 T. vanilla

Bring margarine and cocoa to a boil. Add remaining ingredients. Mix well. Spread over cake.

Gayle Tindol, Rainbow Mountain

TUNNEL-OF-FUDGE CAKE

1½ cups soft butter*
6 eggs
1½ cups sugar

2 cups flour
1 pkg. dark chocolate buttercream frosting mix (2-layer size)
2 cups chopped pecans

Set oven at 350 degrees. Cream butter in large mixer bowl at high speed. Add eggs, 1 at a time, beating well after each. Gradually add sugar; continue creaming at high speed until light and fluffy. *By hand*, stir in flour, frosting mix, and pecans until well blended. Pour batter into greased bundt pan or 10-inch tube pan. Bake for 60 to 65 minutes. Cool 2 hours; remove from pan. Cool completely before serving. *Please use butter only in this recipe, as this cake has a soft, fudgy interior. Test for doneness after 60 minutes by observing dry, shiny, brownie-type crust.

Doris B. Sells, South Parkway

COCONUT CAKES

FRESH COCONUT CAKE

Save the milk from 1 large coconut; remove the coconut from the shell. Grate the coconut and set aside. Use the standard butter cake recipe for cake. Mix batter and bake in layers. Mix coconut, milk, and about ½ cup sugar; spread between layers and on top of cake. Keep refrigerated.

Nora Hawkins, Central

COCONUT CAKE I

1 box Duncan Hines white cake mix
1 T. sugar
1 T. vanilla

Mix according to directions on box and bake in 8-inch round cake pans.

Icing

1 box powdered sugar
6 level T. any vegetable shortening
1 T. almond flavoring

Pinch of salt
Coconut juice to make a smooth paste or hot water
Fresh coconut

Put all ingredients except fresh coconut in mixer and mix thoroughly. Ice and spread coconut on layers and top of cake. I use fresh coconut or large package frozen coconut.

Mary Frances Mitchell, Madison Cross Roads

COCONUT CAKE II

1½ cups sugar
16 ozs. sour cream

18 ozs. frozen coconut
1 box yellow cake mix

Mix sugar, sour cream, and coconut and let set 24 hours. Bake cake mix in two layers and then split each (4 layers). Spread the frosting on cake and refrigerate for 3 days.

Adelaide Steinberg, Blossomwood
Dovie Moore, New Sharon
Cheryl Reid, South Parkway

EASY REFRIGERATOR COCONUT CAKE

Bake your favorite white cake mix in 9x14-inch pan. While hot, pierce with meat fork and pour 1 can Eagle Brand milk over it. Frost with Cool Whip and sprinkle 1 small can coconut over the top. Store in refrigerator.

Shelia Pearce, South Huntsville

FRUIT CAKES

CHRISTMAS CAKE

2 cups pecans
2 cups white raisins
4 cups flour

1 lb. butter
2 cups sugar
6 eggs

3 T. lemon extract

Dredge chopped nuts and raisins in 1 cup of the flour. Cream butter and sugar thoroughly and add eggs 1 at a time. Add remaining ingredients, except extract. Mix thoroughly and add extract. Pour in tube pan and bake in slow oven 1½ to 2 hours at 275 degrees or bake in 2 1-pound loaf pans. This can easily be halved and baked in 1-pound loaves.

Maxie Wilbourn, Central

DARK FRUIT CAKE

1 lb. butter
3 cups brown sugar
1 cup dark Karo syrup
1 cup sour milk*
1 tsp. baking soda
9 eggs

6 cups flour (use 2 cups of this
 amount to flour fruit)
2 tsp. cinnamon
1 tsp. nutmeg
1 tsp. allspice
1 tsp. cloves
1 tsp. salt

Mix until batter is thick enough to drop from a spoon. *If you do not have sour milk, you can make it by adding a little vinegar to milk.

Fruit

2 lbs. raisins	¼ lb. lemon peel
1 lb. seeded muscats	1 lb. candied cherries, chopped
1 lb. currants	½ lb. candied pineapple, chopped
½ lb. citron	2 lbs. dates, chopped
¼ lb. orange peel	3 cups walnuts, chopped

Prepare fruit the day before. Let stand in covered container. Pour 2 cups or more whiskey or brandy over fruit. May add 1 or 2 pints preserves if you like (last year's that may have darkened will do). Dredge fruit in reserved flour, then mix fruit and batter. This will make 3 loaves and 1 10-inch round tube pan. Line each pan with 2 or 3 layers of heavy greased butcher paper or brown paper sacks and bake 2½ to 3 hours or until wooden pick inserted in center comes out clean. May require longer if baking all at once. If necessary cover with foil to prevent excessive browning. Put a pan of water in bottom of oven when baking the cake. It will make cake more moist. Remove from pans; cool. Wrap in plastic wrap or foil; store in a cool place for at least 2 weeks to mellow.

Mary Anne Riley, South Parkway

GOLDEN FRUIT CAKE

16 ozs. red candied cherries (2 cups)
8 ozs. candied orange peel, diced (1 cup)
10 ozs. pitted dates, diced
1 cup California walnuts, chopped
8 ozs. candied lemon peel, diced (1 cup)
8 ozs. candied pineapple, diced (1 cup)
2 cups golden raisins

3¾ cups all-purpose flour
2 cups sugar
1 cup butter or margarine, softened
6 eggs
1 cup cream sherry
½ tsp. salt
2 tsp. double-acting baking powder
2 whole angelica for garnish
2 cups powdered sugar
About 2 T. lemon juice

Up to 2 months before serving: Preheat oven to 300 degrees. Line 10-inch tube pan with foil. Cut cherries in half. Reserve 15 halves for garnish. In large bowl, combine remaining cherries, next 6 ingredients, and ¾ cups of the flour. In another large bowl with mixer at medium speed, beat sugar and butter until fluffy. Add eggs, sherry, salt, baking powder, and remaining flour. Beat at low speed until mixed. Beat 4 minutes at medium speed. Stir in fruit mix. Spoon batter into pan. Bake 3 hours until toothpick inserted in center comes out clean. Cool on rack; remove from pan and peel off foil; wrap tightly with plastic wrap. (You also may use a sherry-moistened cloth for wrapping if you prefer.) Refrigerate cake up to 2 months. (I have also left these, wrapped in sherry cloth and then in foil, on a cool shelf from Halloween until Christmas.) To serve: Cut angelica into 15 leaves. In small bowl, stir lemon juice, a little at a time into powdered sugar until spreading consistency; garnish cake with glaze, leaves, and reserved cherry halves. (If you can not find angelica, you may use green cherries cut into fourths to form leaves for the red cherries.) Makes a 7-pound cake.

Bonnie Riley, South Huntsville-Saddleback Valley, California

Cakes and Frostings

MRS. BRYANT'S FRUIT CAKE

1 box dates, cut-up
1 cup white raisins
1 cup dark raisins
⅔ cup butter
1¼ cup packed brown sugar
¼ cup dark Karo syrup
1 cup water or sweet wine
2 eggs
3 cups flour
1 tsp. cinnamon
½ tsp. nutmeg
1 tsp. baking powder
1 tsp. soda
1 tsp. salt
1 lb. mixed candied fruit
½ lb. whole cherries, red and green
½ lb. candied pineapple, red and green
1 cup pecans

Put first 7 ingredients in pan; bring to boil and let cool. Add remaining ingredients. Mix together and pour into tube pan. Bake slowly at 275 degrees for about 3 hours. Put pan of water in oven while baking. Put brown paper on top of cake for last 2 hours.

Mrs. W. L. Hoover (Barbara), Monrovia

SMALL FRUIT CAKE

3 slices candied pineapple, cut up
24 candied cherries, cut up
1 lb. dates, cut up
1 can moist coconut
1 can Borden's condensed milk
1 cup pecans, cut up
Dash of salt

Mix well. Put in loaf pan and bake 1 hour and 15 minutes at 275 degrees. This is rich. Cut thin slices. This can be eaten immediately.

Wanda Ailor, Blossomwood

WHITE FRUIT CAKE

1 lb. butter
3 cups sugar
13 eggs
6 cups sifted self-rising flour
2 lbs. crystallized cherries
2 lbs. crystallized pineapple
4 cups fresh coconut
2 lbs. broken nut meats
1 tsp. lemon flavoring
1 tsp. almond flavoring
1 tsp. vanilla flavoring

Cream butter and sugar. Add eggs, 1 at a time, beating after each addition. Sift and add flour. Cut cherries and pineapple in small pieces and add to mixture. Add coconut, nuts, and all 3 flavorings. Bake in slow oven (300 degrees) for about 3 hours. Yield: 2 large loaf cakes.

Mrs. Leon Moore, Sr., Big Cove

BLACKBERRY JAM CAKE

1½ cups butter
2 cups sugar
6 eggs
1 cup buttermilk
1 tsp. soda

4 tsp. cloves and cinnamon
3 cups flour
1 cup ground raisins
1 cup ground pecans
1 cup ground coconut
1 cup blackberry jam

Cream butter and sugar; add well-beaten eggs. Add milk and dry ingredients alternately; then add remaining ingredients. Cook 3 layers at 300 degrees.

Fillings

Juice of 3 oranges
Juice of 1 lemon
1½ cups sugar
6 T. flour or cornstarch

Grated rind of 1 orange
1 sm. can pineapple
1 can of angel flake coconut
1 cup nuts

Add enough water to juices to make 3 cups. Mix sugar and cornstarch. Add juice and orange rind. Cook until it begins to thicken, stirring constantly. Add crushed pineapple and coconut. Cook until thick. Add nuts and spread.

Edna McClure, Madison Cross Roads

QUICK AND EASY JAM CAKE

1 box spice cake mix
1 cup raisins
1 cup jam

Mix cake mix according to directions and add raisins and jam. Use German chocolate frosting or carmel.

Mable Sanders, Hurricane

POUND CAKES

CHOCOLATE POUND CAKE

2 sticks margarine
½ cup shortening
3 cups sugar
5 eggs
3 cups flour

½ tsp. baking powder
Pinch of salt
½ cup cocoa
1¼ cups milk
1 tsp. vanilla
¾ cup finely chopped pecans

Cakes and Frostings

Cream margarine and shortening, adding sugar. Add 1 egg at a time, beating after each. Sift dry ingredients twice; add alternately with milk to creamed mixture. Add vanilla and nuts. Bake in large tube pan at 325 degrees for 1¼ hours or until done. Very good with Fudge Bar Chocolate Icing.

Fudge Bar Chocolate Icing

2 ozs. baking chocolate, cut fine
⅔ cup milk
2 cups sugar
½ cup butter
1 tsp. vanilla

Place all ingredients except vanilla in saucepan. Bring to full boil. Cook 1½ minutes. Remove from heat, add vanilla, and beat until thick.

Mrs. L. M. Taylor, Big Cove

COCONUT POUND CAKE

2 sticks margarine
½ cup Crisco
3 cups sugar
5 lg. eggs
½ tsp. almond flavoring
1 tsp. coconut flavoring
3 cups plain flour
1 cup milk
1 can flaked coconut

Cream butter, shortening, and sugar until light and fluffy. Add eggs, 1 at a time, beating well after each. Add flavorings; mix well. Alternately add flour and milk, beating well. Stir in coconut. Spoon into 10-inch greased tube or bundt pan and bake at 350 degrees for 1 hour and 15 minutes.

Linda Nord, Hazel Green

CREAM CHEESE POUND CAKE

1 cup margarine, softened
½ cup butter, softened
1 8-oz. pkg. cream cheese, softened
3 cups sugar
Dash of salt
2 tsp. vanilla
6 lg. eggs
3 cups plain flour

Combine margarine, butter, cream cheese, and sugar; beat well, add salt and vanilla. Add eggs 1 at a time, beating well after each addition. Add flour and mix well. Pour into a greased and floured 10-inch tube pan. Place pan in cold oven and set at 275 degrees. Bake for 1½ hours or until brown. Cool in pan.

Deborah Drake, Big Cove
Barbara Stluka, Davis Hills

FIVE-FLAVOR POUND CAKE

½ lb. butter
½ cup Crisco
3 cups sugar
5 eggs
3 cups all-purpose flour
½ tsp. baking powder
1 cup milk
1 tsp. coconut flavoring
1 tsp. vanilla flavoring
1 tsp. vanilla butter and nut flavoring
1 tsp. rum flavoring
1 tsp. lemon extract

Cream butter, Crisco, and sugar until light and fluffy. Use medium speed. Add eggs 1 at a time and continue beating. Beat fast for 1 minute. Sift flour and baking powder together; add with milk in thirds: start with flour and end with flour. Put in 5 flavorings and continue to beat for about 5 minutes. Grease (Crisco) and flour bundt pan. Pour in batter. Bake at 325 degrees for 1 hour and 15 minutes. Remove cake from pan immediately and place on aluminum foil or wax paper (to catch icing). Pour icing over hot cake and wait to cool.

Icing

½ cup sugar
½ cup water
1 tsp. each of above five flavors

Put all together and boil 2 or 3 minutes. Pour over hot cake.

Maude Taylor, Central
Clara Wall, Central

GRANDMOTHER'S POUND CAKE

1 cup butter
1⅔ cups sugar
5 eggs
2 cups flour
½ tsp. flavoring

Work butter until creamy; beat in sugar and eggs, 1 at a time. When creamy fold in flour and flavoring (vanilla, almond, rum, or any you choose) with a spoon. Spread in buttered and floured loaf pan. Bake for 1½ hours at 300 degrees.

Alma DeShazo, South Parkway
Clara Wall, Central

GRANNY'S OLD-FASHIONED POUND CAKE

3½ cups unsifted all-purpose flour
¼ tsp. baking soda
1½ cups sugar for dry mixture
1 lb. sweet cream butter
10 eggs
1½ T. lemon juice
1 tsp. lemon flavoring
1½ cups sugar for egg whites
2 tsp. cream of tartar

Sift together flour, soda, and 1½ cups sugar. Cream butter into dry mixture with hands. Add egg yolks, 1 at a time, to mixture. Add lemon juice and flavoring. Beat egg whites at low speed until stand in peaks but are still moist. Add to egg whites remaining 1½ cups sugar and cream of tartar. Fold batter into egg white mixture. This is a very stiff batter and will have to be mixed by hand. Grease tube pan and sprinkle with flour. First cook at 250 degrees for 45 minutes. Then turn to 275 degrees and bake for 1 hour. Let sit in oven for 10 minutes and outside for 10 minutes.

Gracie McCurdy, Madison Cross Roads

KENTUCKY WONDER POUND CAKE

2½ cups sifted self-rising flour
2 cups sugar
1½ cups vegetable oil
1 sm. can crushed pineapple with juice
4 egg yolks
2 T. hot water
1 tsp. vanilla
1 cup chopped nuts (floured)
4 egg whites, beaten stiff

Combine all ingredients except nuts and egg whites. Beat well. Add nuts and fold in egg whites. Pour into well-greased tube pan and bake at 350 degrees for about 1 hour or until done.

Charlene Byrd, South Parkway

ORANGE POUND CAKE

2 sticks margarine
2 cups sugar
6 eggs
3 cups plain flour
½ fluid oz. orange extract

Blend ingredients, adding eggs 1 at a time, beating well after each. Bake in tube pan; put in cold oven then set oven at 325 degrees. Bake 1 hour and 15 minutes. Note: No milk, salt, or soda.

Leta Sims, Vestavia

POUND CAKE I

1 lb. butter or margarine
1 lb. powdered sugar
3 cups plain flour

6 eggs (whole)
1 tsp. vanilla
1 tsp. lemon flavoring

Cream butter and powdered sugar till creamy. Add 1 cup flour, a small amount at a time, then add 2 eggs, alternating flour and eggs and ending with flour. The secret to this recipe is beating after each addition. Add flavoring. Bake in a long narrow pan for 1 hour at 350 degrees.

Estelle Pinion, Central
Cora Lewis, Central

POUND CAKE II

3 cups sugar
1 cup butter or 2 sticks oleo
½ cup Crisco
5 eggs, beaten

3 level cups unsifted flour
½ tsp. baking powder
1 cup sweet milk
1 tsp. vanilla
1 tsp. lemon extract

Cream sugar, butter (oleo), and Crisco until sugar dissolves. Add beaten eggs. Sift flour and baking powder together. Add flour and milk alternately to butter-sugar mixture, beginning and ending with flour. Add flavorings. Place in cold stove and turn oven to 325 degrees. Bake for 1½ hours.

Nell Hereford, Hazel Green
Dot Kay, New Sharon

RED VELVET POUND CAKE

1 cup butter
½ cup shortening
3 cups sugar
7 eggs

2 tsp. vanilla
1 1-oz. btl. red food coloring
3 cups cake flour
¼ tsp. salt
1 cup milk

Combine butter, shortening, and sugar: cream until light. Add eggs 1 at a time, beating well after each addition. Stir in vanilla and food coloring. Combine flour and salt; add to creamed mixture alternately with milk. Pour into a greased and floured 10-inch tube pan. Bake at 325 degrees for 1 hour and 20 minutes. Cool. Frost with cream cheese frosting.

Cakes and Frostings

Cream Cheese Frosting

½ cup butter
2 3-oz. pkgs. cream cheese, softened
1 tsp. vanilla
1 lb. pkg. powdered sugar
1-2 T. milk

Combine butter and cream cheese; blend until smooth. Stir in vanilla and sifted powdered sugar. Beat until creamy, adding milk to make frosting of spreading consistency.

Norma Watts, South Huntsville

SOUR CREAM POUND CAKE

½ lb. butter or margarine
½ cup shortening
3 cups sugar
5 eggs
3 cups cake flour
½ tsp. baking powder
¼ cup milk
1 cup sour cream
1 tsp. vanilla
1 tsp. lemon extract

Cream butter, shortening, and sugar until creamy. Add eggs 1 at a time, beating well after each addition. Sift together the cake flour and baking powder. Add to creamed mixture alternately with milk and sour cream. Add vanilla and lemon extract. Pour into greased and floured tube pan. Bake in preheated oven at 300 degrees for 1 hour and 30 minutes.

Clydia M. Reynolds, Madison Cross Roads

WHITE POUND CAKE

3 cups sugar
½ lb. butter
4 cups sifted plain flour
2 tsp. baking powder
1 ¼ cups milk
8 egg whites
2 tsp. lemon juice
1 tsp. vanilla

Cream sugar and butter well. Add ½ of flour mixed with baking powder alternately with milk. Beat egg whites into stiff, not dry, peaks. Add to mixture with remaining flour alternately. Add vanilla and lemon juice. Mix well but do not overbeat. Bake in tube pan for 1 hour and 15 minutes at 350 degrees. *Start in cold oven.* May be baked in layers. Preheat oven to 350 degrees and bake for 25 to 30 minutes.

Mary Sanders, Central

GENERAL CAKES

APRICOT NECTAR CAKE

1 box Duncan Hines yellow cake mix
⅔ cup Wesson oil
¾ cup apricot nectar
1 T. vanilla extract
4 egg yolks
1 T. lemon extract

Mix the cake mix, Wesson oil, apricot nectar, vanilla extract, egg yolks, and lemon extract into a bowl and beat with mixer 5 minutes. Beat egg whites in a separate bowl and fold into the batter. Pour into lightly greased tube pan. Bake in 350-degree oven for approximately 45 minutes. When cool remove from pan and ice with a mixture of powdered sugar and juice from a lemon that will drizzle over the cake.

Jonnie Azlin, Rainbow Mountain

APRICOT NUT CAKE

1 cup boiling water
1 pkg. dried apricots
¾ cup raisins
1 cup sugar
2 T. softened butter
1 egg
1 tsp. vanilla
1⅓ cups sifted flour
1 tsp. baking soda
¾ cup nuts

Pour boiling water over cut-up apricots and raisins. Cover and let cool. Cream sugar and butter. Add beaten egg and vanilla; add flour and soda; then add raisins and apricots. Fold in nuts. Bake in 1-pound loaf pan at 350 degrees.

Maxie Wilbourn, Central

AUNT LOTTIE'S LANE CAKE

1 cup butter
2 cups sugar
1 tsp. vanilla
3¼ cups sifted all-purpose flour
3½ tsp. baking powder
¾ tsp. salt
1 cup milk
8 egg whites

All ingredients should be at room temperature. Cream butter well; add sugar gradually, beating until light and fluffy. Add vanilla, then sifted dry ingredients alternately with milk, beating until smooth. Fold in egg whites. Pour batter into 4 round 9-inch layer pans, 1-inch deep, lined on bottom with paper then greased. Bake in moderate oven, 375 degrees, for about 15 minutes. (If you have only 2 pans, remaining half of batter may stand while first 2 layers are baking.) Let stand for 5 minutes then turn out on racks to cool. Spread Lane Frosting between layers and on top and sides of cake. Cake is best if it is stored for several days to ripen in a cool place. If stored in an airtight container, cake will keep well for several weeks.

Lane Frosting

8 egg yolks
1¼ cups sugar
½ cup butter
¼ tsp. salt
1 cup shredded fresh coconut
1 cup finely chopped seedless raisins
1 cup finely cut candied cherries
1 cup chopped pecans
⅓ cup orange juice

Beat egg yolks slightly; add sugar and butter. Put into saucepan and cook over medium heat, stirring constantly, for about 5 minutes, or until sugar is dissolved and mixture is slightly thickened. (Do not overcook or let egg yolks become scrambled in appearance. Mixture should remain almost transparent.) Remove from heat and add remaining ingredients. Let stand until cold before spreading on cake.

Mrs. Leon Moore, Sr., Big Cove

BANANA NUT CAKE

½ cup oil
1½ cups mashed banana
2 eggs
1½ cups sifted flour
1½ cups sugar
1 tsp. baking soda
4 T. buttermilk
1 tsp. vanilla flavoring
1 cup chopped nuts (black walnuts)

Mix all ingredients together. Bake in tube pan at 325 degrees for 45 minutes. Pour icing over cake after removing from oven.

Icing

5 T. brown sugar
2 T. cream
3 T. butter

Melt all ingredients and pour over cake. Sprinkle with coconut and return to oven and brown lightly.

Mrs. Claude Bridges (Laura), Monrovia

BISCUIT RING CAKE

1 sm. pkg. cream cheese
2 10-oz. cans Hungry Jack
   Refrigerator Biscuits
½ cup melted oleo
¾ cup sugar
Grated rind of 1 orange
¼ cup chopped nuts

Cut cream cheese into 20 pieces. Separate layers of each biscuit and insert square of cream cheese; then press edges back together. Dip into melted oleo and then into mixture of sugar, orange rind, and nuts. Place on edge of bundt pan which has been greased with oleo. Bake at 350 degrees for 30 to 35 minutes. Invert pan over serving plate immediately. Good warm or cold.

Robbie Hallisey, Piedmont

BUSY DAY CAKE

1 No. 2 can crushed pineapple
1 cup pecans
1 pkg. Jiffy cake mix
1 stick margarine

Pour pineapple in 9-inch square pan, sprinkle cake mix over the pineapple, arrange pecans on top, cut up margarine on top of nuts. Bake at 350 degrees for 45 minutes.

June Cope, Hurricane

BUTTERNUT SQUASH CAKE

2 cups boiled, mashed, and
   drained squash
1 cup oil
4 eggs, beaten
2 cups flour
2 tsp. soda
½ tsp. salt
1 tsp. cinnamon
2 cups sugar or honey

Mix squash, oil, and eggs. Add remaining ingredients. Mix well; pour into tube or bundt pan. Bake at 350 degrees for 1 hour or until cake pulls away from sides of pan.

Mrs. Jessie Little, Harvest

CARROT CAKE

4 eggs
2 cups sugar
2 cups sifted flour
2 tsp. soda
¼ tsp. salt
2 tsp. cinnamon
1½ cups cooking oil
3 cups grated carrots
1 cup chopped pecans

Beat eggs until frothy; add sugar gradually. Mix dry ingredients, saving some of the flour to coat nuts. Gradually mix oil and flour mixture, starting with flour and ending with flour. Fold in carrots and nuts. Put in well-greased wax-paper-lined 9 inch round pans. Bake at 300 degrees for 30 to 40 minutes or until done.

Filling

1 8-oz. pkg. cream cheese
1 stick butter or margarine
1 tsp. vanilla flavoring
1 box powdered sugar
1 cup chopped pecans

Mix cheese, margarine, vanilla, and sugar. Add nuts and spread between layers and on top.

Edna McClure, Madison Cross Roads

CARROT PINEAPPLE CAKE

1½ cups all-purpose flour
1 cup sugar
1 tsp. baking powder
1 tsp. baking soda
1 tsp. ground cinnamon
½ tsp. salt
⅔ cup cooking oil
2 eggs
1 cup finely shredded raw carrot
½ cup crushed pineapple, with juice
1 tsp. vanilla

In large mixer bowl, stir together dry ingredients. Add oil, eggs, carrot, pineapple, and vanilla; mix until all ingredients are moistened. Beat with electric mixer for 2 minutes at medium speed. Pour batter into greased and lightly floured 9x9x2-inch baking pan. Bake in 350-degree oven for about 35 minutes; cool. Frost with Cream Cheese Frosting.

Cream Cheese Frosting

1 3-oz. pkg. cream cheese
4 T. margarine
1 tsp. vanilla
Dash of salt
2½ cups sifted powdered sugar
¼ cup chopped pecans

Cream together softened cream cheese and softened margarine; beat in vanilla and salt. Gradually add powdered sugar; blend in well. Stir in pecans.

Mrs. N. Ray Rohland, Big Cove
Roberta Friedman, Harvest

CHEESECAKE I

3 eggs
2 lg. pkgs. cream cheese
⅔ cup sugar
½ tsp. almond extract
Ritz cracker crumbs

Add 3 eggs gradually to softened cream cheese. Mix in sugar and extract. Beat together until smooth. Butter 10-inch pie pan; pour Ritz crumbs in pan and pour out excess. Add mixture and bake 25 minutes at 350 degrees. Cool 20 minutes.

Topping

1 cup sour cream
3 T. sugar
1 tsp. vanilla

Combine all ingredients. Pour onto pie; return to oven for 10 minutes at 350 degrees.

Mrs. Frank J. Nola (Grace), Westbury

CHEESECAKE II

3 eggs, well beaten
2 8-oz. pkgs. cream cheese, softened
1 cup sugar
¼ tsp. salt
2 tsp. vanilla
½ tsp. almond extract
3 cups dairy sour cream
*1 recipe Gram-Nut Crust

Combine eggs, cheese, sugar, salt, and extracts. Beat until smooth. Blend in sour cream. Pour into crust. Bake at 375 degrees for 35 minutes or until set. Cool. Chill 4 to 5 hours. Serves 10.

Gram-Nut Crust

1¾ cups graham cracker crumbs
¼ cup finely chopped walnuts
½ tsp. cinnamon
½ cup melted butter

Combine ingredients and press on bottom and 2½ inches up the sides of a 9-inch spring-form pan.

Cynthia Blanchard, Athens Pike

CHERRY JUBILEE CAKE

1 Duncan Hines Cherry Supreme Cake Mix
1 cup pear or apricot nectar
½ cup Crisco oil
4 eggs, whole
½ cup sugar
½ tsp. juice of maraschino cherries
3 drops red food coloring

Preheat oven to 350 degrees. Grease and flour a 10-inch tube pan. In large bowl blend all ingredients, except eggs; then add eggs 1 at a time, beat at medium speed for 1 minute after each addition. Spread batter in the tube pan. Bake for 45 minutes or until done. Cool right side up for 15 minutes, then remove from pan.

Glaze

1 cup powdered sugar
2 T. cherry juice
6 maraschino cherries, finely chopped

Mix powdered sugar, maraschino cherries, and cherry juice. Pour over cake while still warm to make a glaze.

Edith Baeder, New Sharon

A recipe that is as old as time itself,
Yet always delightfully new.
They call it simple friendship;
Beloved, tried and true.

CHESS CAKE

1 box yellow cake mix
1 stick oleo
3 eggs
1 8-oz. pkg. cream cheese
1 1-lb. box powdered sugar

Mix cake mix, oleo, and 1 egg. Mixture will be rather stiff. Put batter in 9x12-inch pan. Mix 2 eggs, cream cheese, and powdered sugar. Pour this mixture over the dough already in pan. Bake at 350 degrees for about 30 minutes. When cool, cut into small squares.

Mabel Albright, Darwin Downs

CREAM CHEESE BARS
Bottom
1 box yellow cake mix
1 stick of butter or oleo, melted
1 egg, beaten

Mix all 3 ingredients with electric mixer until dry ingredients are wet. Then press firmly with fork into approximately 8½x11-inch baking dish.

Top
3 eggs
1 8-oz. bar of Philadelphia cream cheese
1 box powdered sugar

Mix with electric mixer until batter is creamy. Pour into same dish over crust. Bake 35 minutes at 350 degrees.

Anne Jones, Hurricane

CRUNCH CAKE

2 cups sugar
2 cups flour
1 cup Crisco
6 eggs
1 tsp. vanilla
½ tsp. lemon extract

Combine all ingredients. Beat 12 minutes. Pour into greased and floured tube pan. Bake at 350 degrees for 1¼ hours. Has crunchy crust on top. Good served with fruit.

Norma Colbath, South Parkway

CLEO'S ORANGE DATE CAKE

1 cup butter or margarine
2 cups sugar
4 eggs
2 T. grated orange rind
3½ cups flour
1 tsp. soda
½ tsp. salt
1⅓ cups buttermilk
½ cup sifted flour
1 cup chopped dates
1 cup chopped pecans

Mix all ingredients. Pour into a sheet cake pan. Bake at 325 to 350 degrees for 1½ hours. Remove from oven and let cool.

Glaze
1½ cups sugar
2 T. orange rind
1 cup orange juice

Boil and pour over cool cake while glaze is still hot.

Mrs. Claude Bridges (Laura), Monrovia

DATE COFFEE CAKE

1 cup chopped dates
½ cup walnuts or pecans
¼ cup sugar
1 T. lemon juice
⅔ cup milk or water
1 pkg. Jiffy yellow cake mix

Add first 5 ingredients to cake mix. Bake at 350 degrees. Then sprinkle with powdered sugar. May add cinnamon to powdered sugar. Sprinkle over cake while warm.

Rachel Sturdivant, University

DUMP CAKE

1 can cherry (or strawberry) pie filling
1 can crushed pineapple, drained
1 box yellow cake mix
1 cup chopped nuts
1 cup coconut
1 cup melted oleo

Use a greased tube pan. Pour ingredients into pan in above order. Do *not* prepare cake mix as directed. Just sprinkle dry ingredients into pan. Finish with the melted oleo also poured over top and bake at 350 degrees for 1 hour. Scoop by spoonful into bowl. Serve warm with whipped topping.

Mrs. Ken Quiggle (Jo Ann), Fleming Hills

FAST FIXIN' FRUIT AND CAKE

1 pkg. Duncan Hines Deluxe II White Cake Mix
¼ cup oil
2 eggs
½ cup water
1 can of your favorite pie filling
Powdered sugar
Whipped cream

Pour oil into a 13x9x2-inch pan; tilt pan to cover bottom. Put cake mix, eggs, and water in pan; stir with fork until blended (about 2 minutes). Scrape sides and spread batter evenly in pan. Spoon pie filling onto batter; use a fork to fold into batter, just enough to create a marble effect. Bake at 350 degrees for 35 to 45 minutes until toothpick inserted near center comes out clean. Cool cake. Sprinkle with powdered sugar. Top each piece with whipped cream.

Terri Bunnell, Piedmont

FIG PRESERVE AND HONEY CAKE

2½ cups all-purpose flour
1 tsp. soda
1 tsp. salt
1 tsp. nutmeg
1 tsp. cinnamon
½ tsp. allspice
½ tsp. cloves

3 eggs
¾ cup vegetable oil
1½ cups honey
¾ cup buttermilk
1 T. vanilla
1 cup fig preserves
½ cup chopped pecans

Buttermilk Glaze

Combine dry ingredients in large mixing bowl. Add eggs and oil; beat well. Add honey and blend well. Add buttermilk and vanilla, mixing thoroughly. Stir in preserves and pecans. Pour batter into greased and floured 10-inch tube pan. Bake at 350 degrees for 1 hour and 15 minutes. Let cool 10 minutes and remove from pan. Pour warm glaze over warm cake.

Buttermilk Glaze

¼ cup buttermilk
½ cup sugar
¼ tsp. soda

1½ tsp. cornstarch
¼ cup margarine
1½ tsp. vanilla

Combine first 5 ingredients in saucepan; bring to a boil and remove from heat. Cool slightly and stir in vanilla.

Helen Maples, Owens Cross Roads

GEORGIA CAKE

1 box Duncan Hines Cake Mix
  (white pudding mix)

1 can mandarin oranges, with juice
½ cup oil

4 eggs, whole

Mix and bake at 350 degrees for 20 to 25 minutes. Cool and ice.

Icing

1 lg. can crushed pineapple
1 box vanilla instant pudding mix

½ cup chopped pecans
1 lg. Cool Whip

Fold other ingredients into Cool Whip. Ice layers and top. Refrigerate.

Nell Long, Big Cove
Laura Betterton, Madison Cross Roads
Gwen Pruitt, Davis Hills

GINGERBREAD

½ cup shortening or margarine
½ cup brown sugar
1 cup molasses
1 egg
2½ cups flour

¼ tsp. cloves
1 tsp. cinnamon
1½ tsp. ginger
1 tsp. soda
½ tsp. salt

1 cup hot water

Mix shortening, sugar, molasses, and egg. Add sifted flour and other dry ingredients and beat well. Then add hot water and bake in 9-inch greased pan for 40 to 50 mininutes at 350 degrees.

Myrtie Reynolds, New Sharon

GOLD AND SILVER CAKE
(A must for Christmas at our house for 3 generations)

Gold Cake

1 cup sugar
½ cup butter or oleo
5 egg yolks
2 cups plain flour

½ tsp. soda
1 tsp. cream of tartar
½ cup sweet milk
1 tsp. vanilla

Cream sugar and butter. Add egg yolks and beat well. Sift dry ingredients and add to batter. Alternate with the milk. Add flavoring. Bake in 2 8-inch layer pans at 350 degrees until done.

Silver Cake

½ cup butter
1½ cups sugar
1 tsp. cream of tartar
½ tsp. soda

3 cups flour
1 cup sweet milk
1 tsp. vanilla
6 egg whites, beaten to a froth

Cream butter and sugar. Add dry ingredients to creamed mixture alternately with milk and vanilla. Beat eggs whites to a froth and fold into batter. Bake in three 8-inch pans that have been greased and floured. The layers will be thin. Ice with 7-minute frosting and fresh coconut. Alternate 1 white and 1 yellow layer until you have stacked all 5 layers.

Shirley Milam, Pulaski Pike

GOOEY BUTTER CAKE

1 box yellow cake mix
1 egg
1 stick oleo

Mix together and spread in greased pan, approximately 9x14x3. Spread with topping. Bake at 350 degrees until golden brown for about 45 minutes. Serve in squares.

Topping

2 eggs
1 lb. powdered sugar
1 8-oz. pkg. creamed cheese, softened

Mix thoroughly and heat on medium heat until smooth.

Evelyn Ryan, Harvest

HERMIT CAKE

1 lb. butter
3 cups brown sugar
6 eggs
5 cups flour
2 tsp. baking powder
2 tsp. cinnamon
2 lbs. dates, chopped
1⅓ lbs. chopped nuts (pecans)
2 tsp. vanilla
Juice of 1 lemon

Cream butter and sugar, and add eggs 1 at a time; mix well. Sift dry ingredients. Add small portions to chopped dates and nuts; add remaining ingredients to creamed mixture. Line tube pan with wax paper and bake at 275 degrees for 2½ hours. Best when wrapped for 2 to 3 weeks in cheesecloth soaked with rum.

Oneita Craighead, Fleming Hills

HONEY CAKES

2½ cups flour
½ tsp. salt
1 tsp. ginger
1 cup honey
½ cup oleo
1½ tsp. baking soda

Sift together the flour, salt, and ginger. Bring the honey and oleo to a boil and cool. Add the baking soda and beat well, until it foams. Pour the honey mixture into the flour and mix well. Chill dough for several hours or overnight. Knead the dough until it does not stick to the hands. Roll thin and cut into small cakes. Bake at 400 degrees until light brown.

Clara Wall, Central

HUMMINGBIRD CAKE

3 cups all-purpose flour
2 cups sugar
1 tsp. salt
1 tsp. soda
1 tsp. ground cinnamon
3 eggs, beaten
1½ cups salad oil
1½ tsp. vanilla
1 8-oz. can crushed pineapple, undrained
2 cups chopped pecans, divided
2 cups chopped bananas

Combine dry ingredients in a large bowl; add eggs and salad oil, stirring until dry ingredients are moistened. Do not beat. Stir in vanilla and pineapple, 1 cup chopped pecans, and bananas. Spoon batter into 3 well-greased and floured 9-inch cake pans. Bake at 350 degrees for 25 to 30 minutes or until cake tests done. Cool in pans 10 minutes. Remove from pans and cool completely. Spread frosting between layers, on top and sides of cake. Sprinkle pecans (1 cup) on top of cake.

Cream Cheese Frosting

1 8-oz. pkg. cream cheese, softened
½ cup butter or margarine, softened
1 16-oz. pkg. powdered sugar
1 tsp. vanilla

Combine cream cheese and butter; cream until smooth. Add powdered sugar, beating until light and fluffy. Stir in vanilla.

Pam Hudson, Fleming Hills

JESSIE SANDERSON'S ROYAL SPONGE CAKE
(A family recipe dating from about 1940)

1 cup sugar
½ cup water
3 eggs
1 cup cake flour
1 tsp. salt
2 tsp. baking powder
1 tsp. vanilla
⅛ cup cold water

Boil sugar and water without stirring until syrup spins a thread. Beat egg whites and add sugar and water mixture, slowly. Beat until mixture is cool. Sift together flour, salt, and baking powder. Add egg yolks and flour mixture a little at a time, alternating, into egg white mixture. Add flavoring and cold water. Mix. Bake at 200 to 250 degrees for 30 minutes.

Glenn Sanderson, Harvest

ITALIAN CREAM CAKE

½ cup margarine	1 tsp. soda
½ cup vegetable shortening	1 cup buttermilk
2 cups sugar	1 tsp. vanilla or maple flavoring
5 egg yolks	1 can angel flake coconut
2 cups plain flour	1 cup chopped nuts

5 egg whites

Cream margarine and shortening; add sugar and beat until mixture is smooth. Add egg yolks and beat well. Combine flour and soda and add to creamed mixture alternately with buttermilk. Stir in vanilla (or maple flavoring). Add coconut and chopped nuts. Fold in stiffly beaten egg whites. Bake in 3 greased 8-inch pans at 350 degrees for 25 minutes or until done. When cool, frost with Cream Cheese Icing.

Icing

1 8-oz. pkg. cream cheese	1 box powdered sugar
¼ cup margarine	1 tsp. vanilla flavoring

½ cup chopped nuts

Blend cream cheese and margarine that has been softened until smooth. Add the sifted powdered sugar and mix well. Add the vanilla and beat until smooth. Add the chopped nuts. Spread between layers and on top and sides of cake.

Sandy Hughey, New Sharon

LEMON CHEESECAKE

1 pkg. lemon Jello	1 8-oz. pkg. cream cheese
1 cup hot water	Graham cracker pie crusts
¼ cup sugar	1 lg. can Carnation milk, chilled

Dissolve Jello in hot water. Add ¼ cup sugar. Cut up cheese in Jello while you make graham cracker pie crusts. Heat cheese mixture on low until mixed well. Whip can of milk until milk peaks. Fold in cheese mixture and pour into pie crusts.

Ira M. Hughes, Owens Cross Roads

NEAPOLITAN CAKE

1 purchased 19¼-oz. angel food cake	1 cup whipping cream
	2 T. powdered sugar
1 qt. strawberry ice cream, softened	2 T. cocoa
	½ tsp. vanilla

Slice top from cake about 1-inch down; set aside. Hollow out cake, leaving 1-inch base and sides. Place in freezer for 1 hour. Spoon ice cream into cavity. Replace top; press down gently. Wrap; freeze for several hours.

To serve: Combine whipping cream, sugar, and cocoa. Chill 30 minutes. Add vanilla. Whip until stiff. Frost sides and top of cake. Freeze until 15 to 20 minutes before serving. Serves 8 to 10.

Dyral Eaton, Piedmont

1-2-3-4 CAKE
(Yellow Cake)

1 cup butter (shortening or margarine)	3 cups flour
2 cups sugar	1 cup milk
4 eggs	3 tsp. baking powder
	1 tsp. vanilla
	Pinch of salt

Cream butter and sugar. Add eggs, 1 at a time. Add flour alternately with milk. Add baking powder, vanilla, and salt. Pour into greased and floured 9-inch cake pans. Makes 3 good layers. Bake at 350 degrees until done. Frost as desired.

Mrs. Ernest F. Dilday, Jr., Davis Hills

ORANGE DATE CAKE

1 cup butter	1½ cups buttermilk
2 cups sugar	4 cups flour
4 eggs	1 T. grated orange rind
1 tsp. baking soda	1 lb. chopped dates
Pinch of salt	1 cup chopped pecans

Cream butter and sugar; beat in eggs 1 at a time. Dissolve soda and salt in buttermilk. Add flour and milk alternately. Beat batter until smooth. Add orange rind, dates, and nuts which have been dredged in some of the flour for the cake. Bake in tube pan for 1½ hours at 325 degrees. When done pour orange sauce over hot cake and let cool in pan.

Orange Sauce

2 cups sugar	2 T. orange rind
	1 cup orange juice

Stir until dissolved. Do not heat.

Mrs. Marvin Sharp, Central

PLUM GOOD CAKE

2 cups self-rising flour
2 cups sugar
1 cup vegetable oil
3 eggs

2 sm. jars plum tapioca baby food
1 tsp. cinnamon
1 tsp. cloves
1 cup chopped pecans

Mix well, pour into greased tube pan. Bake 60 minutes at 325 degrees.

Frosting

2 cups powdered sugar   ½ stick margarine
Enough lemon juice to spread

May use just lemon juice and sugar or sprinkle with powdered sugar only, if desired.

Anna Lee Rogers, Madison Cross Roads
Linda DeHaye, Vestavia

POPPY SEED REFRIGERATOR TORTE

Crust

1 cup graham cracker crumbs
1 cup sifted flour

½ cup chopped nuts
½ cup butter, melted

Mix all ingredients. Spread 1 cup of mixture on a pan (9x9x2 inches) and toast in a preheated 350-degree oven for about 7 minutes. Pat remaining mixture into another pan and bake at 325 degrees for 12 minutes. Cool and reserve cold, toasted crumbs for topping.

Filling

1 cup sugar
¼ cup poppy seed
2 T. cornstarch
¼-½ tsp. salt
2 eggs, beaten

1½ cup milk
1 T. unflavored gelatin
¼ cup cold water
½ tsp. vanilla
1 cup whipping cream

Combine sugar, poppy seed, cornstarch, and salt in saucepan; add eggs and milk. Cook until thick. Add gelatin and cold water. Fold in extract and whipped whipping cream. Spread on crust. Sprinkle crumbs on top. Chill.

Darlene Reichmann, Rainbow Mountain

PRUNE CAKE

1½ cups sugar	1 cup buttermilk
2 cups flour	1 cup Wesson Oil
1 tsp. baking soda	1 tsp. vanilla
1 tsp. cinnamon	3 eggs
1 tsp. allspice	1 cup cooked prunes
1 cup nuts	

Sift dry ingredients. Add milk, oil, and vanilla. Beat well. Add eggs and beat again. Fold in prunes and nuts. *Do not beat!* Bake at 350 degrees for 45 minutes to 1 hour.

Icing

1 cup sugar	1 tsp. white syrup
½ cup buttermilk	½ stick butter
½ tsp. baking soda	½ tsp. vanilla

Boil 2 minutes and pour over hot cake. Let set 45 minutes before cutting.

Ira M. Hughes, Owens Cross Roads

RIBBON ICEBOX CAKE

1 pkg. cherry gelatin	1 egg, separated
Graham crackers	½ cup crushed pineapple, drained
½ cup powdered sugar	
¼ cup butter	¼ cup broken walnut meats

Prepare gelatin; set aside to cool. Into a spring-mold or loaf pan place a layer of graham crackers, fitting them snugly. Spread over them a layer of pineapple filling, made by mixing the powdered sugar, butter, beaten egg yolk, crushed pineapple, and walnut meats and folding in the egg white beaten into stiff peaks. Continue alternating layers of filling and crackers until you have 3 layers of crackers and 2 of filling. When the gelatin has begun to stiffen, pour ½ over cake and allow to stiffen completely. Whip remaining gelatin to a froth and pour over top. Let stand in refrigerator overnight. Serve sliced with whipped cream.

Mary Anne Riley, South Parkway

PINEAPPLE CAKE I

½ cup shortening
1½ cups sugar
2½ cups flour
½ tsp. salt

3 tsp. baking powder
½ cup milk
½ cup pineapple syrup
3 egg whites

Cream shortening and sugar. Sift the dry ingredients together. Add alternately with milk and syrup to creamed mixture. Fold in egg whites that have been beaten but not dry. Bake at 350 degrees. Makes 2 9-inch layers.

Filling

2 T. flour
½ cup milk

¼ cup sugar
1 cup crushed pineapple, drained

Cook until thick. Spread between layers. Frost with 7-minute frosting.

Shirley Milam, Pulaski Pike

PINEAPPLE CAKE II

2 eggs
2 cups sugar
¼ cup oil

1 tsp. vanilla
2½ cups flour
2 tsp. baking soda

1 No. 2 can crushed pineapple

Beat eggs, sugar, oil, and vanilla. Add flour sifted with baking soda and mix well. Add crushed pineapple and spread in greased 9x13 pan. Bake at 325 degrees for 40 minutes.

Icing

½ stick margarine
½ 8-oz. pkg. cream cheese, softened

2 cups powdered sugar
1 tsp. vanilla
½ cup chopped nuts

Cream first 4 ingredients together in mixer and spread over cake. Sprinkle with ½ cup chopped nuts.

Sue Kachelhofer, University

PINEAPPLE UPSIDE-DOWN CAKE

½ cup brown sugar
¼ cup margarine
1 can sliced pineapple
A few cherries
¼ cup nuts
½ cup shortening
1 cup sugar

2 eggs, beaten
1¾ cups flour
½ tsp. salt
2½ tsp. baking powder
½ cup milk
1 tsp. vanilla
3 T. water

Heat brown sugar and margarine until dissolved. Arrange with pineapple, cherries, and nuts in bottom of 9 inch skillet or 9 inch round or square pan. Blend shortening, sugar, and eggs together. Blend flour, salt, and baking powder. Combine the 2 mixtures, alternating flour mixture with the milk. Add vanilla and water. Pour batter over fruit. Bake for about 45 minutes at 375 degrees.

Susanne Green, Athens Pike

ROTTEN CAKE

1 pkg. yellow cake mix
18 ozs. frozen coconut (or 2
   7-oz. pkgs.)

16 ozs. sour cream
1½ cups powdered sugar
9 ozs. Cool Whip

Bake yellow cake in 2 layers. Split crosswise to make 4 layers. Drain coconut on paper towel as it thaws. Mix sour cream, sugar, and ⅔ of coconut together. Leave in refrigerator 12 to 24 hours. To ice cake, put sour cream mixture between layers. Spread Cool Whip on sides and top. Sprinkle remainder of coconut on cake. Put in tight-fitting container, such as Tupperware, and refrigerate 3 to 5 days before eating.

Louise Sanford, Piedmont

Watch the man ahead of you and you will soon learn why he is ahead.

We should so live and labor in our time that what came to us as seed may go to the next generation as blossom and that which came to us as blossoms may go to them as fruit. That is what we mean by progress.

SELF-FILLING CUPCAKES

1 pkg., 2-layer size, chocolate cake mix

Mix according to package directions.

Filling

1 8-oz. pkg. cream cheese, softened
⅓ cup sugar
1 egg
Dash of salt
1 6-oz. pkg. semi-sweet chocolate pieces
½ cup chopped pecans (optional)

Cream sugar with cream cheese. Beat in egg and salt. Stir in chocolate pieces and nuts. Fill paper bake cups in muffin pans ⅔ full of cake batter. Drop 1 rounded teaspoon of cream cheese mixture into each cupcake. Bake as package directs. Yield: 30.

Anna Bernice Broad, Big Cove

SEVEN-UP CAKE

1 box pineapple cake mix
1 box pineapple pudding
½ cup oil
4 eggs, unbeaten

1 10 oz. btl. Seven-Up.

Beat together and bake.

Icing

1 stick margarine
1 can pineapple, crushed
1½ cups sugar
2 T. flour
1 egg
1 can coconut

1 cup nuts

Mix and cook all together, except coconut and nuts. Spread mixture on cake while hot; sprinkle nuts and coconut on top.

Mrs. Eugene Smith (Nina), Monrovia

SNIPPY DOODLE COFFEE CAKE

½ cup margarine
1 cup sugar
2 eggs, beaten
2 cups flour
3 level tsp. baking powder
¾ cup milk (approximately)
1 tsp. vanilla
Cinnamon
Sugar
Oleo

Cream oleo and sugar. Add eggs and beat well. Sift flour and baking powder together. Add flour and baking powder and milk alternately. Add vanilla or other flavoring. Makes a thin batter. There is enough batter for 2 9-inch or 2 8-inch cake pans. Sprinkle sugar and cinnamon mixed together on top and dot with oleo before baking at 350 degrees for approximately 35 minutes.

Betty Cothran, Athens Pike

Friends are like flowers. A perennial on whom hearts can depend.

SOUR CREAM WALNUT CAKE

3 cups all-purpose flour
1½ tsp. baking powder
1½ tsp. baking soda
½ tsp. salt
¾ cup butter or margarine
   (1½ sticks)
1½ cups granulated sugar

3 eggs
2 tsp. vanilla extract
1 pt. dairy sour cream
¾ cup packed light brown sugar
2 tsp. cinnamon
1 cup coarsely chopped walnuts
Powdered sugar frosting

Mix flour, baking powder, soda, and salt and set aside. Cream butter in large bowl of electric mixer until soft. Gradually add granulated sugar and beat well. Add eggs 1 at a time, beating thoroughly after each; add vanilla. Then add flour mixture alternately with sour cream, blending after each addition until smooth. Mix brown sugar, cinnamon, and walnuts together. Put about ⅓ of batter in well-greased 10-inch tube pan or bundt pan. Sprinkle with ⅓ of nut mix. Repeat until all batter and sugar mixture are used. Bake at 350 degrees for 1 hour or until done. Let stand on wire rack about 5 minutes. Then turn out of pan, leaving cake bottom up. When still warm, frost with powdered sugar frosting.

Powdered Sugar Frosting

1⅓ cups powdered sugar   ½ tsp. vanilla
                                       Water to thin

Blend ingredients.

Ruth W. Chambers, Darwin Downs

STRAWBERRY CAKE

1 box white cake mix
1 cup oil
4 eggs

1 3-oz. pkg. strawberry Jello
½ cup warm water
½ pt. frozen strawberries

Blend cake mix and oil. Add 1 egg at a time. Add Jello dissolved in warm water; add strawberries. Do not overbeat. Bake in 9 x 13 inch pan at 350 degrees for 25 minutes.

Icing

1 box powdered sugar   1 stick margarine
½ pt. frozen strawberries

Mix and spread on cool cake.

Mrs. Earl Willcut (Maude), Monrovia
Marie Stramiello, Darwin Downs
Larue Wallace, New Sharon
Mary Jo Dreaden, Fleming Hills

WATERGATE CAKE

1 box white cake mix
1 box pistachio instant pudding
3 eggs

1 cup Wesson oil
1 cup club soda or milk
½ cup nuts

Mix first 5 ingredients with mixer at medium speed for 2 minutes; fold in nuts; pour into greased tube pan or oblong pan. Bake at 350 degrees for 55 minutes.

Icing

2 env. Dream Whip
1 box pistachio pudding, instant

1 cup cold water
10 drops green food coloring

Use Dream Whip dry, as it comes from the box. Mix with other ingredients. Whip thoroughly. Spread on cake and sprinkle nuts on top if desired. This is a heavy moist cake.

Jean Moore, Big Cove

WHITE CAKE

1½ cups sugar
½ cup Crisco
1 cup milk

2½ cups self-rising flour
4 egg whites
1 tsp. lemon juice

Cream sugar and Crisco. Add milk and flour. Beat egg whites until stiff. Fold in whites and lemon juice. Bake in layers or oblong pan in moderate oven for 30 to 35 minutes or until done. Test by pricking with toothpick.

Alta Newman, Central

YELLOW ANGEL FOOD CAKE

1½ cups sugar
½ cup water
6 eggs
¼ tsp. salt
1 cup flour
¾ tsp. cream of tartar
1 tsp. lemon or orange flavoring

Boil sugar and water until mixture threads when dropped from spoon. Separate eggs. Pour syrup over beaten egg whites with salt. When mixture is cool, add beaten yolks. Sift flour once; add cream of tartar and sift 3 more times. Fold carefully into egg mixture; add flavoring. Pour into ungreased pan. Bake for 50 to 60 minutes in moderate oven.

Alta Newman, Central

ICINGS/FROSTINGS

CARAMEL FROSTING

3 cups brown sugar
1 stick butter
1 sm. can Pet milk

Boil for 8 minutes and stir. Beat until spreadable.

Gail Hutcheson, Rainbow Mountain

CARAMEL ICING

2 cups white sugar
1 cup buttermilk
1 tsp. soda
½ cup butter or oleo
1 tsp. vanilla

Mix together and cook slowly after mixture boils. Cook to soft ball stage; cool and beat until thick and creamy. Add flavoring. Will ice 2-layer cake.

Ruth Whitt, Madison Cross Roads

FLUFFY WHITE NOT TOO SWEET

4 T. flour
1 cup milk
½ cup margarine or butter
½ cup Crisco
1 cup sugar
1 tsp. vanilla

Mix flour and milk. Cook until forms a thick paste. Set aside to cool. Beat margarine and Crisco for 4 minutes on high speed. Add sugar; mix on high for 4 minutes. Mix paste mixture with Crisco mixture; Beat for 4 minutes. Add vanilla; beat for 2 minutes. Spread on cooled cake. Yields frosting for 3-layer cake.

Chocolate Icing

Add cocoa to sugar before beating into other mixture.

La Juan Blevins, South Huntsville

ICING

¼ cup powdered sugar, sifted ¼ cup grated chocolate, sifted

Mix ingredients together then sprinkle over cake.

Mrs. Tom Baker, Hurricane

MAMA NELL'S CAKE FROSTING

2 cups sugar
1 cup buttermilk
3 lg. ripe bananas
⅓ stick butter
1 tsp. vanilla

Cook sugar and buttermilk until reaches hard rolling boil; add mashed bananas. Cook for 3 or 4 minutes. Add butter and vanilla. Spread on chocolate layers.

Mrs. Claude Bridges (Laura), Monrovia

DESSERTS

AFTERNOON FESTIVE DESSERT

Use 8-oz. new flower (glazed) pots. *Ahead Of Time*: Place a piece of plain cake in the bottom of each. Fill ¾ full with ice cream. Push a straw into mixture and cut off straw even with top of pot. *Freeze*. Before serving add an egg white meringue and brown in the oven at 400 degrees for a few minutes. Place a fresh flower in each straw and serve.

Kathy Albers, Fleming Hills

ANGEL BAVARIAN CAKE

1 cup sugar
2 T. flour
⅛ tsp. salt
4 egg yolks
1 pt. whole milk
1 env. Knox plain gelatin

½ cup cold water
4 egg whites
1½ pt. whipping cream
1 lg. angel food cake
Powdered sugar
½ tsp. vanilla

1 cup grated coconut

Prepare custard from first 5 ingredients. Add gelatin dissolved in cold water and stir into custard while hot. Let cool. Fold in 4 stiffly beaten egg whites and 1 pint whipping cream. Break up 1 large angel food cake and line 13x9x2-inch pan. Pour in custard; repeat layers until full. Refrigerate overnight. Ice with ½ pint cream whipped (sweeten to taste with powdered sugar and vanilla). Top with frozen or fresh coconut. Serves 12.

Blanche Harper, Vestavia

ANGEL FOOD LEMON FLUFF

6 egg yolks
¾ cup granulated sugar
¾ cup lemon juice
¼ tsp. salt
1 env. gelatin
¼ cup cold water

6 egg whites
¾ cup granulated sugar
1 angel food cake
2 cups whipping cream
2 T. powdered sugar
1 tsp. vanilla

Mix first 4 ingredients and cook in double boiler until slightly thick. Remove and add gelatin softened in cold water. Set in refrigerator to cool. Beat egg whites until stiff; gradually add sugar. Fold into cooled custard. Shred 1 angel food cake into flakes with fork. Mix with custard mixture. Pour into lightly greased angel food cake mold. Chill for 8 hours. Unmold and ice with whipping cream which has been whipped with powdered sugar and vanilla. Serves 12.

Marie Stramiello, Darwin Downs

CHOCOLATE ANGEL CAKE

1¼ cups egg whites
1½ cups sugar
¾ cup cake flour (sift before measuring)
¼ cup cocoa
½ tsp. cream of tartar
¼ tsp. salt
1½ tsp. vanilla

Add salt to egg whites and beat until foaming. Add cream of tartar and continue beating until stiff. Fold in sugar carefully. Add vanilla. Sift flour and cocoa together 3 times and fold in carefully. Pour into ungreased tube pan. Bake at 325° for 1 to 1¼ hours. When taken from oven invert pan. When cool remove from pan.

Beulah Kennamer, University

LEMON SPONGE CUPS

8 small baking cups — Preheated 350° F. — Baking time 45 minutes

2 tbsp. softened butter or margarine
1 cup sugar
4 tbsp. flour
¼ tsp. salt
3 egg yolks
5 tbsp. lemon juice
grated rind of lemon
1½ cups milk
3 egg whites

Cream butter or oleo, add sugar, flour, salt, lemon juice and rind. Add well beaten egg yolks which have been mixed with milk. Lastly, add the stiffly beaten egg whites. Pour in greased custard cups. Set cups in a pan of water and bake. When done, each cup will contain lemon custard at bottom of cup and sponge cake on top. Cool — Unmold. This may be baked in a two-quart pyrex baking dish. Serves 8.

Nancy O. Kramer, University

STRAWBERRY SODA POP CAKE

¾ cup shortening
2 cups sugar
3 cups all purpose flour
2 tsp. baking powder
½ tsp. salt
5 egg whites
1 cup strawberry pop

Cream shortening and sugar until fluffy; add ½ cup of pop. Mix well. Sift together flour, baking powder, and salt. Add alternately the remaining pop and flour mixture to creamed mixture. In separate bowl beat egg whites until stiff. Fold into batter. Pour batter into two 9" pans. Bake at 350° for 30 minutes.

Libby Livingston, Big Cove

YELLOW ANGEL FOOD

Boil 1½ cups sugar with ¾ cup water until it spins a thread. Pour syrup over 6 egg whites, beaten. Beat until cool. Add yolks of 6 eggs, well beaten. Fold in 1 cup of flour, 1 tsp. cream of tartar and ½ tsp. vanilla. Bake at 325° for 1 hour.

Beulah Kennamer, University

DELA'S PUMPKIN ROLL

3 large eggs
1 cup sugar
⅔ cup pumpkin
1 tsp. baking powder
½ tsp. nutmeg
¾ cup flour
2 tsp. cinnamon
1 tsp. ginger
1 cup finely chopped nuts

Beat eggs 5 min. on high speed. Slowly beat in sugar. Stir in pumpkin. Stir together flour, baking powder, salt and spices. Fold dry ingredients into pumpkin mixture. Line a greased 15x10 cookie sheet with waxed paper. Grease the paper. Spread batter evenly over paper in pan. **Sprinkle with nuts.** Bake at 350° 12-15 min. or until cake tests done. Turn cake upside down on a dish towel that has been sprinkled with sifted powdered sugar. Roll cake up in towel, let cool. Unroll cake and spread with cream cheese filling. Roll cake and filling like a jelly roll, wrap in Saran wrap or foil and chill. Keep cake roll well wrapped to keep moist.

Cream Cheese filling:

1 cup sifted powdered sugar
6 oz. cream cheese, softened
4 tbsp. softened margarine
1½ tsp. vanilla

Mix all ingredients thoroughly and spread on cooled cake.

Beth Sidnam, Hurricane

CHOCOLATE FOUR LAYER CAKE

Bake 2 layers of chocolate cake and split the layers.

Frosting:

Cook until thick, then cool, 1 cup milk, 3 tbsp. flour

Beat at high speed for 10 min. the cooled mixture, 1 cup sugar, ½ cup solid shortening, ¼ cup butter or margarine, 1 tsp. flavoring

Janice Coombe, Hurricane

NO NAME CAKE

1 box Duncan Hinds butter yellow cake mix
½ cup oil
1 can mandarin oranges, chopped
4 eggs

Beat at medium speed until blended. Grease and flour 3, 9" cake pans. Bake at 350° oven 25 to 30 min.

Topping:
2 9 oz. Cool Whip
1 pkg. vanilla instant pudding mix
1 med. can crushed pineapple, juice and all

Blend by hand and put on cake.

Shelby Gipson, Hurricane

CHOCOLATE CHEESECAKE

3 8 oz. pkg. cream cheese, softened
12 oz. semi-sweet chocolate chips, melted and cooled
1 tsp. vanilla
1 cup sugar
1/8 tsp. salt
3 eggs
1 cup sour cream

In large bowl beat cream cheese very smooth. Add vanilla, salt, sugar, beat well. Add chocolate and beat smooth. Add eggs 1 at a time, beating well. Add sour cream, beat smooth. Spoon into crust, smooth top. Bake in lower ⅓ of 375° oven 1 hour (will be soft). Leave in pan. Cool completely. Cover with foil. Refrigerate overnight.

Crust:
1 8 oz. pkg. chocolate wafer cookies (I use Oreos with white removed)
6 tbsp. butter, melted

In blender make 2 cups fine cookie crumbs. Put in small bowl, stir in butter and mix well. Grease sides only 9x3 springform pan. Press ⅔ of crumbs 2" up sides and ⅓ of crumbs in bottom.

Faye Hardin, Hurricane

CHEESE CAKE (I halve this recipe)

2 lbs. cream cheese (4 8 oz. pkgs.)
1½ cup sugar
½ cup cornstarch
juice of 2 med. lemons

1 stick (real) butter
½ qt. heavy cream (I use whipping cream)
6 whole eggs
vanilla flavoring

Beat cheese slowly and thoroughly. Beat in sugar, then butter, cornstarch, lemon juice, eggs, cream, vanilla (this should take 10-15 min.). Beat until well mixed. Grease a 12x12x2-inch pan (I use a round spring form pan for half a recipe) with Crisco. Fill with batter, place pan in another pan with 1" of water in it. Bake at 350° until golden brown on top (about 40 min.). Don't overcook, it will solidify as it cools.

Faye Hardin, Hurricane

CRANBERRY COFFEE CAKE

½ cup butter
1 cup sugar

2 eggs

Mix together.

2 cups flour
1 tsp. baking powder
1 cup (8 oz.) sour cream

1 tsp. soda
½ tsp. salt

Alternate dry ingredients and sour cream into sugar mixture.

1 tsp. almond or vanilla flavoring — add to batter.

1 16 oz. can wholeberry cranberry sauce

½ cup (or so) chopped pecans

Put ⅓ flour mixture in greased tube pan and alternate with cranberries and nuts, ending with nuts. (Do not let the cranberries touch the side of the pan or it will stick.) Bake 1 hour at 350°, let cool and glaze.

Glaze:
¾ cup powdered sugar
½ tsp. almond flavoring

1 tbsp. warm water

Faye Hardin, Hurricane

FRUIT CAKE

½ cup butter
1 #2 can apple pie filling
1 cup sugar
2 cups flour
2 tsp. soda
1 tsp. cinnamon
½ tsp. nutmeg

½ tsp. ground cloves
1½ cup raisins
1½ cup currents — I use 3 cups raisins
1 cup pecans
2 cups chopped cherries (or mixed fruit)

Melt butter, add pie filling and sugar. Heat until sugar melts. Cool this while sifting dry ingredients together. Use some of dry ingredients to coat nuts, raisins & cherries. Mix everything together and spoon in loaf pan lined with greased brown paper. Bake for 1½ hours in 300° oven.

Fay Hardin, Hurricane

WHITE FRUIT CAKE

2 cups sifted sugar
1½ cups butter
6 eggs
4 cups sifted flour
3 tsp. baking powder
1 tsp. nutmeg
1 tsp. vanilla

pinch salt
1 lb. candied pineapple, chopped
1 lb. candied red cherries, chopped
4 cups chopped pecans
1 cup whiskey

Heat oven to 300°. Cream sugar and butter, add eggs one at a time, beating well after each addition. Sift flour, salt, baking powder together saving ½ cup to coat fruits and nuts. Add whiskey and vanilla to sugar/butter/egg mixture and mix well. Add remaining dry ingredients and mix. Add floured fruit and nuts and spoon into two loaf pans that have been lined with greased brown paper. Bake for 1½ hour or until lightly browned.

Pat Johnson, South Parkway

APPLE CHEESE DESSERT

5 cups apple slices, peeled
1 T. lemon juice
¾ cup sugar
¼ tsp. cinnamon
½ cup sifted flour
¼ tsp. salt
¼ cup margarine
⅔ cup grated cheese

Fill shallow baking dish with apples. Sprinkle with lemon juice and ¼ cup of sugar. Mix cinnamon, flour, salt, and the other ½ cup sugar. Cut in margarine until mixture is granular. Stir in cheese; spread over apples. Bake at 350 degrees until apples are tender, about 40 minutes. Cool before cutting to serve. Serve with plain cream or ice cream. Serves: 6.

Jean Moore, Big Cove

APPLE CRISP

6 cups thinly sliced apples, peeled
⅓ cup sugar
2 T. butter
1 tsp. ground cinnamon
½ tsp. salt
6 T. butter
½ cup sugar
2 T. flour
3 cups raisin bran cereal

Mix together the apples, ⅓ cup sugar, and melted butter, cinnamon, and salt. Place in a greased 8-inch square pan. Set aside; cream butter; blend in ½ cup sugar; add flour and cereal. Crumble together and sprinkle over apple mix. Cover and bake at 350 degrees for 30 minutes. Remove cover and bake 15 minutes longer or until apples are tender.

Dot Atwell, Athens Pike

APPLE DUMPLINGS

1 lg. can biscuits
1 can apple pie filling
1 cup sugar
Cinnamon
Butter or margarine (about ½ stick)
Warm water (about 1 cup)

Use rolling pin to roll biscuits thin, about the size of a saucer. Divide apple pie filling equally among the biscuits, putting about 1 heaping tablespoon in center of each rolled thin biscuit. Pinch up edges of dough over center of filling and overlap edges; secure with toothpick, making sure apples are covered. Place in pan large enough to hold all dumplings. Sift or sprinkle 1 cup sugar, sprinkle of cinnamon, and dots of butter or margarine around and over dumplings. Put enough warm water to just cover, then bake until dumplings brown on top. Good served warm with ice cream on top. Bake at 350 degrees for about ½ hour or a little longer.

Cora Bodie, Blossomwood

BAKELESS PUDDING

½ cup butter
1 cup sugar
2 eggs
1 cup chopped nuts
1 sm. can crushed pineapple (undrained)
½ lb. graham crackers

Cream butter and sugar; add well-beaten eggs, nuts, and pineapple. Crush crackers; alternate layer of crackers and mixture in a dish. Let set for 12 hours in refrigerator. Serve with whipped cream topping or an orange sauce.

Mrs. Wall Johnston (Ruby), Monrovia

BANANA PUDDING

2 cups milk
3 T. flour
3 egg yolks
1 cup sugar
1½ tsp. vanilla flavoring
Milk
Vanilla wafers
Bananas
3 egg whites

Cook first 4 ingredients together until thick. Add vanilla flavoring. Thin to right consistency if too thick, with milk. Layer 1 thin layer vanilla wafers, then 1 layer bananas. Pour a layer of pudding, then 1 layer of wafers, and the rest of pudding. Make meringue topping out of whites and brown.

Gail Hutcheson, Rainbow Mountain

BOILED CUSTARD

4 eggs
1 cup sugar
1 T. flour or cornstarch
1 qt. scalded milk
1 tsp. vanilla

Beat eggs. Combine sugar and flour and add to eggs. Have scalded milk in a double boiler. Stir in egg mixture into hot milk, stirring continuously until thickens. Remove from heat and add flavoring. If cooled too long, custard will curdle, but it can be restored by beating.

Alta Newman, Central

BREAD PUDDING I

3 cups old bread
1½ cups hot milk
2 eggs, beaten
Sugar to taste
2 T. cinnamon
¾ cup raisins
1 cup cooked apples (optional)

Grease a pan or baking dish well with margarine. Use enough to make bread wet. Mix ingredients and bake in a 350-degree oven until pudding is as solid as you want it. Stir twice while in the oven.

Marie Barcus, Central

BREAD PUDDING II

3-4 slices loaf bread, cubed, day-old or stale
⅓ cup sweet tidbits: dried fruit, or raisins, or chocolate pieces, or coconut, or nuts
4 eggs
2 cups milk
⅓ cup sugar
¼ tsp. salt

Cube bread; place in 8-inch round baking dish or 6 6-oz. round custard cups. Add choice of sweet tidbits. Beat together eggs, milk, sugar, and salt into a sweet custard. Pour custard over bread. Bake at 325 degrees for 25 to 30 minutes till nearly set in center. Serve warm or chilled.

Gladys Bragg, Hazel Green

BUTTER BRICKLE DESSERT

¾ cup graham cracker crumbs ¾ cup soda cracker crumbs
½ cup oleo, melted

Press in 9x13 dish. Do not bake.

Filling

1 qt. butter brickle ice cream, softened
2 pkgs. vanilla pudding, instant
2 cups milk
Cool Whip
1 Heath bar

Mix ice cream, pudding, and milk; put in crust and let cool. Top with Cool Whip and a crushed Heath candy bar. (If butter brickle ice cream is not available, substitute an ice cream similar to it.)

Ella Schwerman, South Parkway

CHERRY DELIGHT

1¼ cups sugar
2 T. milk
8 ozs. cream cheese

1 graham cracker crust
1 cup chopped nuts
1 container Cool Whip
1 can cherry pie filling

Mix sugar, milk, and cheese in small mixing bowl. Beat with mixer until creamy and smooth. Spread over cool pie crust. Sprinkle chopped nuts on top and refrigerate for 30 minutes. Spread with Cool Whip and top with cherry pie filling. Refrigerate until ready to serve.

Monteen Dowdey, Twickenham

CHOCOLATE FLOAT

1 cup plain flour
½ tsp. salt
¾ cup sugar
2 tsp. baking powder
½ cup milk
1 tsp. vanilla

3 T. cocoa
2 T. melted margarine
½ cup white sugar
½ cup brown sugar
2 T. cocoa
Nuts (optional)

Mix first 8 ingredients together, making sure batter is well mixed. Pour into 6x10-inch baking pan. Mix sugars, cocoa, and nuts; spread mixture over batter in pan. Bring water to a boil and pour 1 cup over all. Cake batter will rise on top and pudding will be on bottom of dessert. Bake at 350 degrees for 20 to 25 minutes.

Mabel Albright, Darwin Downs

CHOCOLATE MOUSSE

12 ozs. chocolate chips
¾ cup boiling water
8 egg yolks

2 tsp. almond extract
¼ cup sugar
8 egg whites
Cool Whip

Process all ingredients except egg whites and Cool Whip in blender. Fold in stiffly beaten egg whites. Chill. Serve with Cool Whip.

JoAnn Quiggle, Fleming Hills

CHOCOLATE PECAN TORTE

6 eggs, separated
½ cup sugar
1 T. instant coffee dissolved in 3 T. cold water
1 cup chopped pecans
2 T. graham cracker crumbs
2 T. flour
2 tsp. baking powder
¼ tsp. salt
½ tsp. vanilla
2 T. sugar

Beat egg yolks until smooth and lemon colored. Beat in the ½ cup sugar gradually, then beat for 5 minutes. Beat in coffee. Stir in chopped pecans, crumbs, flour, baking powder, salt, and vanilla. Beat egg whites until stiff. Beat in 2 tablespoons sugar and fold into yolk mixture. Turn into 3 9-inch pans, greased and floured. Bake at 300 degrees for 30 minutes. Turn out and cool.

Chocolate Filling

1 6-oz. pkg. semi-sweet chocolate morsels
2 cups milk
2 tsp. instant coffee
2 eggs
2 T. cornstarch
2 T. cold water
½ tsp. vanilla
½ cup whipping cream

Melt chocolate morsels in milk, along with instant coffee, in top of double boiler. Beat eggs and mix in cornstarch dissolved in cold water; stir in part of chocolate milk mixture at a time. Return to double boiler and cook until thickened. Stir in vanilla. Cool. Spread between layers. Serve with whipping cream.

Darlene Reichmann, Rainbow Mountain

DATE ROLL

3 cups sugar
1 cup diluted evap. milk
6 candied cherries, chopped
1 pkg. chopped dates
1 cup chopped pecans
1 T. butter
¼ tsp. vanilla

Cook first 4 ingredients together until mixture forms a soft ball in cold water; then add remaining ingredients. Beat until thick and stiff, pour out on cold damp cloth, and roll up; put in refrigerator until ready to cut; slice thin.

Beryl Tidwell, Big Cove

EAGLE BRAND CUSTARD

1 can Eagle Brand milk
3½ cans hot water
½ cup sugar

1 T. cornstarch
5 eggs
½ tsp. salt
2 T. vanilla

Dissolve milk in 3 cans of hot water in a double boiler. Mix sugar with cornstarch dissolved in the additional ½ can hot water. Add to first mixture in the double boiler. Beat 5 eggs well and stir into double boiler. Cook until thick and coats spoon. Cool a little and add salt and vanilla. If it looks like it will curdle, beat and strain.

Ira M. Hughes, Owens Cross Roads

FIVE-LAYER BLUEBERRY TART

First Layer

2 cups graham cracker crumbs   ½ cup melted butter or margarine

Blend together and press into 9x13-inch pan. Bake for 15 minutes at 300 degrees. Cool.

Second Layer

½ cup soft butter or margarine   1½ cups powdered sugar
2 eggs

Cream butter or margarine. Add powdered sugar. Beat in eggs until light. Spread over first layer.

Third Layer

Spread 1 can blueberry pie filling over second layer.

Fourth Layer

1 lg. can crushed pineapple, drained
1 cup whipped topping

Fold together and spread over third layer.

Fifth Layer

½ cup graham cracker crumbs

Sprinkle graham cracker crumbs on top. Let stand in refrigerator 3 hours or overnight. Easy and delicious. Serves 16.

Cathy Gilbert, Davis Hills

FOUR-LAYER CHOCOLATE PUDDING

First Layer

1½ cups plain flour
1½ sticks butter
3 T. sugar
½ cup pecans

Mix and spread in 9x13-inch slightly greased pan. Bake at 375 degrees until edges are slightly brown. Cool.

Second Layer

8 ozs. cream cheese, softened
1 cup powdered sugar
1 cup Cool Whip

Blend and spread on top of crust.

Third Layer

2 pkgs. chocolate pudding, instant
3 cups cold milk

Beat until thick and spread on second layer.

Fourth Layer

Spread Cool Whip on top and sprinkle with nuts.

Mrs. Janice Robinson, Heritage

FRESH STRAWBERRY FROST

3 pt. hulled fresh strawberries
2 cups sugar
1½ cups orange juice
½ cup lemon juice
¼ cup Grand Marnier

Several days before serving: Put half the strawberries, sugar, orange juice, and lemon juice in an electric blender. Blend on high for 30 seconds. Pour into 12x8x2-inch baking dish. Repeat, using remaining strawberries, sugar, and juices. Stir in Grand Marnier; freeze until partially frozen. Beat with electric mixer at medium until smooth, return to baking dish, and freeze. Cover with foil and store in freezer. Its tart flavor mellows with refreezing. At serving time: Let strawberry frost sit out for 10 minutes or until just soft enough to spoon into sherbet glasses or scoop into chilled bowl and store in freezer until ready to serve at buffet party.

Mary Anne Riley, South Parkway

FROSTY STRAWBERRY DESSERT

Crust

1 cup flour	½ cup chopped pecans
¼ cup brown sugar	1 stick butter

Mix well and bake at 325 degrees for 20 minutes until brown; cool.

Filling

2 egg whites	2 T. lemon juice
Sugar	1 lg. container Cool Whip
	1 16-oz. pkg. strawberries

Beat egg whites well, adding sugar. Add lemon juice; blend; fold in Cool Whip and strawberries; mix well. Crumble crust mixture, put ⅔ mixture in bottom of oblong dish. Pour strawberry mixture over this, sprinkle remaining crust mixture evenly on top and freeze.

Margaret Mann, Owens Cross Roads
Debbie Hawkins, Vestavia

FROZEN DATE DELIGHT

1 8½-oz. can crushed pineapple	2 T. sugar
1 8-oz. pkg. cream cheese, softened	½ cup chopped pecans
	1 8-oz. pkg. diced dates
¼ cup pineapple juice	1 cup whipping cream

Drain pineapple well; reserve ¼ cup liquid. Cream the cream cheese with pineapple juice, gradually add the crushed pineapple, sugar, pecans, and dates; mix thoroughly. Whip cream using chilled bowl and beaters. Fold whipped cream into date mixture. Spoon into 8x8-inch pan or mold. Freeze until firm. To serve thaw slightly and cut into squares or unmold. (This recipe can be used as a salad or dessert.)

Sue David, South Parkway

Desserts

FROZEN DESSERT

2¼ cups crushed Rice Chex
1 cup brown sugar
1 stick margarine, softened
1 can angel flake coconut
½ cup finely chopped nuts
½ gal. ice cream
Whipped cream
Cherries

Mix first 5 ingredients and press ¾ of mixture into oblong dish or pan. Cover with ice cream. Cherry vanilla is good. Sprinkle top with ¼ of mixture. Place in freezer until shortly before time to serve. Top with whipped cream and a cherry.

Mary Alice Clark, Westbury

FRUIT CRUSH

3 cups soft fruit, peaches, or cantaloupe
1 cup vanilla ice cream
1 cup crushed ice

Blend and serve at once.

Lila M. Brown, Harvest

GRAHAM CRACKER PUDDING

⅔ pkg. graham cracker crumbs
1 stick butter, melted
1 sm. can pineapple
1 cup miniature marshmallows
1 egg, beaten
1 cup sugar
1 cup nuts
Whipped cream

Mix graham cracker crumbs and butter. Mix remaining ingredients, except whipped cream, together. Starting with graham cracker crumb mixture, alternate layers of crumbs and pineapple mixture. Top with whipped cream. Chill.

Glenn Sanderson, Harvest

GRANNY'S SPICED APPLES

4 or 5 lg. apples
½ cup sugar
¾ tsp. cinnamon
⅛ tsp. ginger
1 tsp. vanilla

Peel and slice apples. Place in dish and sprinkle with remaining ingredients. Cover with water. Cover and cook on top of stove for about 30 minutes. Remove cover and continue cooking until water has almost all cooked away—about 30 minutes more.

Yvonne Whitman, Heritage

GRAPE-NUT PUDDING

1 or 2 eggs
3/8 cup sugar
½ tsp. vanilla
Few grains salt

⅛ tsp. nutmeg
½ cup Grape Nuts (or less)
1½ cups milk
Whipped cream
Few drops lemon extract

Beat eggs; add sugar, vanilla, and next 4 ingredients. Turn into buttered baking dish; let stand for 15 minutes. Set in pan of hot water. Bake for 45 minutes in moderate oven. Serve with whipped cream with lemon extract added.

Helen Hann, Piedmont

HEAVENLY HASH

2 cups Kraft miniature marshmallows
2 cups cooked rice, chilled
1 8¼-oz. can crushed pineapple, drained

½ cup maraschino cherry halves
¼ cup slivered, toasted almonds
1 cup heavy cream
½ cup sugar
1 tsp. vanilla

Combine marshmallows, rice, fruit, and nuts. Whip cream, gradually adding sugar and vanilla; fold into rice mixture. Chill. Serves 8.

Mary Alice Clark, Westbury

ICEBOX DESSERT

1 sm. box vanilla wafers
2 pt. whipping cream
1 cup sugar
1 tsp. vanilla

8 med. ripe bananas, mashed
1 No. 2 can crushed pineapple, well drained
Pecans, crushed
24 cherries with stems

Line 14x17-inch Pyrex dish with wafers. Whip cream until stiff, gradually adding sugar. Add vanilla and fold in bananas and drained pineapple. Bananas may be sprinkled with lemon juice to keep from turning dark. Sprinkle top with crushed pecans and wafers. When ready to serve cut in 24 squares and top with cherry on stem.

Blanche Harper, Vestavia

ICEBOX PUDDING

1 sm. box vanilla wafers
1 sm. can crushed pineapple, undrained

½ cup sugar or honey
1 stick butter, melted
1 cup chopped pecans

Crush vanilla wafers in bottom of square pan. Drain off ½ of pineapple juice. Mix pineapple, remaining juice, and wafers with rest of ingredients. Chill until firm.

Jeanie Marsh, Harvest

LEMON FRUIT FREEZE

⅔ cup butter or margarine
½ cup sugar
7 cups Corn Chex cereal (3 cups crushed
1 14-oz. can Eagle Brand milk

½ cup lemon juice (bottled)
1 21-oz. can lemon pie filling
1 17-oz. can fruit cocktail, well drained
2 cups whipped topping

Melt margarine; add sugar, then crumbs. Reserve ⅓ cup crumbs for garnish. Pat crumbs firmly in 13x9-inch baking dish. Bake for 12 minutes at 300 degrees; cool. In bowl, mix milk and lemon juice; stir in pie filling and fruit cocktail. Pour over crust, then top with whipped topping; add crumbs. Freeze for 4 hours. Remove at least 20 minutes before cutting in squares. Serves 15.

Ruth Whitt, Madison Cross Roads

LEMON SNOW FREEZE

Crust

16⅔-oz. pkg. vanilla wafers, crushed
2 T. sugar
2 T. melted butter

Mix. Press into pan. Refrigerate for 2 hours. Wesson oil or Pam brushed on pan or freezer tray makes for easy removal.

Filling

2 egg yolks
1 can sweetened condensed milk
2 T. grated lemon rind
½ cup lemon juice
2 egg whites, stiffly beaten
4 T. sugar
Coconut, grated
Vanilla wafers, crushed

Combine first 4 ingredients. Whip egg whites until stiff. Fold in sugar. Then fold in lemon mixture. Pour on top of crust in freezer tray. Top with grated coconut and additional crushed wafers. Freeze overnight. Serves 6.

Blanche Harper, Vestavia

Think only of yourself and others will soon forget you.

Money will buy a fine dog, but only love will make him wag his tail.

LEMON SQUARES

½ cup margarine
1 cup sifted flour
¼ cup powdered sugar
1 cup granulated sugar
2 T. flour
½ tsp. baking powder
Juice of 1 sm. lemon
Lemon rind, grated
2 eggs, beaten

Melt margarine; add sifted flour and powdered sugar. Mix well and spread in 9x9-inch pan. Bake at 350 degrees for 15 minutes. Sift together granulated sugar, flour, and baking powder. Add lemon juice, rind, and beaten eggs. Pour over baked crust and bake for 25 minutes. Cut into squares while warm.

Connie Kramer, Darwin Downs

MACAROON WHIP

½ cup sugar
½ cup cognac or rum
1½ cups crumbled macaroons
1 pt. whipping cream

Stir together ½ cup sugar and ½ cup cognac. Mix well with macaroons to soak. Whip 1 pint whipping cream until very stiff. Fold in macaroon mixture and mix well. Spoon into sherbet or parfait glasses and freeze for 3 hours. May be made ahead as mixture will not harden, even after several days in the freezer. Very rich and potent! Serves 4 to 5. (Yield: Approximately 1 pint.)

Mrs. Lyle Needham, South Huntsville

MOCK BOILED CUSTARD

⅔ cup sugar
1 pkg. vanilla pudding, instant
6 cups cold sweet milk

Combine the sugar and instant pudding mix in the large bowl from the electric mixer, mixing thoroughly with a spoon. Add 1 cup of milk. Start the mixer on low so it will not splatter. Add remaining milk 1 cup at a time. Beat or mix for at least 10 minutes or until it is the consistency of boiled custard. Refrigerate and serve with cake as you would boiled custard.

Mrs. Wall Johnston (Ruby), Monrovia

MAMA'S CHOCOLATE BREAD PUDDING

10 biscuits
¾ cup sugar
⅓ cup cocoa
2 eggs
2 cups milk
1 tsp. vanilla
¾ to 1 cup miniature marshmallows

Crumble biscuits until fine texture. Add sugar and cocoa and beat in eggs; then add milk and vanilla. Pour into well-buttered dish (9-inch pie plate works fine). Dot with butter and bake at 350 degrees for approximately 1 hour; remove from oven. Spread marshmallows over pudding. Return to oven to let marshmallows brown slightly. Slice as you would a pie. (You can test with toothpick for doneness.)

Pat Smith, South Huntsville

ORANGE CREAM TRIFLE

1 11-oz. can mandarin orange sections
2 3½-oz. pkgs. vanilla instant pudding
2 env. whipped dessert topping mix
4 cups milk
1 cup heavy cream
1 tsp. almond extract
2 3-oz. pkgs. ladyfingers

Drain orange sections, reserving syrup. In large bowl with mixer at low speed, beat pudding, topping mix, milk, cream, and extract until blended. Increase to medium high and beat for 5 minutes. Line bowl with ladyfinger halves and drizzle with syrup. Spoon part of mixture on top to cover; add a layer of ladyfingers; repeat; top with orange sections. Delicious light dessert for large crowd.

Ruth W. Chambers, Darwin Downs

PEACHES WITH BOURBON

1½ cups sugar
1½ cups water
6-8 ripe peaches
¼ cup bourbon

Boil sugar and water together for 10 minutes. Peel peaches and put into syrup; cook until just tender. Add bourbon. Serve cold with whipped cream or Cool Whip.

Jeanette Kromis, Westbury

PINK ARCTIC FREEZE

1 8-oz. pkg. cream cheese, softened
2 T. mayonnaise
2 T. sugar
1 16-oz. can whole berry cranberry sauce
1 cup crushed pineapple, drained
1 cup heavy cream, whipped

Beat cream cheese, mayonnaise, and sugar with electric mixer. Add cranberry sauce and pineapple. Mix well. Fold in whipped cream. Freeze in a 9x9-inch dish. Cut into squares to serve.

Virginia Laux, Madison Cross Roads

PLUM PUDDING

1 cup suet
1 cup bread crumbs
1 cup flour
1 cup brown sugar
1 cup raisins

1 tsp. nutmeg
1 tsp. grated lemon
½ tsp. soda
⅓ cup boiling water
Hard sauce or lemon sauce

Grind suet and bread crumbs together. Mix with next 5 ingredients. Add enough water to stiffen mixture. Add ½ teaspoon soda and ⅓ cup boiling water. Add to mixture and pour into a well-greased 1-quart mold. Cover; steam for 1 hour. Serve with hard sauce or lemon sauce or both.

Mary Lou Pfeiffer, Westbury

SUGAR PLUM PUDDING

1 cup flour
¾ tsp. cinnamon
1½ tsp. nutmeg
¾ tsp. soda

½ cup margarine
¾ cup sugar
1 egg, well beaten
½ cup buttermilk

½ cup cooked chopped prunes

Mix flour, spices, and soda. Chop margarine and add to dry ingredients. Add sugar and mix well. Add beaten egg and buttermilk to prunes, mix well. Add this mixture to dry ingredients. Mix well. Pour into buttered pan and bake at 350 degrees until firm. Remove from oven and pour glaze over it while warm.

Glaze

½ stick margarine
¼ cup buttermilk

½ cup sugar
¾ tsp. vanilla

Whipped cream or Cool Whip

Bring margarine, buttermilk, and sugar to a full boil. Remove from heat and add vanilla and pour over pudding. Leave in pan until ready to serve. Top with whipped cream or Cool Whip.

Martha R. Sparks, Rainbow Mountain

STRAWBERRY DELIGHT

First Layer

½ cup butter
1 cup flour

¼ cup sugar
¾ cup finely chopped nuts

Brown butter. Mix ingredients as pie crust. Put in 9x13-inch pan. Bake at 350 degrees for 15 minutes. (NOTE: WATCH—BURNS EASILY.)

Second Layer

24 marshmallows ⅔ cup milk
1 cup whipping cream

Melt marshmallows and milk in top of double boiler. Cool. Whip cream until stiff and fold into marshmallow mixture. Spread on top of FIRST layer.

Third Layer

2 sm. pkgs. strawberry Jello 1 pkg. frozen strawberries
2 cups boiling water Whipped cream

Dissolve gelatin in boiling water; add frozen berries; let stand until thick. Spread on top of SECOND layer. Refrigerate overnight or at least 3 hours before using. Cut into squares and serve with whipped cream on top.

Mrs. Bettye T. Burns, Harvest

SUPER PEACH CRISP

4 cups peach slices, peeled ½ cup flour
⅔ cup packed brown sugar 1 tsp. cinnamon
½ cup old-fashioned or quick ⅓ cup margarine
  oats, uncooked ½ cup chopped nuts
Whipped cream

Place peaches in a 10x6-inch baking dish. Combine dry ingredients; cut in margarine until mixture resembles coarse crumbs. Stir in nuts. Sprinkle over peaches. Bake at 350 degrees for 30 minutes. Serve with whipped cream, if desired. Serves 6 to 8. *Variation*: Substitute 4 cups peeled apple slices for peaches.

Mrs. N. Ray Rohland, Big Cove

What the future has in store for you depends largely on what you place in store for the future.

TEXAS DELIGHT DESSERT

First Layer

1 cup flour   1 cup pecans
1 stick margarine

Mix and put in 9x13-inch pan. Bake for 20 mintues at 300 degrees. Cool.

Second Layer

1 cup Cool Whip (from lg. size)   1 cup powdered sugar
8 ozs. cream cheese, softened

Beat until fluffy. Spread on the above crust when cooled.

Third Layer

2 pkgs. vanilla pudding mix, instant
3 cups milk

Mix for 2 minutes and spread on second layer.

Fourth Layer

Spread the remainder of the Cool Whip from container on top of all of this. Refrigerate for several hours.

Nell Williams, Piedmont

TROPICAL FREEZE

5 cups water   1 cup orange juice
3 cups sugar   ½ cup lemon juice
½ tsp. salt   3 cups mashed bananas (8)

Combine 2 cups water, sugar, and salt in saucepan; bring to a boil. Cool. Add additional water, orange and lemon juice, and mashed bananas. Freeze as usual in home freezer.

Mrs. W. L. Kennedy, Hazel Green

NUT TORTE

6 eggs, separated
sugar
⅓ cup dried bread crumbs
¼ cup all-purpose flour
⅔ cup ground pecans
1 pt. whipping cream
1 tsp. vanilla extract

1. Preheat oven to 325° F. In large bowl, with mixer at high speed, beat egg whites until soft peaks form. Beating at high speed, gradually sprinkle in ½ cup sugar, beating well after each addition. Whites should stand in still peaks.
2. In small bowl, with mixer at medium speed, beat egg yolks until thick and lemon colored. Gradually beat in ½ cup sugar until blended. Stir in bread crumbs, flour and ⅔ cup ground nuts; with wire whisk or rubber spatula, fold into beaten egg whites. Pour batter into 10" by 3" springform pan, lined on the bottom with wax-paper, and spread evenly.
3. Bake 40 minutes or until cake springs back when lightly touched with finger. Invert cake in pan on wire rack: cool completely.
4. In small bowl, with mixer at medium speed, beat whipping cream, vanilla extract and 4 tbsp. sugar until stiff peaks form.
5. Remove cake from pan; with a long sharp knife, slice cake horizontally into two layers. Place bottom layer on cake platter; spread with one-fourth whipped cream mixture; top with second layer. Frost side of cake with half of remaining whipped cream mixture. With hand, gently press ground nuts onto cream.
6. Spoon remaining whipped cream mixture into a pastry bag with a large rosette tube; use to decorate top of cake. Use marachino cherries to decorate the top. 8 half marachino cherries to go around the edge and one whole cherry for the middle.

Louise K. Jackson, University

JESSE'S CHERRY DESSERT

FILLING:
1 pkg. (8 oz.) cream cheese, whipped
¾ cup sugar
1 tsp. vanilla
dash of salt
4½ oz. of Cool Whip

CRUST:
¼ cup brown sugar
1 cup flour
1 cup finely chopped pecans
½ cup softened margarine

TOPPING:
2 cans cherry pie filling
1 tsp. almond flavoring

Additional Cool Whip to dollop on serving squares (if desired). Mix crust ingredients together, press into 9X13 baking dish. Bake 15-18 minutes in 350° oven. Cool. Mix filling ingredients together, spread over cooled crust. Add almond flavoring to pie filling and spread over filling. Refrigerate, cut into squares for serving, add dollops of additional Cool Whip if desired.

Mrs. Marshall (Mabel) Byrd, Jr.
Madison Cross Roads

OLD FASHIONED BREAD PUDDING WITH RUM SAUCE

3 eggs slightly beaten
3 cups milk
3 cups crumbled day old biscuits
½ cup sugar
½ cup raisins
¼ cup butter or margarine
½ tsp. salt
1 tbsp. grated lemon rind
¼ tsp. ground nutmeg

Combine eggs and milk, stir well, add crumbled biscuits and next 5 ingredients, stir gently. Spoon mixture into a greased 2-qt. baking dish and sprinkle with nutmeg. Place dish in a larger shallow pan; add water to depth of 1 inch. Bake at 350° for 50 minutes or until knife comes out clean when inserted. Serve warm with rum sauce. 6 to 8 servings.

RUM SAUCE
¾ cup sugar
1 tbsp. cornstarch
⅔ cup water
½ cup rum
½ tsp. lemon juice
1 tbsp. butter or margarine

Combine first 4 ingredients into a small saucepan; bring to a boil over medium heat, cook 1 minute, stirring constantly. Add lemon juice and butter, stir until butter melts. Serve warm. Yields 1½ cup.

Margaret Hornsby, Hurrican

STRAWBERRY OR PEACH DREAM ICE CREAM

This must be made in a 6 qt. ice cream freezer.

3 cups sugar
4 eggs
1 large can evaporated milk
1 can sweetened condensed milk
1 tsp. vanilla

3 cups chopped peaches or 2 pkg. frozen strawberries (10 oz.)
1 large (6 oz.) pkg. strawberry or peach gelatin
milk

Mix first five ingredients until well blended. Put into a 6 qt. freezer and add milk to make ¾ full. Blend until set.

Patsy A. Vaughn, South Parkway

CHERRY YUM YUM

1 pkg. Cameo cookies (crumbled)
1 tsp. vanilla flavoring
¾ cup sugar

8 oz. pkg. cream cheese (whipped)
1½ stick margarine (melted)
8 cups Dream Whip

Mix cookie crumbs in melted butter. Line bottom of 9X13) baking dish with ½ of mixture. Blend cream cheese, sugar, vanilla, whipped Dream Whip and fold into cheese mixture. Pour ½ mixture over crumbs in dish. Spread cherry pie filling over top, add remaining dream whip and sprinkle with additional, crumbled cookie crumbs. Refrigerate over night.

Ann F. Vaughn, Monrovia

MY MAMA TONEY'S CARROT PUDDING

1 cup grated carrot
1 cup grated potatoes
1 cup very finely chopped suet
1 cup brown sugar
1⅔ cup flour

1 tsp. soda
2 cups chopped seeded raisins
½ cup chopped dried cherries
or ½ cup chopped almonds

Steam 3 hours. No spices are used. Do not let water stop boiling. This is a good substitute for a plum pudding, and much more wholesome.

Beverly Brown, Monrovia 2

FRUIT DESSERT

1 can crushed pineapple with juice
2 tbsp. cornstarch (use to thicken pineapple juice)
1 banana sliced (in lemon juice to keep from discoloring)
strawberries
kiwie fruit
graham cracker crust (pie or individual or put in casserole)

Put sliced bananas in graham cracker crust. Pour thickened pineapple mixture over banana. Top with sliced strawberries and kiwie fruit.

Mildred Fanning, Monrovia
Martha Fanning, San Antonio, TX

WAR TACK

2 eggs	1 tsp. vanilla
1 cup sugar	1 cup dates, chopped
1 cup self-rising flour	1 cup walnuts
3 T. sweet milk	Powdered sugar

Beat eggs and sugar well until creamy. Add flour, milk, and flavoring and beat well. Fold in dates and nuts. Bake in greased pan 7x11x1-inch at 325 degrees until done. Cut in squares and sprinkle with powdered sugar. If light brown—will be sticky—this is better; if dark brown—will be firm.

Marcy Jones, South Huntsville

ICE CREAM AND SHERBET

CHERRY ICE CREAM

4 eggs	1 T. vanilla
2 cups sugar	1 10-oz. jar maraschino cherries, cut up
1 15-oz. can sweetened condensed milk	Juice from cherries
1½ qts. homogenized milk	

Beat eggs until fluffy. Add sugar and beat until creamy. Add sweetened condensed milk and vanilla; blend well. Stir in cherries, juice, and half of homogenized milk. Pour mixture into freezer container; add remaining milk. Yield: 1 gallon.

Earlene Britt, Rainbow Mountain

GELATIN ICE CREAM

2 cups milk	1 pkg. gelatin, unflavored
2 eggs, separated	1 pt. cream
¾ cup sugar	1 tsp. vanilla

Make boiled custard with milk, egg yolks, and ½ cup sugar. Dissolve gelatin in boiled custard. When cool add cream, whipped, and vanilla. Put in refrigerator until set, then beat egg whites with ¼ cup sugar. Fold in the congealed mixture and freeze.

Glenn Sanderson, Harvest

HOMEMADE PEACH ICE CREAM

1½ cups sugar
2 T. flour
½ tsp. salt
3 eggs, beaten

1 qt. whole milk
½ pt. whipping cream
6 cups chopped peaches sweetened with 1 cup sugar
1 T. vanilla extract

Combine sugar, flour, and salt; add eggs and blend well. Add milk and cook slowly until slightly thickened. Let cool. Add the whipping cream (unwhipped), peaches, and vanilla. Pour into freezer and freeze.
Virginia Laux, Madison Cross Roads

ICE CREAM

1 can condensed milk
6 cans orange soda
1 can 7-up

Mix and freeze.
Gloria Radke, South Huntsville

LEMON ICE CREAM

6 eggs
3½ cups sugar

Juice of 6 lemons (may use frozen lemon juice)
1 pt. whipping cream

Fill freezer to fill line with regular milk. Cream eggs and sugar and add everything to the ice cream freezer. Note: For an even richer mix use evaporated milk instead of regular milk.
Pat Zurasky, South Parkway-Rainbow Mountain

ORANGE SHERBET

2 cups buttermilk
1 cup sugar

1 med. can crushed pineapple
Juice of 3-4 oranges and 2 lemons

Mix ingredients together. Stir once when ice forms—freeze again.
Margie Spencer, Vestavia

STRAWBERRY ICE CREAM

3 pts. milk
1 13-oz. can Pet milk
3½ cups sugar

5 eggs
1 pt. strawberries
1½ T. vanilla

Mix the milks and sugar with electric mixer; beat well. Beat the whites and yolks of eggs separately, the yolks until lemon color and whites until stiff. Add to milk mixture and beat again. Crush berries in blender and add to milk mixture; add vanilla and mix well. Freeze in ice cream freezer. Let set to mellow for 1 hour before serving.

Mrs. Paul Bledsoe, Hurricane

VANILLA ICE CREAM I

2 cups sugar
6 eggs, beaten
1 can sweetened condensed milk

1 lg. can evap. milk
2 qts. milk
1 T. vanilla

Combine all ingredients, mixing well. Pour into electric freezer container and freeze.

Margaret Mann, Owens Cross Roads

VANILLA ICE CREAM II

2 cups Eagle Brand milk
5 eggs
3 lg. cans evap. milk
1 cup sugar or ¾ cup honey

3 T. vanilla flavoring
2 pkgs. Dream Whip, prepared as directed
Skim milk

Blend Eagle Brand milk, eggs, and 1 can of evaporated milk in blender. Pour into large bowl. Blend sugar and flavoring with Dream Whip and 2 cans evaporated milk. Add to first mixture. Mix well with spoon. Pour in freezer can. Finish filling can with skim milk. Freeze in hand or electric freezer. For a firmer cream let mellow overnight in deep freeze.

FRUIT CREAM:
Puree fruit in blender, leave out eggs. Makes 2 quarts puree fruit; may not need to add any milk to fill freezer. Yield: 5 quarts.

Mrs. C. W. Fanning (Mildred), Monrovia

YUMMY ICE CREAM DESSERT

½ gal. vanilla ice cream
1 sm. pkg. Oreo cookies, crumbled
1 can Hershey's Chocolate Syrup
1 carton Cool Whip
Nuts

Layer in a 9x13-inch pan and freeze.

Mrs. Herschel Moore (Judy), Heritage

PIES

PIE CRUST

PASTRY

CHOCOLATE CHIP COOKIE CRUST

1 cup chocolate chip cookie crumbs
¼ cup sugar
¼ cup butter or margarine, softened
½ cup chopped nuts

Blend crumbs, sugar, butter, and nuts and press firmly against bottom and sides of a 9-inch pie plate. Bake at 375 degrees for 8 minutes. Cool before filling.

Barbara Webster, Owens Cross Roads

CRISCO PIE CRUST MIX

6 cups sifted flour
1 T. salt
1 lb. Crisco (about 2½ cups)

Mix flour and salt in a large mixing bowl. Cut Crisco into flour with two knives or pastry blender until mixture is uniform and very fine. Store in covered container such as a 3-pound Crisco can. No refrigeration is needed.

Single 8 or 9-inch crust: 1½ cups Crisco mix
3 T. cold water

Double 8 or 9-inch crust: 2¼ cups Crisco mix
4 T. cold water

Double 10-inch crusts: 3 cups Crisco mix
6 T. cold water

Lila M. Brown, Harvest

FLAKY PASTRY

4 cups all-purpose flour
1¾ cups vegetable shortening
   (not oil)
1 T. sugar
1 tsp. salt
1 T. vinegar
1 egg
½ cup water

Mix first 4 ingredients using a fork. In small bowl, mix remaining ingredients. Add to first mixture and blend with fork. Mold dough with hands and chill at least 15 minutes. May be kept in refrigerator or freezer. Hint: Roll out pie crusts, stack between wax paper, and freeze in a large plastic bag.

Pat Zurasky, Rainbow Mountain-South Parkway
Mary Frances Mitchell, Madison Cross Roads

PAT-IN-THE-PAN PIE CRUST

1 cup plain or self-rising flour
½ cup soft butter
¼ cup finely chopped pecans
¼ cup powdered sugar

Heat oven to 400 degrees. With hands, mix all ingredients to a soft dough. Press firmly and evenly against bottom and sides of a 9-inch pie pan. Do not press on rim. Bake 12 to 15 minutes or until light brown. Cool.

Josie Asquith, South Parkway

PERFECT PIE CRUST

⅛ cup boiling water
¼ cup Crisco
⅔ cup sifted self-rising flour
3 ozs. cream cheese
1 T. sugar

Pour boiling water over shortening and beat until creamy. Sift in flour. Stir together. Roll out dough to ⅛-inch thickness on lightly floured board. Place in pie pan and prick with a fork and bake. While crust is still warm rub bottom and sides with cream cheese and sugar. Only use with pies that require a prebaked crust. (May be used with fresh strawberry pie.)

Jean McComb, Central

PIE CRUST

2 cups flour
¾ cup Crisco
¼ tsp. salt

Mix until as coarse as cornmeal. Add sweet milk to moisten and roll out. Yield: 1 10-inch crust.

Mrs. Earl Willcutt (Maude), Monrovia

PIE PASTRY

¾ cup plain flour
½ tsp. salt
3 level T. Crisco
3 T. cold water

Mix flour, salt, and Crisco with pastry blender. Add cold water. Roll dough and line pie pan. Press the pastry around the sides of the pan with a fork. Also prick bottom of pastry-lined pan with fork several times for air to escape. Bake in moderate oven until brown. For a two-crust pie, double recipe.

Maxie Wilbourn, Central

To those who talk and talk and talk
This proverb should appeal.
The steam that blows the whistle
Will never turn the wheel.

CHOCOLATE PIES

CHOCOLATE CHESS PIE I

1½ cup butter
1½ 1-oz. sq. chocolate, unsweetened
1 cup firmly packed brown sugar
½ cup white sugar
2 eggs, slightly beaten
1 tsp. all-purpose flour
1 T. milk
1 tsp. vanilla
1 9-inch pastry shell, unbaked

Melt butter and chocolate in a small pan over low heat. Combine sugars, eggs, flour, milk, and vanilla. Gradually add chocolate mixture, stirring constantly. Pour into pastry shell. Bake at 325 degrees for 40 to 45 minutes.

Evelyn Kaylor, Hazel Green

CHOCOLATE CHESS PIE II

1½ cups sugar
3 T. cocoa
2 eggs
Pinch of salt
1 tsp. vanilla
1 sm. can evap. milk
1 pie shell, unbaked

Mix together and pour in pie shell. Bake at 350 degrees for 40 minutes.

Brenda Bourland, South Huntsville

CHOCOLATE CREAM PIE

4 T. flour
1 T. cornstarch
1½ cups sugar
½ tsp. salt
2½ cups milk
3 egg yolks, slightly beaten
1 T. margarine
1½ tsp. vanilla
4 T. cocoa
Pie shell, baked
Meringue

Blend flour and cornstarch. Mix sugar and salt with flour. Gradually stir in milk. Stir constantly until it begins to thicken. Add egg yolks and continue to stir until thick. Remove from heat and add margarine, vanilla, and cocoa. Pour into baked pie shell and top with meringue.

Clydia M. Reynolds, Madison Cross Roads

CHOCOLATE PIE I

1¼ cups sugar
3 T. flour
4 T. cocoa
¼ tsp. salt
2 cups milk

3 eggs
2 T. butter
1 tsp. vanilla
3 T. additional sugar
Pie shell, baked

Mix dry ingredients; add a little milk, then the egg yolks, then the remainder of the milk. Cook in double boiler until will flake off spoon. Add butter and vanilla and beat well. Pour in baked pie shell and top with beaten egg whites with 3 tablespoons sugar. Bake slowly to brown.

Maxie Wilbourn, Central

CHOCOLATE PIE II

½ cup sugar
3 T. flour
4 T. cocoa
¼ tsp. salt

2 cups hot milk (diluted evap. milk)
3 egg yolks
2 T. margarine
½ tsp. vanilla
Pie shell, baked

Mix together sugar, flour, cocoa, and salt. Add hot milk; on medium heat, stir until thick. Add beaten egg yolks and cook until thick. Remove from heat and add margarine and vanilla. Pour into pie shell.

Meringue

3 egg whites
6 T. sugar

¼ tsp. salt
¼ tsp. cream of tartar

Beat egg whites until stiff. Beat in sugar, salt, and cream of tartar. Beat until smooth and glossy. Bake at 325 degrees until brown.

Beryl Tidwell, Big Cove

CHOCOLATE PIE III

Filling

1¼ cups sugar
3 T. cornstarch or flour
6 T. cocoa
½ tsp. salt

2 cups milk
3 egg yolks
1 tsp. vanilla flavoring
1 pie shell, baked

Blend together sugar, cornstarch, cocoa powder, and salt. Stir into hot milk and cook in double boiler until thick. Beat egg yolks; stir in a small amount of the cooked mixture and return to main mixture. Cook 2 minutes longer; cool; add vanilla. Pour in pie shell.

Meringue

3 egg whites   4 T. sugar

Beat egg whites until frothy; add sugar gradually; beat to stiff form. Spread over pie, having meringue touching pastry rims at points. Bake in preheated oven at 350 degrees until browned lightly.

This recipe presented in memory of Mrs. J. D. Widley, my Home Ec teacher, Riverton High School 1940-1942.

Mrs. Gustavus N. Brown (Eva), Monrovia

FROZEN CHO-PIE

1½ sqs. chocolate   1 tsp. vanilla
¾ cup butter   Graham cracker crust
1 cup + 1 T. sugar   Whipping cream
3 eggs   Nuts

Melt chocolate. Cream butter until light. Add sugar to butter, and continue creaming; add 1 egg at a time, beating for 3 minutes after each. Blend with melted chocolate and vanilla. Beat well. Pour into graham cracker crust and freeze. Top with whipped whipping cream and nuts. (*Rich.*) Serves 6 to 8

Ruth Cornell, Kittleson, Hazel Green

CHOCOLATE YOGURT PIE

Chocolate chip cookie crust   ¼ cup chopped chocolate candy
2 8-oz. cartons plain yogurt   bar (any kind)
½ 12-oz. jar chocolate fudge   Whipped cream topping or non-
   topping   dairy whipped topping
            Chocolate curls or chopped nuts

Stir yogurt gently then fold in half of the fudge topping until blended. Fold in candy bar. Turn into chocolate chip cookie crust and freeze until firm. Spread remaining fudge topping on pie and freeze. When ready to serve, dollop with whipped topping and decorate with chocolate curls or chopped nuts.

Barbara Webster, Owens Cross Roads

CHOCOLATE SATIN PIE

¾ cup butter
1 cup extra-fine sugar
¾ cup cocoa

4 eggs
1 tsp. vanilla
½ tsp. almond extract
Pie shell, baked

Place butter in mixer and whip. Sift sugar and cocoa together. Add slowly to whipped butter on low speed. If mixture is too stiff, add 1 egg and continue beating. Add eggs 1 at a time, then vanilla and almond extract. Beat well. Whip on high speed until the consistency of whipped cream. Pour into pie shell and chill 2 hours.

Evelyn Kaylor, Hazel Green

FUDGE PIE

1 stick butter
2 sqs. chocolate
¼ cup flour

2 eggs
1 cup sugar
Pinch of salt
1 tsp. vanilla

Mix and bake in slightly greased pie pan at 350 degrees until firm. While warm serve with ice cream. Serves 6 to 8.

Reba Cornell, Hazel Green

CUSTARD, CHESS, LEMON PIES/TARTS

BUTTERMILK PIE

1½ cups sugar
2 T. flour
½ cup buttermilk

2 eggs
1½ tsp. vanilla
¾ stick margarine, melted
1 pie shell, unbaked

Mix together and pour into unbaked pie shell. Bake at 375 degrees for 40 minutes or till firm in middle.

Gracie McCurdy, Madison Cross Roads

BUTTERMILK COCONUT PIE

1½ cups sugar
¼ lb. margarine, melted
½ cup buttermilk
2 T. flour

3 whole eggs, well beaten
1 tsp. vanilla
1 can coconut (½ cup or more)
Pie shell, unbaked

Mix all ingredients together and pour into pie shell. Bake for 1 hour at 325 degrees.

Shelia Pearce, South Huntsville
Mrs. L. M. Taylor, Big Cove

BUTTERSCOTCH PIE

1 cup firmly packed brown sugar
½ cup white sugar
4 T. flour
3 egg yolks

2 cups milk
1 tsp. vanilla
½ stick margarine
Pie shell, baked
Meringue

Blend sugars and flour; add beaten egg yolks and milk. Cook slowly until thick. Remove from heat and add vanilla and margarine. Cool. Pour into pie shell. Cover with meringue and bake in slow oven until the meringue is a golden color.

Mrs. Paul Bledsoe, Hurricane

CARAMEL PIE

2 cups sugar
3 cups milk
6 eggs

4 T. flour
2 tsp. vanilla
2 pie crusts, baked
Meringue

Brown ½ cup of sugar. Scald milk. Beat egg yolks until light. Mix sugar and flour. Add to milk. Add egg yolks and vanilla, stirring constantly. Add carmelized sugar. Don't be alarmed if sugar lumps. It will melt with cooking. Cook until thick. Pour into baked pie crusts and top with meringue made from the egg whites. Makes 2 pies.

Sue Carter, Hazel Green

CHESS PIE I

1½ cups sugar
⅓ cup buttermilk
Pinch of salt
1 tsp. vanilla or lemon flavoring

¼ cup butter, softened
2 T. cornmeal
3 eggs
Pie shell, unbaked

Combine all ingredients except eggs and beat well. Beat each egg separately, then beat each 1 in with other ingredients separately. Bake at 350 degrees for 40 to 50 minutes.

Mrs. Carl Vaughn (Helen)
Submitted by daughter, Mrs. Bob Irwin (Virginia), Monrovia

CHESS PIE II

½ cup butter or margarine
1½ cup sugar
3 eggs, well beaten
1½ tsp. vanilla

Dash of salt
1 T. vinegar
1 T. self-rising meal
1 T. self-rising flour
Pie shell, unbaked

Cream butter and sugar. Add beaten eggs. Add vanilla, salt, vinegar, meal, and flour. Pour into unbaked pie shell. Start cooking at 300 degrees for 10 minutes. Turn oven up to 350 degrees and continue baking for 35 minutes longer.

Bonnie Nelson, Heritage

CHESS PIE III

½ stick margarine, melted
3 eggs
1¼ cups sugar

1 T. vinegar
1 tsp. vanilla
Pie shell, unbaked

Mix all together and bake for 1 hour at 300 degrees, starting with a cold oven. You do not have to check this pie while baking.

Mary Frances Mitchell, Madison Cross Roads

CHEWY CHESS PIE

½ cup melted butter
1 cup brown sugar
½ cup white sugar
1 T. flour

2 eggs, unbeaten
2 T. milk
1 tsp. vanilla
Pie shell, unbaked

Melt butter. Mix white and brown sugar and flour. Break eggs into mixture. Add milk and vanilla. Add melted butter. Bake in an unbaked pie shell for 40 minutes at 350 degrees.

Evelyn Kaylor, Hazel Green

COCONUT PIE SUPREME

1 cup sugar	2 tsp. vanilla
⅛ tsp. salt	½ stick butter or margarine
4 T. flour	⅔ cup coconut
2 egg yolks	1 9-inch pie shell, baked
2 cups milk	Meringue

Combine sugar, salt, and flour. Beat egg yolks and add milk to eggs. Add milk-egg mixture to dry ingredients. Mix thoroughly. Add vanilla and margarine. Cook in double boiler until mixture is very thick. Remove from heat and add coconut. Pour into baked pie shell and top with meringue.

Meringue

2 egg whites	¼ tsp. cream of tartar
	3 T. sugar

Whip egg whites until frothy. Add cream of tartar. Whip until stiff but not dry, until they stand in peaks that lean over slightly when the beater is removed. Beat in sugar, ½ teaspoon at a time. Bake in a 350-degree oven for 10 to 15 minutes, depending upon thickness of meringue.

Faye C. Gwin, Madison Cross Roads

COCONUT PIE (MAKES OWN CRUST)

4 eggs	2 cups milk
½ cup self-rising flour	¼ cup butter, melted
1¾ cups sugar	1½ cups coconut
	1 tsp. vanilla

Combine all ingredients in order and mix well. Pour into a well-greased 10-inch glass pie pan and bake from 45 minutes to 1 hour at 350 degrees, until golden brown. For best results, mix flour and sugar together before adding to other ingredients.

Rachel Koger, Hurricane

ESTELLE COCONUT PIE

⅓ cup cornstarch
1 cup sugar
⅓ cup butter or margarine
3 cups milk
2 cups coconut
4 eggs
1½ tsp. vanilla
1 pie shell, baked

Heat cornstarch, sugar, and butter until thickened. Add milk and 1 cup of coconut. Beat egg yolks and add a little at a time to the hot mixture. Add vanilla. Pour into pie shell. Make a merignue with the egg whites and put over filling. Sprinkle with remaining cup of coconut and brown in a slow oven until deep brown.

Estelle Pinion, Central

FRENCH COCONUT PIE I

1 stick butter, melted
1 cup sugar
3 whole eggs
1 can flake coconut
1 T. vinegar
1 tsp. vanilla
1 pie shell, unbaked

Combine all ingredients and pour into an unbaked pie shell. Bake for 1 hour at 350 degrees.

Cynthia Rich, Heritage
Mrs. Tom Baker, Hurricane

FRENCH COCONUT PIE II

½ stick butter
1⅓ cups sugar
3 whole eggs
¼ cup buttermilk
1 tsp. vanilla flavoring
2 cups coconut
1 pie shell, unbaked

Blend butter and sugar together. Add eggs 1 at a time and beat well. Then mix in buttermilk, vanilla, and coconut. Pour into unbaked pie shell. Bake at 325 degrees for 45 minutes.

Anna Lee Pogue, Central

IMPOSSIBLE PIE

½ cup Bisquick
½ cup sugar
4 eggs
2 cups milk
1 tsp. vanilla
3 T. butter
1 3½-oz. can coconut

Put all in a blender or mix well. Pour into a 9-inch buttered pie pan. Bake for 30 minutes at 350 degrees until custard is firm.

Ethel Huse, Davis Hills

INCREDIBLE COCONUT PIE

½ cup self-rising flour
1⅓ cups sugar
4 eggs, beaten
2 cups milk
1 tsp. vanilla
¼ cup melted margarine
1 7-oz. can flaked coconut

Combine flour and sugar; add eggs, milk, vanilla, and margarine. Mix well and stir in coconut. Pour into a deep-dish 9-inch pie pan. No pie shell needed. Bake at 375 degrees for 30 to 35 minutes.

Laura O'Neal, Blossomwood

JELLO PIE

Shell

1 stick *butter*
¼ cup brown sugar
1 cup flour
¼ cup ground pecans

Cream *butter* and brown sugar and add flour; add pecans and mix. Press into a 9x13-inch pan and bake at 350 degrees for 15 minutes. Let cool.

Filling

1 8-oz. pkg. cream cheese
¾ cup sugar
1 pt. whipping cream, whipped
1 cup boiling water
1 sm. box Jello, lemon
1 box Jello, any flavor

Cream the cream cheese with sugar. Whip cream and fold into cheese mixture. Add boiling water to Jello and let cool. Add to cheese and cream mixture. Pour into cooled crust. Chill for 2 hours and add second box of Jello (mixed according to directions on box). I like cherry Jello; it looks pretty. Add to pie and chill until Jello sets.

Carol Hix, Westbury

LAZY PIE

1 stick butter
¾ cup sugar
1 cup flour

1½ tsp. baking powder
¾ cup sweet milk
2-3 cups fruit
¾ cup sugar

Melt butter in flat pan. Mix next 4 ingredients; pour into pan over melted butter. Over this, pour the fruit. Sprinkle ¼ cup sugar over top. Bake at 350 degrees for 30 minutes or until brown.

Dorothy Broad, Big Cove

LEMONADE PIE

1 6-oz. can of frozen lemonade, thawed

1 lg. Cool Whip
1 can Eagle Brand milk
2 graham cracker crusts

Mix first 3 ingredients and pour into crust.

Jean Moore, Big Cove

LEMON CHESS PIE

4 whole eggs
2 cups sugar
1 T. flour
1 T. cornmeal
Dash of salt

¼ cup melted butter
¼ cup sweet milk
2 T. lemon rind
¼ cup lemon juice
Pie shell, unbaked

Beat eggs well; add sugar gradually. Then add other ingredients as listed. Put in pie shell and bake at 350 degrees until filling is firm or tests done with a knife. Delicious.

Mrs. Peggy Barber, Fleming Hills

GRANNY B'S OLD-FASHIONED CUSTARD PIE

4 eggs
1½ cups scalded milk
2 T. flour
1 cup sugar

4 T. butter
¼ tsp. salt
Nutmeg to taste
1 pie crust, unbaked

Mix. Pour into crust. Bake at 300 degrees until knife inserted in center comes out clean.

Winnie Beck, Davis Hills

MAMA'S EGG CUSTARD

3 eggs plus 1 egg white
1¼ cups sugar
1 tsp. flour
⅔ cup milk
1 tsp vanilla extract
¼ tsp. lemon extract
1 pie shell

Beat 3 egg yolks and 1 egg white until light yellow. Mix sugar and flour together; add to eggs, a small amount at a time, beating after each addition. Gradually add milk; mix well. Add extracts. Pour into prepared crust. Cook until set at 325 degrees. Top with meringue.

Meringue

3 egg whites
6 T. sugar
1 tsp. meringue powder
1 tsp. vanilla

Mrs. Carlos Cole (Lillian), Monrovia

MERINGUE

Use 2 tablespoons sugar for each egg white. A little cream of tartar can be added if whites are not stiff enough. Bake at 350 degrees for 10 minutes or until tips start to brown.

Jesse Little, Harvest

MOTHER'S EGG PIE

4 eggs
½ cup sugar
Vanilla
Pinch of salt
2½ cups cold milk
9-10-inch pie shell, unbaked

Beat eggs; add sugar, then remaining ingredients. Pour into pie shell. Bake at 425 degrees for approximately 30 minutes. (Tips: I take a metal spoon and remove foam on top of pie before cooking. At the end of 30 minutes, pie may still be shaky in the middle but should finish cooking after being removed. Baking too long causes it to turn watery.)

Louise Sanford, Piedmont

OLD-FASHIONED EGG CUSTARD I

3 eggs
1 tsp. vanilla
1½ cups sugar
3 tsp. flour
2 cups milk
1 pie shell, baked
Meringue

Beat egg yolks and vanilla; add sugar, flour, and milk. Boil in double boiler until thick. Pour into pie shell, top with meringue, and brown.

Patsy O'Neal, Blossomwood

OLD-FASHIONED EGG CUSTARD II

1 cup milk
1 T. butter
1 tsp. vanilla
1 scant cup sugar
4 egg yolks
1 pie shell, unbaked
4 egg whites
4 T. sugar

Heat milk and butter together in saucepan. Beat vanilla and sugar with egg yolks. Add milk to egg mixture and pour into pie shell. Bake for 10 minutes in 400-degree oven. Reduce heat and bake at 325 degrees until firm. Top with meringue made from 4 egg whites and sugar beaten stiff. Brown in oven. Serves 6.

Reba Cornell, Hazel Green

OLD-FASHIONED EGG PIE

3 whole eggs
¾ cup sugar
1¼ cups milk
1 pie shell, unbaked
Nutmeg

Mix eggs, sugar, and milk. Pour into unbaked pie shell. Sprinkle with nutmeg. Bake at 275 degrees or 300 degrees for 1 hour.

Gracie McCurdy, Madison Cross Roads

RACHEL'S EGG CUSTARD

3 eggs
1 stick butter or margarine, melted
1¾ cups sugar
1 T. flour
1 sm. can evap. Pet milk
Vanilla flavoring to taste

1 deep-crust pie shell, unbaked

Beat eggs well. Then add next 5 ingredients in order. Pour into pie shell. Bake at 350 degrees until brown and barely shakes in center.

Rachel Sturdivant, Darwin Downs

PEANUT PIE

1 sm. pkg. cream cheese
½ cup peanut butter (chunky or smooth)
1 cup powdered sugar
1 reg. Cool Whip
1 pie shell, preheated
Peanuts, ground

Mix well cream cheese, peanut butter, and powdered sugar Fold in Cool Whip. Fill pie shell; sprinkle liberally with ground peanuts. Refrigerate 3 or 4 hours before serving.

Earlene Britt, Rainbow Mountain

SARATOGA TART

3 egg whites
1 tsp. vanilla
1 cup sugar
14 single saltine crackers
¾ cup walnut pieces
1 tsp. baking powder

Beat egg whites until like meringue. Add vanilla and sugar gradually while still beating. Set aside. Mix together saltine crackers mashed coarsely with walnut pieces and baking powder. Fold cracker mixture into egg whites. Pour into greased pie pan and bake at 350 degrees for 40 to 45 minutes. Let cool completely.

Topping

½ pt. whipping cream
3 T. sugar
¼ tsp. maple flavoring

Beat until it will hold peaks. Cover pie and top with shavings from a Hershey chocolate candy bar. Refrigerate.

Carlla Hooper, Heritage

Happiness does not come from doing what we like —.

SPICE PIE

3 eggs, slightly beaten
1½ cups sugar
1 tsp. cinnamon
1 tsp. allspice
1 tsp. nutmeg

1 tsp. lemon juice
1 T. butter
1 T. flour
1 cup milk
Pie shell, unbaked

Bake in pie shell at 300 degrees for 1 hour.

Laura O'Neal, Blossomwood

TOFFEE ICE CREAM PIE

17-18 vanilla wafers ½ gal. vanilla ice cream
1 cup chopped toffee bars

Line bottom and sides of buttered, 9-inch pie pan with wafers. Spoon ice cream into wafer shell; repeat, making 2 layers. Sprinkle ½ cup of chopped toffee between the 2 layers. Store in freezer until serving time.

Toffee Sundae Sauce

1½ cups sugar
1 cup evap. milk, undiluted

¼ cup margarine or butter
¼ cup light corn syrup
Dash of salt

Combine, sugar, milk, margarine, syrup, and salt. Bring to boil over low heat; boil 1 minute. Remove from heat and cool, stirring occasionally. Serve sauce over pie wedges. Yield: 1 9-inch pie (serves 6 to 8) and 2½ cups sauce.

Mildred Prince, Pulaski Pike

VELVETY LEMON TARTS

3 eggs
¼ cup soft butter
¾ cup sugar
Dash of salt

Juice of 1 lemon
Yellow rind of 1 lemon
8 tart shells (about 3-inch), baked
Cool Whip

Put all ingredients except tart shells and Cool Whip into electric blender.

Blend on high speed for 15 seconds. Pour into a heavy saucepan or double boiler and cook, stirring constantly, until thickened. (Cooks quickly.) Pour into 8 baked shells. Cool. Top with Cool Whip.

Cynthia Rich, Heritage

FRUIT PIES

APPLE PIE I

1⅓ cups of sugar
1 T. flour
½ tsp. cinnamon

½ stick margarine
1 egg
1½ cups grated apples

1 pie shell, uncooked

Mix sugar, flour, and cinnamon. Add egg, melted margarine, and apples. Mix well with spoon and pour into pie shell. Cook 1 hour at 325 to 350 degrees.

Monteen Dowdey, Twickenham

APPLE PIE II

1 cup sugar
1 stick margarine
1 tsp. cinnamon
Dash of salt

2 T. flour
1 egg, beaten
1½ cups grated apples
1 pie shell, unbaked

Mix first 5 ingredients together. In a separate bowl mix egg and apples. Combine both mixtures. Pour into pie shell and bake at 400 degrees for 15 minutes. Reduce heat to 350 degrees and bake for 45 minutes.

Evelyn Kaylor, Hazel Green

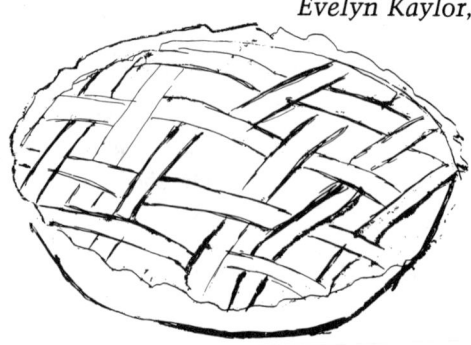

GOLDEN DELICIOUS APPLE PIE

6 apples, grated (yellow Delicious)
½ cup powdered sugar
Juice of 1 lemon
Cinnamon
9-inch pie shell, baked
Whipped cream

Mix apples, sugar, and lemon juice. Sprinkle with cinnamon and put in baked pie shell. Top with whipped cream sprinkled with cinnamon. Serves 6 to 8. Easy and delicious.

Judy Walthall, Fleming Hills

SOUR CREAM APPLE PIE

2 T. flour
⅛ tsp. salt
¾ cup sugar
1 egg
1 cup sour cream
1 tsp. vanilla
¼ tsp. nutmeg
¼ tsp. cinnamon
2 cups sliced apples
1 9-inch pie shell, unbaked

Mix flour, salt, and sugar well in a bowl. Add unbeaten egg, sour cream, vanilla, nutmeg, and cinnamon. Beat to a smooth, thin batter. Blend in apples and pour into pastry-lined pan. Bake at 400 degrees for 15 minutes, then at 350 degrees for 30 minutes. Remove from oven.

Topping

⅓ cup sugar
½ cup flour
1 tsp. cinnamon
¼ cup margarine

Mix until coarse and sprinkle over pie. Brown for 10 minutes in 400-degree oven.

Ila Wilkinson, Central

BLUEBERRY CHEESE PIE

1 stick margarine, softened
1 cup flour
1 cup chopped pecans (optional)

Mix these together well for crust. Press into pan or baking dish and bake till brown; cool.

Filling

1 8-oz. and 1 3-oz. box cream cheese
1 1-lb. box powdered sugar
1 med. Cool Whip
1 can blueberry pie filling

Cream cream cheese and sugar together. Add Cool Whip; spread on baked crust then spoon 1 can blueberry pie filling over top. Refrigerate till ready to serve. Strawberries or peaches may be used.

Mrs. O. V. Mitchell, Central
Winnie Beck, Davis Hills

CHERRY PARTY PIE

1 can pie cherries
1 flat can crushed pineapple
7 T. cornstarch
2 cups sugar
8 T. red food coloring
¾ cup chopped pecans
1 pie shell, baked
Whipped topping

Drain fruit. Add enough water to juice to make 2 cups. Mix cornstarch, sugar, fruit, and liquid. Add food coloring. Cook over low heat, stirring constantly until thickened. Cool. Add pecans. Pour ingredients into a baked pie shell. Top with whipped topping and refrigerate for 3 or 4 hours until serving time.

JoAnn Wester, Fleming Hills

COMPANY PIE

½ cup seedless raisins
½ cup chopped pecans
1 tsp. vinegar
½ cup margarine
¾ cup sugar
2 eggs
½ tsp. cinnamon
½ tsp. nutmeg
¼ tsp. salt
9-inch pie shell, unbaked

Mix raisins, nuts, and vinegar and let stand. Combine margarine, sugar, and eggs and heat until thick. Beat in spices and salt. Stir in raisin mixture. Put mixture into unbaked pie shell. Bake in oven at 400 degrees for 30 to 35 minutes.

Marie Barcus, Central

GRAPE JUICE PIE

¾ cup sugar
¼ cup cornstarch
1⅓ cups grape juice
1 egg, slightly beaten

2 T. butter or oleo
2 T. lemon juice
1 9-inch pastry shell, baked
1 cup whipping cream
1 T. sugar

Combine sugar and cornstarch in a 2-quart saucepan. Stir in grape juice; cook over medium heat, stirring constantly, until thickened and bubbly. Cook 1 additional minute. Add a small amount of hot mixture to egg, mixing well; stir egg mixture into remaining hot mixture. Add butter and lemon juice; returning to heat. Bring to a boil, stirring constantly; boil gently for 1 minute. Cool. Pour into pastry shell; chill thoroughly. Combine whipping cream and sugar, beating until light and fluffy. Spread on pie; chill. Cool Whip can be used.

Mary Frances Mitchell, Madison Cross Roads

GRASSHOPPER PIE

Crust

20 Oreo cookies

4 T. melted butter

Crush cookies until fine crumbs. Mix with melted butter and press into a pie shell.

Filling

25 lg. marshmallows
½ cup milk
⅛ tsp. salt

½ pt. whipping cream
1 oz. green creme de menthe
1 oz. white creme de cocoa

Melt marshmallows, milk, and salt in double boiler and allow to cool. Whip cream. Add liqueurs and add to marshmallow mixture. Pour filling into crust; refrigerate or freeze.

Mrs. Frank J. Nola (Grace), Westbury

HAWAIIAN PIE

Bananas
Graham cracker crust
1 can condensed milk
⅓ cup lemon juice

1 can crushed pineapple
1 cup chopped nuts
1 box Dream Whip
Angel flake coconut
Cherries (optional)

Slice bananas all over the bottom of graham cracker crust. Mix condensed milk and lemon juice and pour over bananas. Drain pineapple and spread over this. Next add a layer of chopped nuts. Mix Dream Whip according to package directions and spread over the top. Sprinkle angel flake coconut over this and decorate, if desired, with cherries.

Patsy Whitt, New Sharon

HEAVENLY FRUIT PIE

1 sm. can pineapple
1 sm. can peaches
1 can Eagle Brand milk
⅓ cup lemon juice
1 lg. Cool Whip
1 sm. orange
2 pie shells, baked

Drain pineapple and peaches. Combine with milk. Fold in lemon juice, Cool Whip, and orange and pour into pie shells. Yield: 2 8-inch pies.

Dorothy Broad, Big Cove
Nora Drake, Big Cove

ICEBOX PIE I

1 lg. Cool Whip
1 lg. can crushed pineapple
1 cup chopped nuts
1 can strawberry filling
1 can Eagle Brand milk

Mix together and pour into 2 pie crusts. Refrigerate overnight and freeze.

Diane McFarland, Harvest

ICEBOX PIE II

1 med. can crushed pineapple
¾ cup sugar
1 pkg. lemon Jello
1 can Topic or Milnot, whipped

Heat pineapple, sugar, and Jello. Cool, then fold in Topic or Milnot. Pour ingredients in crust and refrigerate.

Crust

20 graham crackers
¼ cup butter
¼ cup sugar

Roll crackers fine; add softened butter and sugar.

Ella Schwerman, South Parkway

JIFFY COBBLER

1 stick margarine
1 cup sugar
1 cup flour
1 tsp. salt
1½ tsp. baking powder
1 cup milk
1 lg. can fruit
½ cup sugar

Melt margarine in oblong pan. Combine other ingredients except fruit and ½ cup sugar. Pour mixture over melted margarine. Then pour the fruit over the dough mixture; sprinkle sugar on top. Cook at 350 degrees for ½ hour or until brown.

Jimmie Covington, Central

MAC'S SOUR CREAM RAISIN PIE

1 cup sugar
3 T. flour
⅛ tsp. salt
3 egg yolks
1 cup sour cream
1 cup plumped raisins
½ cup nuts (optional)
1 tsp. vanilla
1 pie shell, baked
Meringue or Cool Whip

Combine sugar, flour, and salt. Beat egg yolks and combine with sour cream. Add to first mixture and cook over low heat until thick. Add raisins, nuts, and vanilla. Cool. Pour into a baked pie shell. Put meringue or Cool Whip on top and serve.

Faye Gwin, Madison Cross Roads

MARSHMALLOW TORTE PIE

½ cup milk
36 Campfire marshmallows
1 cup whipping cream
1 lg. can Del Monte fruit cocktail
Graham cracker pie shell

Heat milk; add marshmallows; dissolve and cool. Fold in whipped cream and cold drained fruit. Fold into graham cracker pie shell. (Save some of the crumbs for topping.)

Helen Hann, Piedmont

MILE-HIGH PIE

Crumb Mixture

2 cups flour   1 cup melted margarine

Mix flour and margarine and spread flat on a cookie sheet. Bake at 350 degrees for 15 minutes. Set this crumb mixture aside.

Filling

2 egg whites   1 tsp. lemon juice
1 10-oz. box frozen strawberries   1 cup white sugar
            1 lg. carton Cool Whip

Beat egg whites until fluffy. *Add* thawed strawberries, lemon juice, and white sugar. Beat this together at high speed for 15 minutes. Fold in Cool Whip. Crumble ⅔ crumb mixture in 9x13 dish. Pour strawberry mixture on crumbs. Top with rest of crumbs. Put in freezer. Does not freeze hard, so can be taken out and eaten right away.

Ella Schwerman, South Parkway

MILLION-DOLLAR PIE

1 can sweetened condensed milk   2 cups mandarin oranges
¼ cup lemon juice   ¾ cup nuts
1 No. 2 can pineapple   1 lg. Cool Whip
            3 graham cracker crusts

Mix milk and lemon juice. Drain fruit. Add to mixture with nuts. Fold in Cool Whip. Pour into pie crusts. This freezes well.

Mary Jo Dreaden, Fleming Hills

MILLIONAIRE PIE

1 can condensed milk   1 lg. can pineapple
¼ cup lemon juice   1 cup chopped nuts
1 9-oz. Cool Whip   2 9-inch graham cracker crusts

Mix milk and lemon juice. Add whipped topping and mix well. Add pineapple and nuts. Pour into 2 crusts and keep in the refrigerator overnight before serving.

Cheryl Reid, South Parkway

OATMEAL AND MINCEMEAT PIE

3 eggs
¾ cup firmly packed brown sugar
1 cup quick or old-fashioned oats, uncooked

2 cups ready-to-eat mincemeat
2 T. brandy, if desired
¼ cup butter or margarine, melted
1 9-inch pie shell, unbaked

Beat eggs until foamy. Gradually add sugar; beat until thick. Stir in remaining ingredients; mix well. Pour into pie shell. Bake in preheated moderate oven at 350 degrees for 35 to 40 minutes or until center of pie is set.

Kathleen Tyson, New Sharon

PEACH COBBLER

2 cups sliced peaches
1 cup sugar
1 stick butter

¾ cup plain flour
2 tsp. baking powder
¾ cup milk
Pinch of salt

Mix peaches with ½ cup sugar and set aside. Put butter in deep 2-quart baking dish, and set in a 350-degree oven to melt. Make batter of ½ cup sugar, flour, baking powder, milk, and salt. Pour this batter over melted butter but do not stir. Put peaches on top of batter but do not stir. Bake 1 hour at 350. Batter will rise to top and brown while baking. Serve with vanilla ice cream.

Diane McFarland, Harvest

FRESH PEACH PIE
(Or Other Fruit)

¾ - 1 cup sugar
3 T. all-purpose flour

5 cups peaches, sliced
2 T. butter or margarine
Pastry for 2-crust pie

Mix sugar and flour. Place peaches in dish lined with ½ unbaked pastry; sprinkle flour and sugar mixture over peaches; dot with butter or margarine. Place top crust on; cut slits to allow steam to escape. Bake at 425 degrees for 35 to 45 minutes.

Beryl Tidwell, Big Cove

PEACH PIE SUPREME

1 pastry shell
4-6 peaches
½-⅔ cup sugar
⅛ tsp. cinnamon
½ cup sour cream
2 T. flour
½ cup grated sharp cheese

Line Pyrex pie pan with pastry. Cut peaches into eighths or leave in halves. Arrange in pastry-lined pan. Mix the sugar, cinnamon, sour cream, and flour. Pour the mixture over the peaches. Bake at 425 degrees for 40 to 50 minutes. When serving, sprinkle with cheese. Variation: Substitute apples for peaches.

Vicki Coffee, Extension Agent

QUICK PEACH PIE

1 stick margarine
1 cup self-rising flour
1 cup sugar
½ tsp. cinnamon
1 cup sweet milk
1 lg. can sliced peaches

Dot bottom of baking dish with margarine. Combine next 4 ingredients. Pour mixture into baking dish. Pour peaches over the top. Bake at 350 degrees until golden brown. (Bottom rises to top for crust.)

Leta Sims, Vestavia

PECAN PIE I

3 whole eggs, well beaten
½ cup granulated sugar
½ cup white Karo syrup
½ cup red Karo syrup
Pinch of salt
1 tsp. vanilla flavoring
1 cup cut-up pecans
Pastry shell, unbaked

Mix filling ingredients; put in pastry shell; bake on low heat for 30 minutes at 350°.

Cora Lewis, Central

So all the good things seem to happen
To the other fellow round about—
And your payload never does come steaming in!
Are you sure you sent a vessel out?

PECAN PIE II

3 eggs
1 cup pecans, chopped
½ cup sugar
½ tsp. salt

1 tsp. vanilla
1 cup Karo syrup
3 T. margarine, chipped
Pie shell, unbaked

Beat eggs slightly. Add nuts, sugar, salt, vanilla, syrup, and chipped margarine. Put into unbaked pie shell and bake for 50 to 55 minutes in oven at 350 degrees.

Pie Pastry

1 cup flour
4 T. shortening

½ tsp. salt
3 T. water

Deborah Drake, Big Cove

PECAN PIE III

3 eggs
½ cup dark Karo syrup
1 tsp. vanilla

1 cup pecans
Pinch of salt
Pie crust, unbaked

Beat filling ingredients together and bake in pie crust at 325 degrees for 35 minutes.

Lottie Power, Harvest

CRACKER PECAN PIE

1 cup chopped pecans
16 saltine crackers, crushed
1 T. baking powder

3 egg whites
1 cup sugar
1 T. vanilla extract

Ice cream or whipped topping

In first bowl mix pecans, saltine crackers, and baking powder. In second, smaller bowl, lightly beat egg whites. Add sugar and vanilla extract. Fold second bowl into first bowl. Pour into well-buttered 10-inch pie pan or 2 8-inch pie pans. Bake at 350 degrees for 20 minutes (in glass dish bake at 325 degrees for 20 minutes) or until lightly browned and a good consistency. Cool and serve with ice cream or whipped topping.

Julie Linderman, Vestavia

DATE-PECAN PIE

2 cups sugar
1 cup butter
4 eggs
½ cup cold water

2 T. vanilla flavoring
Flour
1 cup pecans
1 cup dates

2 pie shells, unbaked

Cream sugar and butter; add well-beaten egg yolks; add water and vanilla gradually. Flour nuts and dates, then add to mixture. Fold stiffly beaten egg whites into mixture. Put mixture in pie shells and cook at 350 degrees for about 35 or 40 minutes. Yield: 2 pies.

Mrs. Wall Johnston (Ruby), Monrovia

DELUXE PECAN PIE

3 eggs
2 T. margarine
1 tsp. salt
1 cup dark corn syrup

1 tsp. vanilla
1 cup sugar
1 cup pecans
Pie shell, unbaked

Mix filling ingredients and pour into pie shell. Bake at 350 degrees for 45 minutes or until a knife inserted in center comes out clean.

Mrs. Marvin Sharp, Central

PECAN SLICES

Crust

1 cup pre-sifted flour ½ cup butter

Blend and spread this mixture in a small pie pan. Bake it in a moderate oven at 350 degrees for 12 minutes.

Filling

2 eggs, beaten
½ cup grated coconut
2 T. flour
½ tsp. salt

1½ cups brown sugar
1 cup chopped pecans
½ tsp. baking powder
1 tsp. vanilla

Bake in a 350-degree oven for 25 minutes. When cool, spread with 1 cup powdered sugar thinned to spread with juice of 1 lemon.

Nell Goodjohn, Darwin Downs

PINEAPPLE CREAM PIE

1 lg. can crushed pineapple, in own juice
1 pt. dairy sour cream
1 lg. pkg. vanilla pudding, instant
1 pie shell, baked
Whipped topping

Drain pineapple; add juice with sour cream to pudding mix and beat well. Fold in pineapple and put it into shell. Chill and serve. May be served with dollops of whipped topping. Super easy.
Ruth W. Chambers, Darwin Downs

PINTO BEAN PIE

2 eggs
1½ cups sugar
1 stick butter, melted
½ cup coconut
1 tsp. vanilla
½ cup mashed pinto beans
Pie shell, unbaked

Beat eggs; add sugar, butter, coconut, and vanilla. Blend pintos in blender and add to other ingredients. Pour in pie shell and bake for 45 minutes in 350 degree oven.
Patsy O'Neal, Blossomwood
Naomi Hicks, New Sharon

PUMPKIN PIE

2 cups fresh pumpkin or 1 can pumpkin
1 lg. can evap. milk (about 2 cups)
1 cup sugar
¼ tsp. salt
¼ tsp. allspice
¼ tsp. cinnamon
2 eggs, slightly beaten
2 T. melted butter
¼ cup brown sugar
½ cup raisins (optional)
1 unbaked pie shell

If using fresh pumpkin, pass through a sieve to remove strings. Mix pumpkin with remaining filling ingredients and pour into a pie shell. Bake at 425 degrees for about 25 minutes or until knife inserted in center comes out clean. May serve with whipped cream.
Madison County

GLAZED STRAWBERRY PIE
(Fresh, ripe peaches may be used)

1 qt. strawberries
1⅓ cups sugar
½ cup water
¼ cup cornstarch
¾ cup cold water

⅛ tsp. salt
1 T. lemon juice
Red vegetable coloring
1 pie shell, baked
Whipped topping

Wash and drain strawberries and remove stems. Bring sugar and water to boiling point in a saucepan over medium heat. Dissolve cornstarch in the ¾ cup cold water; add to syrup mixture and cook about 10 minutes over low heat or until clear. Stir occasionally. Blend in salt, lemon juice, and enough red coloring to produce a light red shade; pour glaze over strawberries and mix gently. When cool place in baked pie shell. Garnish with whipped cream or topping.

Dorothy Mellette, Central

OLD-TIME SWEET POTATO COBBLER

2 cups peeled and sliced sweet potatoes
Pastry for double-crust pie
1½ cups sugar

1 tsp. vanilla
½ cup melted margarine
Dash of nutmeg
1 tsp. grated orange rind

Put potatoes in just enough water to cover and cook for 10 minutes or until tender. Roll pastry to ⅛-inch thickness. Line a greased 10x6-inch pan with ½ of pastry. Cover with potato slices and liquid; add sugar, vanilla, and ¼ cup melted margarine. Sprinkle with nutmeg and grated orange rind. Top with remaining pastry, pressing edges to seal. Make several slits in top crust for steam to escape. Brush top crust with remaining margarine and sprinkle lightly with sugar. Bake in moderate oven until brown.

Mrs. O. V. Mitchell, Central

DELICIOUS SWEET POTATO PIE

1 cup mashed potatotes
1 cup sugar
1 tsp. vanilla flavoring

1 cup butter
1 egg, unbeaten
Pie shell, unbaked

Mix filling ingredients; pour into unbaked pie shell. Cook for 1 hour at 325 degrees.

Mrs. Eugene Smith (Nina), Monrovia

SWEET POTATO PIE I

2 cups cooked, mashed sweet potatoes
2 cups sugar
3 eggs

1 tsp. vanilla
1 stick butter
1 can Eagle Brand milk
2 pie shells, unbaked

Mix all filling ingredients together and pour into pie shells. Bake at 350 degrees until set.

Carolyn Underwood, Hazel Green

SWEET POTATO PIE II

Sweet potatoes
1½ cups sugar
1½ tsp. vanilla
1 T. butter

½ - 1 can condensed milk
½ cup milk
Pinch of salt
Pie shell, unbaked

Ice cream, whipped topping, or meringue

Boil sweet potatoes until well done, then peel and mash. Put 2 cups mashed sweet potatoes in bowl with sugar, vanilla, butter, condensed milk, milk, and salt. Mix, then pour into pie shell and bake at 350 degrees until crust is well browned around the edges, about 30 to 35 minutes. Top with ice cream, whipped topping, or meringue.

Lottie Power, Harvest

THOUSAND ISLANDS PIE

1 No. 2 can fruit cocktail, drained
1 No. 2 can crushed pineapple, drained
1 can Eagle Brand milk

1 cup Cool Whip
1 cup sour cream
2 T. lemon juice
2 graham cracker crusts, baked

Mix ingredients in order given above. Add lemon juice last. Mix well. Pour into crusts. Chill until set. Yield: 2 8-inch pies. Serves 12 to 16.

Mrs. Peggy Barber, Fleming Hills

FRIED APPLE PIES

1 8 oz. package dried apples
2 tbsp. melted butter or margarine
½ to 1 cup sugar
1 tsp. ground cinnamon
2 tbsp. lemon juice
pastry and salad oil

Soak apples overnight. Drain and rinse well. Cover apples with water and cook about one hour until soft. Add remaining ingredients; Mash to combine. Roll out pastry, ⅓ at a time. Cut out pastry, using a five-inch saucer. Place about 3 tbsp. of apple mixture on half each circle. Fold over other half and seal with a fork. To seal pies dip finger in water and moisten edges of circle before folding over. Use a fork dipped in flour and press pastry edges firmly together. Heat 1-inch of salad oil to 375°. cook pies until golden brown on both sides, turning only once. Drain well on paper towel. Yield: About 1½ dozen.

Pastry for 10 pies saucer size.

2 cups flour
1 tsp. salt
¾ cup Crisco
⅓ cup ice water

Mix flour and salt together. Take out ½ cup flour mix and set aside. Cut shortening into remaining flour. Mix until thoroughly mixed. Make a paste with the ½ cup flour and ⅓ cup ice water. Add to shortening and flour and mix with a fork. Place lightly on floured board or wax paper. Divide the dough into 4 or 5 balls. Roll out each ball into the size of two saucers. Cut around each saucer and follow above directions for filling. To bake instead of fry cook in 450° oven for 10-15 minutes on greased cookie sheet.

PECAN PIE

1 raw pie shell (10″)

Filling: Mix in bowl

3 eggs
¾ cup sugar
2 tsp. vanilla
3 tbsp. flour
3 tbsp. butter
1½ tbsp. white karo
1 tsp. salt
2 cups pecans

Bake at 450° for 10 minutes 325° for 30-40 minutes.

Idana Devenish, Westbury

MYSTERY PECAN PIE

1 9" deep pie crust (bake
  6 min. & cool)
1 8 oz. pkg. cream cheese
  (softened)
⅓ cup sugar

4 eggs
2 tsp. vanilla
¼ tsp. salt
1 cup chopped pecans

In a small bowl, beat cream cheese, sugar, 1 egg and 1 tsp. vanilla until creamy, add salt. Spread in the bottom of the pie shell. Sprinkle with 1 cup chopped pecans. Beat 3 eggs, corn syrup and 1 tsp. vanilla. Pour carefully over cheese and nuts. Bake 350° for 10 minutes then reduce heat to 325° for 35 minutes. Cool and serve.

Mrs. Charles Linn, University Homemakers

MY MAMA TONEY'S NUT PIE

standard self-rising flour
  pastry
2 tbsp. self-rising flour
½ tsp. allspice
⅔ cup sugar
4 eggs

1 cup seeded dates
1 cup pecan or hickory nut
  meats
1 tbsp. vinegar
4 tbsp. butter
1 tsp. vanilla

Mix the flour, spice and sugar. Add the beaten eggs and all other ingredients except the butter and vanilla. Cook until the mixture begins to thicken. Remove it from the fire. Add the vanilla and butter and cool slightly. Pour into pastry lined pie pans and bake in a hot oven (400°F) until the pastry is brown and custard firm. Serve cold with hard sauce or whipped cream. Or cook the above mixture until quite thick. Pour into baked pastry shells and set in a slow oven (300°F) about 15 minutes.

Beverly Brown, Monrovia II Homemakers

GIBSON'S COCONUT PIE

Bake pie shell

¾ cup sugar
3 egg yolks
2 tbsp. butter
pinch salt
3 heaping tbsp. flour

2 cups milk scalded (almost boiling)
1 tsp. vanilla
1 cup flaked coconut

Scald milk in thick pan. Mix sugar, flour, egg yolks, salt. Add small amount with milk, remove from heat when doing this. Mix **good** then add remaining mixture and cook until it thickens. Remove from heat, add vanilla, butter and coconut. Put in pie shell. Top with meringue (P. 129) Add cream of tarter to egg whites. (½ tsp.) Put some coconut on top.

Shelby Gipson, Hurricane

MY MAMA TONEY'S CARAMEL PIE

pastry shell
2 cups scalded milk
2 cups sugar
4 tbsp. self-rising flour

3 eggs (reserve 2 whites for meringue
2 tbsp. butter
1 tsp. vanilla

Caramelize 1 cup of sugar, add hot milk to caramelized sugar. Cook til smooth, add the remaining sugar, flour and beaten eggs. Cook the mixture until it's of the consistency of thick cream. Remove it from fire. Add the vanilla and butter. Pour into pastry lined pan and bake in hot oven (400°F) until pastry is a pale brown. Remove from oven and spread with meringue and bake in slow oven (300°F) about 15 minutes or cook the custard mixture until quite thick. Pour into a baked shell. Cover with meringue and bake in a slow oven (300°F) 15-20 minutes.

Beverly Brown, Monrovia II Homemakers

"SHREDDED" APPLE PIE

2 cups cooking (firm) apples, shredded with grater
1¼ cups sugar
1 stick margarine, melted
1 egg, beaten
2 tsp. cinnamon

Mix all ingredients together. Pour in uncooked deep pie shell. Bake 350° for 25-35 minutes until golden. NOTE: The shredding is what makes the difference.

Verne Ernst, Pulaski Pike

CANDIES AND COOKIES

CANDY

CHRIS'S BUTTERSCOTCH PRALINE CANDY

1 pkg. butterscotch pudding mix
   (not instant)
1 cup sugar
½ cup evap. milk
1 T. butter
1 cup pecans

Mix all ingredients except pecans. Cook until soft ball stage. Remove from heat. Beat until thickens and loses some of its gloss. Drop by spoonfuls on wax paper. Pecans may be pressed on top of each piece or added just before dropping.

Mrs. Marshall Byrd, Madison Cross Roads

CHOCOLATE NUT BALLS

2 sticks butter, melted
2 cups crushed graham crackers
1 cup nuts, chopped
1½ cups chunky peanut butter
1 tsp. vanilla
1 box powdered sugar
2 sm. (or 1 lg.) pkgs. semi-sweet chocolate bits
½ cake paraffin wax

Mix first 6 ingredients and cool in refrigerator. Thoroughly melt chocolate bits and paraffin together. Form balls from first mixture. Dip into chocolate. Drop on wax paper to cool. Yield: 50 balls.

Debbie Maples, Owens Cross Roads

DATE BALLS

2 pkgs. chopped dates
1 cup nuts
¾ lb. sm. marshmallows
1 can Eagle Brand milk
3 cups graham cracker crumbs
1 sm. pkg. coconut

Mix first 5 ingredients together, roll into balls, and roll in coconut. Place on wax paper and chill. May be frozen also.

Anna Lee Rogers, Madison Cross Roads

DIVINITY CANDY

2 cups sugar
½ cup light corn syrup
½ cup water

2 egg whites, at room temperature
Dash of salt
1 tsp. vanilla
½ cup walnuts, chopped (optional)

Mix sugar, syrup, and water together; do not stir after mixing. Cook to crack stage when dropped into cold water. Beat egg whites and salt together until egg whites stand in peaks; add syrup mixture slowly. Beating constantly, add vanilla and beat until thick. Add walnuts; drop batter from teaspoon onto wax paper.

Mrs. Burns Drake, Big Cove

NO-COOK DIVINITY

1 box fluffy white icing mix
⅓ cup white syrup
½ cup boiling water

1 tsp. vanilla
1 box powdered sugar
1 cup nuts

Beat icing mix, syrup, boiling water, and vanilla for 5 minutes until stiff. Add sugar and nuts. Drop by a spoon onto wax paper. Let dry for 12 hours. Turn over; let dry another 12 hours. Store in airtight container.

Jimmie Sue Moore, New Sharon

COCONUT FUDGE

1 cup coconut juice (from fresh coconut)
3 cups sugar

¼ cup light Karo syrup
2 or 3 cups grated fresh coconut
Butter, size of walnut

Boil coconut juice, sugar, and Karo until forms soft ball. Add coconut and cook until steam comes out of bubbles then add butter. Set aside and let cool. Beat until begins to look dull. Pour on greased tray and cut in squares.

Margie Brooks, Vestavia

OLD-FASHIONED CHOCOLATE FUDGE

1½ cups milk
4 sq. unsweetened chocolate (4 oz.)
4 cups sugar
3 T. light corn syrup
¼ tsp. salt
1½ tsp. vanilla
3 T. butter or margarine

Combine milk and chocolate in medium-size heavy saucepan; cook over low heat until chocolate is melted. Add sugar, corn syrup, and salt and cook, stirring constantly, to boiling. Cook without stirring to 234 degrees on a candy thermometer. (A teaspoonful of syrup will form a soft ball when dropped in cold water.) Remove from heat at once. Add vanilla and butter, but do not stir in. Leave thermometer in pan while fudge is cooling. Let mixture cool to 110 degrees. When cool enough, you can rest bottom of pan comfortably on hand. Beat with wooden spoon until mixture thickens and just begins to lose its gloss. Mixture will lighten in color as you beat. Beating will take about 15 minutes. Spread in a buttered 8x8x2-inch pan. Let stand until set and cool; cut into squares. Yield: 2 pounds.

Madison County

FIVE-MINUTE FUDGE

2 cups sugar
4 T. cocoa
¼ cup white syrup
½ cup milk
¼ lb. butter or margarine
1 tsp. vanilla
Pecans or peanuts

Mix sugar, cocoa, syrup, and milk. Bring mixture to a boil, then turn to low and boil for 5 minutes, stirring all the time. Remove from heat and add butter and vanilla; add nuts. Beat until firm and pour on platter.

Edith Baeder, New Sharon

QUICK, SURE FUDGE

12 oz. chocolate chips
1 can Eagle Brand milk
1 tsp. vanilla
Nuts to taste

Heat chips and milk and stir until the chips are melted. Add milk and beat in vanilla and nuts as desired.

Mary Ellen Anderson, Madison

GOOD-FOR-YOU CANDY

½ cup creamy peanut butter
2 T. cocoa
2 T. honey
⅛ tsp. salt
1 tsp. vanilla
1¼ cup wheat germ

With spoon mix above ingredients, reserving ¼ cup wheat germ. Sprinkle ¼ cup wheat germ on wax paper. Roll the mixture in small balls with hands. Cover and refrigerate. Yield: 70 balls.

Mrs. Hugh Tipton (Bessie Mae), Monrovia

HAND-DIPPED CHOCOLATES

2 boxes powdered sugar
1 can Eagle Brand milk
1 stick butter
1 cup chopped pecans
1 cup coconut
1 block paraffin
1 lg. bag chocolate chips

Roll first 5 ingredients into small balls. Melt paraffin and chocolate chips. Dip balls into chocolate mixture to coat.

Elaine Story, Pulaski Pike

HEALTH BALLS

1 lb. butter, melted
1 cup peanut butter
3 cups wheat germ
1 T. vanilla flavoring
2 lb. powdered sugar
1 lb. raisins
1 pkg. coconut
1 cup chopped nuts

Mix well, roll into 1-inch balls.

Chocolate Glaze

1 cup semi-sweet chocolate bits   1 stick paraffin

Melt together in top of double boiler. DO NOT add any water. Roll balls in glaze using a fork.

Mrs. C. W. Fanning (Mildred), Monrovia

MARY BALL CANDY

1 lg. can Pet milk
4 cups sugar
3 6-oz. pkgs. semi-sweet chocolate bits
2 sticks butter or margarine
1 jar marshmallow creme (10 or 12 oz.)
1½ tsp. vanilla
3 cups nuts

Bring milk and sugar to boil and let boil for 12 minutes, stirring constantly. While cooking milk and sugar mix chocolate bits, butter, and marshmallow creme. Pour milk and sugar over mixture. (Just dump it all in.) Turn beater on low speed and mix, then turn beater on high and beat until thick. Add vanilla and nuts. Drop on wax paper. Yield: 5 pounds.

Yvonne Whitman, Heritage

NO-FAIL PEANUT BRITTLE

2 cups shelled raw peanuts
1½ cups sugar
⅔ cup white Karo syrup
2 tsp. soda

Mix peanuts, sugar, and Karo. Boil over medium heat in skillet until honey colored and peanuts begin to pop. Remove from heat and stir in soda. Beat vigorously (work fast). Pour on buttered cookie sheet. Cool. Break into pieces.

Mrs. Herschel Moore (Judy), Heritage

OLD-FASHIONED HICKORY NUT CANDY

2 cups sugar
3 tsp. flour
1 cup milk
⅛ lb. butter or margarine
1 cup nuts

Mix sugar and flour in iron skillet; add milk and butter. Cook until ball forms when dropped in cold water. Remove from heat and beat vigorously; add nuts and pour on buttered platter or dish.

Mrs. Bob Freeman, Poplar Ridge

PEANUT BRITTLE

1 cup sugar
½ cup white Karo syrup
¼ cup hot water
1 tsp. margarine
2 cups raw peanuts
1 tsp. soda
1 tsp. vanilla

Bring sugar, syrup, and water to a boil. Add margarine and peanuts; boil and stir constantly until peanuts start to pop and syrup turns brown. Remove from heat and add soda and vanilla. Work real fast. Pour onto a greased cookie sheet, smooth out, and let cool. Break into pieces and store. Never fails.

Mary Moore, Central

BUCKEY'S CANDY

3 lb. powdered sugar
2 lb. peanut butter
1 lb. margarine or butter
12 oz. chocolate
⅔ block paraffin

Combine sugar, peanut butter, and margarine. Roll into small balls. Refrigerate overnight. Combine chocolate and paraffin in double boiler and melt. Use toothpick to dip balls in chocolate mixture. Let cool on wax paper.

Marie Barcus, Central

REESE CUP BALLS

1 box powdered sugar
1 cup peanut butter
1 stick butter
1 T. vanilla
½ block paraffin wax
½ bar Bakers' sweet chocolate

Combine sugar and peanut butter. Add melted butter and vanilla. Mix well (use hands). Roll into little balls and cool on cookie sheet. Melt wax and chocolate in double boiler. Dip balls into chocolate using toothpicks.

La Juan Blevins, South Huntsville

REESE PEANUT BUTTER CUPS

1½ cups graham cracker crumbs
1 box powdered sugar
1 cup peanut butter
2 sticks margarine
6 ozs. chocolate chips

Mix crumbs and sugar. Melt peanut butter; add 1½ sticks margarine and mix with crumb mixture. Spread in 9x13 buttered pan. Be sure to press down. Melt ½ stick margarine with chocolate chips and spread on top.

Norma Colbath, South Parkway

WHITE PRALINES

2 cups sugar
1 T. Karo
⅔ cup whipping cream

¼ tsp. cream of tartar
1 tsp. vanilla
2 cups pecan halves

Place in saucepan all ingredients except vanilla and pecans and bring to boil. Boil for 2 minutes. Remove from heat and let cool for a minute or so. Add vanilla and beat by hand until thick. Pour in pecans and dip a spoonful at a time on wax paper. Note: After mixture has thickened work very quickly or it will become too stiff before it is all spooned onto wax paper. If this happens, add a small amount of milk or leftover whipping cream to make mixture workable again.

Jeanne Peters, South Parkway

COOKIES

ARMENIAN COOKIES

1½ cups powdered sugar
1 cup chopped walnuts

½ tsp. vanilla extract
2 cups unsalted butter, melted

4½ cups all-purpose flour

In a very large bowl, add sugar, nuts, and vanilla extract to butter and mix by hand thoroughly. Add flour, finally mixing with hand until a soft dough is formed. Shape into small finger shapes or round shapes placing on ungreased cookie sheet. Bake at 350 degrees until cookies are lightly browned on the bottoms, approximately 13 minutes. Cool and roll in powdered sugar. Yield: Approximately 120 cookies.

Julie Linderman, Vestavia

BOILED CANDY COOKIES

2 cups sugar
½ lb. margarine
½ cup milk
4 T. cocoa

2½ cups quick oats
½ cup peanut butter
½ cup nuts
2 tsp. vanilla

Combine sugar, margarine, milk, and cocoa in a heavy saucepan. Bring to a rolling boil and boil for 1½ minutes. Remove from stove and quickly add oats, peanut butter, nuts, and vanilla. Beat well until blended. (Helps to keep hot it you set pan in a larger pan of hot water.) Drop by ice teaspoon onto wax paper or foil. (Half portions of this work fine but still boil for 1½ minutes. May be poured into buttered pan. Cut while warm. Take up after it is cool.)

Mrs. Ernest F. Dilday, Jr., Davis Hills

BOURBON BALLS

1 lb. powdered sugar
1 stick butter
¼ cup Eagle Brand milk
4 T. bourbon
2 cups chopped pecans
1 box semi-sweet chocolate
½ block paraffin

Cream butter and sugar together. Add milk, bourbon, and pecans. Roll balls and chill overnight. Stick toothpick into balls before chilling. Melt semi-sweet chocolate and paraffin in double boiler. Dip balls in chocolate mix.

Patsy Brazelton, Owens Cross Roads

BROWNIES

1 cup self-rising flour
4 T. cocoa
1 cup sugar
2 eggs, well beaten
⅔ cup Wesson oil
1 tsp. vanilla
1 cup pecans

Mix all ingredients, adding vanilla and nuts last. Bake in greased and floured 8x12-inch pan for 20 minutes at 350 degrees. Let cool in pan and cut into squares. Yield: 24 brownies.

Glenda Patterson, Owens Cross Roads

HILMA'S BROWNIES

1 stick butter
1 cup sugar
¾ cup self-rising flour
3 heaping T. cocoa
2 eggs
Butter
1 tsp. vanilla
1 cup nuts

Melt butter in 8x11-inch pan. In bowl mix sugar, self-rising flour, and cocoa. Mix well with fork, add eggs, butter, vanilla, and nuts. Bake 20 minutes at 350 degrees.

Opaline West, Madison Cross Roads

CATHEDRAL WINDOW COOKIES

2 6-oz. pkgs. chocolate chips
2 T. margarine
2 eggs
1¾ cups chopped pecans
1 10½-oz. pkg. colored marshmallows
Powdered sugar

Melt chocolate chips and oleo in double boiler. Add well-beaten eggs. Cook until eggs are done—2 or 3 minutes. *Cool* and add nuts and marshmallows. (Be sure it is cool enough not to melt marshmallows). Roll in powdered sugar on wax paper and cool in refrigerator. Cut in slices. Yield: 2 or 3 rolls.

Evelyn Hall, Athens Pike

CHESS SQUARES

1 box yellow cake mix
1 stick margarine
4 eggs
1 8-oz. pkg. cream cheese
1 box powdered sugar

Mix cake mix, margarine, and 1 egg until crumbly. Put mixture in bottom of 13x8 inch pan. Mix cream cheese, powdered sugar, and 3 eggs and pour over first mixture. Bake at 350 degrees for 40 minutes. Cut into squares when cool.

Jimmie Covington, Central

CINNAMON SQUARES

1 stick butter
½ stick margarine
1 cup sugar
1 egg
2 cups flour
2 tsp. cinnamon
½ tsp. vanilla
1 cup finely chopped nuts

Cream butter and margarine; add sugar; cream. Add egg yolk and mix well. Sift flour with cinnamon; add vanilla and flour mixture. Knead this mixture; spread on shallow cookie sheet. Glaze top with beaten egg white. Drain off excess and spread with finely chopped nuts. Bake at 325 degrees for 30 minutes. Cut into squares while still warm as cookies will get very crisp.

Margaret Stickland, Westbury

CHIP PAN COOKIES

1 cup margarine
¾ cup sugar
¾ cup brown sugar
1 tsp. vanilla

2 eggs
2¼ cups self-rising flour
1 12-oz. pkg. chocolate chips
1 cup chopped nuts

Combine margarine, sugar, brown sugar, and vanilla. Beat until creamy. Beat in eggs. Gradually add flour mixture and mix well. Stir in chocolate chips and nuts. Spread into greased 15x10x1-inch baking sheet. Bake at 375 degrees for 20 minutes. Cool; cut into squares. Yield: 35 squares.

Joan Mitchell, Piedmont

CHOCOLATE COOKIES BOILED

4 cups sugar
1 cup milk
½ cup cocoa
½ lb. butter

1 cup peanut butter
5 cups oats
1 cup nuts
1 cup coconut

3 T. vanilla

Add first 4 ingredients and boil from 5 to 7 minutes. Add peanut butter and mix. Add the remaining ingredients. Spoon onto wax paper and cool.

Carlene Chandler, New Sharon

MAGIC COOKIE BARS

1 stick margarine
1-1½ cups graham cracker crumbs
1 can condensed milk
1 12-oz. pkg. chocolate chips
1 7 or 8-oz. pkg. flaked coconut
¾ cup chopped nut meats (optional)

Use 13x9x1-inch pan. Melt margarine in pan on low heat. Remove pan from heat. Spread margarine evenly. Next add each ingredient as listed by spreading evenly in layers in pan. Bake for 20 to 30 minutes at 350 degrees.

Brenda Williams, Harvest

NO-BAKE THREE-LAYER COOKIES

1 cup plus 1½ T. margarine
¼ cup sugar
⅓ cup cocoa
1 tsp. vanilla
1 egg
2 cups graham cracker crumbs
½ cup chopped pecans
½ cup flaked coconut
3 T. milk
3 T. vanilla pudding, instant
2 cups powdered sugar
4 ozs. semi-sweet chocolate squares

Place ½ cup margarine, sugar, cocoa, and vanilla in top of double boiler. Cook until blended. Add egg and cook for 5 minutes longer, stirring constantly. Add cracker crumbs, nuts, and coconut. Press firmly into a 9x9x2-inch pan. Let stand for 15 minutes. Cream ½ cup margarine until light and fluffy. Mix milk and pudding mix together; add to margarine. Blend well. Add sugar gradually; beat until smooth. Spread over first layer. Let stand about 15 minutes in refrigerator until set. Melt chocolate and remaining margarine; cool. Spread over second layer. Cool and cut into bars.

Barbara Keller, Westbury

COCONUT MACAROONS

½ cup sweetened condensed milk
1 tsp. vanilla
2 cups flaked coconut

Combine all ingredients; mix well. Drop by spoonful 1 inch apart on greased baking sheet. Bake at 350 degrees for 10 minutes or until delicate brown. Remove at once from sheet. Yield: 24 cookies.

La Juan Blevins, South Huntsville

LORI'S ORANGE BALL COOKIES

1 lb. orange slices (candy)
7 ozs. coconut
2 cans Eagle Brand milk
1 cup chopped nuts
1 tsp. orange flavoring
1 tsp. vanilla flavoring

Chop orange slices. Mix all ingredients together. Pour into baking pan. Cook for 30 minutes in 350-degree oven. Cool slightly. Roll into walnut-size balls; roll in powdered sugar. Can be stored in refrigerator.

Mrs. Marshall Byrd, Jr., Madison Cross Roads

CREAM CHEESE COOKIES

½ cup butter or margarine
8 ozs. cream cheese, softened
1 cup sugar
2 cups sifted flour
½ cup finely chopped pecans

Beat butter or margarine, cream cheese, and sugar together. Add flour and pecans. Drop by teaspoonfuls onto cookie sheet and mash thin with fingers dipped in water. Cook at 350 degrees for 10 minutes or until slightly brown on edges.

Anne Weaver, Fleming Hills

DATE BALLS

1 cup chopped dates
1 cup sugar
1 stick oleo
3 cups Rice Krispies
1 can coconut
1 cup chopped nuts

Cook dates, sugar, and oleo until mixture bubbles well. Pour over Rice Krispies. Mix and let cool. Roll into small balls. Roll balls in coconut or powdered sugar. Yield: 6 dozen.

Ila Wilkinson, Central

FORGOTTEN COOKIES

2 egg whites
½ cup sugar
1 cup nuts
1 cup chocolate bits

Preheat oven to 350 degrees. Beat egg whites; gradually add sugar. Fold in nuts and chocolate bits. Drop by ½ teaspoonfuls on wax paper or cookie sheet. Turn oven off and leave cookies in the oven overnight. Forget about them till morning.

Mary Ward, Fleming Hills

FRUIT CAKE COOKIES

4 cups flour
1 tsp. soda
1 tsp. salt
1 cup shortening
2 cups firmly packed brown sugar

2 eggs
⅔ cup buttermilk
1 cup chopped pecans
1 cup quartered candied cherries
2 cups cut-up dates
1 cup any other candied fruits

Sift flour; measure; sift again with soda and salt. Cream shortening; add sugar and eggs. Beat until light and fluffy. Add milk and flour. Add nuts, cherries, and other fruits. Chill dough for several hours. Drop by teaspoon about 2 inches apart, on lightly greased cookie sheet. Top each cookie with ½ red and green cherries or pecans halves. Bake 8 to 10 minutes at 375 degrees. Yield: 8 dozen.

Mrs. Hugh Tipton (Bessie Mae), Monrovia

FRUIT COOKIES

1 cup brown sugar
1 stick oleo
2 eggs
1½ tsp. soda dissolved in 1½ T. milk
⅓ cup whiskey or brandy

1½ cups flour, sifted
½ tsp. cinnamon, cloves, nutmeg (each)
½ lb. candied cherries
½ lb. candied pineapple
3 cups pecans
1 box white raisins

Mix thoroughly. Cook at 300 degress for 20 minutes. Drop on cookie sheet. Store in airtight container.

Lucille Mitchell, Madison Cross Roads

It was a wise man who said, "The picture of health requires a happy frame of mind."

GRANOLA COOKIES

½ cup salad oil
⅓ cup molasses
¼ cup water
2 eggs
1 cup honey
1 T. dried milk
1 cup raisins
½ cup oatmeal

1 cup unbleached flour
¼ cup buckwheat flour
¾ cup triticale flour
1 tsp. salt
1 tsp. soda
1 tsp. cinnamon
2 cups granola
¼ cup chopped nuts

Heat oven to 375 degrees. Mix oil, molasses, water, eggs, and honey thoroughly. Stir in remaining ingredients. Drop dough by rounded teaspoonfuls 2 inches apart on lightly greased baking sheet. Bake 8 to 10 minutes.

Janice Coombe, Hurricane

ICEBOX COOKIES

½ tsp. salt
1 tsp. soda
3½ cups flour

1 cup oleo or butter
2 eggs
2 cups sifted, packed brown sugar
1 cup chopped nuts

Sift salt and soda with flour. Mix the butter while firm with flour until mixture looks like fine crumbs. Beat eggs together, add brown sugar, and mix very well. Mix flour mixture with egg mixture; add nuts. Divide this dough on piece of wax paper and roll into a roll. Place these rolls of cookie dough on cookie sheet and refrigerate. Remember the dough is wrapped in the wax paper, closing the ends of paper to make airtight. After refrigerating or placing in freezer overnight, take out 1 roll at a time, slice thin, and bake at 350 degrees or 375 degrees.

Sue Price, Westbury

LIZZIES

¼ cup margarine
½ cup light brown sugar
2 eggs
1½ cups sifted flour
1½ tsp. soda
1½ tsp. cinnamon

1½ tsp. nutmeg
½ tsp. cloves
1 lb. raisins
½ cup bourbon
1 lb. pecans
½ lb. citron, diced
1 lb. candied cherries

Cream margarine; gradually beat in sugar. Add eggs, 1 at a time; beat well after each addition; sift flour with soda and spices. Add to batter mixture. SOAK raisins in bourbon at least 1 hour to plump, then add to batter mixture along with nuts and fruit. Drop from teaspoon on buttered cookie sheet and bake at 325 degrees for about 15 minutes. Store in airtight containers. Can be frozen. Yield: 120. These are especially good with eggnog.

Winnie Linney, South Huntsville

BOILED OATMEAL COOKIES

1½ sticks butter	Pinch of salt
2 cups sugar	3 cups uncooked Quick Quaker
½ cup cocoa	Oats
½ cup sweet milk	½ cup chopped pecans (optional)

Melt butter on low heat. Add sugar, cocoa, sweet milk, and salt. Put on high heat and while stirring bring to full rolling boil for 1 minute. Remove from heat and add oats and pecans if desired. For caramel cookies omit cocoa and use 1 cup dark brown sugar, 1 cup white sugar, and 1 teaspoon vanilla. Drop by teaspoonfuls on wax paper.

Jeanie Marsh, Harvest

BOYFRIEND COOKIES

1 cup butter or margarine	1½ cups flour
1⅓ cups sugar	1 tsp. baking soda
1⅓ cups packed brown sugar	3 cups quick-cooking oats
2 eggs	1 6-oz. pkg. semi-sweet chocolate
1 tsp. vanilla	bits
1½ cups chopped peanuts	

Allow butter or margarine to come to room temperature. In a large mixing bowl cream butter and sugar. Add eggs and vanilla. Beat until fluffy. Sift flour and soda into a large bowl, add oats, and toss to coat oats with flour. Add to first mixture 1 cup at a time until completely mixed. Stir in peanuts and chocolate bits. (Batter will be stiff.) Drop from a teaspoon onto a cookie sheet. Bake in a preheated 375-degree oven for 10 to 12 minutes. Yield: 6 dozen. (I have substituted M & Ms for chocolate and pecans for peanuts.)

Mrs. Erle Douglass (Evelyn), Monrovia

CINNAMON CRISPIES

3 cups plus 3 T. plain flour
½ tsp. soda
⅔ T. baking powder
½ tsp. salt
⅔ T. cinnamon
2½ cups dry oats

1 cup nuts (optional)
1¼ cups Crisco
2½ cups sugar
2⅓ T. molasses
½ T. vanilla
2 lg. eggs

Blend first 6 ingredients in mixer. Then add nuts. Cream shortening and sugar until well blended; add molasses, vanilla, and eggs to creamed mixture. Beat until blended. Add to dry ingredients; mix. Drop on greased cookie sheet with teaspoon. Press with fork. Cook for 15 minutes at 350 degrees.

Mrs. Erle Douglass (Evelyn), Monrovia

OATMEAL CRISPS

¾ cup sifted flour
½ tsp. salt
½ tsp. soda
½ cup shortening
½ cup brown sugar

½ cup granulated sugar
1 egg
1 tsp. vanilla
1½ cup quick oats
¼ cup chopped nuts

Sift first 3 ingredients together; cream shortening. Add sugars; blend thoroughly. Add egg and vanilla; beat well, add dry ingredients, oats, and nuts. Mix well. Form into rolls 3 inches in diameter. Wrap in wax paper. Chill several hours or overnight (may be frozen). Cut into ⅛-inch slices and place on lightly greased cookie sheets. Bake at 375 degrees for 10 to 12 minutes. Yield: 3½ dozen cookies.

Ruth W. Chambers, Darwin Downs

CHEWY PEANUT BUTTER BARS

⅓ cup shortening
½ cup peanut butter, smooth
¼ cup light brown sugar
1 cup granulated sugar
1 tsp. vanilla

2 eggs
1 cup sifted plain flour
1 tsp. baking powder
¼ tsp. salt
1⅓ cups coconut

Cream together the shortening, peanut butter, and sugars until light and fluffy. Add vanilla and eggs. Beat well. Mix in flour, baking powder, and salt. Stir only until blended. Stir in coconut. Spread evenly into a 13x9x2-inch greased pan. Bake at 350 degrees for 25 minutes or until golden brown. Cut into bars.

Vivian Lee, University

CHOCOLATE-COVERED PEANUT BUTTER BALLS

1¼ cups butter
⅞ cup peanut butter
⅛ cup oatmeal
1¼ lbs. powdered sugar

½ box raisins
½ cup coconut
½ cup crushed nuts
1 tsp. vanilla

Melt butter, add ingredients, and mix well. Shape into small balls. Put each on a toothpick before freezing. Freeze. Then dip in chocolate glaze; put on wax paper. Remove toothpicks and fill holes with remaining chocolate.

Glaze

3 6-oz. pkgs. butterscotch or chocolate chips
¾ stick of paraffin

Melt chips and paraffin together in double boiler. Keep hot while coating peanut balls. Hold balls on a toothpick or skewer and dip into coating. Place on wax paper or aluminum foil while coating hardens.

Burlene Childers, New Sharon

EASY PEANUT BUTTER COOKIES

1 cup peanut butter
1 cup sugar

1 egg
1 tsp. vanilla

Preheat oven to 300 degrees. Mix peanut butter and sugar. Add egg and vanilla and mix thoroughly. Roll into balls the size of walnuts. Place on lightly greased cookie sheets. Flatten with fork dipped in flour, crisscross. Bake for 13 minutes.

Polly Hay, New Sharon

PEANUT BUTTER COOKIES

1 cup shortening
1 cup sugar
1 cup brown sugar
2 eggs, beaten
1 cup peanut butter
1 tsp. soda
½ tsp. salt
3 cups flour

Combine all ingredients. Shape into walnut-sized balls. Flatten with tines of fork (crisscrossed). Bake at 325 degrees for approximately 10 minutes.
Betty Cothran, Athens Pike

RICH PEANUT BUTTER BARS

½ cup peanut butter
½ cup margarine
1½ cups sugar
2 eggs
1 tsp. vanilla
1 cup self-rising flour

Heat oven to 350 degrees. Grease and flour 9x13x2-inch pan. Melt peanut butter and margarine in bowl over hot water. Add remaining ingredients. Stir until blended. Bake for 25 to 30 minutes. Cool and cut into squares. Yield: 2 dozen squares.
Glenda Patterson, Owens Cross Roads

PEANUT BLOSSOMS

1 cup shortening
1 cup peanut butter
1 cup sugar
1 cup brown sugar
2 eggs
¼ cup milk
2 tsp. vanilla
3½ cups flour
1 tsp. soda
1 tsp. salt
2 4½-oz. pkgs. milk chocolate stars

Cream shortening, peanut butter, and sugars. Blend in eggs, milk, and vanilla. Mix in flour, soda, and salt. Shape dôugh in balls, roll in sugar, and place on ungreased cookie sheet. Bake at 375 degrees for 10 to 12 minutes. Top each with a candy star immediately and press down firmly. Yield: 6 dozen.
Patty Shepard, South Parkway

SALTED PEANUT COOKIES

1 cup shortening
1 cup white sugar
1 cup brown sugar
2 eggs, beaten
1½ cups flour

1 tsp. soda
1 tsp. baking powder
1 cup salted peanuts
3 cups oatmeal
1 tsp. vanilla

Mix in order given. Drop from spoon onto greased cookie sheet and bake at 350 degrees for 8 to 10 minutes.

Linda Nord, Hazel Green

PECAN BUTTERBALLS

2 cups finely chopped pecans
2 cups flour
2 tsp. vanilla

1 cup butter or margarine, softened
½ cup granulated sugar
¼ tsp. salt
Powdered sugar

Combine blender-chopped pecans with remainder of ingredients, except powdered sugar. Mix well. Roll into 1-inch balls. Bake on ungreased cookie sheet for 20 minutes in preheated 325-degree oven. Let cool slightly and roll in powdered sugar a few at a time. If you like pecans, you will like this one.

Linda Warren, South Huntsville

PECAN CRUNCH

3 egg whites
1 cup sugar
½ tsp. vanilla

1 cup graham cracker crumbs
1 cup chopped pecans
Cool Whip or whipped cream

Beat eggs until stiff. Fold in sugar and vanilla and beat until very stiff. Mix crumbs and pecans together. Fold into egg whites. Pour into buttered Pyrex pie plate. Bake at 350 degrees for 30 minutes. Cool thoroughly and cover with whipped cream. (Cool Whip may be used.) Keep in refrigerator 4½ hours. Cut in wedges to serve.

Anna Bernice Broad, Big Cove

PECAN PIE SURPRISE BARS

1 pkg. yellow cake mix
1 egg
½ cup butter or margarine, softened
1 cup chopped pecans

Grease bottom and sides of 13x9-inch baking pan. Reserve ⅔ cup dry cake mix for filling. In large mixing bowl, combine remaining dry cake mix, egg, and butter. Reserve pecans for topping. Mix until crumbly; press in prepared pan. Bake at 350 degrees for 15 to 20 minutes until light golden brown. Meanwhile prepare filling. Pour filling over partially baked crust; sprinkle with pecans. Return to oven and bake for 30 to 35 minutes until filling is set. Cool; cut into 36 bars.

Filling

⅔ cup reserved cake mix
1½ cups dark corn syrup
3 eggs
½ cup firmly packed brown sugar
1 tsp. vanilla

In large mixer bowl, combine all ingredients and beat at medium speed for 1 to 2 minutes.

Bonnie Riley, South Huntsville-Saddleback Valley

POTATO CHIP COOKIES

1 lb. margarine
1 cup sugar
3½ cups flour
1 cup crushed potato chips
2 tsp. vanilla

Combine margarine and sugar; cream together. Add flour; add potato chips; add vanilla. Drop from teaspoon on greased cookie sheet. Bake at 350 degrees for 15 minutes. Yield: 76 cookies.

Nancy Teasdale, South Huntsville

RICE KRISPIES COOKIES

1½ sticks margarine
1 8-oz. pkg. dates
1 cup sugar
1 cup chopped pecans
2½ cups Rice Krispies
¾ cup coconut

Boil first 4 ingredients until thick. Remove from heat and pour over Rice Krispies and coconut. When cool enough to touch, shape into balls with buttered hands. Roll in powdered sugar.

Jeanette Schlernitzauer, Athens Pike

SKILLET COOKIES

1 stick margarine
1 cup chopped dates
1 egg, well beaten
1 cup sugar

1 cup nuts
2 cups Rice Krispies
1 T. vanilla
Flaked coconut

Cook margarine, dates, egg, and sugar for 5 minutes. Remove and add nuts, Rice Krispies, and vanilla. Mix and drop by teaspoon. Roll in coconut.

Margaret Hay, New Sharon

SNICKERDOODLES

1 cup soft shortening
1½ cups sugar
2 eggs
2¾ cups flour

2 tsp. cream of tartar
½ tsp. salt
1 tsp. soda
2 T. sugar
2 tsp. cinnamon

Cream shortening and 1½ cups sugar together. Add eggs and beat well. Sift flour, cream of tartar, salt, and soda together and add to shortening, sugar, and eggs. Roll into balls, walnut size, and roll in sugar and cinnamon. Space about 2 inches apart on ungreased cookie sheet. Bake at 400 degrees for 8 to 10 minutes (until lightly browned, but still soft).

Eloise Pittman, Blossomwood
Ginny McKinney, Owens Cross Roads

CLARA COOKIES FROM TEXAS

1 box brown sugar
2 eggs
1 cup nuts

1 lb. butter
6 cups flour
1 tsp. vanilla

Mix; place in refrigerator until partly set; roll into rolls about 1 inch in diameter. Wrap in wax paper, set in freezer, and let freeze. Frozen dough will keep for as long as a month. Remove a few rolls at a time, cutting while still frozen. Slice thin and bake for about 10 minutes at 350 degrees. Yield: 12 or 13 rolls.

Clara Wells, Central

SPRY SUGAR COOKIES

½ cup shortening
½ tsp. grated lemon rind
1 cup sugar
1 tsp. baking powder
½ tsp. salt
½ tsp. nutmeg
2 cups sifted flour
½ tsp. soda
2 T. milk

Beat first 6 ingredients thoroughly. Sift together flour and soda. Add with milk to creamed mixture and mix well. Measure out level tablespoons of dough on greased baking sheets. Flatten cookies by stamping with a flat-bottomed glass covered with a damp cloth. Bake at 375 degrees for 10 to 12 minutes. Yield: 3½ dozen.

Ruth W. Chambers, Darwin Downs

SUGAR COOKIES

1 cup butter or margarine
1 cup sugar
¼ cup Egg Beaters or 1 egg
1 tsp. almond extract
½ tsp. vanilla extract
2⅓ cups flour
2 tsp. baking powder
Sugar

Cream together butter and sugar. Add Egg Beaters or egg and extracts. Combine flour and baking powder. Add to butter-egg mixture. Bake at 350 degrees for about 15 minutes. Sprinkle hot cookies with sugar.

Opaline West, Madison Cross Roads

TEA CAKES

THE BEST TEA CAKES

1 cup sugar
⅔ cup Crisco
½ tsp. soda in ½ cup buttermilk
3 egg yolks
1 tsp. baking powder
1 tsp. vanilla
Pinch of salt
2 cups flour

Sift together sugar, flour, baking powder & salt. Blend Crisco into flour mixture. Dissolve soda in buttermilk and mix with flour dough. Gradually stir in egg yolks and vanilla. Drop spoonful onto cookie sheet. Bake 375° until lightly browned.

Betty Butcher, Athens Pike

MOTHER'S TEA CAKES I

2 cups sugar
1 cup butter
2 eggs
3 cups flour
2 tsp. vanilla

Cream sugar and butter; add eggs and mix well; stir in flour and vanilla. Put in refrigerator at least 1 hour or overnight before cutting out. Roll out on floured wax paper and cut with large cookie cutter. Place on greased cookie sheet. Cook for about 10 minutes at 350 degrees.

Dot Atwell, Athens Pike

MOTHER'S TEA CAKES II

½ cup butter
½ cup shortening
1 cup sugar
1 tsp. vanilla
1 egg
2½ cups sifted flour
½ tsp. soda
¾ tsp. salt
2 T. buttermilk

Have all ingredients at room temperature. Cream together butter, shortening, sugar, and flavoring. Add egg and cream until fluffy. Sift together dry ingredients; stir into mixture until smooth; blend in buttermilk. Drop by teaspoonfuls onto ungreased cookie sheet; flatten with bottom of glass dipped in sugar. Bake at 400 degrees for about 12 minutes. Cool. Yield: 5½ dozen cookies. My mother's recipe, more than 100 years old.

Mrs. Grinell Vaughn (Kathleen), Monrovia

OLD-FASHIONED TEA CAKES

6 cups flour
2 cups sugar
¼ cup buttermilk
2 T. vanilla
Pinch of soda
½ cup margarine, melted
½ cup shortening
2 eggs

Mix together all ingredients except flour and pour in well of flour. Beat until very stiff. Roll out and cut with biscuit cutter. Bake at 350 degrees for about 15 minutes on greased cookie sheet.

Gracie McCurdy, Madison Cross Roads

RUSSIAN TEA COOKIES

2 cups margarine
1 cup powdered sugar
4½ cups flour
½ tsp. salt
2 T. vanilla
1½ cups nuts, chopped

Cream margarine and sugar. Add flour, then other ingredients. Shape into small balls. Bake 10 to 15 minutes at 400 degrees. Roll in powdered sugar while hot. Yield: 8 dozen.

Linda Nord, Hazel Green

BUTTERMILK TEA CAKES

2½ cups sugar
2 eggs (beaten)
2 cups flour
1 tsp. baking powder
¾ cup shortening
¾ cup buttermilk
1 tsp. soda
1 tsp. vanilla

Cream shortening and sugar. Stir in beaten eggs, vanilla and buttermilk. Sift dry ingredients together, then stir these dry ingredients into shortening mixture: add enough flour to make dough stiff enough to roll out on a floured board or surface. Cut with large cookie cutter. Bake on slightly greased cookie sheet: bake at 375° for about 10 minutes.

Maude Lynch, Monrovia

CHOCOLATE FUDGE BOILED COOKIES

2 cups sugar
4 tsp. cocoa
½ cup peanut butter
½ cup milk
1 stick margarine
2½ cups oats
1 tsp. vanilla

Put sugar, butter, cocoa, and milk in large pan and cook on medium 3 minutes after full boil. Remove from heat. Add remaining ingredients. Drop by teaspoon onto wax paper. Let cool about 1½ hours.

Pam Lyle, Owens Cross Roads

SHINGLES OR BARK CANDY

2 sticks butter (or margarine)
½ cup sugar   Boil 2 minutes stirring

Line 15x10x1 pan with foil, and then with saltines or graham crackers. Pour butter and sugar mixture over crackers. Bake 9-10 minutes at 350°. Take out and pour onto this a 12 oz. package of sweet chocolate chips. Let this sit for a few minutes, then smooth chocolate to edges of pan. Freeze 15 minutes. Break apart. Makes 3-4 dozen.

Variation: Use butterscotch or peanut butter chips instead of chocolate.

Jeanne Peters, South Parkway

AUNT ANNIE'S ELEPHANT DROPS

1 box (1 pound) powdered sugar
1 stick melted butter or margarine (may need to add ½ stick more)
1 cup coconut
1-½ cup Graham crackers, crushed
1 cup chopped nuts
1 small jar crunchy peanut butter
6 oz. semi-sweet chocolate chips
1 block of paraffin

Mix first six ingredients form into small balls. Melt semi-sweet chocolate chips and block of paraffin in top of double boiler. Dip balls into mixture with a toothpick and allow to set on waxed paper until set.

Janice Mazikowski, University

PRIZE WINNING COOKIES

1 cup sugar
1 cup brown sugar
1 cup butter
2 eggs
1 cup raisins (barely cover with water and boil until almost dry, drain and cool)
2 cups oatmeal (quick-cooking or regular)
2½ cups flour
1 tsp. soda
½ tsp. cinnamon and dash of nutmeg

Cream butter and sugars, add eggs, raisins and flour mixed with soda and spices. Mix well. Add oatmeal and mix. Roll into balls (golf-ball size) and then roll balls in sugar. Place on greased cookie sheet and flatten with bottom of glass. Bake at 375° for 10-12 minutes until cookies turn slightly golden. (Do not overbake). Store in tightly covered container. This is a very moist and chewy cookie.

Doris Sells, South Parkway

COOKING LITE

CHERRY TORTONIS

⅔ cup crushed granola (any flavor)
20 lg. maraschino cherries, finely chopped (about ⅓ cup)
1 tsp. almond extract
Dash of salt
1 9 oz. carton frozen whipped topping, thawed
3 maraschino cherries, quartered

Fold ½ cup of the granola, the chopped cherries, extract, and salt into whipped topping. Divide among 12 small baking cups. Freeze uncovered until firm, about 2 hours. Sprinkle tortonis with remaining granola; garnish with cherries. Serves 12 at less than 100 calories per serving.

Dorothy Mellette, Central

CHICKEN SALAD

2 T. minced onion
1 cup diced lettuce
2 T. chopped green pepper
1 cup diced cooked chicken, unsalted
Low-calorie mayonnaise
1 hard-cooked egg (optional)

Add onion, lettuce, and green pepper to unsalted chicken. Add low-calorie mayonnaise and mix well. Add egg, if desired.

Louise McGehee, Hurricane

CHICKEN/YOGURT BAKE

2-2½ lb. chicken
1 cup plain yogurt
½ cup chopped green onions
1 pkg. onion bouillon

Cut chicken into serving pieces. Mix yogurt, green onions, and onion bouillon and pour over the chicken in a casserole. Put in refrigerator overnight. Cover and bake at 325 degrees for approximately 45 minutes or until chicken is done.

Marjorie Jones, Athens Pike

DEVILED HAM DIP

1 cup diet cottage cheese
1 2¼-oz. can deviled ham
1 tsp. prepared horseradish

Blend cottage cheese, deviled ham, and prepared horseradish. Yield: 1¼ cups, 18 calories per tablespoon.

Evelyn Hall, Athens Pike

DIABETIC DATE-NUT CAKE

½ cup butter	2 tsp. soda
1 egg	½ tsp. cinnamon
1 T. Sucaryl	¼ tsp. cloves
1 tsp. vanilla	1 cup dates
2 cups flour	1 cup pecans, coarsely chopped

1½ cups *diabetic* applesauce (2 sm. cans)

Cream butter. Add egg, Sucaryl, and vanilla which have been beaten together. Sift dry ingredients together and add to other mixture. Mix in dates, nuts, and applesauce—beat (everything) with an electric mixer at medium to high speed for several minutes until well blended. Turn into a buttered loaf pan. Bake in moderate oven (350 degrees) for 1 hour or until wooden pick comes out clean. Serves 8. I count 1 serving as 1 bread, 1 fruit, and 1 fat exchange.

Judy Walthall, Fleming Hills

DIET SALAD

1 can unsweetened pineapple, undrained	1 lg. pkg. Jello, any flavor
	2 cups buttermilk

Heat 1 can pineapple, pour over Jello, and stir until Jello is dissolved. Cool, and add buttermilk. Chill until firm. (If not on a diet use large Dream Whip instead of buttermilk and use sweetened pineapple.)

Jean McComb, Central

FIVE-CUP SALAD

1 6-oz. can mandarin oranges	1 cup shredded coconut
1 can crushed pineapple (no sugar added)	1 cup sour cream
	1 cup pecan pieces

Combine ingredients and chill. This is good for diabetic diets. The only sugar is in the coconut.

Jimmie Covington, Central

FRESH VEGETABLE OMELET
(For weight watchers)

2 cups diced carrots
1 cup sliced onions
2 cups sliced fresh mushrooms
¾ tsp. salt

⅛ tsp. ginger
8 eggs, beaten (4 to a bowl)
4 T. skimmed milk
Dash of pepper

Cook carrots in small amount of water for 2 minutes. Add onions and cook 3 minutes longer. Add mushrooms, salt, and ginger. Mix well, cover, and cook over low heat for 5 minutes or until vegetables are tender and dry. Combine 4 eggs, 2 tablespoons milk, and pepper and cook over low heat. When eggs are almost dry, add ½ of vegetables on ½ the omelet and fold over. Remove to warm platter and repeat remaining ingredients for second omelet. Spray skillet with Pam.

Mary Sanders, Central

FRUIT BREAD FOR DIABETICS

1 cup raisins
1 cup pecans, chopped
1 cup apple, chopped
1 cup unsweetened pineapple, drained, chopped
1 T. grated orange rind
1 T. grated lemon rind
1½ tsp. liquid sugar substitute
½ cup orange juice, unsweetened

2 T. margarine, melted
1½ cups all-purpose flour, sifted
½ tsp. salt
1 tsp. baking soda
½ tsp. allspice
½ tsp. cinnamon
½ tsp. nutmeg
1 T. vanilla extract
2 T. rum extract

Combine raisins, pecans, apple, pineapple, orange rind, lemon rind, sugar substitute, and orange juice. Add melted margarine. Sift and measure flour. Add salt, soda, allspice, cinnamon, and nutmeg to flour and sift again. Add dry ingredients to fruit mixture with extracts and stir until thoroughly mixed. Pour into lightly greased loaf pan. Bake in preheated oven at 350 degrees for about 1 hour. The recipe may be doubled and baked in a tube pan. Keep refrigerated or may be frozen. Yield: 20 slices; 1 slice = 1 bread and 1 fat exchange.

Stella Miller, Fleming Hills

GOLDEN CAKE—FOR DIABETICS

1 cup sifted flour	½ cup frozen orange juice
1½ tsp. baking powder	concentrate, undiluted
½ tsp. salt	1 T. Sucaryl solution
¼ cup cooking oil	4 egg whites
4 egg yolks	¼ tsp. cream of tartar

Mix and sift first 3 ingredients thoroughly several times. Make a well in mixture and add in order the oil, egg yolks, orange juice concentrate, and Sucaryl solution. Beat until smooth. Place egg whites in large bowl, add cream of tartar, and beat until stiff. Pour egg yolk mixture gradually over egg whites and fold in gently. Pour into greased and floured tube pan and bake at 325 degrees for 35 minutes.

LADYFINGERS

⅓ cup sugar	3 T. water
3 eggs, separated	½ tsp. vanilla
¾ cup all-purpose flour	¼ tsp. lemon extract
¼ tsp. baking powder	¼ tsp. cream of tartar
⅛ tsp. salt	¼ cup sugar

Heat oven to 350 degrees. Grease and flour 2 baking sheets. Beat ⅓ cup sugar and egg yolks in small mixer bowl on medium speed until very thick and lemon colored, about 3 minutes. Beat in flour, baking powder, and salt alternately with water, vanilla, and lemon extract on low speed. Beat egg whites and cream of tartar in large mixer bowl until foamy. Beat in ¼ cup sugar gradually; continue beating until stiff and glossy. Fold egg yolk mixture into egg whites. Shape with teaspoon or pastry bag into fingers 3x1-inch, on baking sheets. Bake for 10 to 12 minutes. Low-calorie.

Dorothy Mellette, Central

The blossom cannot tell what becomes of its odor, and no man can tell what becomes of his influence and example that roll away from him and go beyond his view.

LEAN AND LIGHT PANCAKES

1 egg
1½ cups instant nonfat dry milk
2 T. oleo
1½ cups unsifted flour
2 T. sugar
1½ tsp. baking powder
1 tsp. salt
½ tsp. baking soda

Mix together egg, milk, and melted oleo. Combine flour, sugar, baking powder, salt, and baking soda. Add liquid mixture to dry ingredients and beat with a rotary beater until all dry ingredients are moistened. (Batter may be lumpy.) Pour into a hot lightly oiled griddle, using about ¼ cup batter for each pancake; cook until pancakes are puffy and bubbly; turn and cook until nicely brown on underside. Yield: 12.

Marie Barcus, Central

LEMON-NUTMEG CARROTS

12 med. carrots
2 tsp. grated lemon peel
½ tsp. nutmeg
⅛ tsp. salt
¼ tsp. sweetener
½ cup water

Peel carrots; cut in half lengthwise. Place in saucepan with remaining ingredients. Cook covered for 20 to 30 minutes or until tender. Serves 6 at 25 calories per ½ cup.

Evelyn Hall, Athens Pike

LO-CAL BAKED CHICKEN

1 frying chicken
Salt
Black pepper
Thyme
½ celery stalk

Cut chicken into pieces. Salt lightly and place in 8 or 10-inch casserole or 10-inch baking dish. Sprinkle with black pepper, thyme, and any spice you wish. Break celery in pieces and stick here and there. Cover dish and bake for 1½ hours at 350 degrees.

Alma DeShazo, South Parkway

LOW-CALORIE COTTAGE CHEESE DIP

1 sm. carton diet cottage cheese
¼ tsp. curry powder
1 tsp. yellow salad mustard
Crisp vegetables

Blend cottage cheese, curry powder, and yellow salad mustard well. Serve with raw cauliflower, fresh mushrooms, or any crisp vegetable. Ten calories per tablespoon.

Evelyn Hall, Athens Pike

LOW-CALORIE ONION SOUP DIP

1 cup yogurt
1 cup diet cottage cheese
3 T. dry onion soup mix
¼ tsp. chili powder

In medium bowl mix yogurt and cottage cheese until blended. Stir in soup mix and chili powder. Refrigerate the dip covered for 3 hours to let flavor develop. Arrange on tray with an assortment of vegetables or shrimp. Yield: 2 cups; 13 calories per tablespoon.

Evelyn Hall, Athens Pike

LOW-CALORIE WALDORF SALAD

5 drops sweetener
¼ cup diet mayonnaise (or salad dressing)
2 cups diced apple
1 cup chopped celery
½ cup chopped walnuts
½ cup grated coconut (optional)

Add sweetener to salad dressing. Toss with apple, celery, walnuts, and coconut. Serves 8.

Cathy Gilbert, Davis Hills

LOW-FAT ORANGE SALAD

1 lg. Cool Whip
1 12-oz. carton cottage cheese
1 sm. pkg. orange Jello
1 can mandarin oranges, well-drained
1 sm. can crushed pineapple, well-drained

Mix Cool Whip and cottage cheese. Add dry Jello, oranges, and pineapple. Mix well. Chill for 24 hours. Serve on greens.

Cynthia Rich, Heritage

LOW-SODIUM MAYONNAISE

2 egg yolks
2 cups salad oil
4 T. vinegar or lemon juice

Beat egg yolks. Add 2 tablespoons lemon juice or vinegar and mix well. Add salad oil, 1 teaspoon at a time, beating with rotating beater, until ¼ cup has been used. Add remaining salad oil in increasing amounts, alternating last ½ cup with the juice or vinegar. Yield: 2½ cups.

Louise McGehee, Hurricane

OATMEAL DROPS

1½ cups quick-cooking oats
½ cup sugar
3 T. butter or oleo, softened
1 tsp. vanilla
½ tsp. baking powder
½ tsp. ground cinnamon
¼ tsp. salt
1 egg

Heat oven to 350 degrees. Mix all ingredients. Drop dough by teaspoonfuls 2 inches apart onto greased baking sheet. Bake until tops are dry and edges are light brown, 8 to 10 minutes. Cool slightly; remove from baking sheet. When baking a second batch, be sure baking sheet is cool to keep dough from spreading. Yield: 3 dozen cookies; less than 50 calories each.

Dorothy Mellette, Central

OLD-FASHIONED GINGER SQUARES

2¼ cups unsifted self-rising flour
½ tsp. ground ginger
½ tsp. ground cinnamon
⅓ cup oleo (lo-cal)
⅔ cup firmly packed brown sugar
½ cup sorghum molasses
¾ cup water
½ cup dark seedless raisins

Sift flour, ginger, and cinnamon together and set aside. Cream oleo and brown sugar together until fluffy. Add molasses and beat well. Add dry ingredients alternating with water. Beat until blended. Fold in raisins. Spread mixture into greased 15½x10½x1-inch jelly roll pan. Bake at 375 degrees for 15 to 20 minutes. Glaze and cool in pan. 2x2-inch square is 110 calories.

Glaze

1 cup powdered sugar
2 T. water

Do not over bake!

Evelyn Hall, Athens Pike

ORANGE COTTAGE CHEESE SALAD

1 lg. container cottage cheese
1 lg. can crushed pineapple in juice, drained
1 lg. can mandarin oranges, drained, cut up
1 9-oz. container whipped topping
1 3-oz. box diet orange gelatin

Mix all ingredients together including the dry gelatin. Chill well before serving.

Linda Dehaye, Vestavia

PEANUT BUTTER FUDGE

1 18-oz. jar natural peanut butter
2 cups nonfat dry milk
2 heaping T. frozen apple juice concentrate, unsweetened
½ cup walnuts or pecans chopped (optional)

Combine peanut butter and dry milk in bowl, mashing well. Add apple juice concentrate—continue mashing together until well mixed. Add nuts, if desired. Using a tablespoon or wooden spoon, press into a flat pan until mixture gives appearance of fudge. Store covered in refrigerator. Cut into squares to serve.

Sheryl Daniels, Heritage

COOKIES FOR A DIABETIC

1 cup pitted dates
1 cup seedless raisins
1 cup flour
1 tsp. soda
1 tsp. baking powder
½ tsp. cinnamon
½ tsp. nutmeg
⅛ tsp. salt
2 eggs
¼ cup melted butter or oleo
⅓ cup evap. milk
2 tsp. vanilla
2 tsp. Sucaryl

Cut up dates. Soften dates and raisins by soaking in warm water for ½ hour. Drain. (Or grind without soaking.) Mix all ingredients. Drop by teaspoonfuls on greased cookie sheet. Bake in 450-degree oven for 7 minutes. *One* cookie is *66 calories*. May add cut-up pecans or walnuts or shredded coconut. Makes 32. I count 3 cookies as 1 bread exchange, 1 fruit exchange, and 1 fat exchange.

Judy Walthall, Fleming Hills

PUDDING COOKIES

1 egg
1 tsp. Sweet & Low sweetener
1 tsp. vanilla

1 cup self-rising flour
¼ cup shortening
1 pkg. dessert pudding

Beat egg, sweetener, and vanilla until light and fluffy and add flour, shortening, and pudding mix. Mix well. Place dough on wax paper in a 2-inch roll. Set to chill. Cut in ⅛-inch slices. Bake on ungreased cookie sheet at 350 to 375 degrees for 8 to 10 minutes or until cookies begin to brown about the edges. Yield: 2 dozen.

Josie Davis, New Sharon

RED APPLE SALAD

1 can Red Apple Shasta
1 8¾-oz. can crushed pineapple

1 env. plain gelatin
1 apple, chopped

Plain yogurt

Use enough pineapple juice and Shasta to equal 2 cups. Bring to boil. Add plain gelatin and dissolve over low heat. Refrigerate until partially set. Add pineapple and 1 chopped apple. Use as dessert with plain yogurt as topping. Serves 6.

Evelyn Hall, Athens Pike

SAUERKRAUT SALAD

½ cup green pepper or 3 tsp. dehydrated pepper
½ cup salad onions or 3 tsp. dehydrated salad onions

Sweetener to equal 1 cup sugar
¼ cup vinegar
¼ tsp. salt
2 tsp. cooking oil

1 can kraut, drained

Mix all ingredients except sauerkraut and let stand for about 5 minutes. Add drained kraut and toss well with other ingredients; chill. Will keep in refrigerator for about a week.

Dot Atwell, Athens Pike

SKILLET CABBAGE
(Low Calorie)

1 T. salad oil	1 sm. green pepper, chopped
3 cups finely shredded cabbage	1 sm. onion, chopped
1 cup chopped celery	½ tsp. salt
	Dash of pepper

In 10-inch skillet over medium-low heat in hot oil, stir all ingredients until well mixed. Cover pan and cook for 5 minutes, stirring occasionally. Serve immediately. Vegetables will be crisp. Takes approximately 20 minutes to prepare. Makes 4 servings of 50 calories per serving.

Sarah M. Irvin, Monrovia

STRAWBERRY PIE

3 T. cornstarch	1 20-oz. pkg. strawberries,
1 Shasta strawberry diet drink	unsweetened
8 ½-grain saccharin tablets or	1 pie shell, baked
16 ¼-grain tablets	D-Zerta topping

Mix cornstarch in a little Shasta. Heat Shasta in saucepan until thick. Add saccharin and strawberries. Pour into 9-inch baked pie shell. Let cool. Top with D-Zerta topping. Refrigerate.

Mrs. Ernest F. Dilday, Jr., Davis Hills

SUGARLESS POUND CAKE—FOR DIABETICS

21 ½-grain saccharin tablets	2 tsp. baking powder
1 T. milk	6 eggs
3 cups plain flour	1½ cups skim milk
½ tsp. salt	½ cup Crisco oil
	1 T. lemon flavoring

Dissolve saccharin tablets in 1 tablespoon milk. Combine dry ingredients and mix with eggs, milk, oil, sweetener, and flavoring. Beat with electric mixer about 10 minutes. Pour into a greased and floured tube pan and bake at 350 degrees for 1 hour. This cake freezes well. (If desired, may be frozen in individual slices for diabetics.)

Debbie Maples, Owens Cross Roads
Florence Moore, Monrovia

SUNSHINE SALAD

1 pkg. plain gelatin
1 med. can crushed pineapple
1 can orange diet drink (Shasta)

Soften gelatin in ¼ cup diet drink. Heat balance of drink to boiling point. Add softened gelatin. Add pineapple. Refrigerate until firm. Serve as a salad on lettuce with diet dressing or serve as a dessert with diet whipped topping.

Marjorie Jones, Athens Pike

SURPRISE CHOCOLATE CAKE

2 eggs
½ cup butter or margarine, softened
5 tsp. Sweet & Low (= 1¼ cups sugar)
2 cups self-rising flour
½ cup cocoa
1 pkg. dry yeast
1¼ cup skimmed milk
1 tsp. vanilla

Combine eggs, butter, and sweetener. Mix well. Add dry ingredients with milk and vanilla. Cover with foil. Put in bundt pan in warm place for 30 minutes. Bake 15 minutes with foil over it. Remove foil and bake 15 to 20 minutes at 350 degrees.

Larue Wallace, New Sharon

SOUTHERN SPOON BREAD (4 Servings) (1 Bread)

1 cup boiling water
½ cup skim milk
1½ tsp. baking powder
2 eggs, separated
1 tbsp. vegetable oil
½ cup cornmeal
½ tsp. salt

Preheat oven to 375°. Pour boiling water over cornmeal. Stir until smooth. Beat in remaining ingredients, except egg whites. Beat egg whites until stiff; fold into mixture. Turn into casserole sprayed with pan spray. Spoon into serving dishes.

Evelyn Hall, Athens Pike

CHERRY CRISP (Serves 4)

Fruit Layer:
1 16 oz. red sour pitted cherries
1½ tbsp. cornstarch
4 tsp. sugar
¼ tsp. almond extract

Topping:
½ cup quick-cooking rolled oats
2 tbsp. chopped walnuts
1 tbsp. margarine, melted

Fruit Layer:
Drain cherries, reserving ¾ cup juice. Combine small amount of juice, cornstarch and sugar in saucepan. Stir in remaining juice. Cook over moderate heat, stirring constantly until thickened and clear. Remove from heat, add cherries and extract, and spread in 8" pan.

Topping:
Preheat over 375°. Mix oats and walnuts in small bowl, add margarine; mix well with fork. Mixture will be crumbly. Sprinkle topping over fruit layer. Bake for 20 minutes or until topping is browned. Serve warm or chilled.

Evelyn Hall, Athens Pike

TROPICAL DELIGHT (1 Serving)

1 cup pineapple cubes (juice pack)
1 tbsp. All-Bran
½ banana
2 tbsp. Cool Whip

Place fruit in dish, add Cool Whip, stir. Sprinkle All-Bran on top.

Evelyn Hall, Athens Pike

LEMON CHICKEN (Serves 4)

4 chicken breasts
½ tsp. onion powder
½ tsp. crushed thyme
½ tsp. crushed marjoran
2 tsp. grated lemon peel
⅓ cup fresh lemon juice
½ cup water
lemon quarters
dash of paprika
snipped parsley

Place chicken breasts in non-stick baking pan. In separate bowl, combine the seasonings, lemon peel and lemon juice with ½ cup water. Pour this mixture over the chicken and bake, uncovered at 350° for about 30 minutes, basting once or twice with the pan liquid. Bake another 30 minutes until the chicken is done and the skin is crispy. Garnish with lemon wedges and parsley.

Evelyn Hall, Athens Pike

PINEAPPLE - MINT DESSERT (Serves 8)

Thoroughly drain 1 20-oz. can crushed pineapple (juice-pack), reserving 1 cup juice. In saucepan, mix ¼ cup sugar and 1 envelope unflavored gelatin (1 tbsp.). Stir in reserved juice. Stir over low heat until gelatin and sugar dissolve. Remove from heat; stir in ¼ tsp. vanilla, several drops peppermint extract and a few drops green food coloring. Chill mixture until partially set. In mixing bowl combine ⅓ cup non-fat dry milk powder and ⅓ cup ice water; beat at high speed until stiff peaks form. Carefully fold in gelatin mixture and pineapple. Chill, if necessary, until mixture mounds. Spoon into dessert dishes; chill until firm.

Evelyn Hall, Athens Pike

PEACH CASSEROLE

2 large cans peach halves
1 box brown sugar
1 stick butter (sliced)

1½ - 2 tubes Ritz crackers (crushed lightly)
1 stick butter

Drain peaches well, place in 2 qt. dish; spread brown sugar over peaches, then slices of butter; mix Ritz crackers and 1 stick of butter and pour over butter slices. Bake at 200° for 2 hours or longer.

Kelly S. Brewer, Monrovia II

GOO GOO CLUSTERS

1 pkg chocolate Alba
1 tbsp. chunky peanut butter
1½ tbsp. water

2 tbsp. raisins
¾ oz. rolled oats (oatmeal)
½ tsp. honey

Mix and shape into clusters. Freeze. Makes 1 serving. Equals: 1 milk, 1 protein, 1 fat, 1 fruit, 1 bread, and 10 calories. Instead of chocolate Alba and raisins, vanilla Alba and sunflower seeds can be used.

Eunice Bellingrath, Rocket City.

FRUIT DESSERT

1 can Lite fruit cocktail
1 can Lite peaches
1 can crushed pineapple, in own juice
2 small bananas, sliced (optional)

1 6 oz. pkg. vanilla Jello Instant Pudding w/Nutrasweet
1 3 oz. pkg. vanilla and 1 3 oz. pkg. lemon Jello Instant Pudding w/Nutrasweet

Pour fruit and juice in bowl. Add **DRY** pudding and mix well.
1 cup w/bananas = 135 cal, 1 cup w/fruit = 125 cal.

Patsy A. Vaughn, South Parkway

CHOCOLATE DELIGHT

1 cup crushed pineapple
1 banana, diced

4 pkg. Alba 77 (Chocolate)
4 tbsp. Cool Whip

Mix together and freeze in 4 small containers. Makes 4 servings. Each serving counts as 1 fruit and 1 milk. + 12 optional calories.

Eunice Bellingrath, Rocket City

BLUEBERRY (or BLACKBERRY) COBBLER
(Serves 4)

½ cup Bisquick
2 cups berries

2 tbsp. sugar
3 pkg. artificial sweetener

Mix berries, artificial sweetner and ¼ cup water. Refrigerate for several hours or overnight. Mix bisquick with approximately ⅓ cup water, (soupy). Pour into casserole dish. Spread berries on top. Sprinkle 1 tbsp. sugar over berries. Bake at $375°$ for 20 minutes. Sprinkle 1 tbsp. sugar and cook 5 minutes then turn on broiler until browned.

¼ cobbler = 125 calories
1 serving topped with 2 tbsp. La Creme = 149 calories

Jeanne Peters, South Parkway

APPLESAUCE TREAT

Dissolve contents of a large package of banana-strawberry flavored diet Jello in 1½ cups boiling water. Add 3½ cups unsweetened chilled applesauce and 2 tsp. lemon juice; mix well. Chill in 10 dessert dishes, about 45 minutes. 45 calories per serving.

Eunice Bellingrath, Rocket City

FROZEN AMBROSIA DELIGHT

1 cup crushed pineapple
1 cup orange juice
½ cup sweetener
2 medium bananas, diced
1 tbsp. lemon juice
¼-½ tsp. coconut extract

Combine well and freeze in 8 containers. Makes 8 servings. Let set out of the freezer 10 minutes before serving. Counts as 1 fruit.

Eunice Bellingrath, Rocket City

PISTACHIO PUDDING DESSERT

1 3 oz. instant Jello Pistachio Pudding w/Nutrasweet
1 lg. can crushed pineapple, in own juice
1 cup La Creme Whipped Topping

Mix all ingredients together.

¼ of recipe is 105 cal.

Patsy A. Vaughn, South Parkway

LOW CAL STRAWBERRY PIE

1½ cup cold water
1 or 2 tbsp. corn starch

Stir over medium heat until bubbly.

Add:
4 pkg. sugar substitute
1 small box of Nutrasweet strawberry gelatin

Let mixture cool. Stir in 3 cups sliced strawberries. Chill. Serves 4. Put into ready-made crust.

Crust:
8 graham crackers, crushed
4 tsp. diet margarine

Melt margarine. Mix with graham crackers. Put in pie pan. Bake 15 minutes. Cool. Cool Whip can be added to top of pie.

Norma Colbath, South Parkway

ORANGE ROUGHY FISH

Orange Roughy
1 tbsp. Parmesan cheese
1 tbsp. diet margarine
1 tsp. mustard
1 tsp. lemon juice

Bake fish about 12 minutes at $375°$. Spread mixture of margarine, cheese, lemon juice and mustard on fish during the last 3 minutes of baking time. Orange Roughy and sauce for 5 oz. is 150 calories.

Patsy A. Vaughn, South Parkway

VEGETABLE COD-BAKE (Serves 4)

Thaw one 16 oz. package frozen cod fillets; cut into 4 portions. Place in greased 10 x 6¾-inch baking dish; sprinkle with 3 tbsp. lemon juice, ½ tsp. paprika. Combine ½ cup sliced fresh mushrooms, ¼ cup chopped tomatoes, ¼ cup chopped green pepper and 1 tbsp. snipped parsley; sprinkle over fish. Bake, covered, at $350°$ until fish flakes easily with a fork, about 25 minutes. Serve with lemon wedges.

Evelyn Hall, Athens Pike

OVEN BAKED OMELET (Serves 4)

4 slices bacon
3 1 oz. slices processed American Cheese
6 eggs
¾ cup skim milk
Dash pepper

Preheat oven to $350°$. Cook bacon until crisp; drain and crumble. Spray 8-inch pie pan with pan spray. Arrange cheese slices to cover bottom of pan. Beat together eggs, milk, pepper, with fork. Add bacon, pour over cheese. Bake for 30 minutes. Let stand 5 minutes before cutting into wedges.

Evelyn Hall, Athens Pike

FRANK-KRAUT SKILLET (Serves 4)

4 Frankfurters (beef)
1 16 oz. can sauerkraut (rinsed)
½ tsp. caraway seeds
½ cup (2 oz.) shredded Swiss cheese

Slice franks in half and brown in skillet. Add sauerkraut and caraway seed. Cook and stir over medium heat until most liquids are gone. Stir in cheese, heat until melted, 2 or 3 minutes.

Evelyn Hall, Athens Pike

SWEDISH STEW

1½ to 2 lbs. ground beef
4 to 6 medium, potatoes,
1 lb. frozen mixed vegetables
1 large onion, sliced

1 to 2 cans tomato soup or
    tomato sauce
salt and pepper to taste

In large greased casserole place layers of small meatballs; sliced raw potatoes; mixed vegetables; sliced onion, salt and pepper. Add more layers of each as size of casserole will permit. Top with tomato soup or tomato sauce. Cover and bake at 350° approximately 2 hours or until potatoes are tender.

Janice Mizikowski, University

TOPS-STYLE CHILI

½ lb. lean ground beef
sliced mushrooms
¼ cup chopped celery
1 cup green beans (reg. cut)

¼ cup green pepper, chopped
2 cups tomato juice, pepper
    and chili powder to taste.

Cook ground beef and drain fat. Add remaining ingredients and simmer for ½ hour.

Evelyn Hall, Athens Pike

SPAGHETTI SAUCE (Serves 4)

2 tbsp. olive oil
1 clove garlic, minced
½ tsp. salt
½ tsp. thyme
½ tsp. sugar
¼ cup chopped onion

8 oz. tomato sauce
16 oz. can of tomatoes
½ cup tomato paste
½ tsp. basil
½ tsp. oregano
1 lb. ground turkey

Brown ground turkey. Drain fat. Add remaining ingredients. Simmer for 2 hrs.
Counts as 2½ proteins, 1½ fat, 1 veg. 35 optional cal.

Eunice Bellingrath, Rocket City

CHICKEN POULETT

1 pkg. Pepperidge Farms Stuffing Mix (8 oz.)	¾ tsp. salt
1 stick butter	2½ cups cooked chicken, diced
1 cup hot water	2 eggs
¼ cup green onions, chopped	1½ cups milk
½ cup celery, chopped	1 can mushroom soup
½ cup mayonnaise	cheddar cheese

Mix above ingredients together and place ½ of mixture in a greased baking dish. Add 2½ cups diced cooked chicken on top and then the rest of the bread mixture over this. Beat 2 eggs and 1½ cups milk, pour over chicken. Refrigerate over night, take out 1 hour before baking. Pour 1 can of mushroom soup over top and bake 40 minutes at 350°, add grated cheddar cheese and bake 10 minutes.

Judy Case, Rainbow Mountain

TURKEY & DRESSING (Serves 1)

¾ oz. self-rising cornmeal (¼ cup)	½ tsp. sage
1/8 tsp. garlic powder	½ tsp. poultry seasoning
⅓ cup chopped onion	4 oz. cooked turkey, diced
	1 tsp. vegetable oil

Combine all ingredients and mix well. Spoon into a small casserole dish that has been sprayed with a pan spray. Bake at 400° for 35 min.

Counts as: 1 bread, 2 veg, 4 protein, 1 fat.

Eunice Bellingrath, Rocket City

STROMBOLI

1 loaf frozen bread dough	½ lb. provolone cheese, grated
1 small onion, chopped	½ lb. thinly sliced ham
1 green pepper, chopped	½ lb. mozarella cheese, grated
½ lb. pork sausage	

Defrost bread dough but do not let rise. Oil bread dough, flatten and roll into a rectangle about 12"x15". Brown pork sausage, onion and green pepper. Drain. Spread on bread dough, then layer provolone cheese, ham and mozarella cheese on dough. Roll lengthwise like a jelly roll and seal edges and tuck in ends. Roll will be approximately 15" long. Place seam side down on an oiled cookie sheet and bake at 350° for 30-45 minutes until golden brown. Slice into serving size pieces. Great with a green salad. Serves 6-8.

Pat Johnson, South Parkway

LOW-CALORIE EGGPLANT PARNIAGAM

1 large eggplant, cut into ½ inch slices
1 tbsp. olive oil
3 tbsp. grated parmesan cheese
1 tsp. pepper
½ cup Italian seasoned bread crumbs
pinch garlic powder
1 tsp. leaf oregano, crumbled
1 8 oz. can tomato sauce
3 oz. mozzarella cheese, thin sliced.

Boil large kettle of water; remove from heat; drop in eggplant slices and let stand for 5 minutes. Drain slices, blot dry with paper toweling. Heat oil in non-stick skillet; add eggplant to oil and brown both sides. Combine parmesan, pepper, garlic powder and oregano with tomato sauce mixture over bottom of 9" square shallow baking dish. Arrange eggplant in layers with mozzarella cheese. Pour remaining sauce over all and top with bread crumbs. Bake at 350º for thirty minutes.

Evelyn Hall, Athens Pike

SCALLOPED CORN (Serves 8)

1 17 oz. can cream style corn
1 cup skim milk
1 egg beaten
1 cup cracker crumbs, divided
2 tbsp. chopped pimento
¼ cup chopped onion
dash pepper
1 tsp. margarine

Preheat oven to 350º. Combine corn and milk. Stir in egg. Add ¾ cup of crumbs, pimento, onion, and pepper. Mix well. Pour into baking dish sprayed with pan spray. Melt margarine. Add remaining ¼ cup cracker crumbs. Spread over corn mixture. Bake 45 minutes.

Evelyn Hall, Athens Pike

BAKED ACORN SQUASH WITH APPLE STUFFING
(Serves 2)

1 med. acorn squash
2 tbsp. diced celery
2 tsp. margarine, melted
2 small apples, unpeeled, diced
2 tsp. minced onion
2 tbsp. water

Preheat oven to 400º. Cut squash in half. Remove seeds. Place cut side down on baking sheet sprayed with pan spray. Combine apples, celery, and onion. Add margarine and water. Place in baking dish. Cover. Bake squash and apple stuffing for 45 minutes or until tender. Remove from oven. Fill with apple mixture.

Evelyn Hall, Athens Pike

SCALLOPED CORN

1 17 oz. can cream style corn
1 cup skim milk
1 egg beaten
1 cup cracker crumbs, divided
2 tbsp. chopped pimento
¼ cup chopped onion
dash pepper
1 tsp. margarine

Preheat oven to 350°, combine corn and milk. Stir in egg. Add ¾ cups of crumbs, pimento, onion, pepper. Mix well. Pour into baking dish sprayed with pan spray. Melt margarine. Add remaining ¼ cup cracker crumbs. Spread over corn mixture. Bake 45 minutes. Serves 8.

Evelyn Hall, Athens Pike

MY MOTHER-IN-LAW'S WILD RICE CASSEROLE

3 cups cooked wild rice
(1 cup raw = 3 cups cooked)
1 cup cooked white rice
(⅓ cup raw = 1 cup cooked)
1 can sliced water chestnuts, drained
2 tbsp. soy sauce
¼ cup green pepper
1 can cream of celery soup
1 tbsp. chopped pimento
2 tbsp. chopped parsley
1 tbsp. minced onion
salt and pepper to taste

Mix all the ingredients and bake at 350° for 1 hour. Also a good stuffing for Cornish hens.

Clare Welden, Monrovia II

PUMPKIN OR CARROT MUFFINS (Serves 2)

2 slices raisin bread (crumbled)
½ cup pumpkin or ½ cup baby food carrots
⅔ cup dry non-fat milk
2 eggs
1 tsp. pumpkin spice
4 pkg. Sweet & Low or 8 tsp. brown sugar replacement
1 tsp. baking powder

Beat eggs until light. Add remaining ingredients and mix well. Fill Pam sprayed muffin tin ⅔ full makes 6 muffins. Bake at 400° 15 minutes. Serves 2.

LIME GELATIN SALAD

1 3 oz. pkg. lime Jello (sugar free)
1 cup cottage cheese (1% milkfat)
2 cups crushed pineapple (in its own juice), drained
2 tbsp. diet mayonnaise
8 tbsp. La Creme

Prepare Jello according to package directions. Add rest of ingredients. Serves 8 at 120 calories each.

Jeanne Peters, South Parkway

HARVARD BEETS (Serves 4)

1 1 lb. can beets, sliced (save liquid)
1 tbsp. cornstarch
Dash of pepper
¼ cup vinegar
1 tbsp. sugar

Drain beets reserving liquid. Add enough water to beet juice to make ⅔ cup liquid. Combine cornstarch and pepper in saucepan. Add liquid and vinegar. Stir until smooth. Cook, stirring constantly, until mixture thickens and boils. Boil 1 minute, stirring. Add sliced beets and sugar, heat through.

Evelyn Hall, Athens Pike

EGGS

BEST DEVILED EGGS

6 hard-boiled eggs
¼ cup mayonnaise
2 T. onion, chopped
1 T. green pepper, chopped (optional)
1 tsp. prepared mustard
⅛ tsp. salt
Dash of pepper
Dash of paprika

Slice eggs lengthwise in half and carefully remove yolks. Mash yolks with mayonnaise and remaining ingredients and stir well. Stuff eggs whites with mixture and garnish with paprika. Could be party food.

Mrs. O. V. Mitchell, Central

FRENCH COUNTRY OMELET

3 T. butter or margarine
¼ cup bacon, diced
2 med. potatoes, diced
¼ cup onion, minced
3 eggs
½ tsp. salt
¼ tsp. seasoned salt
1 tsp. parsley, snipped

In skillet, in 1 tablespoon butter, cook bacon until brown. Add potatoes and onion; saute until tender and golden. In bowl beat eggs with seasonings, parsley, and 3 tablespoons water. In hot skillet, melt 1 tablespoon butter and add half of eggs. When eggs begin to set, add half of potato mix and fold omelet. Turn onto plate and brush top with butter. Repeat for remaining eggs and potato mixture, using 1 tablespoon butter in hot skillet.

Mary Anne Riley, South Parkway

CHEESE BAKED EGGS

2 T. butter
Bread crumbs
8 eggs
Salt, pepper, and paprika to taste
1 cup Cheddar cheese, grated
1 cup heavy cream
Parsley, chopped

Grease 7x11-inch baking dish with butter. Spread bread crumbs to cover bottom of dish. Carefully break eggs onto saucer and slide onto bread crumbs. Season with salt, pepper, and paprika. Sprinkle grated cheese over eggs. Pour on cream. Bake in moderate oven at 350 degrees for 25 minutes until eggs are firm. Just before serving, garnish with chopped parsley.

Vicki Coffee, Extension Agent

CONFETTI-FILLED EGGS

8 hard-cooked eggs
1 8-oz. pkg. cream cheese
½ cup mayonnaise
½ cup sweet pickle relish
Salt and pepper to taste
Paprika

Remove egg yolks; mash with cream cheese, mayonnaise, pickle relish, salt, and pepper. Fill egg whites with yolk mixture and sprinkle with paprika.

Mrs. Claude Bridges (Laura), Monrovia

GARLIC GRITS

1 cup grits
4 cups water
1 tsp. salt
1 roll garlic cheese
1 stick oleo
2 eggs
Milk

Add grits to water with salt. When boiling, add garlic cheese cut in pieces and 1 stick oleo. Beat eggs; add enough milk to eggs to measure 1 cup. Stir in grits. Pour in a buttered 2-quart casserole. Bake for 45 minutes at 350 degrees. Serves 12.

Evelyn Hall, Athens Pike

QUICHE

Basic Custard:
3 eggs
1½ cups milk
1½ cups cheese, shredded

9-inch pie shell
1 cup cooked meat and/or vegetables
Herbs of choice

Combine eggs, milk, and cheese. Partially bake pie shell at 450 degrees for 5 to 6 minutes. Fill shell with custard mixture and meat and/or vegetables. Can use leftovers, such as cubed, sliced, diced bacon; ham; sausage; chicken; broccoli; mushrooms; onion; corn; peas; carrots. If using fresh vegetables, cook them slightly first. Season quiche with herbs. Bake 50 minutes or until center is nearly set.

Linda Nord, Hazel Green

QUICHE LORRAINE

1 tsp. butter
1 cup cooked ham or Canadian bacon, diced
1 med. onion, grated
1 pie shell, unbaked
½ cup Swiss cheese, grated

4 eggs, slightly beaten
½ cup evap. milk with 1 cup milk
½ cup water and ½ cup cream
½ tsp. salt
½ tsp. pepper
Pinch of nutmeg

Melt butter in a skillet. Add meat and cook until golden brown. Remove meat; add onion and cool for 5 minutes. Cover bottom of crust with meat, onions, and cheese. Combine the remaining ingredients and pour into shell. Bake at 450 degrees for 15 minutes. Reduce heat to 350 degrees and continue baking for 15 to 20 minutes or until custard is set. Do not over bake. Serve hot as hors d'oeuvres or main luncheon dish with a salad. Serves 6 to 8.

Marie Stramiello, Darwin Downs

QUICHE SUPREME

9-inch pie shell
2 T. butter
1 med. onion, chopped
1 cup mushrooms, sliced

8 ozs. Cheddar cheese, shredded
3 eggs
½ cup milk
1 T. parsley flakes
½ cup bacon-flavored protein

Bake pie shell 10 minutes at 400 degrees. Heat butter and saute onion and mushrooms till soft. Spoon into baked crust. Sprinkle cheese over vegetables. Beat eggs in small bowl until frothy, stir in milk, and pour mixture over vegetables. Top with parsley and bacon bits. Bake in 400-degree oven for 15 minutes. Lower temperature to 350 degrees and bake 20 minutes more. Let stand about 5 minutes before serving.

Carolyn Griner, Rainbow Mountain

SPANISH EGG SUPREME

2 eggs per person
1 T. catchup
1 T. milk

1 tsp. sweet relish
⅓ Cheddar cheese
Dash salt, pepper, and garlic salt

Beat all ingredients well. Heat a buttered skillet, running spatula down center, allowing eggs to drain into center slowly. Turn off heat before eggs are set and allow them to cook by pan heat.

Mrs. W. L. Vaughn, Sr. (Frances), Monrovia

HOT HOLIDAY DEVILED EGGS

20 hard-cooked eggs
1 T. prepared mustard
¼ tsp. pepper
¼ cup mayonnaise

1½ T. vinegar
Salt and pepper to taste
Pimiento strips
½-1 cup broth (any kind)

Cut eggs in half lengthwise, remove yolks and sieve. Place in bowl; add mustard, pepper, mayonnaise, and vinegar. Beat until smooth; add salt and pepper and mix. Fill egg whites and garnish with pimiento. Place in chafing dish and add just enough broth to cover bottom of dish. Cover and heat for 15 minutes. Serves 40.

Jacquelyn Outlaw, Extension Agent

GERTRUDE'S CHEESE CASSEROLE OR STRATA

8 slices bread
½ lb. sliced American Cheese
or grated cheese
3 eggs, beaten
2 cups rich milk
pinch salt

Remove bread crust. In small buttered casserole, layer three bread slices, whole or in bits, then ½ of cheese. Repeat once. Mix eggs, milk and salt. Pour over bread. Refrigerate over night or several hours. Set in pan of hot water (to avoid scorching); bake 40 to 60 minutes at 325 degrees or until knife stick in center comes out clean.

Mildred Fanning, Monrovia

MEATS

GROUND BEEF

AMERICAN LASAGNA

2 lbs. ground beef	¾ tsp. pepper
2 garlic cloves, minced	¾ tsp. oregano
1 sm. onion, chopped	16 ozs. lasagna noodles
2 8-oz. cans tomato sauce	8 ozs. American cheese, shredded
1 tsp. salt	8 ozs. mozzarella cheese, shredded
12 ozs. cottage cheese	

Brown hamburger, garlic, and onion. Add tomato sauce, salt, pepper, and oregano. Cover and cook 20 minutes. Cook noodles according to package directions. Layer in 13x9x2-inch pan: Noodles, shredded cheese, cottage cheese, and meat sauce. Bake for 20 to 30 minutes at 350 degrees.

Patty Shepard, South Parkway

APPLESAUCE BEEF LOAF

1 egg, slightly beaten	1 tsp. dried celery flakes (or
1 cup soft bread crumbs	finely chopped celery)
½ cup applesauce	½ tsp. salt
2 T. onion, finely chopped	Dash of pepper
1 tsp. Dijon-style mustard	1 lb. ground beef

Sauce

½ cup applesauce	1 T. vinegar
1 T. brown sugar	1 tsp. Dijon-style mustard

Combine first 8 ingredients; add beef and mix well. Shape into round loaf in 9x9x2-inch pan. With a spoon make a depression in top of loaf. Combine remaining ingredients into a sauce; pour into depression in meat loaf. Bake in 350-degree oven 1 hour. Serves 4 or 5.

Lila M. Brown, Harvest

A man's mind is like his car; if it gets to knocking too much, he had better have it overhauled or change it.

BAR B-Q GROUND BEEF CUPS

¾ lb. ground beef
½ cup barbecue sauce
1 T. instant minced onion

2 T. brown sugar
1 8-oz. can Pillsbury Tender Flake biscuits

¾ cup sharp cheese, grated

Brown ground beef and drain. Add barbecue sauce, onion, and brown sugar. Mix. Turn off stove and let mixture simmer while preparing dough. Put each biscuit in a muffin tin (press each one out flat and up to edge of muffin cup). Pour meat mixture into muffin tin. Sprinkle with cheese. Bake at 400 degrees for 10 to 12 minutes until brown.

Kathy Albers, Fleming Hills
Mary Jo Dreaden, Fleming Hills

BARBECUED BEANS AND HAMBURGER MEAT

2 lbs. ground beef
1 green pepper
1 onion

1 lg. can kidney beans
1 cup barbecue sauce
½ lb. Cheddar cheese

Brown ground beef with onion and green pepper. Mix all items; top with cheese. (May have to add a little catchup to make it thinner.)

Mrs. R. D. Sibley, Big Cove

BARBECUED BURGERS

1 lg. onion, chopped
1 lb. ground beef

Salt to taste
1 can corned beef, diced

½ btl. barbecue sauce

Saute the onion in a skillet until tender. Add the ground beef, salt, and corned beef and cook until meats are brown. Add the barbecue sauce. Simmer for 10 to 15 minutes; then serve in hot buns.

Burlene Childers, New Sharon

BRUNO SPECIAL

1 onion, chopped
1 or 2 garlic cloves, diced
Olive oil

1 lb. hamburger
2 eggs, beaten with a fork
1 pkg. spinach, cooked

Salt to taste

Fry onion and garlic in olive oil. When yellowed add hamburger; cook but do not let brown. Add eggs, mixing until solid; add spinach and cook through. Serve with sourdough French bread and Italian salad.

Mary Lou Pfeiffer, Westbury

CHEESEBURGER LOAF

1½ lbs. ground beef
1 5-oz. can evap. milk
½ cup cracker crumbs
1 cup American cheese, shredded
1 egg, beaten
¼ cup onion, chopped
¼ cup green pepper, chopped
¾ tsp. salt
¼ tsp. pepper
¼ tsp. dried basil leaves
2 slices American cheese

Combine all ingredients except cheese slices in a large mixing bowl and mix well. Place mixture in a loaf pan and shape into a loaf. Bake at 350 degrees for 1 hour. Remove from oven. Cut each cheese slice into 2 triangles and arrange on top of loaf. Return to oven for 2 minutes or until cheese melts. Let stand for 10 minutes before slicing. Serves 6 to 8.

Kay Bass, Big Cove

CHEROKEE CASSEROLE

1 lb. ground beef
1 T. oil
¾ cup onion, finely chopped
1½ tsp. salt
Dash of pepper
½ sm. bay leaf
⅛ tsp. each of garlic powder, thyme, oregano
1 16-oz. can tomatoes
1 can cream of mushroom soup
1 cup Minute Rice
Cheddar cheese strips

Brown meat in oil; add onions and cook until tender. Stir in ingredients in order given, reserving cheese. Bring to a boil, reduce heat, and simmer for 5 minutes, stirring occasionally. Spoon into a 2-quart baking dish and top with cheese. Bake at 350 degrees for 25 minutes.

Charlotte Still, Westbury

There are two things to aim at in life: first, to get what you want; and after that, to enjoy it. Only the wisest of mankind achieve the second.

CHILI I

1 lg. onion, minced
2 garlic cloves
Butter
2 lbs. ground beef
1 lg. can tomatoes
1 sm. can tomato sauce

1 sm. can tomato paste
2 tsp. chili powder
½ tsp. black pepper
¼ tsp. salt
6 ozs. water
2 cans Van Camp's kidney beans

Brown onions and garlic in butter. Brown ground beef and drain grease. Mix onions, garlic, ground beef, tomatoes, tomato sauce, tomato paste, chili powder, pepper, salt, and water. Drain kidney beans and rinse them before adding to the above mixture. Let simmer 1½ to 2 hours.

Martha R. Sparks, Rainbow Mountain

CHILI II

2 lbs. lean ground beef
1 lg. onion, chopped
2 T. butter

1 qt. tomato juice
1 can kidney beans, drained
1 tsp. brown sugar

2 T. chili powder

Melt butter in large pan, add chopped onion, and brown. Add ground beef and brown well. Add remaining ingredients and simmer.

Jimmie Moore, New Sharon
Lottie Power, Harvest

CHILI CHEESE FESTIVITY

1 lb. ground beef
1 med. onion, chopped (½ cup)
1 env. chili seasoning mix
1 10¾-oz. can cream of tomato soup
½ cup water
2 eggs, beaten

1 cup milk
1 6-oz. pkg. Fritos, crushed
1 cup Monterey Jack cheese, shredded (4 oz.)
1 cup sour cream
½ cup Cheddar cheese, shredded (2 oz.)

In large skillet cook hamburger and onion. Drain excess fat. Add chili mix, tomato soup, and water. Simmer 5 minutes. Blend eggs and milk into meat mixture. Cook and stir until thickened and bubbly. Stir in corn chips and Monterey Jack cheese. Pour into 2-quart casserole. Bake uncovered in 350-degree oven for 30 to 35 minutes. Spread top with sour cream. Sprinkle with Cheddar cheese. Return to oven until cheese melts. Garnish with red and green chili peppers. Serves 6.

Gwen Pruitt, Davis Hills

EASY CHILI

1½ lbs. ground beef, browned
1 can tomatoes
1 can tomato sauce
1 can kidney beans
2 cans red beans
1 T. chili powder
Salt and pepper to taste
1 sm. onion, chopped

Mix together and cook slowly on stove for 2 hours.

Diane McFarland, Harvest
Susan Fulda, Rainbow Mountain

FRITOS, CHILI CASSEROLE

3 cups Fritos corn chips
1 lg. onion, chopped
1 cup American cheese, grated
1 can chili with beans
1 can chili without beans

Place 2 cups Fritos in baking dish. Arrange chopped onion and one half of cheese over Fritos. Pour heated chili over and top with remaining cheese and Fritos. Bake at 350 degrees for 10 minutes. Serves 6. This is a good meatless casserole.

Mrs. Leo Wall (Lawsie), Monrovia

CHINESE BEEF

1½ lbs. ground beef
1 celery rib, diced
1 lg. onion, diced
2 T. soy sauce
Chow mein noodles
1 can cream of chicken or mushroom soup
½ cup milk

Brown ground chuck, celery, onion, and soy sauce. Layer meat mixture in buttered casserole with chow mein noodles. Dilute soup with milk and pour over casserole. Bake 45 to 50 minutes at 350 degrees. Serves 8 to 10.

Doris Smith, Davis Hills

CHINESE CASSEROLE

¼ cup onion, chopped
½ cup celery
1 lb. ground beef
1 T. soy sauce

1 can tomato soup
1 can cream of mushroom soup
1 1-lb. can Chinese vegetables
1 can chow mein noodles

Cook onions and celery in small amount of oil just until soft. Brown ground beef; add next 4 ingredients. Pour into 2-quart casserole. Spread noodles on top. Bake for 30 minutes at 350 degrees.

Josie Asquith, South Parkway

CHOPPED SUEY, AMERICAN STYLE

1 lb. ground beef
1 cup raw rice
1 cup carrots, diced
1 cup celery, chopped

1 med. onion, sliced
1 sm. can mushrooms and juice
1 lg. can tomatoes
Salt and pepper
Butter

Brown ground beef; add next 5 ingredients in layers starting with rice. Pour tomatoes over all. Add salt and pepper to taste. Dot with butter. Cook covered for 45 minutes on medium heat.

Jeanie Marsh, Harvest

DINNER IN A POCKET

1 lb. ground beef
½ cup onion, chopped
3½ ozs. tomato paste
1 egg, beaten

¾ cup cottage cheese
½ cup Parmesan cheese
1 pkg. crescent dinner rolls
2 slices American cheese

Brown beef and onions, stir in tomato paste, and set aside. Combine egg, cottage cheese, and Parmesan cheese and set aside. Separate crescent dinner rolls into 4 rectangles. Spread them evenly on a cookie sheet and pinch together all openings. The dough should make one solid rectangle. Spread meat mixture over half the dough. Spread cheese mixture atop meat and lay American cheese slices atop the cheese mixture. Fold dough over meat and pinch edges together to form a roll. Follow oven directions for time and temperature which are given on the crescent dinner rolls. Serve immediately. Serves 4.

Linda Clark, Owens Cross Roads

EASY STROGANOFF CASSEROLE

1½ lbs. ground chuck
2 T. instant minced onion
1-2 T. parsley flakes
¼ tsp. garlic salt
1 tsp. salt

¼ tsp. pepper
1 7-oz. can sliced mushrooms, drained
1 10½-oz. can vegetable soup
1 cup sour cream
½ cup milk

Brown first 6 ingredients in 2½-quart casserole; drain. Stir mushrooms and vegetable soup into casserole and simmer for 15 minutes. Blend in sour cream and milk. Heat thoroughly. Add topping.

Topping

1½ cups flour
2 tsp. baking powder
1 tsp. paprika
½ tsp. salt

½ tsp. celery seed
¼ tsp. pepper
¼ cup shortening
¾ cup milk
1 tsp. poppy seeds

Sift first 6 ingredients together in mixing bowl. Cut in shortening. Add milk and stir only until all particles are moistened. Drop by tablespoonful on top of casserole and sprinkle poppy seeds over all. Bake in 475-degree oven for 15 to 20 minutes until golden brown.

Lynn Bolin, Vestavia

FAZLINE

1 pkg. broad noodles
1 onion, minced fine
1 green pepper, minced fine
1 garlic clove, minced fine

1½ lbs. hamburger
1 No. 2 can corn, drained
1 can tomato soup
1 sm. can ripe olives
1 lb. cheese, grated

Cook noodles 20 minutes in salted water; drain. Fry onion, pepper, and garlic and add meat in bits. Fry until meat is light brown and vegetables are tender. Add corn and tomato soup; simmer for 10 minutes. Add olives and most of cheese. Pour into wide, shallow casserole dish; top with remaining cheese. Bake at 350 degreees for 30 minutes. Serves 6.

Cynthia Blanchard, Athens Pike

GHOST-TOWN BURGERS

½ lb. ground beef
2 T. onion, finely chopped
⅓ cup tomato paste

½ tsp. salt
¼ tsp. oregano
6 sandwich buns, sliced

12 1-oz. slices sharp process cheese

Combine beef, onion, tomato paste, salt, and oregano. Spread 2 tablespoons of mixture over the cut side of each bun half. Put buns on cookie sheet; brown in hot oven (400 degrees) for 12 minutes. Cut ghost faces from cheese slices, using tiny cutters or a paring knife. Place a cheese face over browned meat. Return to oven for 1 to 2 minutes, until cheese faces start to soften. Yield: 1 dozen.

Debbie Maples, Owens Cross Roads

GRECO

1 yellow onion, chopped
1 green pepper, chopped
1 lb. ground beef
2 sm. cans mushrooms, drained

2 cups shell macaroni
3 cups tomato sauce
1 can cream-style corn
Sharp cheese

Saute onions and green pepper in a small amount of oil until glossy. Brown meat and add mushrooms. Boil macaroni until tender and add to meat. Add tomato sauce and corn and mix well. Place in a greased casserole and refrigerate. When ready to bake, grate lots of cheese and cover casserole top with cheese. Bake at 300 degrees for 1 hour. Serves 6.

Vicki Coffee, Extension Agent

GROUND BEEF CASSEROLE

1 2½-oz. jar mushrooms, sliced
Margarine

1 lb. ground chuck
4 ozs. egg noodles

Saute mushrooms in margarine. Brown meat separately and drain. Cook noodles.

Sauce

8 ozs. Philadelphia cream cheese
½ cup milk

½ tsp. flavor-all seasoning or
1 T. Worcestershire sauce

⅓ cup Romano cheese, grated

Cook milk and cream cheese over low heat until cheese is melted. Add seasoning and grated cheese. Combine sauce, noodles, mushrooms, and meat in a casserole dish. Bake at 300 degrees for 25 minutes. Top with croutons.

Connie Wagner, Rainbow Mountain

HAMBURGER FAVORITE

1 lb. hamburger meat
Salt and pepper
2 16-oz. cans whole kernel corn
1 can tomato sauce
1 lg. onion, diced
3 tsp. chili seasoning
1 can water

Mix above ingredients. Bake for 40 minutes at 325 degrees.

Alta Neely, New Sharon

HAMBURGER PIE I

1 cup onion, chopped
1 lb. ground round or chuck
2 T. butter or margarine
1 tsp. salt
¼ tsp. pepper
1 T. Worcestershire sauce
2 T. catchup or chili sauce
1 9 or 10-inch pie shell, unbaked
1 cup cottage cheese
½ cup sour cream
2 eggs, beaten
Paprika
Parsley or chives, chopped

Cook onions and beef in butter for about 5 minutes, breaking up meat with a fork. Stir in next 4 ingredients. Turn meat into pie shell. Blend together cottage cheese, sour cream, and eggs. Pour over meat. Bake at 350 degrees for 30 to 40 minutes. Remove from oven; sprinkle with paprika and parsley *or* chives. Serves 6.

Mrs. W. B. Whitt, Heritage

HAMBURGER PIE II

1 med. onion, chopped
1 lb. ground beef
Salt and pepper
1 No. 2 can green beans, cooked (2½ cups)
1 10½-oz. can tomato soup
5 med. potatoes, cooked
½ cup warm milk
1 egg, beaten
Salt and pepper

Cook onion in fat until golden; add meat and seasoning and brown. Add drained green beans and soup. Pour into greased 1½-quart casserole. Mash potatoes and add milk, egg, and seasoning. Spoon in mounds over meat. Bake at 350 degrees for 30 minutes. Serves 6.

Cynthia Blanchard, Athens Pike
Mrs. Ruth Gump, Monrovia

HAMBURGER STROGANOFF

½ cup onion, minced
1 clove garlic, minced
Butter
1 lb. ground beef
2 T. flour
1 tsp. salt
¼ tsp. pepper
1 3-oz. can sliced mushrooms
1 can cream of chicken soup
1 cup sour cream
Chow mein noodles

Saute onion and garlic in butter; stir in ground beef, flour, salt, pepper, and mushrooms. Cook 5 minutes; add soup and simmer for 10 minutes. Remove from heat. Stir in sour cream. Serve over chow mein noodles. Serves 4 to 6.

Maxie Wilbourn, Central

HOLIDAY SPAGHETTI

1 cup onions, minced
¾ cup green pepper, minced
1 cup mushrooms, sliced
3 T. drippings
1 lb. ground beef
2 tsp. salt (or to taste)
1 tsp. sugar
1½ T. Worcestershire sauce
Dash or 2 of paprika, black pepper, and monosodium-glutamate
3½-4 cups cooked tomatoes
¼ lb. spaghetti
Parmesan cheese

Cook first 3 ingredients in drippings until onions are yellow. Add ground beef and cook until browned. Then add seasonings and tomatoes and heat. Break raw spaghetti into small pieces; add to boiling water, cook, and drain. Toss with a little Parmesan cheese. Mix meat mixture with spaghetti, and pour into well-greased casserole. Sprinkle with Parmesan cheese. Bake in a 325 to 350-degree oven for about 20 minutes. Turn off oven and let sit for 10 minutes or longer before serving. Serve hot. Garnish with crisp bacon if desired.

Teddie Johnston, Pulaski Pike

Today having a change of heart is more than a figure of speech.

Let a smile be your umbrella, but do not get a mouthful of rain.

HOT TAMALE BALLS

3 cans tomatoes
2 T. chili powder
4 tsp. salt
1 lb. ground beef

1 lb. ground pork
¾ cup tomato juice
¼ cup flour
1½ cups cornmeal
Garlic to taste

Mix tomatoes, 1 tablespoon chili powder, and 2 teaspoons salt in large pot and heat. Meanwhile mix ground meat, tomato juice, flour, cornmeal, garlic, 1 tablespoon chili powder, and 2 teaspoons salt together and form into small balls. Drop in sauce and simmer for 2 hours. Skim fat; serve in chafing dish with cocktail picks. Makes 150 balls.

Birdie Hubbard, Pulaski Pike

HUNTER'S STEW

1½ lbs. ground beef
1 med. onion
1 can alphabet soup

Garlic salt
Catchup
Hamburger buns

Brown ground beef; pour off grease. Add onion and soup, sprinkle with garlic salt, and add catchup to taste. Simmer 20 to 30 minutes. Serve over hamburger buns with salad and choice of potato.

Martha R. Sparks, Rainbow Mountain

JULIE'S BEEF ROUNDS

1 lb. ground beef, cooked, cooled
1 lb. sharp Cheddar cheese, chopped
1 lg. onion, chopped
1 can tomato soup
½ cup salad oil
1 tsp. garlic salt
1 tsp. oregano
Italian bread

Mix ingredients (except bread) well and let stand in refrigerator overnight. Spread on sliced Italian bread, broil about 2 minutes or until cheese melts.

Mrs. Marshall Byrd, Jr., Madison Cross Roads

MACARONI AND BEEF CASSEROLE

7 ozs. elbow macaroni
1 lb. ground beef
1 10¾-oz. can cream of mushroom soup
1 14½-oz. can whole tomatoes
¾ cup cheese, shredded
¼ cup bell pepper, chopped
¾ tsp. seasoned salt
1 can French fried onions

Cook macaroni and drain; brown meat and drain; combine all ingredients except onions. Pour half into 2-quart dish and add half of the onions. Pour the remainder of mixture over onions. Cover and bake at 350 degrees for 30 minutes. Top with remainder of onions and bake uncovered for 5 minutes.

Glenda Beard, Harvest

MEAL IN ONE

2 T. onion, chopped
1 T. shortening, melted
1 lb. ground beef
1 tsp. salt
1 tsp. pepper
½ T. chili powder
1 pt. canned tomatoes
1 cup spaghetti, cooked
Cheese

Brown onion in shortening; add beef, salt, and pepper. Cook until brown. Remove from heat. Add chili powder, tomatoes, and spaghetti and mix well. Cover with cheese and cook 15 minutes on 375 degrees or until cheese is melted.

Lorene P. Butler, Poplar Ridge

MEATBALLS I

1 lb. ground beef
1 sm. onion, chopped
½ cup tomato catchup

1 egg
½ cup sweet milk
2 cups toasted bread crumbs
Salt and pepper to taste

Work all ingredients together. Roll into walnut-size balls. When all balls are made, roll in flour and fry in cooking oil until brown. Have ready 1 can tomato paste diluted with ½ can water; heat and let simmer 20 to 30 minutes. Serve with creamed potatoes and slaw or with spaghetti or place balls as browned into a pan, 1 layer deep. Make 1½ cups white flour gravy, then pour gravy over meatballs and spoon 1 can mushroom soup over all. Sprinkle with cheese if you like (optional). Cover pan with foil and cook in a preheated oven for 20 minutes at 450 degrees. Meatballs can be made a day ahead and browned. I have been using this recipe for 36 to 37 years.

Mrs. O. V. Mitchell, Central

MEATBALLS II

1½ lbs. ground beef
½ cup uncooked rice
1 T. salt
⅛ tsp. pepper

1 T. onion, grated
1 can tomato soup
½ can water
1 green pepper, chopped

Mix meat, rice, and seasonings. Shape into balls; drop into tomato soup to which has been added the onion and pepper. Cook slowly for about 30 to 40 minutes.

Jeanette Schlernitzauer, Athens Pike

PORCUPINE MEATBALLS

1 lb. ground beef
¼ cup uncooked rice
1 egg

2 T. onion
Salt and pepper
1 tsp. Worcestershire sauce
1 can tomato soup

Mix all ingredients except soup. Add ¼ cup soup or catchup to meat. Roll into balls. Brown in small amount grease. Pour soup and same amount of water over meat and simmer till done. Makes 2 dozen small meatballs.

Opaline West, Madison Cross Roads

SAUCEPOT MEATBALLS

1 pkg. dry onion soup mix	½ tsp. garlic salt
½ cup water	¼ tsp. pepper
2 cups tomato sauce	¼ tsp. ground thyme
1 lb. lean ground beef	1 T. parsley, chopped

In deep, heavy saucepan or skillet combine soup mix, water, and tomato sauce. Bring to a boil and simmer covered for 15 minutes. Mix beef, seasonings, and parsley. Shape into 16 meatballs; place in sauce. Simmer uncovered for 30 to 40 minutes, turning occasionally. Serve over hot, cooked noodles, spaghetti, or rice. Serves 4.

Gladys Bragg, Hazel Green

MEAT LOAF I

2½ cups oats	½ cup celery
⅓ cup butter	⅓ cup onion
1½ lbs. ground meat	⅓ cup green pepper
1 8-oz. can tomato sauce	1 tsp. marjoram
2 eggs, beaten	½ tsp. pepper
½ cup carrots	1 T. salt

Chop carrots, celery, onion, and green pepper. Mix all ingredients. Bake at 400 degrees for 1¼ hours. Serves 8.

Dovie Moore, New Sharon

MEAT LOAF II

1 cup Kellogg's Croutettes	1 lb. ground beef
Milk	1 egg

Cover croutettes with milk and allow to stand about 5 minutes to soften. Add ground beef and beaten egg. Mix well. Form into loaf. Bake at 350 degrees for about 1½ hours.

Pauline Schock, Blossomwood

PRIZE-WINNING MEAT LOAF

1½ lb. ground beef	1½ tsp. salt
1 egg, beaten	1 cup tomato juice
¾ cup 1-minute oats	¼ tsp. pepper
¼ cup onions, chopped	

Mix above ingredients, form into loaf. Place in shallow pan in moderate oven and bake about 1 hour. Good with catchup poured on top.

Mrs. Marvin Sharp, Central

MEXICAN MEAT CUPS

1 pkg. refrigerated biscuits (10)
1 lb. ground beef
1 15½-oz. can chili beans
¼ cup water
1 15¼-oz. can Mexican-style sandwich sauce
1 cup shredded Cheddar cheese
Lettuce
Tomato

Roll or pat each biscuit into a 4-inch circle. Fit over backs of well-greased muffin pans and bake 8 minutes in a 400-degree oven. Brown and drain meat. Stir in beans, water, and sandwich sauce and heat to boiling. Remove biscuits from pans and fill with meat sauce. Top with cheese, lettuce, and tomato. Yield: 10.

Glenda Patterson, Owens Cross Roads

PIZZA

Meat Sauce

1 lb. ground beef
1 garlic clove, minced, or garlic salt
Onion to taste, chopped
1 15-oz. can tomato sauce
Pinch of oregano
Pinch of pepper

Brown ground beef with garlic and onion, drain off fat. Add tomato sauce, oregano, and pepper. Simmer 15 minutes. Cool to lukewarm. While meat sauce is cooking, prepare crust.

Crust

1 pkg. active dry yeast
½ cup warm water
1½ tsp. sugar
½ tsp. salt
1 T. cooking oil
1¼ to 1½ cups all-purpose flour, if self-rising omit salt

Soften yeast in warm water in mixing bowl. Add sugar, salt, and oil; mix well. Gradually add flour to form stiff dough. Knead on floured surface just until smooth, about 2 minutes. Let dough rest on greased 15x10-inch pan for 10 minutes. Pat crust over bottom of greased pan; spread with meat sauce. Bake at 425 degrees for 10 minutes; remove from oven and add a topping of 2 cups (½ lb.) shredded mozzarella cheese and ¼ cup grated Parmesan cheese. Return to oven and bake for 10 more minutes until brown and cheese is melted thoroughly.

Peggy S. Wallace, Poplar Ridge

RAGU BEEF CASSEROLE

1½ lbs. yellow squash
1 lg. onion
1½ lbs. ground beef
1 med. jar Ragu spaghetti sauce

Cook squash until tender; chop and put in bottom of long casserole dish; top with sliced onions. Then add browned ground beef. Add Ragu spaghetti sauce on top of meat and sprinkle with Parmesan cheese. Bake at 350 degrees for 30 minutes. Serve with salad.

Doris Moore, Madison Cross Roads

RUSHING STEW

1 med. onion, chopped
1 T. cooking oil
1 lb. hamburger meat
1 cup water
1 can tomatoes, cut in pieces
1 can creamed corn
1 sm. pkg. noodles
Salt
American cheese

Brown onion in oil. Brown hamburger meat; add water, tomatoes, corn, and noodles. Cook until noodles are done and liquid is cooked down. Stir occasionally to keep from sticking. Pour into casserole dish, season, and cover with grated American cheese. Cover; cheese will melt from heat of the stew.

Dot Atwell, Athens Pike

SHEPHERD'S PIE

NOTE: *All vegetables must be pre-cooked!*

1 lb. ground beef
2 T. flour
2 T. onions, minced
1 tsp. salt
1 16-oz. can tomato paste
2 cups green beans
2 cups whole-kernel corn
2 cups English peas
2 cups carrots
2 T. oleo
Potatoes, whipped

Brown meat, *drain off fat*, add flour, minced onions, and salt. Pour tomato paste over this mixture and cook 3 or 4 minutes. Put one-half of meat in bottom of 2-quart casserole dish. Layer green beans, then whole-kernel corn, then English peas, and then carrots (be sure to use in the order given). Add the remaining one-half of the meat on top of the vegetables. Then top this with the oleo drizzled over the top. Top this with the amount of whipped potatoes you use to serve 6 people. Bake in oven at 375 degrees until bubbling. If you like cheese, sprinkle with cheese of your choice. Serves 8 to 12.

Edith T. Dobbs, Hurricane

SOUTHERN BEEF ROLL

2 cups cooked ground beef
1 cup gravy or tomato sauce
2 T. onion, minced
2 T. green pepper, chopped
2 cups sifted flour
3 tsp. baking powder
¼ cup shortening
1 tsp. salt
⅔ cup sweet milk

Combine meat, gravy, onion, and pepper. Make biscuit dough with remaining ingredients. Roll dough into a rectangular sheet about ⅓-inch thick. Spread with beef mixture and roll *as for butter roll*. Bake in hot oven, 400 degrees, for about 30 minutes or until well browned. Slice thick and serve with extra gravy or tomato sauce. (Note: Demonstrated this at club meeting several years ago, and it went over big. Had to give several copies of recipe to members.)

Mrs. O. V. Mitchell, Central

SPAGHETTI SAUCE

1 med. onion
1 green pepper, chopped
2 garlic cloves
2 T. Wesson oil
1 lb. ground chuck
1 can tomatoes
1 can tomato puree or sauce

Cut onion, green pepper, and garlic and fry them in oil; add meat and cook until brown; then add tomatoes and sauce. Turn heat down and simmer it for about 3 or 4 hours.

Jeannette Broad, Big Cove

SPANISH DELIGHT CASSEROLE

1 lg. onion, chopped
1 green pepper, chopped
3 stalks celery, chopped
1 T. salad oil
1 lb. ground beef
1 tsp. salt
2 6-oz. cans tomato sauce
1 4-oz. can mushroom stems and pieces
1 8¾-oz. can whole-kernel corn
2 T. chili powder
2 or 3 drops hot sauce
1 8-oz. pkg. noodles
Cheese

Saute onion, pepper, and celery in hot salad oil. Add meat and salt and cook until meat is white. Drain excess fat. Add tomato sauce, mushrooms, corn, chili powder, and hot sauce. Simmer 30 minutes. Cook noodles and drain. Add to meat. Pour half of the mixture into casserole. Add slices or chips of cheese. Add the rest and more cheese. Bake until cheese melts. This freezes well. If frozen, thaw and bake at 350 degrees until thoroughly heated and cheese is melted.

Gwen Pruitt, Davis Hills

SPANISH RICE PRONTO

1 lb. hamburger, browned
1 med. onion, thinly sliced
½ med. green pepper, diced
1⅓ cups Minute Rice
1¾ cups hot water
2 cans Hunt's tomato sauce
1 tsp. salt
Dash of pepper
1 tsp. prepared mustard (optional)

Brown hamburger in saucepan or skillet. Add onion, green pepper, and Minute Rice. Cook and stir over heat until lightly browned. Add hot water, tomato sauce, and seasonings; mix well. Bring quickly to a boil, cover tightly, and simmer 10 minutes. Serves 4.

Mildred Kuykendall, Darwin Downs

STUFFED BEEF ROLLS

2 eggs, beaten
2 lbs. ground beef
1¼ tsp. salt
½ cup fine, dry bread crumbs
2 T. onion, chopped
½ tsp. sage
⅛ tsp. pepper
½ cup water
2 T. flour
Oil
2 cans golden mushroom soup
2 T. snipped parsley
2 T. pimiento, chopped
2 T. water
1 3-oz. can sliced mushrooms, drained

Combine eggs, ground beef, and 1 teaspoon salt. Combine bread crumbs, onion, sage, ¼ teaspoon salt, pepper, and water. Divide meat into 8 portions. On wax paper pat each into a 4-inch square. Top with 2 tablespoons crumb mixture. Roll up; seal. Make 8 to 12 rolls; coat with flour. Brown in small amount of hot oil; remove and drain. In skillet bring to boil soup, parsley, pimiento, and water. Add meat and mushrooms. Reduce heat, cover, and simmer 25 minutes, stirring occasionally. Serves 12.

Mrs. Herman Johnston (Mildred), Monrovia

SUPER SUPPER

1 5¼-oz. pkg. instant potatoes
1½ cups sour cream
1 cup water
1 lb. ground beef
2 8-oz. cans tomato sauce
1 T. onion, minced
1 12-oz. can corn with sweet peppers, undrained
1 tsp. salt
¼ tsp. pepper
⅙ tsp. oregano
½ cup cheese, grated

In ungreased 13x9-inch baking dish, blend potatoes with sour cream and ½ cup water until crumbly. Pat firmly on bottom of dish. In large skillet, brown ground beef, and stir in ½ cup water and remaining ingredients except cheese. Spoon mixture over potato mixture. Sprinkle with cheese. Bake at 350 degrees for 25 to 30 minutes or until cheese is melted and bubbly.

Mary Jo Dreaden, Fleming Hills

TEXAS BEEF LOAF

2 eggs, beaten
½ cup evap. milk
1 sm. onion, chopped
1 tsp. salt
1 T. Worcestershire sauce
1½ cups crackers, crushed
1½ cups chopped celery
1½ lbs. ground beef

Combine all ingredients and mix well. Pack in a baking dish. Bake at 350 degrees for 45 minutes. Let set for several minutes before slicing.

Peggy Wallace, New Sharon

TEXAS HASH

1 lb. ground beef
3 lg. onions, sliced
1 lg. green pepper, chopped
1 16-oz. can tomatoes
½ cup cooked regular rice
2 tsp. salt
1 to 2 tsp. chili powder
⅛ tsp. pepper

Heat oven to 350 degrees. In large skillet cook and stir meat, onion, and green pepper until meat is brown. Drain off fat. Stir in tomatoes, rice, salt, chili powder, and pepper; heat through. Pour into greased 2-quart casserole. Cover and bake 1 hour. Serves 4 to 6.

Gisa Hall, Westbury

TWO-BEAN/BEEF BAKE

1 10-oz. pkg. frozen lima beans
1 lb. ground beef
½ cup chopped celery
1 cup chopped onion
1 6-oz. can tomato paste
1 1-lb. can pork and beans in tomato sauce
1 cup water
1 T. chili powder
½ tsp. salt

Cook lima beans until almost tender. Drain well. Brown ground beef in skillet; drain off fat. Add celery and onion; cook until almost tender and meat is well browned. Stir in cooked lima beans, tomato paste, pork and beans, water, chili powder, and salt. Turn mixture into 2-quart casserole. Bake at 350 degrees for 30 minutes or until hot and bubbly. Serves 8.

Dorothy Baker, Poplar Ridge

WESTERN MAC CASSEROLE

1 box cheese and macaroni
1 lb. ground beef
¼ cup chopped onion
8 ozs. tomato sauce or tomatoes
Salt and pepper to season
15-oz. can whole kernel corn

Prepare cheese and macaroni as directed; brown ground beef and onions and drain. Mix all ingredients and pour into casserole (2½-quart). Bake at 425 degrees for 15 to 20 minutes. A little grated cheese sprinkled on top adds to the taste.

Opaline West, Madison Cross Roads

BEEF, STEAK, AND ROASTS

BEEF STROGANOFF I

6 generous servings steak (sirloin, tenderloin, or round)
Flour
Salt
Pepper
2 med. onions, chopped
1 beef bouillon cube
2 cups water

2 T. sherry
1 4-oz. can mushrooms with liquid
1 bay leaf
½ tsp. thyme
½ tsp. marjoram
2¼ cups instant rice
2 cups boiling water
½ pt. sour cream

Place meat, flour, salt, and pepper in bag and shake. Brown meat and onions, add bouillon dissolved in 1½ cups water, ½ cup water, sherry, mushrooms, bay leaf, thyme, and marjoram. Simmer 1 hour. Add rice and boiling water, simmer until rice is done. Five minutes before serving add sour cream. Serves 6.

Jeanie Marsh, Harvest

BEEF STROGANOFF II

2 lbs. beef tenderloin or sirloin steak
¼ cup butter
1 6-oz. can sliced mushrooms, drained
2 10½-oz. cans beef bouillon broth

⅓ cup instant minced onion
¼ cup catchup
1½ tsp. garlic salt
⅓ cup Gold Medal flour
2 cups dairy sour cream
8-10 ozs. med. noodles, uncooked
3 T. butter or margarine

Cut meat across the grain into ¾-inch slices, then into strips 3 inches by ¼ inch. Melt ¼ cup butter in large skillet. Cook and stir mushrooms in butter about 5 minutes; remove. In same skillet, brown meat. Reserving ⅔ cup of the broth, stir in remaining broth, onion, catchup, and garlic salt. Cover and simmer for 15 minutes. Blend reserved broth and the flour; stir into meat. Add mushrooms; heat to boiling, stirring constantly. Boil and stir 1 minute. Stir in sour cream; heat through. Cook noodles as directed on package. Drain. Toss with 3 tablespoons butter. Serve with stroganoff. Serves 6 to 8.

Gisa Hall, Westbury

BAR-B-Q BEEF DINNER

2 cups roasted beef (leftover roast works great), chopped
3 T. salad oil
¾ cup onion, chopped
¼ cup green pepper, chopped
2 No. 303 cans green beans
2 cans sm. whole potatoes
1 tsp. salt
¼ tsp. pepper
Chili-pineapple Bar-B-Q Sauce

Heat oil in a large skillet; add onion and green pepper; cook until tender. Cut potatoes in half. Combine with beef and remaining ingredients (including chili-pineapple sauce—see below); add to onion and green pepper. Cook over low heat, stirring occasionally, until hot and lightly browned. Serves 10.

Chili-Pineapple Bar-B-Q Sauce

¾ cup green onions, chopped
1 cup pineapple juice
1¼ cups catchup
½ tsp. chili powder

Combine ingredients and bring to a boil; simmer for 15 minutes. Spoon over roast beef dinner; continue cooking as stated above.

Mrs. Jess Sanford (Louise), Piedmont

BEEF POT ROAST AND VEGETABLE DINNER

3 lbs. beef pot roast
1 T. shortening
Salt
Black pepper
1½ cups water
1 10¾-oz. can of cream of mushroom soup
6 med. potatoes
6 med. carrots

Heat pressure cooker and melt shortening. Brown roast on all sides. Season with salt and pepper; add water. Close cover on cooker securely and cook for 35 minutes. Take off of heat and let pressure drop. Remove cover and add mushroom soup, potatoes, and whole carrots. Return cover and pressure cook for 15 minutes more. Add a tossed salad and you have a dinner for six people.

Mrs. Paul Bledsoe, Hurricane

COLD FILLET OF BEEF

1 7 to 8-lb. fillet of beef, trimmed of all fat
1 cup soy sauce
1 cup olive or peanut oil
1 cup sherry
6 garlic cloves, chopped
1 tsp. Tabasco sauce
Dash of freshly ground pepper

Marinate the fillet in the rest of the ingredients for 24 hours, turning several times. Remove and dry. Rub with oil and roast on a broiling rack at 475 degrees for 28 to 30 minutes for rare. (Follow standard cooking chart for doneness.) Baste with the marinade 3 to 4 times during the roasting. Allow it to cool. If possible, do not refrigerate. Serves 8 to 16.

Jeanette Kromis, Westbury

CORN BEEF CASSEROLE

1 med. onion
8-oz. pkg. egg noodles
1 can corn beef
1 can cream of celery soup
Cheese for topping

Saute onion until done. Cook noodles. Then in casserole dish layer noodles, beef, onion, and celery soup. Repeat; there should be 2 layers. Then sprinkle with cheese and bake until cheese is melted.

Anna Lee Rogers, Madison Cross Roads

DRIED BEEF SUPREME

1 sm. jar dried beef
2 T. butter or margarine
1 med. green pepper, chopped
1 can mushroom soup
1 sm. can mushroom pieces
½ soup can of milk

Cut dried beef into small pieces. Melt the butter in a saucepan and saute the dried beef and green pepper lightly. Add the soup and mushroom pieces and stir in milk. Heat through. May be served over toast or hot grits.

Carlene Chandler, New Sharon

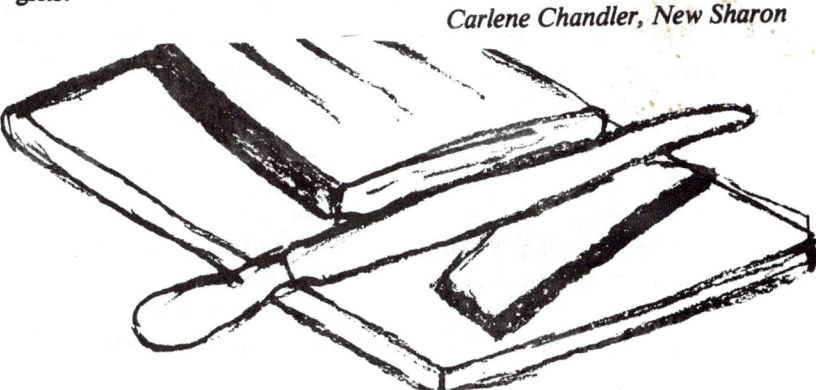

FLANK STEAK ROLL-UPS

1 lb. flank steak
Meat tenderizer
4 slices bacon
Marinade (see below)

Score both sides of steak and use meat tenderizer on both sides, pricking in well with fork. Cut steak in strips the width of bacon strips. Divide steak into 4 portions and roll each, wrapping it with bacon. Hold together with toothpicks. Put into pan and pour marinade over them. Let sit for at least 5 or 6 hours before broiling.

Marinade

¾ cup salad oil
6 T. soy sauce
2 T. Worcestershire sauce
1 T. dry mustard
1 garlic clove, crushed
½ T. coarse black pepper
¼ cup wine vinegar
¾ tsp. dried parsley
1 tsp. salt
¼ cup lemon juice

Combine ingredients and mix well. Pour over steak.

Doris B. Sells, South Parkway

FRIED BEEF SLICES WITH ONIONS

½ lb. beef
1 T. cornstarch
2 T. soy sauce
1 tsp. sherry (optional)
1 egg
½ tsp. sugar
1 T. water
½ onion
4 T. cooking oil
½ tsp. salt

Cut beef into slices or shreds. Mix beef with cornstarch, soy sauce, sherry, egg, sugar, and 1 tablespoon water. Cut onion same shape as meat. Heat 1 tablespoon cooking oil and fry onions with salt for about 3 minutes. Transfer them to a plate. Heat remaining oil and put in seasoned beef. Stir constantly for 1 minute. Add onion and stir another minute. For variation, use green pepper, mushrooms, celery, etc.

Carolyn Griner, Rainbow Mountain

ITALIAN BEEF

3-4 garlic buds
3-4 lbs. sirloin tip, rump, or boneless chuck roast, sliced paper thin
½ tsp. garlic powder
1 T. oregano
1 tsp. crushed red pepper
1-2 bay leaves
1 tsp. salt or to taste
Approx. 1½ cups water

Put pieces of garlic buds between slices of beef and tie beef together as one roast. Put in electric skillet or oven with remaining ingredients and cook covered for 3 hours at 325 degrees. Great for tougher cuts of roast. Serve on buns, with or without juice.

Jonnie Azlin, Rainbow Mountain

MAN-SIZED STEAK SALAD

1½ lb. beef sirloin steak, cut 1½-in. thick
1 4½-oz. jar sliced mushrooms, drained
1 med. green pepper, sliced in rings
⅓ cup red wine vinegar
¼ cup salad oil
1 tsp. salt
½ tsp. onion salt
½ tsp. Worcestershire sauce
¼ tsp. pepper
¼ tsp. tarragon leaves
2 garlic cloves, crushed
Lettuce cups
Cherry tomatoes

Set oven control at broil and/or 550 degrees. Broil meat 3 to 4 inches from heat until medium, about 13 minutes per side; cool. Cut meat into 3/8-inch strips. Arrange in 13½x9x2-inch baking dish. Place mushrooms on meat; top with pepper rings. Combine vinegar, oil, and seasonings; pour over meat and vegetables. Cover and refrigerate at least 3 hours, spooning marinade over vegetables occasionally. With slotted spoon, remove vegetables to lettuce cups on salad plates. Arrange strips of meat beside vegetables; garnish with tomatoes. Serves 4.

Gisa Hall, Westbury

MEAT-RICE CASSEROLE

Flour
1 or 2 lbs. stew beef, boneless
1 can beef bouillon or use bouillon cubes
2 cans onion soup
1 can mushrooms or bits
¼ cup lemon juice (reconstituted, bottled)
1½ cups Minute Rice

Flour and brown and season meat in oil. Add soup and remaining ingredients, except rice. Simmer till tender. Serve over hot rice. Serves 8.

Mildred Kuykendall, Darwin Downs

MEAT SALAD

¾ lb. roast beef, cooked, unsalted
½ cup parsley
1 T. vinegar
2 T. olive oil
½ tsp. dry mustard
¼ tsp. rosemary
½ tsp. sage

Dice meat in small cubes. Add meat to the parsley, vinegar, oil, and dry mustard. Add rosemary and sage. Stir well. Cover and let stand about 3 hours. Garnish and serve with radishes, lettuce wedge, and green pepper rings. Serves 4. Low-sodium dish.

Louise McGehee, Hurricane

ONION-SMOTHERED STEAK

¼ cup flour
1 tsp. salt
⅛ tsp. pepper
1½ lbs. beef, round steak cut ¾-inch thick
2 T. cooking oil
3 med. onions, sliced
¼ tsp. dried thyme, crushed
1 bay leaf
1 cup water
1 T. vinegar
1 clove garlic, minced

Combine flour, salt, and pepper; pound into meat. Cut steaks into serving-sized pieces. Brown meat in hot oil. Top with onion slices and stir in remaining ingredients. Bring to boil; reduce heat and simmer covered for 1 hour. Remove bay leaf. Serves 6.

Jeannette Broad, Big Cove

ORIENTAL BEEF SKILLET

1-2 lbs. round steak, ½-in. thick
1 cup celery slices, bias-cut
½ cup onion, chopped
1 cup carrots, sliced thin
2 pkgs. brown gravy mix
2 T. soy sauce
½ 1-lb. can (1 cup) bean sprouts
Cooked rice
3 cups fresh spinach, torn in pieces

Cut meat in narrow strips and quickly brown meat, half amount at a time. Remove meat; add celery, onions, and carrots. Cook and stir unti' tender-crisp—about 5 minutes. Mix gravy mix as directed and add to above along with soy sauce and bean sprouts; heat through. Serve over hot cooked rice on plates; add good handful of torn fresh spinach; then top with beef mixture.

Doris Moore, Madison Cross Roads

PEPPER STEAK I

1-1½ lbs. round steak
2 T. oil
1 garlic clove, minced
½ tsp. salt
¼ tsp. pepper
¼ cup soy sauce
1 tsp. sugar

1 cup fresh or canned bean sprouts, drained
1 cup canned tomatoes, cut up
4 green onions, sliced
1 can French-style green beans
2 green peppers, seeded
1 T. cornstarch
2 T. cold water

Slice steak into narrow strips. In skillet or slow cooker, brown steak in oil. Combine with garlic, salt, pepper, soy sauce, and sugar in slow cooker. Cook on low for 6 to 8 hours. Turn control to high; add bean sprouts, tomatoes, green onions, green beans, and green pepper cut in strips. Dissolve cornstarch in water. Stir into pot. Cover and cook on high for 15 to 20 minutes or until vegetables are tender and sauce is thickened. Serves 4 to 5.

Dot Atwell, Athens Pike

PEPPER STEAK II

1 lb. round steak, cubed
1 green pepper, sliced
2 T. oil
¼ cup soy sauce
1 med. onion, sliced

1½ cups water
1 tsp. salt
½ tsp. ground pepper
1 4-oz. can mushrooms, drained
2 T. cornstarch

Brown steak in oil. Add remaining ingredients except cornstarch. Cover and cook on low heat for 35 minutes. Add cornstarch and cook a few minutes longer. Serve over rice.

Carolyn Underwood, Hazel Green

PLANKED T-BONE STEAK

1 T-bone steak
Tomatoes

Chives, chopped
Parmesan cheese, grated

Place the steak on rack of a broiler pan. Broil to desired degree of doneness, then place on a heated plank. Cut the tomatoes in half crosswise. Place around steak and sprinkle with chives and Parmesan cheese. Broil until cheese is melted.

Dot Kay, New Sharon

ROLLED STEAKS

6 sandwich or breakfast steaks
Salt
Pepper
Flour
1 cup grated cheese
2 T. parsley
6 bacon strips

Steaks should be 3 to 4 inches wide by 6 to 8 inches long. Lightly flour, salt, and pepper steaks. Brown in frying pan. Remove from pan and sprinkle with cheese and parsley. Roll each steak and secure with toothpick. Wrap with a bacon strip. Return to frying pan at low heat. Roll each steak around occasionally until bacon is done.

Debbie Hawkins, Vestavia

SAUERBRATEN

2 med. onions, sliced
2 cups tomato catchup
1 cup water
2 or 3 bay leaves
1 T. sugar
1 T. dry mustard
1 T. horseradish or more
1 T. vinegar
1 T. Worcestershire sauce
1 tsp. salt
¼ tsp. pepper
3 to 4 lbs. pot roast, brisket, or shoulder

Mix ingredients and pour them over the roast. Cover and store in refrigerator 6 to 24 hours. Remove meat; drain well on towel, and roll meat in flour. Brown in oil on all sides. Add sauce. Cover. Simmer slowly 2½ to 3 hours in 325-degree oven.

Bonnie Nelson, Heritage

SHERRIED BEEF

2 lbs. stew beef
1 can cream of mushroom soup
¼ cup cooking sherry
½ pkg. dry onion soup mix

Cut beef in 1½-inch cubes. Combine all ingredients in casserole. Cover and bake at 325 degrees for 3 hours.

Beth Sidnam, Hurricane

STEAK CASSEROLE

Round steak
Salt
Pepper
Flour
1 can mushroom soup
½ cup water
1 sm. onion, sliced

Meats

Cut meat in bite-sized pieces. Salt and pepper to flavor it. Flour the meat and brown on both sides. Put it in a casserole dish. Combine remaining ingredients and add to the meat. Cover tightly and cook at 350 degrees for 1½ to 2 hours.

Debbie Maples, Owens Cross Roads

SUKIYAKI

1 lb. top sirloin or round steak	¼ lb. mushrooms
2 T. oil	½ cup hot water
1 lg. onion	1 beef bouillon cube
3 celery stalks	1 T. sugar
1 16-oz. can chop suey vegetables	3 T. soy sauce

Cut meat in paper-thin slices (if slightly frozen, the meat cuts more easily; cut meat on the diagonal). Brown meat slices in hot oil in wok or large skillet. Push meat to one side and add sliced onion, celery, chop suey vegetables, and mushrooms. Cook 3 minutes, stirring constantly. To all add bouillon cube dissolved in the hot water, sugar, and soy sauce. Bring to boil and boil 2 minutes. Stir. Serve with boiled rice. Serves 6.

Doris Smith, Davis Hills

LAMB

BUTTERFLY LEG OF LAMB

1 5 or 6-lb. leg of lamb	½ tsp. pepper
1-2 garlic cloves, crushed	½ tsp. crushed thyme
1 tsp. salt	¼ cup grated onion
½ tsp. oregano	½ cup salad oil
½ cup lemon juice	

Remove bone from meat. Your grocer usually will do this at no charge. Split it lengthwise to remove bone yourself. Mix other ingredients. Put meat in marinade and leave at room temperature or overnight in refrigerator, turning occasionally. When ready to cook, remove meat and reserve marinade. Insert 2 long skewers at right angles making an X. This makes the meat easier to handle and keeps it from curling. Cook on medium heat for 1½ to 2 hours, turning every 15 to 20 minutes until done. Basting with reserved marinade frequently. Remove skewers and slice across the grain. Serves 6 or 8.

Katheryn Linn, Twickenham

LAMB STEW

4 carrots, sliced
1 can green peas
1 can lima beans
Lamb broth
Salt
Pepper

2 lbs. cooked, chopped lamb
1 med. onion, chopped
1 tsp. garlic salt
¾ tsp. Worcestershire sauce
2 pinches curry powder
Flour or cornstarch

Place carrots, green peas, and lima beans in broth (may need to add a little water) with salt and pepper and cook for about 20 minutes. Add lamb, onions, garlic salt, Worcestershire sauce, and curry powder and simmer for about 45 minutes. Mix flour or cornstarch with enough water to make a paste, and cook for another 30 minutes.

Opaline West, Madison Cross Roads

LIVER

CHICKEN LIVER

Salt
1½ lbs. chicken livers
Flour

1 sm. onion, sliced (optional)
Oil
1 can cream of mushroom soup
½ soup can water

Salt livers, dredge in flour, and brown with onion in oil on medium heat. Remove livers and onion from pan; drain off oil. Return livers and onions to pan and add soup and water. Let simmer until ingredients are heated through.

Vicky Grimwood, Harvest

LIVER CASSEROLE

1 lb. beef liver, cut in 1-in. pieces
2 T. salad oil
1 onion, chopped
1 cup celery, chopped

1 10¾-oz. can cream of
  mushroom soup, undiluted
1 cup Cheddar cheese, shredded
2 cups cooked lima beans
¼ cup milk

Brown liver in oil. Add onion and celery; simmer 10 minutes. Remove from heat, and stir in remaining ingredients. Spoon mixture into a 1½-quart casserole. Bake at 300 degrees for 30 minutes. Serves 4.

Mrs. Frank Ernst, Pulaski Pike

LIVER SURPRISE

1 lb. liver
½ cup lemon juice
½ cup Parmesan cheese; grated

½ cup wheat germ
1 T. parsley
Salt and pepper to taste

Soak liver in lemon juice for 1 hour. Rinse liver and cut into 1-inch strips. Combine remaining ingredients. Coat liver mixture. Fry until just cooked.

Marianne Mullen, Westbury

PORK

BACON-EGG CASSEROLE

6 slices white bread, crust removed, cubed

¾ lb. sharp cheese, grated
½ lb. bacon

Mix together:
4 eggs
2 cups milk

½ tsp. dry mustard
½ tsp. salt
Dash of pepper

Butter casserole dish. Alternate layers of bread and cheese (2 times). Pour egg mixture over above mixture. Sprinkle bacon, cooked and crumbled, on top. Cover and let stand in refrigerator overnight. Bake uncovered at 350 degrees for 1 hour.

Earlene Britt, Rainbow Mountain

EGG AND BACON SOUFFLE

¼ cup bacon, diced
3 slices bread
3 eggs, slightly beaten

1 cup milk
½ tsp. salt
¼ tsp. each dry mustard and paprika

Fry bacon until light brown. Brush bread with bacon drippings. Cut slices to fit 1½-quart casserole and arrange in layers; sprinkle each with bacon. Combine eggs, milk, and seasonings. Pour over bread. Bake at 350 degrees until mixture does not adhere to inserted knife. About 45 minutes.

Cynthia Blanchard, Athens Pike

DINNER CREPES

Crepe

½ cup flour
½ tsp. salt (if using self-rising flour, use ¼ tsp. salt)
4 eggs
1 cup milk
3 T. melted, cooled butter
1 T. oil

Combine flour and salt; add eggs and ¼ cup milk. Beat until smooth. Blend remaining milk and butter. Cover bowl and set in refrigerator for 1 hour. Put oil in crepe pan and heat on medium for 2 or 3 minutes; wipe out excess. Pour enough crepe batter in pan to coat bottom; pour off excess. Return to heat for 15 to 20 seconds or until surface is dry and edges are lightly browned. Turn pan upside down and tap edge. Crepe should come loose; if not, use a fork tine to get it started then tip it over and tap again. Repeat till all batter is used up. Seal in airtight container and refrigerate till needed. Yield: 24 crepes.

Filling For 8 Crepes

1 can asparagus or green beans
1¼ cup ham pieces
Melted butter
Mornay sauce

Divide ham and asparagus into eight portions and arrange in the center of each crepe. Prepare Mornay Sauce. Place 1½ tablespoon sauce on each crepe with han and asparagus. Roll up crepes and place in buttered casserole; brush with melted butter. Bake at 375 degrees for 20 minutes. Remove from oven, spoon any remaining sauce over crepes, and serve. Yield: 8 small or 4 large servings.

Mornay Sauce

2½ T. butter
2½ T. flour
1¼ cups hot milk
¼ tsp. salt
¼ cup grated Swiss cheese
1 T. Parmesan cheese
¼ tsp. dry mustard

Melt butter in saucepan. Stir in flour and cook for about 1 minute. Remove from heat and stir in milk and salt. Return to heat and add cheeses and mustard. Cook stirring constantly until sauce boils and thickens.

Jeanie Marsh, Harvest

CORN AND HAM CASSEROLE

1 can whole kernel corn
3 cups cooked ham, chopped
2 T. green pepper, minced
2 T. onion, minced
1 cup croutons
1 cup milk

Combine ingredients in casserole; top with grated cheese. Bake at 375 degrees for about 45 minutes.

Pauline Schock, Blossomwood

DROPPED HAM DUMPLINGS

3-4 cups cooked ham scraps
1 red pepper pod, crushed

Simmer ham and pepper in at least 2 quarts water until ham is tender. Add water as necessary to maintain at least 2 quarts in the pot. Remove ham from broth and remove all fat when cool. Set aside.

Dumplings

2 cups self-rising flour
Enough cold water for stiff dough

Mix flour and cold water. While broth is boiling fairly rapidly, drop dough in by small spoonfuls till all dough is used. Return ham to broth, cover, and cook for 2 or 3 minutes longer. Avoid stirring any more than necessary.

Katheryn Linn, Twickenham

FRIED HAM PATTIES

2 cups ham, ground
1 egg, beaten
⅔ cup flour
1½ tsp. baking powder
1 tsp. cinnamon
1 tsp. sugar
½ cup crushed pineapple, drained

Combine all ingredients and mix well. Shape into patties and fry in deep, hot fat until golden brown on both sides.

Kathleen Tyson, New Sharon

HAM AND EGG CASSEROLE

6 slices of bread
12 ozs. sharp cheese, grated
2 cups ham, chopped
3 eggs, beaten
2 cups milk
1 tsp. dry mustard
1 tsp. salt
4 shakes Tabasco sauce

Butter a 3-quart casserole (or 9x13-inch dish). Cut crust off of bread. Cut each slice into 4 squares. Mix cheese with ham. Add eggs plus milk, mustard, salt, and Tabasco. Line the bottom of pan with bread squares. Pour mixture over bread and refrigerate overnight. Bake at 325 degrees for 45 minutes.

Margie Brooks, Vestavia

HAM CONES

1 lb. ham, ground
1 T. onions, grated
1 T. parsley flakes
2 T. orange juice
1 T. prepared mustard
1 egg
½ cup corn flakes, crushed

Mix all ingredients, except corn flakes, and shape into cones. Roll in crushed corn flakes and place in a greased baking pan. Bake at 375 degrees for 45 minutes.

Margaret Hay, New Sharon

HAM KABOB

½ cup catchup
⅓ cup orange marmalade
3 tsp. onion, chopped
2 tsp. olive oil
1 tsp. lemon juice
1 tsp. dry mustard

Mix all ingredients, place enough ham chunks, cherries, mandarin oranges, and chunked pineapple for the number of people you are to serve in sauce, and refrigerate for several hours. Add Kraft Barbeque sauce when ready to grill. Place ham chunks, cherries, mandarin oranges, and chunked pineapple on skewers and grill.

Donna Branan, Owens Cross Roads

HAM LOAF

1 lb. ham, ground
2 eggs
¾ cup milk
1 lb. fresh pork
⅔ cup cracker crumbs *or* oatmeal

Mix ingredients and form into loaf. Pour dressing over loaf and bake at 325 degrees for about 2 hours, basting occasionally. Dressing will become thick and syrupy.

Dressing

¼ cup vinegar
½ cup brown sugar

½ cup water
1 T. prepared mustard

Boil dressing a few minutes before putting over ham loaf. Serves 6.

Doris B. Sells, South Parkway

HAM OMELET

½ cup butter, melted
½ cup flour, sifted
1 tsp. baking powder
1 doz. eggs
Salt and pepper

Tabasco sauce
2 cups cooked ham, diced
1 lb. Munster or Jack cheese, diced
1 pt. cottage cheese

Melt butter in 3-quart Pyrex dish (9x13-inch). Sift flour with baking powder. Beat eggs with wire whip and season lightly. Add 5 to 6 drops Tabasco sauce. Stir in flour, ham, cheese, cottage cheese, and most of melted butter. Turn remaining butter around in dish to cover. Pour in egg mixture. Bake at 400 degrees for 15 minutes. Reduce heat to 350 degrees and bake 10 to 15 minutes, until puffed and golden brown. Cut in squares and serve immediately.

Oneita Craighead, Fleming Hills

HAM PATTIES

1 lb. lean cooked ham, ground
1 cup high protein cereal, crushed
1 egg, lightly beaten
½ cup skim milk

Pinch of black pepper
1 T. prepared mustard
1 cup crushed juice-packed pineapple
1 tsp. cornstarch

Combine ham, cereal, egg, milk, pepper, and mustard. Shape into 6 patties and place in a nonstick roasting pan. Bake in moderate 350-degree oven for 12 to 15 minutes. Stir pineapple and cornstarch together and pour over patties. Bake an additional 10 minutes. Serves 6 with only 179 calories each.

Debbie Maples, Owens Cross Roads

PLANTATION-STYLE HAM SLICES

1½ lbs. ham slices, cooked   1 can Compliment for ham

Place the ham slices in a shallow baking dish and cover with Compliment. Bake at 350 degrees for 35 minutes. Serves 4.

Vernie Holt, New Sharon

LASAGNA I

1 lb. sweet Italian sausages
1 clove garlic, halved
2 lbs. Italian tomatoes
1 6-oz. can tomato paste
1 env. onion soup mix
1 tsp. salt
½ tsp. basil
⅛ tsp. pepper
1-lb. pkg. lasagna noodles
1 T. oil
2 eggs
1 lb. ricotta or cottage cheese
2 8-oz. pkgs. mozzarella cheese, sliced
½ cup Parmesan cheese, grated

Slice sausages; combine with garlic and just enough water to cover in a large frying pan; simmer 10 minutes or until liquid evaporates. Remove from pan and set aside. Break up tomatoes with a fork; combine with tomato paste, onion soup, salt, basil, and pepper in a medium-sized saucepan, and cover. Simmer 1 hour or until slightly thick. Stir in sausages. While sauce simmers, slide lasagna noodles, one at a time, into a large kettle of boiling, salted water; add oil. Cook, stirring often, 15 minutes or until tender. Drain and cover with cold water until ready to layer into baking dish. Beat eggs slightly; stir in ricotta or cottage cheese. Lightly oil two 9x13-inch baking dishes. Line bottom of each dish with a single layer of drained noodles. Cover noodles with portions of ricotta-cheese mixture, tomato sauce, mozzarella cheese slices, and grated Parmesan cheese. Repeat layers of each. Bake in 350-degree oven for 30 minutes. Let stand about 15 minutes. Cut into squares; lift out with wide spatula. Recipe makes a lot, but it reheats nicely.

Lynn Bolin, Vestavia

Something is wrong in the life of the individual who constantly sees wrong in others.

LASAGNA II

1 lb. lasagna noodles
2 lg. onions, chopped
½ lb. hot sausage
1 lb. ground round steak
3 T. olive oil
2 garlic cloves, minced

2 bay leaves
1 can Italian tomatoes
1 6-oz. can tomato paste
Salt and pepper
1 lb. ricotta cheese
¼ lb. Parmesan cheese

1 lb. mozzarella cheese

Cook noodles. Brown onions, sausage, and ground steak in oil. Add all ingredients except noodles and cheeses. Simmer, covered, 1 hour. Layer in 9x13-inch pan, noodles, ricotta, sauce, and cheeses (one half of each). Layer again with other half. Bake at 400 degrees for 20 to 25 mintues. Use no substitutes.

Angie Pamfiles, Westbury

Why is it opportunities always look bigger going than coming?

CHEESY SAUSAGE QUICHE

¾ lb. pork sausage links
½ cup onion, thinly sliced
⅓ cup green pepper, chopped
1½ cups sharp Cheddar cheese, grated
3 T. flour

2 eggs, beaten
1 cup evaporated milk
1 T. parsley flakes
¾ tsp. seasoned salt
¼ tsp. garlic salt
¼ tsp. black pepper

9-inch pie shell, unbaked

Preheat oven to 375 degrees. In medium skillet fry sausage until cooked. Remove sausage and drain on paper towel. Reserve 2 tablespoons fat. Saute onion and green pepper in reserved fat 2 to 3 minutes. Slice sausage. Combine cheese and flour. Stir in sausage slices, green pepper, and onion. Spread in pie crust shell. Mix remaining ingredients and pour into shell. Bake on cookie sheet, 35-40 minutes or until browned and filling is set. Serves 6.

Sue Carter, Hazel Green

SAUSAGE QUICHE

6 slices bread
Butter
1 lb. sausage
4 eggs
1 cup sharp Cheddar cheese, grated

1 tsp. Worcestershire sauce
1 tsp. mustard
½ ts. salt
Dash of paprika
Black pepper
2 cups milk

Trim crusts and butter bread. Cut into fourths. Line 9x14-inch Pyrex dish. Cook sausage; drain and let cool. Spread sausage over bread. Combine eggs. Cheddar cheese, Worcestershire sauce, mustard, salt, paprika, black pepper, and milk. Mix well. Pour over sausage. Let stand in refrigerator overnight. Take out 1 hour before cooking. Bake at 350 degrees for 30-40 minutes. Test with knife.

Louise Sanford, Piedmont

BREAKFAST PIZZA

Biscuit dough
3 eggs, beaten
½ cup cheese, grated

½ cup ham, chopped
1½ T. milk
Salt and pepper to taste

Roll out biscuit dough, thin. Place in small square pan. Mix remaining ingredients and pour mixture on dough. Bake 20 minutes at 350. May use sausage or bacon. Serves 6.

Opaline West, Madison Cross Roads

EASY SAUSAGE PIZZA

1 lb. pork sausage
3 cups Bisquick baking mix
1½ cups water or beer
1 jar spaghetti sauce

1 can ripe olives, sliced
1 green pepper, sliced
1 cup cheese, shredded
¾ cup onion, chopped

1 can mushrooms

Heat oven to 425 degrees. Grease pizza pan. Cook and stir sausage. Drain. Mix baking mix and water until mixed. Spread in pan. Spread sauce, top with sausage and remaining ingredients. Brown crust until golden, 25 to 30 minutes.

Patsy Whitt, New Sharon

HOT LINK SAUSAGE CASSEROLE

4 potatoes
2 onions
1 can whole kernel corn
1 can tomato sauce
4 hot sausage links

Slice potatoes in bottom of a greased casserole dish; slice onion and place over potatoes; cover with corn and tomato sauce. Slice sausage links ¼-inch thick and put over the tomato sauce; bake 1 hour at 350 degrees or until done.

Mary Moore, Central

SAUSAGE AND RICE CASSEROLE

¾ lb. sausage, browned, drained
¼ lg. green pepper, diced
2 cans cream of chicken soup
1 can cream of mushroom soup
1 cup brown rice
½ sm. jar pimiento, drained (optional)
1 tsp. onion, grated

Put sausage in bottom of casserole or baking dish and cover with remaining ingredients. Cover and bake at 350 degrees for 1 hour or until rice is tender.

Diane McFarland, Harvest

SMOKED SAUSAGE AND RICE

Cooked rice
1 lb. smoked sausage
1 onion, sliced
1 green pepper, cut in pieces
1 cup celery, sliced
2 tomatoes, cut in eighths *or* 1 pt. canned tomatoes
1 8-oz. can sliced pineapple, drained
1 cup beef broth
¼ tsp. *each* garlic powder and pepper
1 T. brown sugar
2 T. cornstarch

While rice is cooking, cover and cook sausage in ½ cup water for about 5 minutes. Remove from water and cut in thin slices. Combine sausage, onion, green pepper, and celery in skillet. Cook until vegetables are tender crisp. Add tomatoes, pineapple (drain, cube, and reserve juice), broth, and seasonings. Cover and simmer 5 minutes. Blend cornstarch with pineapple juice. Pour into meat mixture and cook, stirring until clear and thickened, about 2 minutes. Serve over rice. Serves 6.

Doris B. Sells, South Parkway

BAR-B-Q PORK

2 lbs. cooked pork meat
2 T. butter
1 med. onion, chopped, browned
2 T. brown sugar
2 T. vinegar
2 T. Worcestershire sauce

2 T. lemon juice
1 tsp. salt
1 tsp. dry mustard
1 tsp. chili powder
¾ cup catchup
¾ cup water

Pork shoulder is good for this recipe. Mix together all ingredients except meat and simmer for 45 minutes. Add meat to sauce and simmer for another 20 minutes; may need to add a little extra water.

Betty Cothran, Athens Pike

BAR-B-Q SPARERIBS

2 lbs. spareribs
½ cup light brown sugar
½ cup catchup
½ cup chopped onion
1 garlic clove, minced
3 whole cloves

½ tsp. grated orange rind
Juice of ½ orange
1 T. vinegar
1 T. salad oil
1 T. Worcestershire sauce
¼ tsp. Tabasco sauce

Salt and pepper to taste

Roast ribs in shallow pan for 1 hour at 325 degrees. Mix sauce ingredients and boil 5 minutes. Pour fat from ribs. Cover ribs with sauce; increase heat to 400 degrees. Roast uncovered, basting after 45 minutes or until fork tender. Serves 2 or 3.

Elaine Story, Pulaski Pike

EASY BARBECUED PORK CHOPS

4 to 6 pork chops, center-cut
¾ cup water
¼ cup vinegar
1 T. sugar

2 T. Worcestershire sauce
½ cup catchup
1 tsp. salt
Dash of pepper

Place chops evenly in baking dish. Combine all remaining ingredients and pour over chops. Bake 1 hour in 350-degree oven. Serves 4 to 6 people.

Regna Howard, Madison Cross Roads

MANDARIN STUFFED PORK CHOPS

4 double-ribbed pork chops
1 can mandarin oranges
1 cup packaged stuffing
⅓ med. onion, chopped
¼ cup seedless raisins
½ tsp. salt
¼ tsp. pepper
½ cup orange juice

Split chops through the middle from outer edge to bone, leaving meat on bone. Spread open like a book, pound both sides till thin. Drain oranges reserving juice; mix oranges, stuffing, onion, raisins, salt, and pepper. Add ¼ cup orange juice and mix well. Spread on chops, fold over and secure, with toothpicks. Into baking dish pour reserved juice, plus enough extra orange juice to make liquid ¼-inch deep. Cover and bake at 350 degrees for 1½ hours, baste, and continue baking uncovered for 20 to 25 minutes.

Elaine Story, Pulaski Pike

PORK CHOP AND NAVY BEAN CASSEROLE

8 center-cut pork chops
1 16-oz. can stewed tomatoes
4 cups cooked or 2 15-oz. cans navy beans
1 med. onion, sliced
Salt, pepper, and Worcestershire sauce to taste

Brown pork chops quickly; remove from skillet, and drain excess fat. Place tomatoes in skillet. Pour navy beans in a 2½-quart casserole; add onion, seasoning, and tomatoes. Top with pork chops. Bake in a preheated oven until pork chops are tender, about 1 hour and 15 minutes. Serves 4.

Billie Creel, Big Cove

PORK CHOP CASSEROLE

4 thick chops
Dash of thyme
Dash of basil
Salt and pepper
Onions
Green pepper
½ sm. tomato
8 heaping tsp. long grain rice, uncooked
1 can consomme

Brown chops and place in casserole with next 3 ingredients. Stack chops with thick slices of onion, green pepper, and tomato. Add 2 heaping teaspoons uncooked rice per chop. Add 1 can consomme. Cover; cook 1 hour at 350 degrees.

Leta Sims, Vestavia

PORK CHOPS AND RICE I

6 pork chops
1 cup rice, uncooked
1 can chicken gumbo soup
Salt and pepper

Saute pork chops on both sides in skillet. Wash rice and put in bottom of rectangular casserole. Lay chops on rice. Pour the soup over all. Rinse the can with approximately ¼ cup water. Add to casserole and season. Bake in oven 40 minutes at 350 degrees.

Ethel Huse, Davis Hills

PORK CHOPS AND RICE II

6 med. pork chops
2 cups Minute Rice
1 lg. onion, chopped
2 chicken bouillon cubes
2 cups boiling water

Brown pork chops in 2 tablespoons fat, remove from pan, and set aside. Saute onion in fat in pan until lightly browned. Add rice to pan and stir together with onion. Dissolve bouillon cubes in boiling water; add to rice. Bring to quick boil and reduce heat. Place pork chops on top of rice and cover tightly. Turn off heat and let stand until rice is done. Serves 6.

Evelyn Hall, Athens Pike

PORK CHOPS WITH AMBER RICE

8 pork chops
1 T. vegetable oil
1 ⅓ cups packaged precooked rice
1 cup orange juice
Salt and pepper
1 can condensed chicken-and-rice soup, undiluted

Heat oven to 350 degrees. Brown pork chops in oil. Spread rice over bottom of 9x13-inch Pyrex dish. Add orange juice and stir. Salt and pepper pork chops and arrange on top of rice. Pour soup over chops. Cover and bake 45 minutes. Uncover and bake 10 minutes longer.

Virginia Erwin, Monrovia

SAUCY BAKED PORK CHOPS

6 pork chops
1 can cream of chicken soup
1 med. onion, sliced
3 T. catchup
2 tsp. Worcestershire sauce

Trim fat from chops and heat the fat in skillet; remove trimmings. Brown chops in hot fat; season with salt and pepper. Place in a baking dish. Combine remaining ingredients; pour over chops. Cover; bake in 350-degree oven for 50 to 60 minutes or until chops are done. Makes 6 servings.

Mrs. Bob Freeman, Poplar Ridge

SPARERIBS AND KRAUT

3-4 lbs. spareribs
1 lg. can shredded kraut & juice
Salt to taste
½ tsp. caraway seeds

In a frying pan quickly brown ribs in deep fat, browning all sides. As they brown remove from fat and place in Dutch oven. Spread kraut over ribs and salt. Sprinkle with caraway seeds. Add water to top of kraut. Simmer, covered, for 2½ to 3 hours or until liquid is gone.

Katheryn Linn, Twickenham

STUFFED PORK CHOPS

4 thick pork chops
Salt and pepper
2 cups dry bread cubes
1 cup cracker crumbs
½ tsp. poultry seasoning
Sage to taste
¼ cup chopped onion
3 T. butter or margarine
Flour
4 T. oil
1 can mushroom soup

Cut a pocket in each pork chop and sprinkle with salt and pepper to taste. Combine bread cubes, cracker crumbs, ⅛ teaspoon pepper, poultry seasoning, and sage in a bowl. Cook the onion in butter until tender. Add to bread mixture and mix well. Add enough water to moisten. Fill pork chop pockets with bread mixture and secure with toothpicks. Dredge chops with flour and brown in oil in skillet. Add soup and cover skillet. Bake at 350 degrees for 1 hour.

Dorothy Gillespie, Fleming Hills

SWEET AND SOUR PORK CHOPS

6 to 8 pork chops
Salt and pepper
2 lemons
3 onions
Brown sugar

Put pork chops in oblong pan. Salt and pepper. Slice lemons thin; also slice onions thin. Put layer of lemons then layer of onions on top of pork chops, then cover with brown sugar. Bake in a 350-degree oven for one hour. Delicious.

Mary Alice Clark, Westbury

SWEET-SOUR PORK I

3 lbs. pork
3 T. soy sauce
1 clove garlic, minced
¼ tsp. ginger
⅓ cup vinegar
⅓ cup brown sugar
¾ cup pineapple tidbits or chunks and juice
3 cups tomato juice

Cut pork into bite-size pieces and lightly brown in large skillet. Add remaining ingredients. Cover and simmer 45 minutes.

Linda Nord, Hazel Green

SWEET-SOUR PORK II

1 lb. pork, boneless, 1-inch cubes
⅓ cup flour
3 T. oil
1 jar mushroom gravy
¼ cup onion, thinly sliced
2 T. brown sugar
2 T. vinegar
1 T. soy sauce
½ cup green peppers, ½-inch squares
½ cup pineapple chunks

Trim fat from pork, dust with flour, brown in oil in skillet. Add gravy, onion, sugar, vinegar, and soy sauce. Cook over low heat for 30 minutes. Add pepper and pineapple. Cover and simmer 15 minutes, stirring now and then. Serve hot over rice.

Doris B. Sells, South Parkway

VEAL

VEAL CUTLETS

1 pkg. saltines, crushed (may need a few more)
¼ tsp. paprika
4 veal cutlets, ½-inch thick
1 egg
2 T. water
3 T. butter or fat
1 garlic clove (optional)
Tomato Sauce

Mix cracker crumbs with paprika and bread cutlets in mixture. Mix the egg and water; put the cutlets in this and then back in the crumbs. Place on a rack to dry, leaving them out for about 15 minutes, and then place them in the refrigerator for 45 minutes. They need to be well dried to insure that the breading stays on while cooking. After they are dried, brown with garlic in butter over quick heat. Turn down heat, cover, and cook until tender, about 30 minutes. Uncover, turn heat up, and crisp again. Serve with Tomato Sauce and a sprig of parsley.

Tomato Sauce

It can be a canned sauce or made from catchup thinned with water and spiced up with Tabasco, paprika, cayenne pepper, onion salt, chopped bell pepper, or garlic as your tastes favor.

Blanche Harper, Vestavia

VEAL PARMESAN

6 veal cutlets	2 T. water
Salt	Fat
Pepper	1 qt. spaghetti sauce
Italian bread crumbs	Mozzarella cheese
2 eggs	Parmesan cheese

Season veal with salt and pepper. Dip cutlets in bread crumbs, then in eggs mixed with water, then back in bread crumbs. Saute in fat until well browned, about 10 minutes on each side. Put cutlets in large pan and cover with spaghetti sauce and mozzarella cheese. Sprinkle with Parmesan cheese. Bake at 350 degrees for 45 minutes to 1 hour.

Spaghetti/Tomato Sauce

Oil	Salt to taste
1 garlic clove, chopped	Pepper to taste
1 1-lb. 1-oz.-can tomatoes	Pinch of baking soda or sugar
1 can tomato paste	1½ tsp. oregano
1 can Hunt's sauce (optional)	2 tsp. parsley
1 med. onion, chopped	1 bay leaf

Cover bottom of large saucepan with oil. Brown garlic, add tomatoes, and simmer for 20 minutes. Add tomato paste and Hunt's sauce plus 2 tomato paste cans of water. Add remaining ingredients; cover; simmer for about 3 hours. May use after 1 hour, but tastes better after 3 hours.

Marlene Galipean, Vestavia

VEAL SCALLAPINI ALLA CACCIATORE

6 veal shoulder steaks
Flour
Salt
Pepper
3 T. olive oil
2 garlic cloves, crushed
1 sm. can mushrooms
1 No. 2 can whole tomatoes, drained
2 T. chopped parsley

Dredge steaks with flour seasoned with salt and pepper. Heat oil in heavy skillet; cook garlic until golden brown. Add steaks and brown on both sides. Reserving liquid, drain mushrooms and add to meat; cover and cook for 5 minutes. Add tomatoes, mushroom liquid, and parsley. Simmer gently for 25 minutes.

Elaine Story, Pulaski Pike

BARBECUED WEINERS

1 onion, chopped
1 small green pepper, chopped
¾ cup catsup
2 tbsp. butter
2 tbsp. prepared mustard
1 tbsp. worcestershire sauce
1 tsp. salt
2 tbsp. brown sugar
1 pkg. wieners

Score weiners twice on one side and once on the other side. Mix other ingredients together, add weiners and cook until hot.

Joan Shady, Athens Pike

RED BEANS AND RICE WITH SAUSAGE

1 lb. red kidney beans, dry
2 cloves garlic
¼ tsp. cayenne pepper (red)
¼ tsp. basil
1 bayleaf
¼ tsp. cumin
1 bell pepper, chopped
1 onion, chopped
1 stalk celery, chopped
1 to 1¼ lb. smoked sausage, sliced

Cover beans with water and soak overnight. Drain beans and combine all ingredients except sausage. Add water till it covers beans and more (about ½ inch above). Cook slowly two to four hours, until gravy is thick and beans tender. If it gets too thick add more water. Add sausage during the last hour. Serve with rice.

Ruth Ann Stalnaker, Hillwood

GOLDEN BREAST OF TURKEY

1 tbsp. flour
1 medium onion, sliced
¼ cup chopped celery
4½ to 5 lb. turkey breast
2 tbsp. margarine, melted
salt, pepper and paprika to taste

Preheat oven to 350°F. Shake flour in a large size (14"x20") Brown-In-Bag; place in 12"x8"x2" baking dish. Spread onion and celery in bag. Rinse and pat dry turkey breast. Brush turkey with melted butter. Sprinkle with seasoning as desired. Place turkey on top of vegetables in bag. Close bag with twist tie; make 6 half-inch slits in top of bag. Insert meat thermometer through bag into thickest part of turkey breast. Do not let thermometer touch a bone. Cook 1½ to 2 hours or until meat thermometer reads 185°F. Makes approximately 12 servings.

Mildred Fanning, Monrovia

GERMAN SAUERBRATEN

2-3 lbs. rump or sirloin tip roast
cooking oil
Marinade:
1 cup water
½ cup vinegar or less
1-2 large onions, sliced
2-3 tbsp. flour
water

1 tbsp. sugar
1 tbsp. salt
2 bay leaves, peppercorns

Combine marinade ingredients in large ceramic bowl. Add meat; cover tightly. Put marinade in refrigerator 2-4 days, turning meat once daily. Remove meat from marinade, dry and brown in hot oil in heavy pan. Lower heat, add onion and half of marinade. Cover and cook over low heat until tender (2-3 hours). Remove meat, pour off grease and add flour to meat drippings. Season to taste. You may add sour cream and/or white wine. Sirloin steak can be substituted for less expensive meat.

Anneliese Lang, University

TIME TO SPARE SPARERIBS

1 large cooking bag 14"x20"
½ cup flour
1½ cups barbecue sauce
½ cup chopped onions
½ cup chopped green pepper
3½ lbs. pork spareribs (trimmed)

Preheat oven to 325°. Shake flour in cooking bag, place bag in a 13"x9"x2" cooking pan; add onions, green peppers and barbecue sacue. Squeeze bag to blend ingredients. Cut ribs into serving size pieces. Place ribs in bag, turn bag several times to coat ribs with sauce. Arrange ribs in an even layer. Close bag with nylon tie. Make 6 one-half inch slits in bag and bake for 1½ hours or until ribs are tender. Makes 4 to 6 servings.
Variation: Barbecue Sparerib Dinner
add 2 cans (16 oz. each) pork and beans
  1 tbsp. prepared mustard
  2 tsp. chili powder to barbecue sauce
Note: Sauce will cause inside of bag to darken in color. This is a normal reaction and does not indicate burning.

Margaret Hornsby, Hurricane

GAMMA'S GREATEST MEAT LOAF

2 tsp. "Accent" flavor enhancer
1 egg
1 tsp. salt
¼ tsp. pepper
½ tsp. dry basil leaf
¼ cup ketchup
2 tsp. prepared mustard
1½ cups soft bread crumbs
2 beef boullion cubes
1 cup boiling water
½ cup finely chopped onion
½ cup finely chopped celery
1 cup shredded swiss cheese
2 lbs. ground chuck
½ tsp. dry thyme

Beat egg lightly in medium bowl; add Accent, salt, pepper, basil, thyme, ketchup, and bread crumbs. Dissolve boullion cubes in boiling water, add to bowl and mix well until all ingredients are well blended. Mix celery, onion and cheese in bowl. Break up ground chuck and add to bowl mixing lightly but thoroughly with fork. Shape mixture into shallow baking pan (12"x5" oval) or press into 9"x5"x3" loaf pan. Bake uncovered at 375° over 1 hour.

Ann Burke, Hillwood

DUTCH MEAT LOAF

2½ lbs. hamburger
2½ cups bread crumbs
1 cup cheese (cubed small)
1 cup catsup
salt and pepper
½ green pepper, chopped
1 small onion, chopped
2 eggs

Mix all ingredients. Form into two loaves. Pour some catsup over top of loaves. Bake at 350° about 1 hour. May be frozen.

Dottie Cutts, Westbury

HAM ROLLS WITH RICE

12 slices of baked ham
1 cup rice
1 cup sour cream
1 tbsp. mayonnaise
2 tsp. soy sauce
1 can sliced mushrooms
1 small jar of chopped pimento
1 cup shredded cheddar cheese

Cook rice as directed on package. Add sour cream, mayonnaise, soy sauce, mushrooms, pimento and cheese. Mix thoroughly. Take each ham slice and place 1 tbsp. of rice mixture in middle, roll and secure with toothpick. Place in rows in greased 9"x13" pan and cover. Bake 350° for 30 minutes. Can be served as is or with cheese sauce over the top.

Mrs. Charles Linn, University

POULTRY AND GAME

SWEET / SOUR CHICKEN

4-5 boneless chicken breast	1 16 oz. can chunk pineapple
1 tbsp. vegetable oil	(undrained)
1 medium onion, chopped	3 tbsp. brown sugar
1 garlic clove, pressed	3 tbsp. catsup
2 carrots (2 inch. slices)	3 tbsp. soy sauce
1 medium green pepper, chunked	1 tbsp. corn starch
	1 tbsp. ginger

Cut chicken into small chunks, brown in oil. Reduce heat to low, add carrots, onions and garlic, cover and cook 10 minutes. Add peppers and remaining ingredients, cover and simmer 10 minutes longer. Serve over cooked rice.

Cindy Vanderzyl, Athens Pike

MANDARIN CHICKEN SALAD

2 to 3 cups diced cooked chicken	1 (11 oz.) can mandarin oranges, drained
1 cup diced celery	½ cup toasted slivered almonds
2 tbsp. lemon juice	leaf lettuce
1 tbsp minced onion	additional mandarin orange slices (optional)
1 tsp. salt	
⅓ cup mayonnaise or salad dressing	1 cup seedless green grapes

Combine chicken, celery, lemon juice, onion and salt; chill well. Add mayonnaise, grapes, oranges, and almonds to chicken mixture; toss well. Serve on lettuce. Garnish with additional orange slices, if desired. Yield: 6 servings.

Frankie Johnson, Madison Cross Roads

HOT CHICKEN CRUNCH

2 cups diced cooked chicken	1 cup grated cheese
2 cups celery (cut bias)	½ tsp. salt
½ cup grated onion	2½ tsp. tarragon vinegar
½ cup toasted almonds	1 can (8 oz.) water chestnuts (sliced very thin)
½ tsp. Accent	
2 tbsp. lemon juice	crushed potato chips for topping
1 cup Hellman's Mayonnaise	

Mix all ingredients well. Place in baking dish and top with crushed potato chips. Bake 15 minutes in 450° oven. Check after 10 minutes. May need to place foil over top to prevent too much browning. Serves 8-10.

Sue Kachelhafer, University

CHICKEN CASSEROLE

2 cups chopped anc cooked chicken
1 small container sour cream

1 can cream of chicken soup
½ cup sliced water chestnuts

RITZ CRACKER CRUMB MIXTURE

Melt ¾ stick of margarine   mix with crushed Ritz Crackers

Spread in bottom of baking dish (sprayed with Pam) ½ of Ritz Cracker mixture. Pour chicken mixture over the cracker mixture. Top with remaining cracker mixture. Bake at 350° for 25 to 30 minutes.

Virginia Cornelison, Hurrican Club

4-H CHICKEN

4 whole chicken breasts, split
¾ cup parmesan cheese
2 cups bread crumbs
1 tsp. salt

¼ tsp. pepper
¼ cup chopped parsley
½ cup margarine, melted
1/8 tsp. garlic powder

Bone chicken if desired. Combine parmesan cheese, bread crumbs, salt, pepper & chopped parsley to form a crumb mixture. Add garlic powder to margarine. Dip chicken into melted margarine and then coated with both. Arrange pieces in a 13x9x2-inch pan. Do not overlap the pieces. Bake at 350°F for 1 hour until tender. Do not turn chicken. Serve 4-5.

Patsy Brazelton

CHICKEN

APRICOT CORNISH HENS

4 sm. birds (about 1 lb. each)	3½-4 cups cooked rice
Butter	1 can onion soup or 1 can
Salt	chopped mushrooms
1 cup apricot nectar	1 T. butter
1 T. honey	Parsley
2 T. melted butter	Apricot sections

Thaw birds completely and rub inside and outside with butter, then sprinkle insides with salt. Place in glass roasting pan or regular roaster. Cook birds according to time on package, basting with melted butter often. While birds are cooking prepare the apricot sauce and rice. Make the sauce by combining apricot nectar, honey, and 2 tablespoons melted butter. Prepare the rice according to package directions. When fully cooked add 1 can onion soup or 1 can chopped mushrooms and 1 tablespoon butter. Baste the birds with the apricot sauce the last 15 minutes of cooking time. Remove birds to a heated platter, fill cavities with rice, arranging any extra rice around birds on tray. Garnish with fresh parsley and apricot sections. Serves 4 to 6.

Blanche Harper, Vestavia

ARROZ CON POLLO
(Rice With Chicken)

1 fryer, disjointed	1 8-oz. can tomato sauce
¼ cup Wesson oil	1½ cups water
1 cup celery, chopped	2 tsp. salt
1 green pepper, chopped	¼ tsp. pepper
1 onion, chopped	1 tsp. brown sugar
1 clove garlic, minced	1 4-oz. can pimientos, chopped
1 cup raw rice	(optional)

Coat chicken with hot Wesson oil in heavy skillet. Brown over medium heat. Remove chicken, add remaining ingredients except pimiento, and stir well. Replace chicken, cover, and cook slowly 30 to 40 minutes, until rice is done. Fluff rice with fork, add pimiento, and heat through. Serves 4 to 6.

Lila M. Brown, Harvest

BAKED CHICKEN

1 fryer, cup up
1 pkg. dry onion soup mix
1 can mushroom soup

Place meaty pieces of chicken in bottom of baking dish. Sprinkle a package of dry onion soup mix over the chicken. Top with undiluted mushroom soup. Bake at 350 degrees for 1 hour. Serves 6.

Evelyn Hall, Athens Pike

BARBEQUE CHICKEN

Sauce:
6 T. salad dresssing
1 T. vinegar
1 tsp. salt
2 tsp. pepper
1 stick of butter, melted

Mix all ingredients and spread over chicken; bake covered for 30 minutes at 350 degrees. Turn chicken and brush with remaining sauce and cook uncovered for 30 more minutes.

Donna Brannon, Owens Cross Roads

Just think how happy you would be if you lost everything you have right now—then got it back again.

BBQ CHICKEN

1 fryer, cut up
Salt and pepper to taste

Sauce:
1 stick butter
¼ cup vinegar
2 tsp. salt
2 tsp. pepper
2 tsp. Tabasco sauce
2 tsp. dry mustard
1 T. Worcestershire sauce

Cook over low heat until all sauce ingredients are well mixed. Brush on chicken and bake at 375 degrees for 1 hour, turning once, and adding more sauce. Place chicken under broiler until desired brownness is reached adding remaining sauce. Serves 6.

Melinda Ellis, Owens Cross Roads

BRIDE'S CHICKEN SALAD

1 cup sour cream
½ cup mayonnaise
2 T. lemon juice
1 tsp. Worcestershire sauce
1 tsp. salt
7 cups cooked chicken, diced (7 or 8 chicken breasts)
1½ cups celery, diced
1 cup pecans

Combine sour cream, mayonnaise, lemon juice, and Worcestershire sauce, and salt. Combine with chicken, celery, and pecans. Serves 10 to 15.

Bettye Richardson, South Parkway

CHICKEN AND DRESSING

1 onion, chopped
4 celery stems, chopped
2 cups Pepperidge Farm dressing (or 2 cups biscuit and white bread crumbs
4 eggs
4 cups white cornbread crumbs, coarse
6 cups chicken broth
Salt and pepper to taste
½ cup oleo or butter
2 T. raw onion, minced
1 hen, cooked

Cook chopped onion and celery in 1 quart of water until tender. Put cooked onion, celery, and water in dressing, reserving 1 cup of water. Add remaining ingredients, except hen. Mix to the consistency of bread mixture. If too dry, add more broth; pour into *oleo*-greased shallow pan and bake at 400 degrees until brown. Serve with giblet gravy.

Giblet Gravy

Hen giblets and neck meat
2 T. flour
2 T. oleo
1 cup celery-and-onion water
2 cups milk
Salt and pepper to taste
2 T. dressing
2 hard-boiled eggs, chopped

Cook and chop giblet and neck meat; set aside. In boiler mix flour and oleo and simmer until smooth. Add celery-and-onion water, milk, salt and pepper, dressing, and eggs, then giblets. Cook or simmer for 5 minutes, stirring to keep from sticking. Serve over dressing.

Jean McComb, Central

CHICKEN AND DRESSING CASSEROLE

1 8-oz. pkg. cornbread stuffing
1 lg. fryer, cooked, boned
1 can cream of chicken soup
1 can cream of celery soup
2 cans chicken broth (measure in soup can)
1 stick margarine, melted

Put stuffing in baking dish. Place boned chicken on the stuffing. Spoon on the chicken soup and celery soup. Pour on the two cans of chicken broth with melted margarine. Bake at 350 degrees for 45 minutes. Very good.

Nell Goodjohn, Darwin Downs

CHICKEN AND DUMPLINGS

2½ cups flour, sifted
½ tsp. salt
1 tsp. baking powder
Dash of pepper
½ cup shortening
⅔ cup milk or water
1 chicken
2 qts. broth
Salt and pepper to taste

Sift flour, salt, baking powder, and pepper together. Cut in shortening until it looks mealy. Then add milk about ⅓ cup at a time until you have a soft dough that can be handled. Roll out to ⅛ inch in thickness on a cloth or board that has been well floured. Cut dough in 1-inch strips. Then into short 3-inch pieces; let stand for awhile, 10 or 15 minutes. Drop into boiling broth. Cook slowly without stirring, 15 or 20 minutes. Have your chicken cooked with a least 2 quarts broth. Put chicken parts in bottom of vessel in which chicken and dumplings are to be cooked. Drop dumplings on top of chicken. Add salt and black pepper to broth. (From Sam Houston's day. I make them all the time.)

Mrs. O. V. Mitchell, Central

CHICKEN AND KRAUT CASSEROLE

1 lg. jar or can of kraut
1 T. Worcestershire sauce
Salt
8 chicken breasts or any chicken parts
3 lg. onions, sliced
1¼ cup tomato juice

Wash kraut and put in casserole dish. Sprinkle Worcestershire sauce over chicken; salt chicken and put it on top of kraut. Spread onions over chicken. Pour tomato juice over all. Cover with lid or cooking foil. Bake 1½ hours at 450 degrees.

Ina Mae Lawler, Central

CHICKEN AND SPAGHETTI

1 lg. fryer
8 ozs. spaghetti
1 can cream of mushroom soup
1 can cream of celery soup
1 sm. can mushrooms, broiled in butter
1 sm. jar pimiento, drained

Boil fryer in water to cover until tender. Remove from broth. Cook spaghetti in the chicken broth for 10 to 15 minutes. Cup up the chicken. Add cream of mushroom and celery soups, undiluted, mushrooms, and pimiento. Mix in spaghetti which has been drained; put in casserole dish. Sprinkle buttered bread crumbs on top. Bake 30 minutes at 350 degrees.

Mrs. Sonny Moore, Vincent Study Club
Mrs. Warren Moore (Florence), Monrovia

CHICKEN-ASPARAGUS CASSEROLE

1 lb. asparagus, cooked
8 chicken breasts, cooked
1 can cream of chicken soup
1 can cream of mushroom soup
1 cup heavy cream
1 tsp. curry powder
Dash of Tabasco sauce
4 T. pimiento, chopped
4 T. sharp cheese, grated
Paprika

Place asparagus in buttered casserole; arrange chicken which has been cooked, skinned, and boned over asparagus. Combine soups, cream, curry powder, and Tabasco sauce. Heat stirring constantly, until sauce is smooth; add pimiento. Pour over chicken and asparagus, sprinkle with cheese and paprika. Bake in 400-degree oven for 15 minutes. Serves 8.

Mrs. Marshall Byrd, Jr., Madison Cross Roads

CHICKEN BREASTS WELLINGTON

6 whole chicken breasts, boned, split
Seasoned salt
Seasoned pepper
1 6-oz. pkg. long grain and wild rice
¼ cup orange peel, grated
2 eggs, separated
3 8-oz. cans refrigerated crescent dinner rolls
1 T. water
2 10-oz. jars red currant jelly
1 T. prepared mustard
3 T. port wine
¼ cup lemon juice

Pound chicken breasts with meat mallet; sprinkle each with seasoned salt and pepper. Cook rice according to package directions for drier rice; add orange peel. Cool. Beat egg whites until soft peaks form; fold into rice mixture. On floured surface, roll 2 triangular pieces of dinner roll dough into a circle. Repeat with remaining rolls until you have 12 circles. Place a chicken breast in center of each circle. Spoon about ¼ cup rice mixture over chicken; roll chicken jelly-roll fashion. Bring dough up over stuffed breast. Moisten edges of dough with water and press together to seal. Place seam side down on large baking sheet. Slightly beat egg yolks with water; brush over dough. Bake uncovered, at 375 degrees for 45 to 50 minutes or until breasts are tender. If dough browns too quickly, cover loosely with foil. Heat currant jelly in saucepan; gradually stir in mustard, wine, and lemon juice. Serve warm with chicken. Serves 12.
Bonnie Riley, South Huntsville-Saddleback Valley

CHICKEN BREASTS WITH DRIED BEEF

2 jars dried beef
8 whole chicken breasts, boned
8 slices bacon

1½ cans mushroom soup
1½ cartons sour cream
Paprika

Line large flat 2 to 3-quart casserole with dried beef. Place in oven to dry out beef. Roll each chicken breast and wrap with slice of bacon. Place chicken on top of beef. Combine soup and sour cream and pour over chicken. Sprinkle with paprika. Cover dish with foil and bake 3 hours or more in 300-degree oven. Remove foil for last ½ hour to brown. Do not cook too fast or sauce will boil away. Serves 8. Good for luncheons. Variation: Add 2 tablespoons sherry to soup mixture.
Jean Siersma, Piedmont
Margie Spencer, Vestavia

CHICKEN BREASTS WITH ORANGE SAUCE

8 whole chicken breasts
¼ cup butter
Salt and pepper
2 lg. oranges
⅓ cup light brown sugar
Water
Orange juice
½ tsp. dry mustard
1½ tsp. flour
1½ to 2 cups rice, uncooked
Parsley

Allow 1 whole chicken breast per person. Remove all bones except the main breast bone. Cook bones; strain and reserve stock. Brown breasts on all sides in butter. Season lightly with salt and pepper. Put in shallow baking dish, skin side up. Add 1 cup boiling water to chicken. Peel and scrape out white inner pulp from 1 orange and cut rind in thin strips; reserve orange for garnish. Cook rind with brown sugar, ½ cup water, ½ cup orange juice, and mustard until rind is tender and transparent. Pour over chicken. Cover and bake at 325 degrees for 30 minutes. Uncover and bake about 30 minutes longer, basting several times with pan juices. Thicken pan juices with flour mixed with a little cold water. Bake a few minutes longer. Prepare rice according to package directions using 1 cup orange juice, reserved chicken stock, and water. To serve, put rice in center of dish, surround with chicken, and top with gravy. Garnish with parsley and orange sections.

Kathy Albers, Fleming Hills

CHICKEN CACCIATORE

½ cup all-purpose flour
2 tsp. salt
¼ tsp. pepper
3 lb. frying chicken, cut-up
3 T. salad oil
1 qt. canned tomatoes
1 lg. onion, sliced
½ cup green pepper, chopped
2 T. parsley, chopped
¼ tsp. garlic powder
½ tsp. oregano

Combine flour, salt, and pepper and coat the chicken. Brown chicken lightly in hot oil and add all remaining ingredients. Cook over medium heat; bring to a boil then turn heat low; cover and cook for about 40 minutes or until chicken is fork tender.

Lillian Cole, Monrovia

CHICKEN CASSEROLE I

Onion
Celery
6 chicken breasts
1 box Escort crackers
1 stick butter or margarine
1 can water chestnuts, sliced
1 can cream of mushroom soup
1 can cream of chicken soup
1 carton sour cream

Cook small quantity of onion and celery with chicken. Bone chicken; cut in large pieces. Crumb ½ box crackers and line the bottom of a greased 9x13-inch pan. Dot with ½ stick butter. Arrange chicken atop crumbs. Add chestnuts to chicken. Mix soups and sour cream and add to top of chestnuts. Put balance of cracker crumbs on top and dot with butter. Bake at 400 degrees for 30 minutes. Serve hot.

Carlla Hooper, Heritage
Mildred Prince, Pulaski Pike

CHICKEN CASSEROLE II

6 to 8 chicken breasts
8 ozs. sour cream
2 tsp. poppy seed
2 cans cream of chicken soup
1 pkg. Ritz Crackers
1½ sticks butter

Cook and bone chicken. Lay chicken in bottom of casserole dish. Mix sour cream and soup together. Pour over chicken and put poppy seed over this. Crush crackers and then pour melted butter over crumbs. Bake in regular oven at 350 degrees for 45 minutes or until brown on top. Can also be baked in microwave for about 15 or 20 minutes on full power.

Barbara Webster, Owens Cross Roads
Edna McClure, Madison Cross Roads

CHICKEN CASSEROLE III

2 cups cooked chicken, cup up
½ cup celery, chopped
½ cup onion, chopped
½ cup bell pepper, chopped
½ cup mayonnaise

¾ tsp. curry powder
8 slices bread
2 eggs
2 cups milk
1 can mushroom soup
Cheese, grated

Mix first 6 ingredients together. Cube 4 slices of bread and spread on bottom of baking dish. Add chicken mixture. Cube remaining bread and place on top. Beat eggs; add 1½ cups milk and pour over top. Refrigerate overnight. When ready to bake, mix 1 can mushroom soup and ½ cup milk. Heat and pour over top. Cover with grated cheese. Bake 1 hour and 15 minutes at 350 degrees—may want to bake at 300 degrees.

Ruth Whitt, Madison Cross Roads

CHICKEN CASSEROLE IV

5 chicken breasts, cooked, chopped
1 can cream of chicken soup
¾ cup mayonnaise

1¼ cups celery, chopped
½ cup cashew nuts, chopped
1¼ T. onion, minced
1 T. lemon juice
4 hard-boiled eggs, chopped

Mix all together and place in large casserole dish and bake 35 minutes at 350 degrees. Then crumble corn flakes for topping and bake 15 more minutes.

Betty Butcher, Athens Pike
Mrs. Lewis Vaughn (Frances), Monrovia

CHICKEN CASSEROLE V

1 chicken, boned
1 can cream of chicken soup
1 can chicken broth
1 cup sour cream

2 cups cooked noodles
15 Ritz Crackers
1 cup Cheddar cheese, grated
½ stick margarine, melted

Steam boil chicken in pan until tender and remove bones. Mix soup, broth, sour cream, and noodles along with chicken placing all ingredients in a 13x9-inch pan. Crumble crackers and sprinkle over top, baking at

350 degrees for 15 minutes. Sprinkle cheese on top and bake another 5 minutes.

Julie Linderman, Vestavia

CHICKEN ALMOND CASSEROLE

3 cups chicken, diced	3-oz. pkg. almonds, slivered
2½ cups rice, cooked	1 tsp. salt
1 cup mayonnaise	4 T. lemon juice
4 hard-boiled eggs, chopped	1 cup bread crumbs
1 onion, chopped	1 pimiento pepper, chopped
2 cans mushroom soup	2 T. butter

Mix the above and bake 30 to 45 minutes at 350 degrees.

Thelma Freeman, Pulaski Pike

CHICKEN CRUNCH

4 cups chicken, diced	2 cans mushroom soup
¼ cup onion, chopped	1 cup celery, chopped
1 cup chow mein noodles	½ cup chicken broth
1 cup water chestnuts	⅓ cup almonds for garnish

Mix all ingredients together and place in baking dish. Bake about 40 minutes at 325 degrees until bubbly. After baking sprinkle with toasted, slivered almonds.

Adelaide Steinberg, Blossomwood

CHICKEN CHOW MEIN

1 lb. lean pork (cut in sm. pieces)	Salt and pepper
1 cup onions, chopped	1½ T. soy sauce
¾ cup celery, chopped	1 can fried Chinese noodles
1 can chow mein vegetables	1 can cream chicken soup
1½ cups boiled chicken, cut in sm. pieces	1½ cups rice cooked in soup from boiled chicken

Fry pork in hot skillet and pour into large saucepan. Add onion, celery, chow mein vegetables, and cooked chicken and chicken soup from boiled chicken and simmer for 30 minutes. Season with salt, pepper, and soy sauce. Thicken with cream of chicken soup. Serve over fried Chinese noodles and equal amounts of cooked rice. Serve with tossed green salad and rolls.

Martha R. Sparks, Rainbow Mountain

CHICKEN DIVAN

2 10-oz. pkgs. broccoli
3 chicken breasts, cooked
2 cans cream of chicken soup
1 cup mayonnaise
1 tsp. lemon juice
½ lb. sharp Cheddar cheese
1 cup bread crumbs
1 tsp. oleo

Cook broccoli. Arrange broccoli in baking dish. Add boned chicken on top of broccoli. Combine soup, mayonnaise, and lemon juice. Mix well. Pour over chicken. Sprinkle with cheese. Top with buttered bread crumbs. Bake 25 to 30 minutes at 350 degrees. Serves 8 to 10.

Joan Mitchell, Piedmont

CHICKEN HOW-SO

½ cup onion, sliced (1 med.)
½ cup celery, chopped
1 sm. green pepper, cut in strips
2 T. butter or margarine
1 can golden mushroom soup
½ cup water
1 beef bouillon cube
½ tsp. curry powder
1 tsp. Worcestershire sauce
1 T. soy sauce
1 8-oz. can bamboo shoots, drained
2 chicken breasts, cooked, cubed
1 3-oz. can chow mein noodles

In medium skillet brown onion, celery, and pepper in margarine. Stir in soup, water, beef cube, and seasonings, mix well. Cover and simmer for 10 minutes. Stir in bamboo shoots and chicken and heat. Simmer 2 to 3 minutes. Serve over chow mein noodles. Serves 4.

Ruth W. Chambers, Darwin Downs

CHICKEN IN COLA
(Good And Easy)

1 chicken
Oil
1 cup catchup
1 cup cola
1 tsp. onion
Salt and pepper
Worcestershire sauce (optional)

Brown chicken in oil. Add catchup after browning. Add cola, minced onion, seasonings, and Worcestershire sauce. Allow to boil, then lower to simmer until tender, 30 minutes or so. Run under broiler.

Mildred Kuykendall, Darwin Downs

CHICKEN ITALIANO

2 whole chicken breasts (about 1½ lbs.)
Garlic salt and pepper
3 T. butter or margarine
1 15½-oz. jar spaghetti sauce
1 tsp. Italian seasoning
2 cups celery, thinly sliced
½ cup green pepper, thin strips
1 sm. can mushroom pieces
3 cups hot cooked rice

Remove chicken skin and bones and cut meat into strips. Season chicken with garlic salt and pepper. Saute in butter about 4 minutes. Stir in spaghetti sauce and Italiana seasoning. Cover and simmer 10 minutes. Add celery and green pepper and continue cooking until vegetables are tender crisp. Add mushrooms just long enough before serving to heat thoroughly. Serve over rice. Sprinkle with grated Parmesan cheese, if desired. Serves. 6. Budget Saver: Use any type of boneless chicken.

Dixie Nixon, Davis Hills

CHICKEN MAYONNAISE WITH WALNUTS

4 cups chicken, cooked
1 cup walnut meats, broken
1½ to 2½ cups mayonnaise (preferably homemade with touch of sugar)
Salt and pepper
Tabasco sauce
Greens
Hard-cooked eggs

Cut chicken meat into generous pieces. Use all white meat for elegance; white and dark for best flavor. Combine chicken, walnuts, and mayonnaise, reserving about a dozen walnut halves for garnish. Add salt, pepper, and Tabasco to taste. Spoon into bowl lined with greens—garnish with additional mayonnaise, hard-cooked eggs, and walnuts.

Jeanette Kromis, Westbury

CHICKEN 'N RICE BAKE

Salt and pepper
1 chicken, cut for frying
1 stick margarine
1 med. onion, chopped
4 chicken bouillon cubes
1 cup long grain rice
½ tsp. salt
1½ cups water
1 sm. can mushrooms (optional)

Salt and pepper chicken. Brown in margarine. Saute onion in margarine after removing chicken. Crush bouillon cubes with fork. Add to onion. Stir in rice. Add salt, mushrooms, and water. Place in baking pan. Lay chicken on top of rice. Cover with foil. Bake 1½ hours at 325 degrees.

Patty Shepard, South Parkway

CHICKEN ORIENTAL

⅔ cup water
2 tsp. cornstarch
4 chicken breasts, skinned, boned
4 T. oil
2 pkgs. Japanese-style vegetables
4 T. salted peanuts
2 T. soy sauce
1 tsp. ginger

Combine water and cornstarch; set aside. Cut chicken in strips. Saute chicken in oil until it turns white, about 5 minutes. Add vegetables, peanuts, soy sauce, ginger, and cornstarch mixture. Bring to a boil, separating vegetables with a fork and stirring constantly. Reduce heat, cover pan, and simmer for 6 to 8 minutes. Serve with rice. Serves 6.

Adele Arcangeli, Westbury

CHICKEN PARMESAN

1 cup commercial seasoned bread crumbs
¾ cup Parmesan cheese
¼ cup parsley, chopped
⅛ tsp. garlic powder or 1 garlic clove
4 chicken breasts
Butter

Put first 4 ingredients in plastic bag. Shake well. Take chicken breasts and dip in melted butter, then roll in crumb mixture. Put in casserole dish. Bake in oven at 350 degrees until golden brown.

Regna Howard, Madison Cross Roads

CHICKEN OR TURKEY PIE

½ cup cold broth, from stewed chicken
⅓ cup all-purpose flour
1½ cups concentrated chicken broth, hot
2½ cups stewed chicken, boned, cut in large pieces
1 can English peas, drained
¾ cup celery, diced
1 sm. onion
1 sm. diced potato
1 tsp. salt
1 cup all-purpose flour
1½ tsp. baking powder
¼ tsp. salt
3 T. butter
½ cup milk

Make a paste by blending cold chicken stock with ⅓ cup flour. Add paste to hot chicken chicken stock and cook over direct heat stirring constantly until sauce boils and thickens. Cut chicken into large pieces and combine with peas, celery, onions, potato, and 1 teaspoon salt. Pour in 9x13-inch buttered pan. COMBINE 1 cup flour with baking powder and ¼ teaspoon salt. Cut in butter with pastry blender or 2 knives, add milk *all at once*, stirring quickly with a fork until dough just stiffens. Turn dough out onto floured board, knead 8 times and roll or pat out to fit the top of the casserole. Make several slits, for a design near the center to allow the steam to escape, then place on top of the hot filling in the casserole. Bake in moderate oven (425 degrees) for about 20 minutes or until nicely browned and the filling is boiling-hot all the way through. Serves 5.

Mrs. Edith T. Dobbs, Hurricane

CHICKEN PIE

½ cup margarine
½ cup all-purpose flour
1½ tsp. salt
¼ tsp. paprika

3 cups chicken broth
4 cups chicken, cooked, cut up
Pastry to cover
2 or 3 hard-boiled eggs, chopped

Melt margarine in 2-quart pan. Stir in flour, salt, and paprika until smooth. Add chicken broth. Boil, stirring constantly. Remove from heat. Place chicken and eggs in baking dish; pour thickened broth and mix well. Cover with pastry. Bake at 400 degrees for 30 to 35 minutes.

Laura Betterton, Madison Cross Roads

CHICKEN PRONTO

4 chicken breast halves, boneless
¼ cup bottled Italian dressing

⅓ cup Italian-seasoned dry bread crumbs

Dip chicken breast halves (4 ounces each) in Italian dressing. Then in bread crumbs. Cover and bake at 450 degrees for 15 minutes. Uncover; bake 10 minutes more.

Sandy Hughey, New Sharon

CHICKEN SALTIMBOCCA

3 large boneless chicken breasts
6 thin slices boiled ham
3 slices mozzarella cheese, halved
1 med. tomato, seeded, chopped
1 pkg. spaghetti sauce seasonings (dry)
2 T. Parmesan cheese, grated
4 T. margarine or butter, melted
bread crumbs

Remove skin and bones from chicken breasts and halve lengthwise. Place chicken, boned side up, on cutting board. Place plastic wrap over it. Working from the center out, pound lightly with meat mallet to 5-by-5 inches. Remove wrap. Place a ham slice and a half slice of cheese on each cutlet, trimming to fit. Top with some tomato and a dash of spaghetti seasoning. Tuck in sides. Roll up jelly-roll style, pressing to seal. Combine bread crumbs and Parmesan cheese. Dip chicken in butter then roll in crumbs. Place in shallow baking pan. Bake in 350-degree oven for 40 to 45 minutes. Serves 6.

Norma Watts, South Huntsville

CHICKEN SAUTERNE

1 broiler or 6 chicken breasts
Flour
Salt and pepper
1 stick margarine
1 can cream of chicken soup
¾ cup cooking sauterne
1 5-oz. can water chestnuts, drained, sliced
1 3-oz. can mushrooms, undrained
2 T. green pepper

Dredge chicken pieces in flour, salt, and pepper. Saute, until brown, in margarine and remove to a baking dish. Add the remaining ingredients to the margarine and pour over chicken. Cover with foil and bake 25 minutes in 350-degree oven. Remove foil and cook 20 to 25 minutes longer. I usually serve with very fluffy mashed potatoes. You can also use regular wine, and it gives a stronger flavor.

Mrs. Frank J. Nola (Grace), Westbury

CHICKEN SPAGHETTI

1 lg. hen (4-5 lb.)
2 cups onion
2 cups celery
1 pepper, chopped
2 garlic cloves
3 cups stock
1 1-lb. can tomatoes or tomato sauce
Salt and pepper
1 pkg. spaghetti
Cheese, grated

Boil hen until tender; remove bones. Cut up onion, celery, pepper, and garlic in stock and boil until tender. Add tomatoes or sauce. Salt and pepper to taste. Cook spaghetti in salted water. In a 9x13x2-inch casserole dish put alternate layers of chicken, sauce, and spaghetti. Save enough sauce to pour over top. Bake at medium heat until bubbles. Add favorite grated cheese the last few minutes of baking time. This is good made a day early and refrigerated.

Joan Jackson, Piedmont

CHICKEN SUPREME

4 cup cooked chicken breasts, diced
2 cups half-and-half milk
6 T. butter
6 T. flour
1½ tsp. salt
⅛ tsp. white pepper
3 cups milk
6 egg yolks
2 T. onion, chopped
4 T. Parmesan cheese
10 baked pastry shells (Pepperidge Farm)

Simmer chicken in half-and-half until milk is reduced to about half. Melt butter and blend in flour and seasonings. Gradually add milk and cook, stirring, until thickened. Add about 1 cup of this sauce to chicken mixture and stir in 2 egg yolks and the onion. Beat a little of the sauce into remaining egg yolks. Put back in saucepan with remaining sauce and cook for a few minutes longer. Stir in 2 tablespoons of the cheese. Pour chicken mixture into shallow broiler-proof dish, cover with sauce, and top with remaining cheese. Brown under broiler. Serve over baked pastry shells. Delicious luncheon dish for ladies.

Margaret Mann, Owens Cross Roads

CHICKEN WITH CASHEWS

½ chicken
½ T. cornstarch
½ tsp. sugar
1 tsp. salt
2 T. soy sauce
Cooking oil
3-4 mushrooms (optional)
1 cup nuts

Clean and dice chicken (1-inch-square pieces). Mix cornstarch, sugar, salt, and soy sauce. Put 4 tablespoons oil in shallow frying pan and pour in chicken when the oil is hot. Stir constantly for about one minute. Pour soy sauce mixture on top of chicken. Add mushrooms and cook 5 minutes. Remove from fire. Add nuts and serve.

Carolyn Griner, Rainbow Mountain

CHICKEN WITH DRIED BEEF

6 chicken breasts, boned
¾ lb. dried chipped beef

6 strips lean bacon
1 can cream of chicken soup

In bottom of a shallow casserole arrange dried beef. Wrap a strip of bacon around each chicken breast; arrange over beef. Spread undiluted soup over chicken, cover with aluminum foil and bake in 300-degree oven for 2 hours. Increase heat to 350 degrees and bake for another 20 to 30 minutes, basting several times. Serves 6.

Gaynell Geiger, Blossomwood

CHICKEN WITH RICE

1 can cream of chicken soup
½ cup water
1 chicken, cut-up, fryer or parts

Salt and pepper
Paprika
1 sm. box Minute Rice
1 can cream of mushroom soup

Put chicken soup and water in a large casserole. Add chicken and seasonings. Sprinkle with rice, Top with mushroom soup. Cover tightly and bake 1 hour at 375 degrees. Do not open oven while baking.

Ilu Wilkinson, Central

CHINESE CHICKEN

4 chicken breasts, boneless
¼ cup margarine
1 cup water chestnuts, sliced
1 cup bamboo shoots
½ cup celery, diced
1 reg. can green beans

3 cups canned chicken broth
¼ cup soy sauce
½ tsp. salt (or to taste)
1 tsp. sugar
Pepper to taste
2 T. cornstarch

Slice chicken in short strips. Saute in margarine in deep pan. Add water chestnuts, bamboo shoots, celery, and green beans. Pour chicken broth over mixture. Add soy sauce and seasonings. Cover and simmer 15 minutes. Blend 2 tablespoons cornstarch with small amount of water. Add to chicken and cook until broth is thick. Serve over cooked rice and with Chinese noodles.

Margaret Strickland, Westbury

CHOPPED CHICKEN CASSEROLE

2 cups chicken, chopped
4 hard-boiled eggs, chopped
2 cups celery, cut
2 cups frozen peas
1 cup cream

1 cup mayonnaise
½ cup onion, chopped
1 cup Cheddar cheese, grated
½ cup toasted slivered almonds
   or pecans, chopped

1 cup potato chips, crushed

Mix all ingredients well. Sprinkle chips over top. Bake at 450 degrees for 15 minutes (Use 2-quart casserole or baking dish). Serves 8. Can be mixed the day before, adding potato chips to top when ready to bake.

Mrs. L. L. Tuck (Harriet), Madison County

CORNISH HENS

8 Cornish game hens
1½ tsp. salt
1⅓ cups mushroom pieces, drained
½ cup chopped onion
¼ cup chopped bell pepper

¾ cup margarine
3 cups cooked long grain and
   wild rice, mixed
¼ tsp. pepper
Butter

Heat oven to 325 degrees. Sprinkle insides of hens with salt. Saute mushrooms, onions, and pepper in margarine in large saucepan. Add rice, salt, and pepper. Stuff hens. Rub outside of birds with butter and wrap in foil. Cook for 1½ hours covered, then open up foil and cook for 30 minutes longer.

Dorothy Mellette, Central

DOUBLE CHICKEN TETRAZZINI

1 can cream of mushroom soup
1 can cream of chicken soup
1 cup chicken broth
2 cups Cheddar cheese, shredded
4 cups chicken, diced (or 2
   16-oz. cans of boned chicken)

1 12-oz. pkg. spaghetti, cooked,
   drained
1 4-oz. can mushrooms, sliced
½ cup Parmesan cheese
Paprika

Combine undiluted soups and broth; stir in Cheddar cheese, chicken, spaghetti, and mushrooms. Mix well. Pour into greased 9x13-inch baking dish. Sprinkle with Parmesan cheese and paprika. Bake at 350 degrees for 25 to 30 minutes or until bubbly.

Gina Guess, Hazel Green

EASY BROCCOLI AND CHICKEN CASSEROLE

2 cups Minute Rice (cooked in chicken broth)
1 pkg. frozen broccoli
2 cups cooked chicken, diced
1½ cups cheese sauce
Cracker crumbs
Almonds

Place in baking dish in this order: rice, broccoli, and chicken; cover with cheese sauce. Cook about 30 minutes in 350-degree oven. Remove from oven; cover with cracker crumbs (buttered) and almonds. Brown in oven at about 250 degrees for 15 minutes.

Mrs. D. T. Thomas (Mary Lee), Monrovia

EASY CANN HAWAIIAN CHICKEN BREASTS

18 chicken breasts, skinned, boned
½ cup butter or margarine
2 cans cream of mushroom soup
1 can cream of chicken soup
1¼ cups milk
¼ cup cooking sherry
2 chicken bouillon cubes
1 No. 2 can crushed pineapple, drained well
4 ozs. Macadamia nuts, chopped

Brown chicken breasts in butter, slowly. As each piece is browned, place in a single layer in an oven proof casserole. When all chicken is browned, drain excess butter from pan and return to medium heat. Add soups, milk, sherry, and bouillon cubes to pan. Scrape up all brown bits from bottom of pan. Mix soup mixture until smooth and hot; pour over chicken in casserole. Spread pineapple and nuts over mixture. Cover tightly with lid or foil. Bake at 275 degrees for about 3 hours or at 350 degrees for 45 minutes. Serves 8 to 10.

Dyral Eaton, Piedmont

FANTASTIC CHICKEN

1 8-oz. jar apricot preserves
1 pkg. dry onion soup
1 bottle of any thick red salad dressing
2 broiler chickens, quartered

Mix together sauce ingredients. Spread chicken pieces in baking pan: spoon sauce over chicken. Bake at 350 degrees for 1½ hours. Serves 8.

Mrs. Jo Ann Daniels, Heritage
Dorothy Gillespie, Fleming Hills

FRIED CHICKEN

1½ cups buttermilk
1½ tsp. savory
1 tsp. black pepper
2 1½-lb. broiler-fryer chickens
¾ cup flour

1½ tsp. salt
¼ tsp. black pepper
1 tsp. Accent
1½ tsp. paprika
Shortening (use part butter)

Mix buttermilk, savory, and 1 tsp. pepper together in large, shallow dish. Add chicken pieces. Cover and set aside in a cool place to marinate 1 hour, turning the chicken pieces occasionally. Remove chicken from marinade. Coat with a mixture of the flour and next four ingredients, and put on wax paper; allow to stand about 30 minutes. Fill a large heavy skillet half full with fat. Heat slowly to 360 degrees. Put only a few chicken pieces at one time into heated fat. Fry chicken 10 to 13 minutes or until tender and brown; turn pieces with tongs several times during cooking. Drain on paper towel.

Sue Carter, Hazel Green

JELLIED CHICKEN ALMOND

1 T. unflavored gelatin
¼ cup cold water
1 cup mayonnaise
1 cup heavy cream, whipped

½ tsp. salt
1½ cups cooked chicken, diced
¾ cup almonds, blanched, chopped

¾ cup green seedless grapes, halved

Soften gelatin in cold water; dissolve over hot water. Cool slightly; then combine with mayonnaise, whipped cream, and salt. Fold in diced chicken, blanched almonds, and grapes. Spoon into 6 or 8 individual salad molds. Chill until firm. Unmold on lettuce leaves. Garnish with sliced stuffed olives and mayonnaise. Serves 6 to 8.

Nell Long, Big Cove

MOTHER HEN PIE

1 3½-lb. chicken
Pastry for single crust
3 T. butter
3 T. flour
1 cup evap. milk, undiluted
1 cup chicken stock
½ cup almonds, blanched, sliced, or coarsely chopped
1 4-oz. can mushrooms

Cook chicken until tender in salted water. Take the skin and bones out. Cut up into pie crust. Make cream sauce from butter, flour, and evaporated milk. Add remaining ingredients. Bake at 350 degrees at 30 minutes until brown. Serves 6 to 7.

Estelle Pinion, Central

TERESA'S CHICKEN IN SOUR CREAM SAUCE

Salt
Flour
1 2-2½-lb. fryer, cut up
Butter
8 ozs. sour cream
4-oz. can mushrooms, stems and pieces
1 can cream of mushroom soup, undiluted
1 T. lemon juice
1 T. water

Salt and flour chicken, place in buttered baking dish (1 layer). Mix rest of ingredients and pour over chicken. Bake at 325 degrees for 1 hour and 15 minutes, until chicken is tender, basting several times. Sauce will be thick. Serves 4 to 6.

Opaline West, Madison Cross Roads

TURKEY

TURKEY CURRY

2 T. butter or margarine
⅓ cup onion, finely chopped
1 - 2 T. curry powder
1 can condensed cream of chicken soup
Cooked turkey (about 2 cups), diced
1 T. lemon juice
1 cup packaged rice, precooked

Melt butter, add onion, and cook until tender. Stir in curry powder and heat a few seconds. Add ⅔ cup water and the soup and heat, stirring. Add turkey and heat. Add lemon juice. Serve on cooked rice. Serves 4.

Mrs. Lyle Needham, South Huntsville

HOT TURKEY SALAD SOUFFLE

6 slices bread	½ cup mayonnaise
2 cups diced cooked turkey	Salt and pepper to taste
½ cup chopped onion	2 eggs
1 cup chopped green pepper	1½ cups milk
½ cup chopped celery	1 can mushroom soup
¼ cup pimiento	½ cup grated Cheddar cheese

Cube 2 slices of bread and place on bottom of greased casserole dish. Combine turkey, vegetables, mayonnaise, salt, and pepper; spread over cubed bread. Trim crust from remaining 4 slices of bread and place on top of turkey mixture. Combine eggs and milk and pour over casserole. Cover and chill overnight. When ready to bake, spoon undiluted soup over the top. Bake at 325 degrees for 1 hour. Sprinkle cheese over top the last few minutes. Serves 6 to 8.

Margie Brooks, Vestavia

GAME

DOVE OR QUAIL

Prepare 2 birds per person. Soak birds in milk, then salt and pepper them. Shake with flour. Fry as you would chicken. Remove birds and drain off grease. Make gravy with flour and water. Place on rack in broiler pan and steam for one hour, no longer. Serve with gravy while hot.

Marie Buist, Westbury

ROAST WILD DUCK

1 duck	1 carrot
Salt	1 onion
Pepper	2 ribs celery
1 apple	1 No. 2 can pineapple juice
	1 cup red wine

Clean duck inside and out; salt and pepper inside. Stuff with fruit and vegetables. Place in roaster, adding juice and wine. Cover and bake for 3 hours or more at 300 degrees. Serves 2.

Elaine Story, Pulaski Pike

VENISON ROAST

1 roast
Butter
Onion or garlic
¼ - ½ cup port wine or wine vinegar

1 cup olive oil
⅓ cup vinegar (exclude if using wine vinegar)
⅓ cup lemon juice
Salt
Pepper

Rub roast with butter and onion or garlic. Combine remainder of ingredients and marinate meat in it for 8 hours in the refrigerator. Take roast out of marinade and bake covered for 25 to 30 minutes per pound at 300 to 325 degrees. You may use wine to make gravy instead of in marinade if you prefer.

Mrs. Hugh Tipton (Bessie), Monrovia

VENISON SWISS STEAK

¼ cup flour
¾ tsp. salt
⅛ tsp. cayenne pepper
⅛ tsp. thyme
⅛ tsp. nutmeg
⅛ tsp. clove
2 lbs. steak meat
¼ cup oil

2 lg. onions, thinly sliced
2 cups tomatoes or tomato juice
1½ T. Worcestershire sauce
1 cup red wine
1 garlic clove, crushed
⅓ cup chopped carrots
⅓ cup green peppers
⅓ cup celery

1 4-oz. can mushroom pieces

Mix flour, salt, pepper, thyme, nutmeg, and cloves. Cut meat into serving sizes and pound mixture into meat with mallet. Brown meat on both sides in oil, add onions, and let cook for about 3 minutes. Add remaining ingredients. Cover and cook in oven for about 2½ hours at 350 degrees. Serves 6.

Mrs. Hugh Tipton (Bessie), Monrovia

SALADS AND SALAD DRESSINGS

CONGEALED SALADS

APPLE SALAD

1 lg. pkg. cream cheese
2 pkgs. lemon Jello

½ cup chopped nuts
1 or 2 apples, unpeeled, chopped

Soften cream cheese with Jello. Mix ingredients together as listed.

Ursula Bumpus, Central

APRICOT JELLO SALAD

2 No. 2 cans crushed pineapple
½ cup sugar
1 lg. pkg. cream cheese (8 ozs.)
1 lg. box apricot Jello

1 cup diced celery
1 cup nuts
2 pkgs. Dream Whip (not Cool Whip)

Bring pineapple and sugar to a boil. Bring cream cheese to room temperature and beat with some hot pineapple-sugar juice. Add dry apricot Jello and cool. Mix in celery and nuts. Beat Dream Whip and fold into mixture. Refrigerate till set.

Ruth Gump, Monrovia

APRICOT SALAD

1 lg. box orange Jello
1 cup boiling water
1 can apricot halves and juice

½ sm. can frozen orange juice, undiluted
1 lg. pkg. cream cheese

Combine the box of Jello and 1 cup boiling water. In the blender mix apricot halves and juice, orange juice, and cream cheese. Mix the blender mixture with Jello. Fills 12 individual molds.

Emogene Ross, Blossomwood

BUTTERMILK SALAD

6 ozs. orange Jello
1 16-oz. can crushed pineapple

2 cups buttermilk
1 9-oz. carton Cool Whip

Combine orange Jello with crushed pineapple. Boil 1 minute. Let cool until it thickens. Stir in buttermilk. Let thicken again. Stir in 9-oz. carton of Cool Whip. May substitute strawberry for orange Jello.

Nora Drake, Big Cove
Lorene P. Butler, Poplar Ridge

CHERRY CONGEALED SALAD

2 sm. pkgs. cherry Jello
1¾ cups water
1 No. 2 can crushed pineapple, undrained

1 can cherry pie filling
2 3-oz. pkgs cream cheese, softened
Milk
Pecans

Dissolve Jello in water, add pineapple, and cherry pie filling. Pour half in dish and refrigerate until set. Soften cream cheese with a little milk until it can be spread over congealed salad. Press pecans into cream cheese; pour remainder of cherry mix over it and return to refrigerator.

Peggy Barber, Fleming Hills

When a person turns loose and drifts with the current, he soon gets into deep water.

CHERRY SALAD SUPREME

1 3-oz. pkg. raspberry Jello
2 cups boiling water
1 21-oz. can cherry pie filling
1 3-oz. pkg. lemon Jello
1 3-oz. pkg. cream cheese

⅓ cup mayonnaise
1 8¾-oz. can crushed pineapple
½ cup whipping cream, whipped
1 cup miniature marshmallows
2 T. chopped nuts

Dissolve raspberry Jello in 1 cup boiling water; stir in pie filling. Turn into 9x9x2-inch baking dish; chill until partially set. Dissolve lemon Jello in 1 cup boiling water. Beat cheese and mayonnaise together. Add lemon Jello gradually. Stir in pineapple. Fold cream and marshmallows into lemon mixture. Spread over cherry layer; top with nuts. Chill until firm. Serves 12.

Carol Hix, Westbury

COCA-COLA SALAD

1 2½-oz. can black cherries
1 sm. can sliced pineapple
Water
2 pkgs. cherry Jello

2 whole sm. Coca-Colas
1 sm. pkg. cream cheese
1 can nuts
2 bananas

Drain juice from cherries and pineapple; add enough water to juice to make 2 cups. Heat juice and water and dissolve Jello with it while hot. Add Coca-Cola and congeal until thickened. Then add rest of ingredients.

Josie Davis, New Sharon

COOL GELATIN SALAD

1 pkg. lemon gelatin
1 pkg. lime gelatin
1 cup boiling water
1 pt. lg.curd cottage cheese

1 14-oz. can sweetened
   condensed milk
1 13 to 15-oz. can crushed
   pineapple in syrup
1 cup mayonnaise

Empty gelatins into large mixing bowl. Pour in boiling water. Stir until dissolved. Pour in other ingredients, mix, and refrigerate.

Dean Hill, University

CRANBERRY SALAD I

1 qt. cranberries, ground
2 cups sugar
1 pkg. strawberry Jello
1 cup boiling water
1 env. Knox unflavored gelatin

¼ cup water
Rind of 1 orange, grated
Juice of 1 orange or 1 lemon
½ cup miniature marshmallows
1 cup nuts

1 lg. can crushed pineapple

Cover cranberries with sugar and let stand overnight in refrigerator. Dissolve strawberry Jello with boiling water; add unflavored gelatin, dissolved in ¼ cup water, to the mixture. Add orange rind and orange or lemon juice. Combine Jello mixture with cranberries, then add miniature marshmallows, nuts, and crushed pineapple. Mix well and pour in large mold or individual molds.

Faye C. Gwin, Madison Cross Roads

CRANBERRY SALAD II

1 3-oz. pkg. cherry Jello
1 env. plain gelatin
1 cup hot water
½ cup finely chopped celery
½ cup chopped nuts
1 can whole cranberry sauce, drained
1 cup sour cream

Dissolve Jello and gelatin in hot water. Chill until slightly thickened. Break cranberries with a fork; stir into Jello with celery and nuts. Fold in sour cream. Pour into mold and chill until firm.

Mrs. W. L. Vaughn, Sr. (Frances), Monrovia

CUCUMBER SALAD SUPREME

1 3-oz. pkg. lime gelatin
¾ cup boiling water
1 med. cucumber, unpeeled, minced
1 med. onion, chopped
1 cup nuts, coarsely chopped
1 cup sm. curd cottage cheese
2 T. lemon juice
1 cup salad dressing

Mix gelatin and boiling water. Let stand until syrupy. Mix other ingredients in order given. Add to gelatin and pour into mold. Chill overnight. Serves 8.

Doris Smith, Davis Hills

DRY JELLO SALAD

9 ozs. Cool Whip
12 ozs. cottage cheese
1 flat can crushed pineapple
1 pkg. Jello, any flavor

Mix Cool Whip and cottage cheese. Add well-drained pineapple. Stir in dry Jello. Refrigerate. This makes a delicious salad and will keep for several days.

Peggy S. Wallace, Poplar Ridge

FRESCA SALAD

1 can applesauce
2 sm. pkgs. apricot Jello
1 lg. can crushed pineapple
Dash of salt
1 12-oz. can Fresca

Heat applesauce. Add Jello and dissolve. Add pineapple—juice and all. Then add dash of salt and Fresca. Cool and pour into mold. Makes about 15 individual molds. For dressing: Add Durkee's Famous Dressing to sour cream until it suits your taste.

Evelyn Hall, Athens Pike

FROZEN LIME MINT SALAD

1 8¼-oz. can crushed pineapple
1 20-oz. can crushed pineapple
1 3-oz. pkg. lime-flavored gelatin
1 6½-oz. pkg. tiny marshmallows
1 cup buttermints, crushed
1 9-oz. carton frozen whipped dessert topping, thawed

In large bowl, combine both cans *undrained* pineapple, *dry* lime gelatin, marshmallows, and mints. Cover and refrigerate for several hours or until marshmallows begin to melt. Fold in dessert topping. Spoon mixture into 16 paper-lined muffin pans. Cover and freeze overnight. Peel paper off and serve on lettuce-lined platter. Garnish with fresh mint sprigs.

Norma Watts, South Huntsville

FRUIT FLUFF SALAD

1 3-oz. pkg. lemon or orange gelatin (diet type may be used)
½ cup hot water
½ cup orange juice
2 T. lemon juice
¼ tsp. salt
¼ cup chopped nuts
¼ cup crushed pineapple, drained
¼ cup orange segments
2 T. chopped maraschino cherries
¼ cup grape halves
1 cup whipped cream

Dissolve gelatin in hot water. Add fruit juices and salt. Cool. Chill until partially set. Whip with rotary beater until fluffy and light. Fold in fruit, nuts, and cream. Pour into 1-quart mold. Chill until firm. Serves 8.

Ruth W. Chambers, Darwin Downs

ICE CREAM JELLO SALAD

1 pkg. Jello
1 cup hot water
1 qt. vanilla ice cream
1 can crushed pineapple
1 banana
½ cup nuts

Mix; set in refrigerator until firm.

Mrs. D. T. Thomas (Mary Lee), Monrovia

JELLO SALAD

2 boxes cherry Jello
1 sm. jar red cherries, reserve juice
2 cups water, including cherry juice
1 cup Hellman's mayonnaise

2 sm. pkgs. Philadelphia cream cheese
1 sm. can crushed pineapple
1 cup nuts
1 box Dream Whip, not Cool Whip

Mix Jello and water and let set until appears as thick as an egg white. Beat mayonnaise and cream cheese together and fold into Jello mixture when it thickens but is not set. Then fold in pineapple, juice and all, and cut-up cherries, and nuts. Add Dream Whip.

Ruth Gump, Monrovia

JELLO WITH TOPPING

2 3-oz. boxes apricot Jello (or 1 6-oz. box)
2 cups hot water
1½ cups cold water

2 bananas, sliced
1 20-oz. can crushed pineapple, drained, reserving liquid
2 cups miniature marshmallows

Mix Jello with hot water until dissolved. Add the 1½ cups cold water, chill in refrigerator until slightly thickened (about 45 minutes). Add sliced bananas, crushed pineapple, and marshmallows. Let gel in refrigerator.

Topping

¾ cup sugar
1 egg
2 T. flour
1 cup pineapple juice (from crushed pineapple)

1 8-oz. pkg. cream cheese, softened
1 4-oz. pkg. Cool Whip, softened
Coconut for top (frozen or canned)

Cook sugar, flour, egg, and pineapple juice until thick, stirring constantly; remove from heat. Add cream cheese and Cool Whip. Stir until blended or put in blender. Spread on top of gelatin and sprinkle with coconut on top. Return to refrigerator.

Maude Taylor, Central

MOLDED CRANBERRY, ORANGE, AND PINEAPPLE SALAD

2 pkgs. red Jello
1 cup boiling water
1½ cup cold water
1 orange
1 1-lb. can pineapple chunks
1 1-lb. can whole cranberry sauce, slightly beaten
1 cup nuts

Mix Jello; peel orange and cut segments in half. Cut pineapple chunks in thirds; mix fruits and nuts into Jello and pour into a large mold; chill. Serve with sour cream.

Mrs. D. T. Thomas (Mary Lee), Monrovia

1-2-3-4 CONGEALED SALAD

1 3-oz. box lemon Jello
½ cup water
½ cup pineapple juice
1 T. Knox gelatin
1 cup grated American cheese
1 sm. can Carnation milk
½ cup mayonnaise
1 15-oz. can crushed pineapple
½ cup nuts (optional)

Heat liquid; add Jello and dissolved gelatin. Let cool and add cheese, mayonnaise, milk, pineapple, and nuts. Pour in a round mold and refrigerate until congealed. Turn on lettuce leaves and sprinkle paprika on top.

Doris Moore, Madison Cross Roads

ORANGE JELLO SALAD

1 sm. pkg. orange Jello
2 cups hot water
1 sm. can crushed pineapple
1 pkg. miniature marshmallows
1 cup heavy whipping cream
1 T. mayonnaise
Cheese, grated

In an oblong Pyrex dish mix the Jello and 2 cups hot water. Add pineapple and marshmallows. Stir until marshmallows melt. Cool; whip cream and blend with mayonnaise. Spread over cool Jello mixture. Sprinkle with grated cheese.

Mrs. Tom Baker, Hurricane

PEAR SALAD

1 lg. can pears
1 med. can pears
⅓ cup sugar
3 T. lemon juice
Pinch of salt
2 pkgs. gelatin, unflavored
½ cup cold water

Cup up pears. Drain juice and combine 2½ cups of juice with sugar, lemon juice, and salt. Heat until hot, not boiling. Add unflavored gelatin that has been soaked 5 minutes in cold water. Mix well; let cool. Then pour over cut-up pears in long Pyrex dish. Let congeal.

Dressing

½ stick butter
1 T. sugar
8 lg. marshmallows
1 pkg. Dream Whip

Melt butter and add other ingredients. Cook in top of double boiler. Let cook until marshmallows melt and mixture has thickened. Cool. Beat Dream Whip and fold it into dressing. Spread over congealed salad. You can sprinkle top with grated cheese if desired. Keep in refrigerator.

Bonnie Holliman, Piedmont

PINEAPPLE CHEDDAR SALAD

1 3-oz. pkg. lemon gelatin
1 cup boiling water
1 8¼-oz. can crushed pineapple, undrained
¾ cup sugar
1 cup whipping cream, whipped
1 cup shredded mild Cheddar cheese
½ cup chopped pecans

Dissolve gelatin in boiling water. Stir in pineapple and sugar; cool. Fold in remaining ingredients. Spoon into a 9-inch square pan. Chill until formed. Cut into squares to serve. Serves 9.

Dorothy Moore, New Sharon

Hope is like the sun which, as we journey toward it, casts the shadow of burden behind us.

PINEAPPLE CRANBERRY SQUARES

2 3-oz. pkg. raspberry gelatin
1¼ cup boiling water
1 1-lb. 4-oz. can crushed pineapple, undrained
1 lb. can whole cranberry sauce
¾ cup port wine
1 cup chopped pecans
1 8-oz. pkg. cream cheese
1 cup sour cream
Crisp salad greens

Dissolve gelatin in boiling water. Stir in undrained pineapple, cranberry sauce, and wine. Chill until mixture thickens slightly. Fold in pecans and turn into a 9x9x2-inch square pan. Chill until firm. When gelatin is set, soften cream cheese and gradually beat in sour cream until mixture is smooth. Spread over gelatin; chill. When ready to serve, cut into squares and arrange on crisp salad greens. Serves 9.

Mrs. L. M. Taylor, Big Cove

PRETZEL SALAD

2 cups broken thin pretzels
¾ cup melted butter
1 T. sugar
1 6-oz. pkg. strawberry Jello
2 cups boiling water
2 10-oz. pkgs. frozen strawberries
8 oz. cream cheese, softened
1 cup sugar
½ lg. carton Cool Whip

Mix together pretzels, butter, and 1 tablespoon sugar and press in 9x13-inch greased baking dish. Bake at 400 degrees for 8 minutes; let cool completely. Mix Jello, water, and strawberries and refrigerate until thick. Cream together cream cheese and sugar; add Cool Whip, spread over pretzel crust. Pour Jello mixture over second layer and return to refrigerator; let stand overnight.

Sue Carter, Hazel Green
Doris Coward, Harvest

SEA FOAM SALAD

1 pkg. lime jello
1 cup boiling water
1 sm. pkg. cream cheese
3 T. mayonnaise
1 sm. can crushed pineapple
½ cup (sliced or chopped) pecans
1 pkg. miniature marshmallows

Mix Jello and water and let cool. Cream cream cheese and mayonnaise together and mix with Jello mixture and remaining ingredients. Place in mold and chill until firm.

Lottie Power, Harvest

SPARKLING BEETCUPS

1 3-oz. pkg. lemon Jello
1¼ cup water
¾ cup beet juice
1 lb. beets, diced (2 cups)
2 T. vinegar

1 tsp. Worcestershire sauce
1 tsp. horseradish
½ tsp. salt
½ cup chopped celery
1 tsp. grated onion

4 drops Tabasco sauce

Make Jello according to directions, except substitute ¾ cup beet juice for water. Mix in remaining ingredients and gel in cups.

Marie Stramiello, Darwin Downs

SPICED PEACH SALAD

1 1-lb. 13-oz. can spiced peaches
1 6-oz. pkg. lemon Jello

1½ cup orange juice
1 cup chopped pecans

Drain spiced peaches; add enough water to the syrup to make 2 cups. Heat syrup and dissolve Jello in it. Add orange juice; cool until it begins to thicken; add cut-up peaches and nuts. Put into greased molds. Serves 10 to 12.

Laura Mae Wilbourn, Hurricane

STRAWBERRY JELLO SALAD

1 6-oz. box strawberry Jello
1 cup boiling water
1 8-oz. can crushed pineapple

½ cup chopped pecans
1 or 2 10-oz. pkgs. frozen
  strawberries

1 pt. sour cream

Dissolve Jello in hot water. Add whole can of crushed pineapple (juice and all), pecans, and strawberries; stir. Place half of mixture into mold and let congeal. Spread sour cream then other half of mixture on top.

Angie Pamfiles, Westbury
Mrs. L. M. Taylor, Big Cove

VIOLA MARSHMALLOW DELIGHT SALAD

1 box of lime Jello
1 cup boiling water
12 big marshmallows or use miniatures
1 cup grated American cheese
1 cup chopped pecans
1 sm. can crushed pineapple
1 cup Cool Whip or 1 sm. can of evap. milk

Pour boiling water over Jello and mix. Add marshmallows and cheese immediately and stir until all is dissolved; let cool. Add: pecans and pineapple. After it sets stir in Cool Whip or whipped evaporated milk. To use evaporated milk, freeze it around the edges, then beat until fluffy. Pour into a mold.

Margaret Birchfield, Central

YUM YUM SALAD

2 cups boiling water
1 6-oz. pkg. gelatin, any flavor
16 marshmallows
2 cups cold water
1 No. 2 can fruit, pineapple, or fruit cocktail
1 lg. pkg. cream cheese
1 cup nuts

In saucepan bring 2 cups water to a boil; add gelatin. Stir until dissolved. Add marshmallows, lower heat, and stir until melted. Add 1 cup drained fruit juice with cold water to make 2 cups. In bowl mix cheese and fruit with a fork. Add to pot on stove. Mix until cheese is melted. Add nuts. Makes a large salad.

Ethel Huse, Davis Hills

LETTUCE, SLAW, AND KRAUT SALADS

CABBAGE SLAW

3 lbs. cabbage, shredded
1 sm. onion, finely chopped
1 bell pepper, finely chopped
1 tsp. dry mustard
1 tsp. celery seed
2 tsp. salt
1 cup sugar
½ cup oil
1 cup vinegar

Combine cabbage, onion, and bell pepper in a gallon jar or a large bowl. Combine remaining ingredients and heat to boiling—but do not boil. Pour over chopped vegetables and let stand in refrigerator at least overnight. Tastes better on third or fourth day. Keeps about 10 days.

Betty Cothran, Athens Pike

CHINESE SLAW

1 17-oz. can Leseur peas
1 can Chinese vegetables
1 cup green olives
1 cup chopped celery
1 16-17-oz. can French green beans
1 cup water chestnuts
1 chopped red onion
1 cup vinegar
1 cup sugar

Drain vegetables. Boil vinegar and sugar and pour over vegetables. Cover and let stand overnight. Can be made ahead 2 or 3 days.

Mrs. Herschel Moore (Judy), Heritage

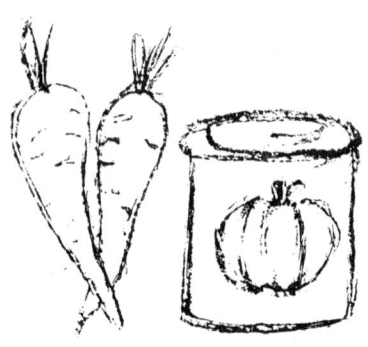

COLE SLAW

2 cups shredded cabbage
1 cup grated carrots
½ green bell pepper
⅓ cup mayonnaise
2 T. sugar
1 T. salt
½ tsp. celery seed
2 tsp. lemon juice or vinegar

In large bowl combine cabbage, carrots, and pepper. Blend mayonnaise, sugar, salt, celery seed, and lemon juice. Pour over cabbage, mix, chill, and serve.

Rachel Sturdivant, University

DAINTY WINTER SALAD
(Cabbage Salad)

Cabbage
1 tsp. salt
Pepper

Mint Sauce (see below)
6 T. olive oil
2 T. tarragon

Shave the cabbage on a slaw cutter in a pan of cold water; let it soak 1 hour then press it dry. Heap in a salad bowl; at serving time at the table dust it first with salt and a little pepper; sprinkle a little Mint Sauce over it and olive oil. With a fork and spoon toss thoroughly until every part of the cabbage is covered with seasoning and oil. Put tarragon over it; mix thoroughly and serve.

Mint Sauce

1½ T. powdered sugar
3 T. hot water

⅓ cup finely minced mint leaves
½ cup very mild wine vinegar

Dissolve sugar in water; let cool. Blend in remaining ingredients; let set ½ hour before using. Yield: 1 cup.

Mrs. Allen Drake (Wilma), Monrovia

KRAUT SALAD

1 lg. can kraut, drained
5 green onions, chopped
1 green pepper, chopped
3 stalks celery, sliced thin

½ cup pimiento, chopped
¼ cup vinegar
1 cup sugar
½ cup oil

Combine all ingredients and refrigerate overnight. Keeps well for weeks in refrigerator.

Elizabeth Nixon, Davis Hills

LETTUCE SALAD

½ head of lettuce
1 red bell pepper
1 cup celery
1 purple onion

1 can sm. English peas, drained
1½ cups mayonnaise
Parmesan cheese
Bacos

Put cut lettuce on bottom of long casserole dish. Add chopped pepper, celery, onions, and English peas. Cover with mayonnaise and sprinkle with Parmesan cheese. Refrigerate for 24 hours. Sprinkle with Bacos when ready to serve.

Lorene P. Butler, Poplar Ridge

LULA'S FREEZER SLAW

1 med. cabbage, shredded fine	1 cup vinegar
1 T. salt	½ cup water
3 lg. celery stems, chopped fine	2 cups sugar
1 med. green pepper, chopped fine	1 tsp. celery seed
1 tsp. mustard seed	

Sprinkle salt over cabbage and let set for 1 hour. Squeeze cabbage out. Mix cabbage, celery, and green pepper well and pack in freezer boxes. Make syrup. Bring last 5 ingredients to a boil for 1 minute. Let cool. Pour over cabbage mixture. Freeze.

Mrs. Ernest F. Dilday, Jr., Davis Hills

SANTA MARIA SALAD

2 cups Italian bread cubes	2 cups cauliflower floweret slices
2 cups KRAFT Italian dressing	2 cups broccoli flowerets
2 qts. torn assorted salad greens	1½ cups zucchini slices

Toss bread cubes with ¼ cup dressing. Bake on cookie sheet at 350 degrees for 20 minutes, turning occasionally. Combine assorted greens, cauliflower, broccoli, zucchini, and bread cubes with ⅓ cup dressing in a salad bowl: toss lightly. Serve with additional dressing if desired. Serves 4 to 6.

Mrs. L. L. Tuck, Harvest

SAUERKRAUT SALAD

1 lg. can sauerkraut, undrained	1 cup chopped celery
1 cup chopped onions	1 sm. jar pimiento, drained
1 cup chopped red and green bell peppers	1 cup sugar
	¼ cup oil

Combine all ingredients in a large mixing bowl. Allow to sit covered in refrigerator 24 hours. Salad is then ready to serve. This will keep a long time in the refrigerator. Very good with dried beans and cornmeal bread or any meal planned.

Margaret Birchfield, Central

Salads and Salad Dressings 319

SEVEN-LAYER SALAD

½ head lettuce
½ head cauliflower flowerets
1 pkg. frozen green peas
Cheddar cheese, grated

½ pkg. dry Italian salad dressing mix
3-4 T. mayonnaise
Bacon bits

Layer the ingredients in a glass bowl (or large salad bowl). Cover and do not disturb. Marinate for 24 hours. Toss and serve.

Evelyn Hall, Athens Pike

VEGETABLE SALADS

BEAN AND BACON SALAD

2 16-oz. cans whole green beans, drained
½ cup chopped onion
⅓ cup salad oil
¼ cup vinegar
½ tsp. salt
¼ tsp. pepper

4 hard-cooked eggs, chopped
¼ cup mayonnaise
1 tsp. prepared mustard
¼ tsp. salt
4 slices bacon, fried crisply, crumbled
Crisp greens
Paprika

Combine beans, onions, salad oil, vinegar, salt, and pepper; toss lightly. Cover and chill. Mix remaining ingredients except bacon, greens, and paprika. Just before serving, drain bean mixture and toss with bacon. Serve on crisp greens; top with a spoonful of egg mixture and sprinkle with paprika. Serves 6.

Gisa Hall, Westbury

BROCCOLI SALAD I

1 bunch fresh broccoli
⅓-½ cup chopped olives, pimiento stuffed

½-⅔ cup mayonnaise
4 boiled eggs, chopped
1 sm. onion, chopped

Wash and drain broccoli. Cut into bite-sized pieces. Add other ingredients. Mix lightly. Chill before serving. (Make day ahead for blending.)

Evelyn Hall, Athens Pike

BROCCOLI SALAD II

1 bunch of broccoli 2 cups celery
½ onion, grated

Cut up broccoli very fine. Use more or less celery, depending on size of broccoli bunch. Mix with enough mayonnaise to moisten.

Mary Kantor, Westbury

CORN SALAD I

1 16-oz. can whole kernel corn ¼ cup chopped celery
½ cup Cheddar cheese ¼ cup chopped onion
¼ cup chopped green peppers ¼ cup chopped cucumber
¼ cup chopped carrots ¼ cup sweet pickle relish
½ cup Thousand Islands salad dressing

Drain corn and cut cheese in ¼-inch cubes. Combine all ingredients. Cover; chill overnight. Serve in lettuce cups. Serves 5 to 6. I usually quadruple this as it keeps very well. Men seem to like it very much.

Emogene Ross, Blossomwood

Whenever a bowl of punch we make, four striking opposites we take, the strong, the weak, the sour, the sweet. Together mixed, most kindly meet.

CORN SALAD II

2 cans shoe peg corn 1 sm. onion, finely chopped
2 sm. or 1 med. green pepper, Mayonnaise to taste
    finely diced 2 med. tomatoes, chopped
Salt and pepper to taste

Drain shoe peg corn and mix pepper and onion. Add mayonnaise and mix well. Refrigerate. Just before serving, add chopped tomatoes. Add salt and pepper to taste. Adjust amounts of onions, pepper, and mayonnaise to suit individual tastes.

Susan Fulda, Rainbow Mountain

CREAMY POTATO SALAD

9 med. potatoes
3 hard-cooked eggs
⅔ cup mayonnaise
1 tsp. prepared mustard
¾ cup commercial sour cream
1 tsp. salt
¼ tsp. pepper
11 slices bacon
¼ cup chopped green onion
½ cup chopped celery
¼ cup commercial Italian salad dressing

Cook potatoes in boiling salt water for about 30 minutes or until tender. Drain well; cool slightly. Peel and cut potatoes into ¾-inch cubes. Remove yolks from eggs and mash; set whites aside. Stir mayonnaise, mustard, sour cream, salt, and pepper into yolks; set aside. Cook bacon until crisp; drain on paper towels and crumble. Chop egg whites, add bacon, potatoes, onion, celery, and Italian dressing. Fold in mayonnaise mixture; chill at least 2 hours. Serves 12.

Oneita Craighead, Fleming Hills

EVELYN'S ARTICHOKES

1 can artichokes
1 can asparagus, drained
1 can cream of mushroom soup
Bread crumbs
Butter

Slice artichokes and cut up asparagus; combine with soup in baking dish. Top with bread crumbs, dot with butter, and bake at 350 degrees until bubbly, about 15 to 20 minutes.

Emogene Ross, Blossomwood

EXTRA BEAN SALAD

1 cup cider vinegar
1 cup sugar
½ cup salad oil
1 can green beans
1 can wax beans
1 can red beans
1 can garbanzo beans
1 can niblet corn
1 cup sliced celery
1 cup sliced onions
1 2-oz. jar pimiento

Mix together vinegar, sugar, and salad oil and bring to a boil; then pour over well-drained vegetables. Place in refrigerator. Keeps well. Should be made a day or two ahead of time.

Anne Weaver, Fleming Hills

GUACAMOLE SALAD

2 avocadoes
¼ tomato
1 T. lemon juice
1 T. chili powder
1 T. garlic salt
1 T. sour cream
1 T. yogurt

Peel and mash avocadoes. Peel and chop tomato fine. Mix together and season to taste with remaining ingredients.

Diane McFarland, Harvest

MARINATED TOMATOES

1 garlic clove, minced
¼ cup sliced green onion tops
1 tsp. salt
¼ tsp. finely ground pepper
¼ cup snipped parsley
½ tsp. thyme leaves
6 fresh tomatoes, peeled
⅔ cup salad oil
¼ cup vinegar

Combine first 6 ingredients and sprinkle over tomatoes, which have been cut in half or in thick slices. Mix oil and vinegar and pour over tomatoes. Cover and chill several hours or overnight. Spoon dressing over tomatoes several times while chilling. Drain before serving. Serves 6.

Mrs. Herschel Moore (Judy), Heritage

MARINATED VEGETABLE SALAD

2 cups cauliflower, bite sized
1 cup cut green beans, drained
4 oz. fresh mushrooms, sliced
1 cup pitted ripe olives, drained
1 med. onion, sliced, separated into rings
½ cup sliced carrots
1 green pepper, sliced

Dressing

⅜ cup lemon juice
¾ cup vinegar
3 T. sugar
1½ tsp. salt
¼ tsp. pepper
1 tsp. dill weed
Italian dressing to taste

Mix ingredients. Prepare dressing, pour over ingredients, and let marinate overnight.

Darlene Reichmann, Rainbow Mountain

OLD-FASHIONED POTATO SALAD

2 lbs. potatoes
½ cup sliced green onion
⅔ cup thinly sliced celery
4 hard-cooked eggs, chopped
1 tsp. salt
1 tsp. celery seed
¼ tsp. pepper
1 cup mayonnaise
1 T. prepared mustard
½ cup sweet pickle relish
Pickle slices
Hard-cooked egg slices

Cook, peel, and cube potatoes. Combine potatoes, onion, celery, chopped eggs, salt, celery seed, and pepper in a large bowl. Blend mayonnaise, mustard, and pickle relish. Gently stir into potato mixture. Chill thoroughly before serving. Garnish with slices of pickles and hard-cooked eggs. Serves about 8.

Kay Bass, Big Cove

OVERNIGHT VEGETABLE SALAD

1 10-oz. pkg. frozen green peas, thawed
1 15-16 oz. can red kidney beans, drained
1 16-oz. can cut green beans, drained
1 12-oz. can white whole corn, drained
1 cup diced celery
1 med. onion, diced
½ cup diced green pepper
1 2-oz. jar pimiento, chopped
¾ cup white vinegar
½ cup sugar
2 T. salad oil
2 tsp. water
½ tsp. paprika

In large bowl combine all vegetables and pimiento. In small bowl, combine remaining ingredients and stir until sugar dissolves. Pour over vegetables and toss. Cover and refrigerate 24 hours, stirring occasionally.

Rachel Koger, Hurricane

POTATO SALAD I

4 cups cooked potatoes
2 boiled eggs
¼ cup chopped pickle
1 onion, chopped
1 tsp. salt
Dash of cayenne pepper

Set aside and make dressing.

Dressing

1½ tsp. salt
1 tsp. mustard
1 egg, beaten

2 T. butter, melted
¾ cup milk
¼ cup vinegar

Mix salt and mustard. Then add beaten egg, melted butter, and milk. Cook slowly until thick. Add vinegar. Pour over potatoes and toss. If a richer dressing is needed, add a little mayonnaise. Sprinkle with paprika and refrigerate.

Debbie Hawkins, Vestavia

POTATO SALAD II

4-6 potatoes
2-4 eggs
¼ cup celery
⅛ cup carrots
⅛ cup green pepper

10 Spanish olives with pimiento
1 T. sweet pickle relish
Salt to taste
Pinch of pepper
Onion powder to taste

1 tsp. mustard or Durkee's Dressing

Boil potatoes. Hard boil the eggs. Cut up potatoes and eggs in a bowl. Add celery, carrots, green pepper, olives, and sweet pickle relish. Add salt, pepper, and onion powder to taste. Add mayonnaise and mustard or Durkee's Dressing and mix all ingredients together. Chill overnight.

Sylvia Elsner, South Huntsville

RICE SALAD

4 cups cooked rice
½ cup finely diced onion

½ cup finely diced cucumber
½ cup finely diced green pepper

Mix well; add vinaigrette sauce.

Vinaigrette Sauce

6 T. olive or vegetable oil
2 T. wine vinegar

½-1 tsp. salt
12 grinds of the pepper mill

Mix all ingredients.

Jeanette Kromis, Westbury

SCANDANAVIAN SALAD

1 No. 2 can English peas, drained
2 No. 2 cans French-style green beans, drained
1 sm. can chopped pimiento
4 big stalks celery
1 med. red or white onion

Mix together.

Dressing

½ cup salad oil
1 cup red vinegar
1 T. salt
1 cup sugar
1 tsp. paprika

Mix ingredients together and pour over salad. Let stand 24 hours. Keeps indefinitely.

Virginia Laux, Madison Cross Roads

JEAN'S SPINACH SALAD

2 minced garlic cloves, or to taste
½ cup French dressing
6 slices bacon
1 lb. spinach, washed
2 hard-boiled eggs, chopped

Ahead of time, put garlic in French dressing. Fry bacon until it is crisp. Tear spinach into bite-size pieces; combine with chopped egg and crumbled bacon. Remove garlic from dressing and discard. Pour dressing over salad and toss. Serves 5.

Emogene Ross, Blossomwood

SPINACH SALAD

2 bunches fresh spinach
2 med. fresh red onions
2 sm. pkgs. frozen green peas
1 sm. carton fresh mushrooms
½ lb. bacon
¼ cup sugar
Mayonnaise

Layer spinach, onions, peas, and mushrooms in large see-through bowl. After layering spinkle with bacon bits and sugar. Cover entire top of salad with mayonnaise. Refrigerate overnight. Serves 8 to 10.

Robbie Hallisey, Piedmont

TABOULI
(Salad)

1½ cups bulgar wheat	Parsley flakes or fresh parsley
2 or 3 green onions with tops	to taste
½ green pepper	½ cup vegetable oil
1 cucumber, peeled	½ cup lemon juice
3 sm. tomatoes	1 tsp. salt

Rinse bulgar wheat with water and drain. Chop onions, green pepper, cucumber, and tomatoes fine. Mix all ingredients together and let set in refrigerator overnight.

Carlla Hooper, Heritage

TOMATO SALAD

2 env. gelatin	1 cup mayonnaise
1 cup cold water	1-1½ cucumbers, chopped
2 lbs. sm. curd cottage cheese	1 onion, grated
1 can tomato soup	1 btl. olives, sliced
½ green pepper, chopped	

Dissolve gelatin in cold water. Heat soup and gelatin. Let cool a little. Add all other ingredients. Mix well and chill. Enjoy!

Piedmont

24-HOUR BEAN SALAD

1 can cut white wax beans	½ cup salad oil
1 can French-style beans	½ cup cider vinegar
1 can red beans	¾ cup sugar or less
1 cup thin-sliced onion	½ tsp. salt
¼ tsp. pepper	

Drain all beans; combine with onion in a big bowl. Put the rest in a jar and mix well. Pour over beans, cover, and refrigerate for 24 hours. Drain well and serve.

Roberta Friedman, Harvest

VEGETABLE SALAD I

1 can whole green beans, drained
1 can green peas, drained
1 can bean sprouts, drained
1 cup chopped celery
1 cup chopped green pepper (may use ½ cup red and ½ cup green)
1 cup chopped green onion

Mix all ingredients together.

Dressing

½ cup water
1 T. salt
1 cup sugar
½ cup Mazola oil
1 tsp. black pepper
¾ cup vinegar

Mix and pour over vegetables. Refrigerate several hours or overnight.

Mrs. Bob Erwin (Virginia), Monrovia

VEGETABLE SALAD II

1 16-oz. can French-cut green beans
1 can whole kernel corn
1 16-oz. can tiny English peas
1 cup chopped celery
1 sm. jar pimiento, cut up
1 cup chopped green peppers
1 sm. onion, diced
1 cup sugar
½ cup cooking oil
1 tsp. celery seed
Salt and pepper to taste
¾ cup vinegar

Drain green beans, corn, and peas. Mix vegetables in large bowl. Heat all other ingredients and cool. Then pour over vegetables and mix well. Refrigerate overnight.

Mrs. Paul Bledsoe, Hurricane

MEAT SALADS

CHICKEN SALAD

4 cups cooked chicken
1 cup chopped celery
1 cup sliced almonds
2 cups green grapes, halved, seeded
¾ cup sour cream
½ cup mayonnaise

Mix and refrigerate for 2 hours or longer. Serve on lettuce with pineapple.

Roberta Friedman, Harvest

CORN BEEF SALAD

1 4-oz. pkg. lemon Jello
1 cup boiling water
3 hard-boiled eggs, chopped fine
½ cup cucumber, chopped fine
1 sm. onion, chopped fine
1½ to 2 cups celery, chopped fine
1 12-oz. can corn beef
1 cup mayonnaise
½ tsp. salt

Dissolve gelatin in boiling water. Chill until thickened. Chop fine: eggs, cucumber, onion, and celery. Add with corn beef, mayonnaise, and salt. Chill several hours and serve. This does mold well.
Pat Zurasky, Rainbow Mountain-South Parkway

HEARTY TUNA SALAD

2 7-oz. cans tuna
1 16-oz. pkg. green peas (English peas), cooked
1 cup thinly sliced celery
¾ cup mayonnaise
1 T. lemon juice
⅛ tsp. curry powder
⅛ tsp. garlic salt
1 tsp. soy sauce
1 cup chow mein noodles
Lettuce cups
½ cup toasted slivered almonds

Mix tuna, peas, and celery; chill. Mix separately: mayonnaise, lemon juice, curry powder, garlic salt, and soy sauce; chill. At serving time combine the 2 mixtures. Add chow mein noodles and serve on lettuce cups. Top with almonds. Serves 6.
Note: This recipe was given to me several years ago by Lois Pittman, the wife of the chaplain of St. Luke's Hospital, Cedar Rapids, Iowa. It's a good salad plus having the make-ahead advantage.
Bonnie Riley, South Huntsville-Saddleback Valley

HOT CHICKEN SALAD I

2 cups diced chicken
½ cup broken cashew nuts
1 cup diced celery
¼ cup chopped onion
1 can mushroom soup
¼ cup water or broth
Dash of pepper
1 3-oz. can chow mein noodles

Cook chicken, dice, and then mix with other ingredients in a greased casserole. If you do not use the broth, you can put a chicken bouillon cube in the water. Put some of the noodles inside and the rest on top. Cook at 325 degrees for 30 minutes.
Evelyn Hall, Athens Pike

HOT CHICKEN SALAD II

1 cup diced chicken (about 4 chicken breasts)
1 cup cooked rice
1 can cream of chicken soup
1 sm. onion, minced
1 cup diced celery
3 boiled eggs, chopped
½ tsp. salt
1 skimpy cup mayonnaise or salad dressing

Mix all ingredients and top with bread crumbs. Bake at 375 degrees for 30 minutes.

Edith T. Dobbs, Hurricane

PATIO SALAD

1 cup cubed cooked pork
4 hard-cooked eggs, chopped
½ cup diced celery
½ cup diced sweet or sour pickle
Mayonnaise
Lettuce

Combine the pork, eggs, celery, and pickles in a bowl. Add enough mayonnaise to moisten and mix well. Serve in lettuce cups and garnish with paprika.

Dean Wilburn, New Sharon

TASTY HOT CRAB SALAD

1 6-oz. pkg. frozen king crab or 1 7½-oz. can
¾ cup diced celery
2 T. minced onion
3 hard-cooked eggs, sliced
1 T. lemon juice
1 can cream of chicken soup
½ cup mayonnaise
Salt and pepper to taste
Potato chips

Combine all the ingredients. Put in baking dish. Top with crushed potato chips. Bake at 350 degrees for 20 to 30 minutes. You can substitute turkey or chicken for the crabmeat.

Bonnie Nelson, Heritage

TUNA FISH SALAD

1 can tuna
4 hard-boiled eggs, grated or chopped
1 carrot, grated
2-3 stalks celery, finely chopped
Sweet pickle or dill pickle, chopped
Sm. amount of pickle juice
Mayonnaise to moisten
1 tsp. mustard
Dash of salt
Dash of pepper

Mix to desired consistency. (Recipe from my mother, Beverly Tucker.)

Sheryl Daniels, Heritage

FRUIT SALAD

CARROT MARSHMALLOW SALAD

4 cups shredded carrots
1 cup tiny marshmallows
½ cup pineapple
1 cup seedless raisins
½ cup shredded coconut
1 cup mayonnaise
1 cup Cool Whip

Scrape carrots and shred with coarse shredder into mixing bowl. Add marshmallows, pineapple cut in ½-inch pieces, raisins, and coconut. Toss lightly to mix. Add the mayonnaise and carefully fold in the Cool Whip. Serves 6 to 8.

Maxie Wilbourn, Central

CURRIED FRUIT CASSEROLE

1 lg. can fruit salad
1 med. can chunk pineapple
1 med. can peach halves
1 cup bing cherries
2 bananas, sliced
½ cup brown sugar or honey
2 T. cornstarch
¼ cup melted butter
1 T. curry powder
½ cup fruit juices

Drain fruits, being sure to save ½ cup of the juices; mix last 5 ingredients in saucepan. Place fruit in a 3-quart casserole that has been well greased. Pour mixture over fruit and bake at 350 degrees for 40 minutes.

Roberta Friedman, Harvest

CHERRY SALAD

1 lg. can crushed pineapple, drained
1 lg. can cherry pie filling
1 can Eagle Brand milk
1 lg. carton Cool Whip

Mix first 3 ingredients and let stand overnight. Add Cool Whip.

Lottie Power, Harvest

FAST AND EASY FRUIT SALAD

1 sm. can mandarin oranges
1 reg. can fruit cocktail
1 reg. can pineapple chunks
2 bananas, sliced
1 lg. pkg. vanilla pudding, instant
Coconut (optional)

Drain mandarin oranges and partially drain fruit cocktail. Mix first 4 ingredients, then add vanilla pudding (dry). Mix thoroughly; add coconut if desired. Chill.

Gina Guess, Hazel Green
Pam Smith, South Huntsville

FROZEN CHERRY SALAD

1 4-oz. pkg. whipped cream cheese
1 4½-oz. carton Cool Whip
1 21-oz. can cherry pie filling
2 11-oz. cans mandarin oranges

Stir cream cheese and Cool Whip together; then fold in pie filling and oranges. Can be served either frozen or chilled. Line pan with wax paper if you want to remove whole from pan.

Pat Zurasky, Rainbow Mountain-South Parkway

FROZEN CRANBERRY SALAD

1 can jellied cranberry sauce
1 apple, grated
1 can crushed pineapple
1 carton whipping cream
1 tsp. powdered sugar
Pecans, chopped

Mash cranberry sauce. Add grated apple and drained, well-mashed crushed pineapple. Place in 8x8-inch cake pan. Whip whipping cream sweetened with powdered sugar. Spread on top of fruit and sprinkle chopped pecans over cream. Put in freezer until hard and slice or square. This was part of a wedding gift of personal recipes from a friend's mother. It is a Thanksgiving tradition at our house and enjoyed all year round.

Linda Warren, South Huntsville

FROZEN PINK SALAD

1 lg. Cool Whip
1 can condensed milk
1 lg. can crushed pineapple
1 can cherry pie filling

Mix together and freeze.

Mrs. Erle Douglass (Evelyn), Monrovia

FROZEN FRUIT SALAD CUPS

1 sm. can crushed pineapple
3 T. chopped maraschino cherries
1 T. lemon juice
¾ cup sugar
2 cups sour cream
1 cup chopped pecans
2 bananas, mashed

Mix all together and freeze in individual cupcake liners.

Margaret Mann, Owens Cross Roads

FROZEN SALAD

⅓ cup mayonnaise
1 sm. pkg. Philadelphia cream cheese
½ pt. whipping cream
1 No. 2 can crushed pineapple, drained
1 lb. marshmallows, small, colored
1 cup chopped nuts

Whip mayonnaise, cream cheese, and whipping cream. Mix in a little pineapple juice. Combine all the ingredients and freeze.

Josie Davis, New Sharon

FRUIT SALAD I

1 can crushed pineapple
1 can mandarin oranges
1 pkg. sm. marshmallows
1 cup nuts
1 pkg. Dream Whip (prepared)
½ cup maraschino cherries, diced
1 sm. pkg. coconut

Drain pineapple and mandarin oranges and save juice. Mix juices with marshmallows and let stand overnight or a few hours. Next mix with remaining ingredients; then fold in Dream Whip. Chill.

Mrs. Ken Quiggle (Joann), Fleming Hills

FRUIT SALAD II

1 lg. can diced peaches
1 lg. can pears
1 pt. strawberries

1 sm. pkg. coconut
1 cup miniature marshmallows
¾ cup sour cream
Nuts

Mix and chill.

Glenn Sanderson, Harvest

FRUIT SALAD WITH SAUCE

1 egg
½ tsp. vinegar
2 T. cornstarch
3 T. sugar

1 lg. can diced pineapple
1 lg. can fruit cocktail
1 sm. can mandarin oranges
Nuts

To make sauce beat egg and add vinegar, cornstarch, sugar, and juice from pineapple; heat over low heat, stirring until thickened and cool. Pour mixture over drained fruits. Add nuts if desired.

Pat Zurasky, Rainbow Mountain-South Parkway

HEAVENLY SALAD

¼ cup lemon juice
1 can Eagle Brand milk
1 cup nuts

1 sm. can crushed pineapple, drained
1 med. carton Cool Whip

Stir lemon juice in milk, add nuts and pineapple; fold in Cool Whip. Pour in an 8x8-inch dish and chill. Chopped, drained cherries may be added for color.

Anna Lee Pogue, Central

POPPY SEED FRUIT SALAD

1 can peach pie filling
2 cans mandarin orange slices, drained

1 can pineapple tidbits, drained
1 box fresh or frozen strawberries
Poppy seed

2 to 3 bananas

Combine all ingredients except bananas and let sit overnight. Before serving, slice and add bananas. Will last several days covered in refrigerator. You may use 1 can strawberry pie filling and fresh peaches as a change.

Sylvia Elsner, South Huntsville

STUFFED PEARS

6 halves canned pears
½ cup chopped nuts
½ tsp. vanilla
½ cup whipping cream
½ T. sugar

Combine stiffly whipped cream, nuts, sugar, and flavoring. Pile lightly into chilled pears.

Mrs. Tom Baker, Hurricane

WATERGATE SALAD

1 pkg. pistachio pudding mix, instant
1 lg. container Cool Whip
1 16-oz. can crushed pineapple, undrained
½ cup chopped nuts
½ cup miniature marshmallows

Mix all ingredients in bowl and chill. Decorate top with whole pecans and cherries.

Mrs. Erle Douglass (Evelyn), Monrovia

WHITE SALAD

1 pt. whipping cream
1 pkg. miniature marshmallows
1 can each: fruit cocktail, pineapple, and peaches

Whip cream until stiff. Mix all ingredients together. May use bananas instead of peaches.

Patsy O'Neal, Poplar Ridge
Sylvia Elsner, South Huntsville

There is no scale or chart on earth to measure what a true friend is worth.

SALAD DRESSINGS

BLUE CHEESE SALAD DRESSING

½ cup plain yogurt
½ cup mayonnaise
⅓ cup crumbled blue cheese
Juice of ½ lemon
½ tsp. poppy seed
¼ tsp. pepper

Stir yogurt and mayonnaise together. Add cheese, lemon juice, poppy seed, and pepper. Refrigerate and use on favorite tossed salad.
Nell Hereford, Hazel Green

DANNY'S ITALIAN DRESSING

½ cup cider vinegar
½ cup plus "smidgen" vegetable oil
¼ tsp. marjoram
½ tsp. oregano
¼ tsp. basil leaves
⅛ tsp. paprika
¼ tsp. parsley
¼ tsp. salt
Pinch of red pepper

Shake well before serving. (My son Danny's recipe.)
Sheryl Daniels, Heritage

ROQUEFORT DRESSING

½ cup sour cream
½ cup mayonnaise or salad dressing
¼ cup grated bleu cheese
1 tsp. vinegar
¼ tsp. sugar
Dash of garlic salt

Blend together and let stand for at least ½ hour.
Doris Smith, Davis Hills

SALAD DRESSING
(100-Year-Old-Recipe)

4 egg yolks
1 egg white
5 T. vinegar
5 T. melted butter

Beat the eggs very lightly; pour boiling hot vinegar on top. Boil until thick; then add 5 tablespoons melted butter. If used for cabbage or lettuce, add sugar; if used for chicken, add mustard, pepper, and salt and thin with cream.

Mrs. Allen Drake (Wilma), Monrovia

CRANBERRY SALAD

1 lb. cranberries, ground
1 orange
¾ cup chopped pecan
4 stalks celery, diced
1 8¼ oz. can crushed pineapple
1 6 oz. can cherry gelatin
4 cups hot water
1 cup sugar
1 tsp. salt
1 envelope unflavored gelatin
½ cup cold water

Combine cranberries, orange, pecan, celery, pineapple. Set aside; dissolve cherry gelatin in hot water; add sugar and salt. Dissolve unflavored gelatin in cold water and stir in cherry gelatin mixture. Combine all ingredients and pour into large molds or 20 to 25 individual molds. Chill until firm. Serve 25.

Patsy Brazelton

APPLE CRUNCH SALAD

2 pkgs. (3 oz.) or 1 pkg. (6 oz.) strawberry gelatin
2 cups boiling water
1½ cups cold water or apple juice
¼ tsp. cinnamon (optional)
1 cup diced celery
1 cup diced peeled apples
¼ cup chopped nuts

Dissolve gelatin in boiling water. Add cold water and cinnamon and chill until thickened. Fold in apples, celery, & nuts. Spoon into a 6 cup jello mold or bowl. Chill until firm about 4 hours. Makes 5 cups or 10 servings.

Evelyn Lorenz, University

WEST INDIES SALAD

1 lb. fresh lump crab meat
1 medium onion (chopped finely)
½ cup oil
⅓ cup cider vinegar
½ cup ice water
salt and pepper

Divide chopped onions in half and spread ½ over bottom of large mixing bowl. Separate crab meat lumps and place on top of onions in bowl. Then spread balance of onions over this. Add salt and pepper to taste. Pour oil, then vinegar, then ice water. Cover and place in refrigerator to marinate from 2 - 12 hours. When ready to serve, toss but do not stir. Serve over fresh lettuce.

Jeanne Peters, South Parkway

LEE'S SEVEN LAYER SALAD

2 cups lettuce
½ cup chopped onion
½ cup chopped celery
1 can English peas, drained
½ cup sliced water chestnuts
8 slices of crisp bacon
1 cup shredded cheese (your favorite)
1½ cup mayonnaise
1 tbsp. sugar

Layer ingredients as listed. Mix mayonnaise and sugar. Cover top of vegetables with this mixture. Sprinkle with cheese and bacon bits.

Mildred R. Fanning, Monrovia

CABBAGE SALAD

This cabbage salad kept covered and refrigerated will keep indefinitely. In a large container, arrange the following ingredients in layers.

1 large head of cabbage, shredded	2 medium onions, thin sliced (separate the onion rings)
1 green pepper, sliced paper thin	1 medium can or jar pimento, drained

(DO NOT STIR)

For the dressing, mix together the following ingredients and boil 2 minutes.

1 cup salad oil	1½ tsp. salt
1 cup sugar	1 tsp. celery seed
¾ cup white vinegar	

Pour the hot dressing over the vegetables. Cover tightly and refrigerate at least 4 hours before serving. Makes 15 servings.

Frankie Johnson, Madison Cross Roads

GRAPE SALAD

2 small black cherry Jello	1 can blueberry pie filling
1 cup hot water	½ cup chopped nuts
1 16 oz. can chunk pineapple with juice	

Mix together and refrigerate until set.

Topping:

½ pt. sour cream	½ cup sugar
8 oz. cream cheese	1 tsp. vanilla

Cream all ingredients and spread on set jello salad.

Debra Segraves, Monrovia II

ORANGE PINEAPPLE SALAD

1 6 oz. pkg. orange jello	1 pt. Half & Half
1 cup hot water	1 cup, grated medium sharp cheese
1 large can crushed pineapple with juice	1 cup nuts, chopped

Mix together and pour into a Jello mold and chill overnite.

Catherine Mitchell, Hurricane

SALAD PARMESAN

Use exact measurements!

Mash in bottom of bowl:
1 clove garlic	¼ tsp. pepper
½ tsp. salt	dash dry mustard

Stir in:
¼ cup salad oil	2 tbsp. parmesan cheese
1 tbsp. lemon juice	

Heap 2 qts. of greens on top. When ready to serve, toss.

Jeanne Peters, South Parkway

ORANGE JELLO SALAD MARSHMELLO DELIGHT

1 6 oz. pkg. orange Jello	2 cups boiling water
2 cups pineapple juice	28 marshmallows (cut fine)
1 cup grated cheese	2 20 oz. cans crushed pineapple or pineapple drained
2 cups whip topping or 1 cup whipping cream, whipped)	1 cup pecans (chopped)

Dissolve Jello in boiling water, add cheese, marshmallows and pineapple juice, stir until cheese and marshmallows are partially dissolved. Set in refrigerator until it starts to congeal, then add pineapple, pecans and fold in whipped topping. Refrigerate until firm. Serves 10 or 12.

Mrs. Leo (Lawsie) Wall, Monrovia

SOUR CREAM POTATO SALAD

4 to 4½ cups peeled and sliced potatoes	2 hard-cooked eggs, sliced
2 stalks celery, finely chopped	½ cup commercial sour cream
12 small radishes, thinly sliced	¾ cup mayonnaise
1 small onion, finely chopped	½ teaspoon dillseeds
	1¼ tsp. prepared mustard
	1½ tsp. salt
	½ tsp. seasoned salt

Cook potatoes in boiling water until tender. Drain; chill thoroughly. Combine potatoes, celery, radishes, onion, and egg slices in a large mixing bowl; set aside. Combine remaining ingredients in a small bowl; mix well, and pour over vegetables. Toss lightly. Yield: about 6 servings.

Louise K. Jackson, University

SWEET AND SOUR DRESSING

2 cups (white) vinegar
1½ cups sugar
2½ tsp. salt
2 tbsp. pepper (white)
garlic powder to taste

Combine all ingredients and mix well. Stir each time you use. Peel cucumbers and slice to suit your purpose. Pour dressing over these and make into sandwiches in any shape you desire. Also is very good on slaw.

Edith Dobbs — Hurricane

CUCUMBERS WITH MUSTARD SAUCE

3 large cucumbers peeled and sliced thin
2 tbsp. Crisco Oil
4 tbsp. vinegar
1 tsp. prepared mustard
1 tsp. salt
½ tsp. pepper

Place cucumbers in covered bowl and cover with ice. Fifteen to twenty minutes before serving time, mix next 5 ingredients together. Drain water and ice cubes from cucumbers. Then pour sauce over them, mix well and chill. This is also good over green beans, cabbage, turnip greens, spinach & dried or fresh cooked, peas.

Rachael Sturdivant, University

SALAD DRESSING

4 cups tomato juice
1 small bell pepper, minced
2 canned green chilies, chopped
¼ tsp. fresh ground pepper
2 tbsp. chopped green onion tops
½ onion, minced
½ large cucumber, minced
1½ tsp. Worcestershire sauce
juice from 2 lemons
1 large tomato, finely diced

Put two cups juice and all other ingredients in blender, blend well: add remaining juice slowly; add juice of 2 lemons and more chopped tomato. Chill thoroughly.

Evelyn Hall, Athens Pike

SEAFOOD

DEVILED CRAB

1½ cups crabmeat
1 10½-oz. can condensed cream
   of celery soup
2 T. green pepper, chopped
1 T. onion, chopped

2 tsp. lemon juice
1 tsp. Worcestershire sauce
½ tsp. prepared mustard
⅓ cup dry bread crumbs
1 T. butter or margarine, melted

Heat oven to 350 degrees. Remove hard membrane from crabmeat. Combine soup, crabmeat, green pepper, onion, lemon juice, Worcestershire sauce, and mustard. Spoon into 1-quart casserole or four 6-ounce baking dishes. Combine bread crumbs and butter. Sprinkle over crabmeat mixture. Bake 20 minutes or until bubbling and lightly browned. Serves 4.

Mrs. Lyle Needham, South Huntsville

FISH PUFFS

1 lb. fish fillets, thawed
Salt and pepper
1 egg white

¼ cup mayonnaise
1 tsp. onion, minced
½ tsp. Worcestershire sauce

Dash of hot sauce

Separate fillets. Arrange skin-side down in a buttered 8-inch square dish. Season with salt and pepper. Beat egg white until stiff but not dry. Fold in other ingredients. Spread mixture on fillets. Bake at 425 degrees for 18 to 20 minutes or until fish flakes easily and sauce is golden brown.

Elizabeth Nixon, Davis Hills

NEW JERSEY SEAFOOD

¼ cup butter
¼ cup flour
1½ cups milk
½ tsp. salt
¼ tsp. dill
⅛ tsp. dry mustard
Pinch of thyme
2 cups Cheddar cheese, grated

2 egg yolks, lightly beaten
½ lb. mushrooms, sliced
3 T. butter
1 lb. shrimp
1 lb. crabmeat
1 qt. oysters in liquid
Juice of 1 lemon
½ cup grated cheese for topping

Make cream sauce from first 3 ingredients and add seasonings. Add cheese and cook until melted. Add egg yolks and cook 5 minutes longer. Keep warm over hot water. Saute mushrooms in butter. Add prepared seafood and heat gently. Add lemon juice. Put into a 3-quart casserole, sprinkle with cheese. Broil under 450 degrees until cheese melts. Serve with rice.

Vicki Coffee, Extension Agent

OCEANBURGERS

1 can Cheddar cheese soup
½ tsp. dried onion flakes
¼ tsp. Tabasco pepper sauce
½ tsp. crushed oregano
2 tsp. lemon juice
1 lb. fish sticks, cooked
6 hamburger buns, slightly toasted
Dill pickle slices

In saucepan, simmer first 5 ingredients for 15 minutes, stirring occasionally. Spoon over fried fish sandwiches. Garnish with pickle slices.

Cathy Gilbert, Davis Hills

PERCH 'N TATERS BAKE

1 lb. ocean perch fillets, fresh or frozen
½ tsp. salt
1 1-lb. can sm. white potatoes, drained
1 8-oz. can tomato sauce
3 T. Parmesan cheese, grated
1 T. parsley, chopped
½ tsp. basil
¼ tsp. oregano

Thaw frozen fish. Sprinkle with salt. Pour half of the tomato sauce over bottom of shallow 1½-quart casserole. Arrange fish in center and potatoes at ends of casserole. Pour remaining tomato sauce over fish. Mix cheese, parsley, basil, and oregano together; sprinkle over fish and potatoes. Bake uncovered in hot oven, 400 degrees, for 22 to 25 minutes or until fish flakes easily when tested with a fork and potatoes are serving temperature. Serves 4.

Madison County

QUICK N' EASY SALMON PATTIES

1 15 to 16-oz. can pink salmon
1 egg
⅓ cup minced onion
½ cup flour
1½ tsp. baking powder
1½ cups Crisco

Drain salmon. In a medium mixing bowl, mix salmon, egg, and onion until sticky. Stir in flour; add baking powder to salmon mixture. Form into small patties and fry until golden brown (about 5 minutes) in hot Crisco. Serve with tartar sauce or Caesar salad dressing. Serves 4 to 6.

Gaynell Geiger, Blossomwood

ROBBIE'S CRAB AND SHRIMP CASSEROLE

1 med. green pepper, chopped
1 med. onion, chopped
1 cup celery, chopped
6½-oz. can flaked crabmeat
½ lb. fresh shrimp, cut in pieces
½ tsp. salt
⅛ tsp. pepper
1 tsp. Worcestershire sauce
1 cup mayonnaise
1 cup crumbs, buttered

Heat oven to 350 degrees. Mix all ingredients. Place in greased 1-quart baking dish. Sprinkle with crumbs. Bake for 30 minutes.

Robbie Hallisey, Piedmont

SALMON FLAKE CASSEROLE

1 5-oz. pkg. macaroni
¼ cup chopped onion
½ cup chopped celery
⅓ cup margarine
¼ cup chopped green sweet pepper
2 cups sweet milk
1 tsp. salt
Dash of pepper
1 1-lb. can pink salmon
Bread crumbs, buttered

Cook macaroni according to directions, drain, and rinse. Saute onion and celery in margarine; add pepper, and slowly add milk. Cook over medium heat, stirring constantly until thick. Add macaroni, salt, and pepper. Flake salmon, add to sauce, and place in casserole dish. Top with buttered bread crumbs. Bake at 350 degrees, covered, for 30 minutes.

Mrs. Frank Ernst, Pulaski Pike

SALMON LOAF

1 cup flaked salmon
1 cup cracker crumbs
1 cup scalded milk
1 tsp. salt
Pepper to taste
1 T. margarine
½ tsp. onion juice or 1 sm. onion
2 egg yolks, beaten
1 tsp. lemon juice
2 egg whites

Flake salmon into a bowl. Combine crumbs, milk, salt, pepper, margarine, onion, egg yolks, and lemon juice. Add this mixture to the salmon. Mix well; then fold in beaten egg whites. Place in well-greased and crumbed loaf pan. Bake at 350 degrees until brown. Serve with lemon slices or with sauce of 2 tablespoons catchup and 2 tablespoons mayonnaise beaten together.

Mildred Prince, Pulaski Pike

SALMON OR TUNA CASSEROLE

1 can salmon or 2 cans tuna
1 can English peas, cooked, drained
1 sm. pkg. egg noodles, cooked, drained
1 can cream of celery soup
½ cup salad dressing
¼ cup onion, chopped
1 egg, beaten
Salt and pepper to taste
⅓ cup buttered bread crumbs, or
⅓ cup cracker crumbs
½ cup cheese, grated (optional)

Mix all ingredients together, except cheese and crumbs. Pour into a 1-quart casserole dish. Spread cheese and crumbs on top. Bake for 25 minutes at 350 degrees. Serves 6.

Nell Hereford, Hazel Green

ESCALLOPED OYSTERS I
(Family Recipe)

3 pts. oysters, drained (reserve liquids)
3 to 4 cups crumbled saltine crackers
½ cup heavy cream or milk
¼ to ½ cup oyster liquid
1 tsp. Worcestershire sauce
Salt and pepper to taste
½ cup butter

In buttered casserole dish place layer of oysters. Sprinkle crumbled crackers over oyster layer. Repeat until oysters are used, finishing with cracker crumbs. Combine cream, oyster liquid, Worcestershire sauce, salt, and pepper. Pour evenly over oysters. Dot top with butter. Bake at 350 degrees for 30 to 40 minutes or until liquid is absorbed.

Margie Spencer, Vestavia

ESCALLOPED OYSTERS II

1 to 2 pts. oysters
2 cups cracker crumbs, med. coarse
½ cup butter, melted
½ tsp. salt
Pepper to taste
½ cup half-and-half
¼ cup oyster liquor
¼ tsp. Worcestershire sauce

Drain oysters; save liquor. Combine crumbs, butter, salt, and pepper.

Spread one-third of buttered crumbs in buttered pan, cover with half of oysters, then spread one-third more crumbs, cover with remaining oysters. Combine cream, oyster liquor, and Worcestershire sauce and pour mixture over oysters. Top with remaining crumbs. Bake in 350-degree oven for 30 to 40 minutes until it starts to bubble.

Adele Arcangeli, Westbury

BOILED SHRIMP

4 bay leaves
20 peppercorns
1 tsp. mustard seeds
12 whole cloves
⅛ tsp. cumin seeds
1 tsp. crushed red pepper
⅛ tsp. celery seeds
⅛ tsp. light fennel seeds

2 tsp. dehydrated onion flakes
⅛ tsp. caraway seeds
¼ tsp. ground marjoram
¼ tsp. whole thyme
1 tsp. salt
1 lemon, halved
2 garlic cloves
5 lbs. med. or lg. shrimp

Put the first 12 ingredients in a muslin bag. Bring 4 to 5 quarts of water to a boil. Add salt, lemon, garlic, and herb bag. Return to a boil and allow to cook for 2 to 3 minutes, then stir in shrimp and cook 3 to 5 minutes. Drain well and chill. Serve in bowl on lettuce leaf and garnish with lemon slices.

Myrtle Breithaupt, Westbury

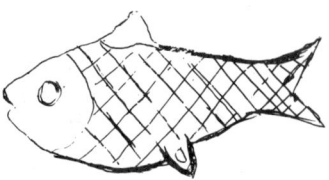

FRENCH-FRIED SHRIMP

1 cup Aunt Jemima Pancake Mix
1 tsp. salt

Dash of pepper
¾ cup cold water

2 lbs. fresh shrimp

Combine pancake mix, salt, pepper, and cold water in bowl. Beat with rotary beater about 2 minutes. Dip shrimp in batter; drain. Fry in hot deep fat (375 degrees) for 2 to 3 minutes. Drain on absorbent paper. Serve with cocktail sauce. Note: Scallops can be used.

Mrs. Jo Ann Daniels, Heritage

SEAFOOD QUICHE

½ cup onion, finely chopped
¼ cup green pepper, finely chopped
¼ cup celery, finely chopped
½ lb. crabmeat, pick out shell
½ lb. shrimp, peeled, deveined, cooked

Pastry for 1 9-inch pie
1 cup Swiss cheese, grated
1¼ cups scalded milk
2 eggs and 2 egg yolks, beaten
1 tsp. salt
Pepper to taste
Pinch of sweet basil

Saute onion, green pepper, and celery in small amount of butter until tender. Combine with crabmeat and shrimp. Pour into prepared crust, sprinkle with grated Swiss cheese. Combine milk, eggs, and seasonings. Pour over all. Sprinkle top with basil. Bake at 325 degrees for 25 to 30 minutes until set. You may use all crab or mix any other seafood—fish, scallops, etc. The more the better. Enjoy!

Adele Arcangeli, Westbury

SHRIMP CREOLE

1 T. margarine
½ cup green pepper
¾ cup onion, chopped
¾ cup celery, chopped
2 garlic cloves, minced
1 can stewed tomatoes
1 can tomato sauce
2 T. Worcestershire sauce

1½ cups water
1 T. salt
¼ tsp. pepper
Dash of Tabasco sauce
1½ lbs. cooked shrimp
1 cup Mateus or Chianti wine
1 T. cornstarch
Cooked rice

In margarine saute peppers, onions, celery, and garlic. Add stewed tomatoes, tomato sauce, Worcestershire sauce, 1½ cups water, salt, pepper, and Tabasco sauce. Simmer uncovered for 45 minutes. Add boiled shrimp and wine. Cover and reduce heat just below simmer; cook for 15 minutes. Add cornstarch to a little water and mix to remove all lumps. Stir into creole until slightly thickened. Serve over cooked rice. Serves 6.

Melenda Ellis, Owens Cross Roads

Try to fix the mistakes—never the blame.

SHRIMP DE JONGHE

⅔ cup butter (not oleo)
2 T. chives
½ tsp. garlic powder
⅛ tsp. pepper
1½ lbs. med. raw shrimp, cleaned
1½ cups crushed bacon-flavored crackers

In a 2-quart saucepan melt butter over medium heat for 4 to 5 minutes. Add chives, garlic powder, and pepper and stir to blend. Dip shrimp into melted butter then roll in crumbs to coat. Layer shrimp in 8-inch (1½-quart) baking dish. Sprinkle shrimp with remaining crumbs. Bake at 350 degrees for 25 to 30 minutes. Delicious!

Adele Arcangeli, Westbury

SHRIMP MOSCA

2 lbs. shrimp, in shells, headless, washed
Pinch of oregano
Pinch of rosemary
Pinch of fresh ground pepper
1 tsp. salt
5 or 6 garlic pods
1½ ozs. olive oil
1 oz. sauterne wine

Place all ingredients except wine in a skillet and saute over hot fire for 15-20 minutes. Add sauterne and cook over lower heat about 10 minutes (or until wine evaporates). Serve in the shells, followed by finger bowls. Italian bread may be served to dip into juice. Serves 4.

Myrtle Breithaupt, Westbury

SHRIMP WRIGGLE

3 T. butter
3 T. flour
2 cups warm milk
Salt
Pepper
1 can shrimp
1 cup canned green peas

Melt butter and flour. Blend with warm milk. Salt and pepper to taste. Cook stirring constantly until nice and thick. Cut up 1 can or more of shrimp and add green peas with some juice for flavor. Serve on toast or unsalted crackers.

Helen Hann, Piedmont

TUNA LOG

1 8-oz. pkg. cream cheese, softened
1 oz. blue cheese
1 T. mayonnaise
2 T. celery, finely chopped
1 T. onion, finely chopped
8 to 10 drops Tabasco sauce
1 7-oz. can of tuna
Pecans, finely chopped

Mix the above and shape in logs, then roll in finely chopped pecans. May be frozen up to two weeks. Serve with town crackers.

Thelma Freeman, Poplar Ridge

TUNA ROLL

Baking-powder biscuit dough
  (using 2 cups flour)
2 cans (or 1 lg. can) flaked tuna
1 onion, minced
1 green pepper, diced small
½ tsp. salt
Milk

Roll biscuit dough to ¼-inch thickness on floured board. Combine tuna, onion, pepper, and salt; moisten slightly with milk, mix well, and spread on dough. Roll as for jelly roll. Bake on greased baking sheet at 400 degrees for a half hour or until brown. Serve with cream sauce.

Mary Lou Pfeiffer, Westbury

TUNA SPOONLETS

¼ tsp. lemon peel, grated
1 T. top milk
1 T. parsley, minced
1 T. onion, minced
Dash of pepper
1 7-oz. can tuna (white albacore), drained, shredded
1 egg, beaten
3 to 4 T. flour

Mix all ingredients thoroughly. Drop by small rounded spoonfuls into 1 inch of Wesson Oil heated to 350 degrees. Fry about 3 minutes, turning to brown evenly. Serves 3 to 4.

Blanche Harper, Vestavia

SHRIMP CREOLE

2½ lb. raw unpeeled shrimp
1½ tbsp. bacon grease
1½ tbsp. flour
½ cup finely chopped onion
⅓ cup finely chopped green pepper
¼ cup finely chopped celery
1 8 oz. can tomato sauce
1 16 oz. can Italian tomatoes with basil
1 clove garlic, minced
3 dashes tabasco
2 tbsp. Worcestershire sauce
1 tsp. sugar
2 tsp. salt
¼ tsp. pepper
2 tbsp. chopped parsley
¾ cup chopped green onion
4 cups cooked rice

Peel and devein shrimp. Set aside. In a heavy pot make a roux by melting the bacon grease and gradually stirring in the flour. Continue stirring until golden brown. Add onions, green pepper, and celery. Cook until tender. Pour in the tomato sauce and tomatoes with liquid. Blend well. Add garlic, tabasco, Worcestershire, sugar, salt and pepper. Simmer, uncovered, over low heat for 30 minutes, stirring occasionally. Add the shrimp, parsley and green onions. Cook about 30 minutes more over low heat until shrimp are done and mixture is thickened. Serve over hot fluffy rice.

Penny Garner, Monrovia II

CANNING AND FREEZING

CANNING AND FREEZING

BANANA BUTTER

3 cups mashed ripe bananas
¼ cup finely chopped
   maraschino cherries
¼ cup lemon juice
6½ cups sugar
1 6-oz. bottle liquid fruit pectin

In saucepan combine mashed bananas, lemon juice, cherries, and sugar. Mix well. Bring to a full rolling boil and boil hard for 1 minute. Quickly stir in pectin. Skim off foam. Ladle fruit butter into hot scalded jars. Adjust jar lids and bands. Process in a boiling waterbath canner (212°F.) for 10 minutes. Fills 7½ pint jars.

Jean Chisorsky, Madison

COUNTRY BUTTER

1 lb. margarine
⅔ cup cooking oil
1 cup buttermilk

Soften margarine and mix all together in mixer. Keep refrigerated.

Mrs. Eugene Smith (Nina), Monrovia

DO-IT-YOURSELF PEANUT BUTTER

Roast 2 cups shelled peanuts on cookie sheet in preheated 350-degree oven for 15 to 20 minutes, stirring occasionally. In the blender, put 1 cup roasted peanuts and 1½ tablespoons oil. Blend until smooth, adding another 1½ tablespoons oil gradually to make the peanut butter the proper consistency. Add ½ teaspoon salt.

Mrs. W. L. Hoover (Barbara), Monrovia

KENTUCKY APPLE BUTTER

7 lbs. tart apples (20-21 med.
   apples)
4 qt. cider
2½ cups sugar
1 tsp. ground allspice
1½ T. cinnamon
1 tsp. ground cloves

Slice and core apples. Add cider and cook until apples are tender, press fruit through sieve to remove skin and seeds. Add sugar and spices to pulp and cook until thick, stirring frequently. Pour into hot jars and ajust jar lids and bands. Process in a boiling waterbath canner (212°F.) for 10 minutes.

Brenda Williams, Harvest

APPLE PIE FILLING

4½ cups sugar
1 cup cornstarch
2 tsp. cinnamon
¼ tsp. nutmeg

3 T. lemon juice
6 lbs. apples
1 tsp. salt
10 cups water

In large saucepan, blend first 4 ingredients. Stir in 10 cups water, cook, and stir until thick and bubbly. Add lemon juice. Pack peeled, cored, and sliced apples into hot canning jars leaving 1-inch headspace. Fill with hot syrup leaving ½-inch headspace. Adjust lids. Process in water-bath canner for 15 minutes (pints) or for 20 minutes (quarts). Yield: 6 quarts. Apple pie: Prepare pastry; add 1 quart filling. Bake for 50 minutes at 400 degrees.

Carolyn Griner, Rainbow Mountain

FIG JAM

Scald 6 quarts figs in 6 quarts boiling water; let stand 15 mintues. Drain; rinse thoroughly in clean, clear water, drying and pressing fruit until all water is out. Remove stems, measure crushed fruit, and add ½ cup sugar for each cup. Add enough water to cover, boil down until thick. May add a little lemon, orange, pressed ginger, 1 large can of pineapple, or 1 box strawberry Jello for variation. Pour in jars and adjust lids and bands. Process in a boiling waterbath canner (212°F.) for 10 minutes.

Brenda Williams, Harvest

FIG STRAWBERRY PRESERVES

3-4 cups mashed, stemmed figs   1 3-oz. pkg. strawberry Jello
3 cups sugar

Thoroughly mash figs. Mix the Jello and sugar. Put on very low heat and stir until sugar dissolves. Then put on medium heat and cook for 30 minutes, stirring often. Quickly pour into hot jars and adjust lids and bands. Process in a boiling waterbath canner (212°F.) for 10 minutes. Makes 6 6-ounce glasses. This is delicious. May also use cherry Jello.

Rachel Sturdivant, Darwin Downs

PEACHES FOR FRIED PIES

2 gal. sliced peaches, unpeeled 6-8 cups sugar
2 cups vinegar

Wash peaches and chop up with peelings on. Pour sugar and vinegar over peaches. Mix and let set overnight. Cook over slow heat stirring occasionally until thick. Fill jars, adjust lids and bands. Process in a waterbath canner (212°F.) for 20 minutes—pints; 25 minutes—quarts. You may also freeze if you wish.

Cora Lewis, Central
Mrs. Ernest F. Dilday, Jr., Davis Hills

PEAR RELISH

1 peck pears
5 green peppers
5 red peppers
3 hot peppers (optional)

5 lg. onions
5 cups vinegar
5 cups sugar
1 tsp. salt

Grind pears through food chopper and drain off juice. Grind peppers and onions. Combine all and bring to a boil and boil for 20 minutes. Pack into hot canning jars and adjust lids and bands. Process in a boiling waterbath canner (212°F.) for 10 minutes."

Mrs. Emmett Bussey (Ellen), Monrovia

STRAWBERRY JAM I

2 cups strawberries
4 cups sugar

1 pkg. Sure-Jell
1 cup water

Mash berries and mix with sugar. Let stand for 2 minutes. Cook Sure-Jell and water till boiling. Pour over berries; stir well. Put into containers and cover. Let stand for 24 hours. Then it is ready for freezer. Will keep 3 weeks in refrigerator. May be thawed and refrozen several times.

Anna Lee Rogers, Madison Cross Roads

STRAWBERRY JAM II

2 T. vinegar
4 cups strawberries
1 tsp. margarine
3½ cups sugar

Put vinegar on strawberries; boil for 1 minute. Add margarine then sugar; boil for 20 minutes more. Stir until cool. Pour into hot jars and adjust lids and bands. Process in boiling waterbath canner (212°F.) for 10 minutes."

Ursula Bumpus, Central

PICKLES

BREAD AND BUTTER PICKLES I

25-30 med. cucumbers
8 or more lg. onions, sliced thin
2 lg. bell peppers, chopped
½ cup salt
5 cups sugar
5 cups vinegar
2 T. mustard seed
1 tsp. tumeric
½ tsp. whole cloves

Chill cucumbers; slice thin. Layer cucumbers, onions, and peppers. Gradually sprinkle salt on this. The secret to these pickles is to cover top with ice and let set for 3 hours in refrigerator if you have room. Drain off water; do not wash. Bring to a boil sugar, vinegar, and spices. Add cucumbers and boil until they begin to change color. Put into hot jars and adjust lids and bands. Process in a boiling waterbath canner (212°F.) for 10 minutes. They are real crispy and real good.

Mary Moore, Central

BREAD AND BUTTER PICKLES II

3 lbs. cucumbers
⅓ cup pure granulated salt
5 cups cold water
½ lb. onions, sliced thin
2 cups apple cider vinegar
1⅓ cups sugar
1 tsp. celery seed
2 tsp. prepared mustard
1 tsp. ginger
¼ tsp. tumeric
⅛ tsp. mace
Few dashes of red pepper

Wash cucumbers thoroughly 2 or 3 times in cold water. Cut into ¼-inch crosswise slices. Put into an enamelware or glass bowl or crock. Sprinkle with salt and water. Cover and let stand overnight. Next morning, turn into a colander and drain 10 to 15 minutes. Put into a large pan or preserving kettle, add onions, vinegar, sugar, and spices. Heat; simmer only 3 or 4 minutes. Pack into hot sterile jars and adjust lids and bands. Process in boiling waterbath canner (212°F.) for 10 minutes. Makes 3 or 4 pints.

Glenda Patterson, Owens Cross Roads

CRISP CUCUMBER STICKS

7 lbs. lg. cucumbers
2½ cups lime
2 gal. water
¼ lb. alum

2 qt. white vinegar
1 qt. water
4 T. salt
5 lbs. sugar

Peel cucumbers and cut in strips. Mix lime and 2 gallons of water. Place cucumbers in this liquid and let set for 24 hours. Wash, then add alum and cover with water; let set 12 hours. Wash and drain. Make syrup of vinegar, 1 quart of water, salt, and sugar; boil and pour over cucumbers. Let set 4 hours. Cook for about 30 minutes. Place in jars and adjust jar lids and bands. Process in boiling waterbath canner (212^oF.) for 10 minutes.

Jesse Little, Harvest

14-DAY CUCUMBER PICKLES

14 lbs. med. cucumbers
2 gal. cold water
2-3 cups salt (enough to float an egg)
1 box alum

1 gal. pure apple vinegar
10 lbs. sugar
1 box pickling spices
1-2 garlic bulbs (optional)
1 T. dill seed

Step 1: Wash cucumbers. Place in stone jar; glass will do. Let stand 14 days in salt and cold water. Cover container with a cloth. Step 2: Remove cucumbers from salt water and wash; slice or cube the cucumbers. Wash crock and return cucumbers to it. Pour 2 gallons of water and 1 box alum over cucumbers. Cover and let stand for 6 hours. Then wash cucumbers 3 or 4 times, let drain. Replace in clean crock and cover with vinegar. Let stand overnight. Pour off vinegar and drain well. Clean and wipe crock dry. Layer cucumbers, then sugar. Repeat with cucumbers, sugar, and spices until all sugar is used. Last layer should be sugar, spices, and small amount of garlic and dill. Cover and let stand overnight. Next day pickles are ready to eat. Keep crock covered and in a cool place.

Mrs. O. V. Mitchell, Central

DILL PICKLES

1 head of dill
1 garlic clove
1 clove
6 peppercorns
⅛ tsp. alum

¼ tsp. tumeric (optional)
¼ tsp. mustard seed (optional)
1 qt. cucumbers
2 qt. vinegar
1 qt. water
1 cup *plain* salt

Place dill garlic, clove, peppercorns, and alum in a sterilized quart jar. If desired, may also add tumeric and/or mustard seed. Tightly pack in cucumbers. In saucepan mix vinegar, water, and salt. Heat to boiling. Pour over cucumbers. Adjust jar lids and bands. Process in a boiling waterbath canner (212°F.) for 10 minutes. This vinegar mixture will cover about 6 quarts of pickles.

Sarah M. Irvin, Monrovia

MIXED VEGETABLE PICKLES

1 qt. apple cider vingar	1 gal. quartered green tomatoes
4 cups sugar	½ gal. green and red bell peppers
½ cup salt	½ gal. onions
1 T. black pepper	1 qt. cauliflower flowerets

Mix vinegar, sugar, salt, and pepper. Bring to boil. Add vegetables. Cook for 5 minutes. Pack in hot jars. Cover with brine. Adjust jar lids and bands. Process in a boiling waterbath canner (212°F.) for 10 minutes.

Mrs. Ernest F. Dilday, Jr., Davis Hills

MUSTARD PICKLES BY ARTE

3 qt. sliced cucumbers *or* 1 gal. dill pickles	1½ lbs. onions, sliced or cubed
	6 bell peppers (red, if possible)
3 lbs. cabbage, shredded	1 cup salt
	1 gal. water

Soak vegetables overnight in brine of salt and water. Rinse in cold water and drain before adding to sauce.

Sauce

1 T. black pepper	1½ lbs. white sugar
3 T. white mustard seed	1 cup flour
3 T. tumeric	1 lg. jar mustard
1½ lbs. brown sugar	2 qt. vinegar

Mix, add vegetables, and cook for 15 minutes. Pack in pint jars and process in boiling water bath for 10 minutes.

Mary Anne Riley, South Parkway

PICKLED MUSHROOMS

1 lb. mushrooms
2 garlic cloves
Vinegar
Olive oil
4 T. chopped onion
4 T. chopped shallots
1 lg. bay leaf
Salt to taste
Pepper to taste
Tabasco sauce
Shake of cayenne pepper

Gently boil mushrooms for 10 minutes. Drain and cover with garlic vinegar made from 1 crushed garlic clove dropped in vinegar. Store in refrigerator for at least 2 days. Drain again and cover with olive oil (or salad oil). Add onion, shallots, bay leaf, 1 crushed garlic clove, salt, Tabasco sauce, and cayenne pepper. Let stand for another 2 days. They will keep indefinitely—if you can keep from eating them all at the first bite!

Norma Watts, South Huntsville

PICKLED OKRA I

3 lbs. sm. okra pods
6 sm. celery leaves
6 sm. hot peppers
6 sm. garlic cloves
1 T. dill seed, divided
2 cups white vinegar (4%-6%)
4 cups water
½ cup pickling salt

Remove part of stem from each okra pod. Firmly pack okra into hot sterilized jars. Place a celery leaf, pepper pod, 1 garlic clove, and a few dill seeds in each jar. Combine vinegar, water, and salt in a medium saucepan; bring to a boil. Pour over okra. Top with lids and screw metal bands tightly. Process in boiling-water bath for 10 minutes. Yield: 6 pints.

Betty Johnson, Hurricane

PICKLED OKRA II

2 lbs. sm. okra
Ice water
3 cups white vinegar
2 cups water
5 T. salt
To each pint jar add:
2 garlic cloves
1 tsp. mustard seed
2 Tabasco peppers
1 tsp. dill seed

Soak okra in ice water for 1 hour. Meanwhile, have pint jars heating in hot water on stove. Blend white vinegar, water, salt and keep hot. Add garlic, mustard seed, Tabasco peppers, and dill seed to the hot jars. Pack okra into hot jars. Pour hot liquid over okra. Seal jars and set them in boiling water for 5 minutes.

Jesse Little, Harvest

SQUASH PICKLES

8 cups sliced sm. yellow squash	Ice water
4 med. white onions, sliced	3 cups vinegar
2 red sweet peppers, cut in strips	2 cups sugar
2 green sweet peppers, cut in strips	1 tsp. celery seed
⅓ cup coarse salt	1 tsp. tumeric

Soak first 4 ingredients in coarse salt and ice water. Drain well. Heat vinegar, sugar, celery seed, and tumeric. Boil this syrup and add vegetables. Boil for 3 minutes. Pack into hot canning jars and adjust jar lids and bands. Process in a boiling waterbath canner (212°F.) for 5 minutes.

Patsy Brazelton, Owens Cross Roads

UM-M-M PICKLES

6 cups sliced cucumbers, unpeeled	1 tsp. celery salt
1 cup sliced onion	1 cup white vinegar
1 cup cut-up bell pepper	2 cups sugar

Put all in large container or jar. Shake well and refrigerate overnight. Read to use and keeps well in refrigerator indefinitely.

Mabel Albright, Darwin Downs

JERRIE'S BEETS

½ gal. beets	2 cups brown sugar
3 cups apple cider vinegar	1 cup white sugar
1 cup water	2 sticks cinnamon
1 tsp. allspice	Dash of salt

Boil beets until tender, peel, and slice or leave baby beets whole. Set aside, mix remaining ingredients and boil for 5 minutes. Add beets and simmer 15 minutes. Pack beets in hot jars; cover with liquids; adjust jar lids and bands. Process in a boiling waterbath canner (212°F.) for 30 minutes. Yield: Approximately 6 pints.

Mrs. Claude Bridges, (Laura), Monrovia

RED BEET JELLY

6 cups red beet juice
½ cup lemon juice
2 pkgs. Sure-Jell
1 6-oz. raspberry Jello
8 cups sugar

When canning red beets, peel the beets before cooking to get juice. The beets peel better than oranges if the tops are cut off first—then the outer skin is easily peeled down. And the beets do not lose the color! Place beet and lemon juices and Sure-Jell in a large pan and bring to a boil. Add Jello and sugar. Bring to a second boil and cook for 6 minutes. Pour into sterile jars. Adjust jar lids and bands. Process in boiling waterbath canner (212°F.) for 5 minutes.

Mabel Albright, Darwin Downs

CHILI SAUCE

8 lb. (4 qt.) skinned ripe tomatoes, cut-up
6 med. onions, chopped
6 green peppers, chopped
1 cup sugar
2 T. salt
3 cups cider vinegar
4 tsp. whole cloves
3 T. whole allspice
1 tsp. Tabasco sauce

Combine the first 6 ingredients in deep kettle; tie spices in cheesecloth bag. Add to kettle; cook uncovered for 2½ to 3 hours or until quite thick, stirring often. Remove spice bag. Stir in Tabasco. Pour sauce at once into hot, clean, sterilized jars. Adjust lids and bands. Process in a boiling waterbath canner (212°F.) for 10 minutes. Yield: 4 to 5 pints.

Estelle Pinion, Central

HOMEMADE CATCHUP

3 tsp. whole cloves
3 tsp. broken cinnamon stick
2 tsp. celery seed
½ tsp. cayenne pepper
3 tsp. salt
½ tsp. garlic salt
2 cups white vinegar
16 lb. ripe tomatoes
1 med. chopped onion
2 cups sugar

Measure spices (except salts); add vinegar, cover, and bring to a boil. Remove and set aside to steep. Wash and quarter tomatoes. Add garlic salt and onion; bring to boil. Cook 15 minutes: Stir occasionally. Press through colander. Add sugar, bring to boil, and simmer until reduced to half. Strain vinegar mixture; discard spices. Add mixture and salt to tomatoes and simmer until as thick as catchup. Pour into sterilized jars and adjust jar lids and bands. Process in a boiling waterbath canner (212°F.) for 10 minutes. Yield: 4 to 5 pints.

Myrtie Reynolds, New Sharon

HOT DOG RELISH

4 cups ground onions
12 green peppers
6 red peppers (not hot)
10 green tomatoes, ground
½ cup salt

6 cups sugar
1½ tsp. tumeric
2 cups water
1 T. celery seed
2 T. mustard seed

4 cups vinegar

After grinding all vegetables using a coarse blade, sprinkle with salt and let stand overnight. Squeeze and drain. Combine remaining ingredients and pour over vegetable mixture. Heat to boiling then simmer for 3 minutes. Pack in sterile jars. Adjust jar lids and bands and process in a boiling waterbath canner (212°F.) for 10 minutes. Yield: 8 or 9 pints.

Mabel Albright, Darwin Downs

HOT PEPPER JELLY

1 cup sweet red peppers
¼-½ cup hot peppers

1½ cups apple cider vinegar
6½ cups sugar

1 btl. Certo

Chop red sweet peppers; add hot peppers and vinegar; put mixture in blender and puree. Pour into large saucepan with sugar and bring to rolling boil. Boil 1 minute. Cool 5 minutes; add Certo and stir until mixture starts to jell. Pour into jars and adjust jar lids and bands. Process in a boiling waterbath canner (212°F.) for 5 minutes. Good with meats, especially pork.

Brenda Williams, Harvest

PEPPER JELLY

½ cup hot green or red peppers
¾ cup red or green bell pepper
1½ cups cider vinegar
5 cups sugar
1 btl. Certo

Grind peppers; then add all ingredients except Certo. Put on stove and bring to a boil. Remove for 10 minutes, then add Certo and bring to another boil. Skim and pour into jars and adjust jar lids and bands. Process in a boiling waterbath canner (212°F.) for 5 minutes.

Barbara Webster, Owens Cross Roads

SLICED CUCUMBERS FOR FREEZER

2 qt. sliced cucumbers, unpeeled
2 T. salt
1 cup vinegar
1½ cups sugar

Put cucumbers in strainer; sprinkle with salt. Use hands to stir 2 or 3 times. Let drain for 2 hours. Put in freezer containers. Cover with mixture of vinegar and sugar. Do not heat anything. Put in freezer. (Very crisp.)

Mrs. Ruth Gump, Monrovia

TOMATO RELISH

1 gal. green tomatoes
8 bell peppers
2 or 3 hot peppers
6 onions
3 cups sugar
2 cups vinegar
2 tsp. salt
1 tsp. cinnamon
1 tsp. cloves
1 tsp. allspice

Grind tomatoes, peppers, and onion in food chopper. Add sugar, vinegar, salt, and spices. Cook until thick. Pour into jars and adjust jar lids and bands. Process in a boiling waterbath canner (212°F.) for 10 minutes.

Brenda Williams, Harvest

TOMATO SAUCE

½ bushel tomatoes, cored
½ tsp. canning salt, per pint
½ tsp. sugar, per pint

Quarter tomatoes. Cook down until only tomato liquid remains but *do not add any water.* Put liquid through a sieve. Return to stove and cook for 2 to 3 hours on medium, stirring occasionally until thick. Pour into hot sterilized jars; cover with seals that have been heated in hot water; put rim in place and tighten. Place in water-bath canner and process for 10 minutes.

Nan Rogers, Madison

HOG'S HEAD STEW

1-1½ hog's head
2 venison shoulders or 6 lbs. ground beef
4 chickens
1 peck onions
1 gal. potatoes
3 lg. cans tomato juice

1 pkg. poultry seasoning
2½ gal. each of tomatoes, peas, corn, carrots
Bay leaves to taste
3 lbs. salt or to taste
3-4 qts. broth, to thin
Worcestershire sauce (optional)

Cook all meats until meat is easily removed from bone. Grind meat in a food processor with remaining ingredients. Place the mixture in a large kettle and heat to boiling. Have quart or pint jars ready. When stew starts to boil, place in hot sterile jars, leaving at least 1-inch head space. Meats do not need to be packed tightly. Process at 10 pounds pressure for 90 minutes for quarts and 75 minutes for pints. This is as good as chili for those long cold winter months.

Doris Coward, Harvest

HOMEMADE HOMINY

Select dried white corn with flat grains; shell about 1 gallon and wash thoroughly. Soak in lukewarm water for an hour. Dissolve 4 tablespoons of lye (Red Devil) in 2 gallons boiling water, using an enamel pot to cook corn in. Add the soaked corn and boil for 30 minutes or long enough to loosen the husks and kernels near the germ. A barrel churn is good to use for 5 to 10 minutes for this purpose. Let stand in fresh water for 2 or 3 hours. Changing the water 7 or 8 times, until all traces of lye are gone. Cover with fresh water and boil until tender. (Will have yellow cast to water when start washing. After lye is gone water will be clear.) May be canned or shared with friends. If canning hominy pack hot hominy into jars to about ½ inch of top. Add ½ teaspoon salt to pints; 1 teaspoon to quarts. Cover with boiling water, leaving ½ inch heat space at top of jars. Adjust jar lids and bands. Process in a pressure canner at 10 pounds pressure (240°F.)—pint jars, 60 minutes; quart jars, 70 minutes.

Mrs. Allen Drake (Wilma), Monrovia

SPICED PEAR BUTTER

6 lbs. firm ripe pears
1¼ cups water
¼ cup. lemon juice
½ tsp. salt

1½ tsp. ground cinnamon
¼ tsp. ground cloves
3½ cups brown sugar, packed

Wash, quarter and core, but do not peel pears. In a 6 quart pan, combine pears, water and lemon juice; cover and simmer until fruit is soft, 20-30 minutes. Whirl mixture in blender. Return to pan and add salt, cinnamon, cloves, and sugar. Simmer, uncovered, stirring frequently as the mixture thickens, until very thick and mixture is reduced to 8 cups — it takes about 2 hrs.. Ladle boiling hot butter into hot clean canning jars to within ¼" of top. Slide spatula between jar and butter, wipe rim; then set on hot lid and screw on ring band. Place filled jars on a rack in canning kettle half filled with hot water; add boiling water to cover jars with an inch of water. Cover kettle. For ½ pints, process 10 minutes after water boils. Remove jars and cool. Makes about 4 pints.

Ruth Ann Stalnaker, Hillwood

MISCELLANEOUS

HOW TO FREEZE IRISH POTATOES

Wash small or large potatoes well. Put them in boiling water and cook until about ¼-done; remove from water; cool; put them in freezer bags or cups and freeze. Use any way you wish. Good. (For large potatoes, peel and cook until ½ done.)

Ina Mae Lawler, Central

MAPLE SYRUP

1 cup boiling water
2 cups sugar
½ tsp. Maplene flavoring
½ tsp. lemon juice

Pour boiling water over sugar and add Maplene flavoring. Add lemon juice and bring to a boil to prevent graining. Stir and syrup is ready to serve over pancakes, waffles, or whatever.

Louise McGehee, Hurricane

CHILDREN'S RECIPES

APPLEWICH I

Apples, sliced
Orange juice
Cheese slices

Dip apple slices in saucer of orange juice (or similar citrus juice) to keep them from turning brown. Place slice of cheese between two slices of apple, and you have an applewich.

Connie Wagner, Rainbow Mountain

APPLEWICH II

1 lg. red or golden delicious apple   Lemon juice
Peanut butter

Have mother slice apple in ¼-inch slices across the diameter. There will be a star in the middle of each slice. Dislodge seeds. Dip slices in lemon juice. Blot and spread with peanut butter, using an apple slice to top. Fun to make and fun to eat!

Sheryl Daniels, Heritage

BACON-ENGLISH MUFFINS

3 English muffins, halved
Butter
12 pieces bacon
6 tomato slices
6 American cheese slices

Spread muffin halves with butter. Place muffins and bacon slices on rack in broiler pan. Broil 3 inches from heat until bacon is brown, about 2 minutes. Remove muffins and turn bacon over and broil 1 minute longer. Top each muffin half with 1 tomato slice, 2 pieces bacon, and 1 slice American cheese. Broil for about 1 minute. Serves 6.

Jeanie Marsh, Harvest

BACON OMELET

1 T. margarine
1 egg
1 T. milk or cream
Dash of salt
Dash of black pepper
1 slice bacon

Heat margarine in skillet over low heat to bubbling. Beat egg with milk or cream, salt, and pepper until fluffy. Pour egg mixture into buttered skillet, cooking slowly over low heat. As undersurface of egg mixture starts to set, lift it slightly with spatula to let the uncooked portion flow under and cook; sprinkle the cooked and crumbled bacon on top of egg mixture. As soon as all of mixture is set, fold and serve. (For a family use 6 measures of each ingredient.)

Mrs. O. V. Mitchell, Central

BARBECUED WIENERS

1 pkg. wieners
Barbecue sauce
Cheese (any kind)

Slice wieners lengthwise; insert a slice of cheese in each. Cover with sauce and bake in 350-degree oven for ½ hour. (Easy and good.)

Jimmie Covington, Central

BELIEVE-IT-OR-NOT COOKIES

1 egg
1 cup brown sugar
1 cup peanut butter (creamy or crunchy)

Mix in bowl; roll into balls and mash with a fork. Place on greased cookie sheet. Bake at 375 degrees for 10 minutes.

Carlla Hooper, Heritage

BREADSTICKS

⅓ cup butter
2 cups Bisquick
½ cup cold water
Additional butter, melted

Melt butter in 13x9x2-inch pan. With a fork, stir Bisquick and cold water in bowl. Smooth dough into a ball on floured surface and knead 5 or 6 times. Roll into rectangle, about 10x6 inches. Cut lengthwise in half; cut each half into 12 equal strips. Dip strips in butter, completely coating each strip. Bake in buttered pan for 12 to 15 minutes at 450 degrees.

Jeanie Marsh, Harvest

BREAKFAST BEFORE

½ lb. sausage
6 eggs
2 cups milk
1 tsp. salt
⅛ tsp. dry mustard
2 slices bread, cubed, or enough to cover bottom of dish
1 cup grated Cheddar cheese

Brown sausage; drain. Beat eggs with milk, salt, and mustard. Layer bread cubes, sausage, and cheese in baking dish. Pour egg mixture on top. Bake at 400 degrees for 25 to 30 minutes. If desired freeze the bread-sausage-and-cheese portion ahead. The day before you wish to bake, remove from freezer, add egg mixture and let set overnight. A good company breakfast.

Diane McFarland, Harvest

FRANKFURTER-NOODLE CASSEROLE

8 all-beef frankfurters, sliced
¼ cup chopped onion
2 T. butter
2 cups cooked med. noodles
1 can tomato soup
½ cup water
1 tsp. mustard
¼ cup buttered bread crumbs

Put frankfurters, onion, and butter in saucepan and cook until onion is tender. Combine above with noodles and mix well. Blend together soup, water, and mustard. Add to noodle mixture and place in 1½-quart casserole dish. Top with crumbs. Bake at 350 degrees for 30 minutes. Serves 4.

Melenda Ellis, Owens Cross Roads

GOLDEN SHELL CAKE

1 stick of butter, melted
2 eggs
1½ cups sugar
2 cups flour
1 tsp. salt
1 cup milk
1 tsp. soda
½ tsp. baking powder
½ tsp. cinnamon (optional)

Mix butter and eggs. Then add sugar, flour, salt, milk, soda, baking powder, and maybe cinnamon. For better taste add the cinnamon. Stir. When ready pour into greased bundt pan. Cook at 350 degrees for 36 minutes on top shelf of oven. Take out and let cool. Then gloss.

Gloss

1½ cups powdered sugar   15 tsp. milk
4 drops yellow food coloring

Mix powdered sugar and milk. Stir until mixture runs from the spoon. Add food coloring then. When cake is cool, pour gloss over it.

Heather Marsh (Age 8), Harvest

GOOD STUFF

1 pie crust, unbaked
Pecans, chopped
8 ozs. cream cheese
9 ozs. Cool Whip
1½ cups powdered sugar
Bananas, sliced
2 pkgs. pudding, instant
Milk
Additional Cool Whip

Make crust for 9x13-inch pan. Sprinkle chopped pecans over crust before baking at 350 degrees for 20 minutes. Mix cream cheese, Cool Whip, and powdered sugar until creamy and spread over crust. Cover this with sliced bananas. Mix instant pudding and spread over the bananas. Garnish with Cool Whip.

Lila M. Brown, Harvest

GRANOLA

½ cup water
3 tsp. salt
½ cup oil
½ tsp. vanilla
½ cup brown sugar
½ cup honey

8 cups oats
1 cup wheat germ
1 cup sesame seeds
1 cup coconut
1 cup raw cashews or sliced almonds

Mix first 6 ingredients. Add to remaining ingredients. Bake for 45 minutes at 325 degrees in shallow pan. Stir every 15 minutes.

Gloria Radke, South Huntsville

HOT DOGS

8 slices of bread
Soft butter
Mustard

8 cheese slices
8 hot dogs, cooked
¼ cup melted butter

Spread 1 side of a slice of bread with soft butter and mustard. Place bread on baking sheet and top with a slice of cheese; put hot dog on cheese. Fold bread over dog to make a triangle shape. Brush with butter. Broil 4 to 5 inches from heat for about 2 minutes.

Jeanie Marsh, Harvest

KIM'S BROWNIES

1 cup margarine
⅓ cup cocoa
2 cups sugar

4 eggs
1½ cups flour
1 tsp. vanilla
½ cup chopped walnuts

Melt margarine and cocoa. Mix sugar and eggs well. Add flour and vanilla. Pour in melted ingredients. Add nuts. Bake in greased 9x13-inch pan at 350 degrees for 15 or 20 minutes.

Kimberly Reichmann, age 11, Rainbow Mountain

OATMEAL MEAT LOAF

1½ lbs. ground chuck
¾ cup quick-cooking oats
1 med. onion, chopped
1 egg

1½ tsp. salt
¼ tsp. pepper
1 can tomato juice

Put ground chuck in bowl and break apart with a fork. Add oats and set aside. Combine remaining ingredients in a blender and liquify. Stir all ingredients together until well blended. Put in a loaf pan and bake for 1 hour and 15 minutes at 350 degrees. Let stand 10 minutes before slicing. Serves 6.

Melenda Ellis, Owens Cross Roads

OLD-TIME POPCORN BALLS

5 qts. popped corn
2 cups sugar
1½ cups water
½ tsp. salt
½ cup light syrup
1 tsp. vinegar
1 tsp. vanilla

Keep corn hot and crisp in slow oven (300 to 325 degrees). Butter sides of saucepan. In it combine remaining ingredients except vanilla. Cook to hard ball stage. Add vanilla. Pour slowly over hot corn, stirring just to mix thoroughly. Butter hands lightly; shape balls. Yield: 15 to 20 balls.

La Juan Blevins, South Huntsville

OVEN-FRIED CHICKEN

⅓ cup shortening
¼ cup flour
Salt to taste
Pepper to taste
½ tsp. paprika
2 lb. chicken legs

Melt shortening and set aside. Mix flour, salt, pepper, and paprika in paper bag. Wash and dry chicken legs. Place 3 or 4 at a time in bag and shake till well coated. Put on ungreased 13x9x2-inch baking pan and drizzle shortening on chicken; bake uncovered for 45 minutes at 425 degrees.

Jeanie Marsh, Harvest

Too many people are looking for rewards from efforts that produce only consequences.

PINK PUNCH

1 qt. btl. Wink 1 sm. can frozen pink lemonade
Crushed ice

Mix using only 1 can of water instead of 3 as directed on lemonade can.
Martha Sparks, Rainbow Mountain

POPSICLES

2 cups cold water 1 pkg. regular Kool Aid
or 1 cup sugar
4 cups very hot tap water 1 pkg. Jello
2 cups boiling water

Mix and keep in pitcher. Shake well before filling forms. Yield: 20 to 24 popsicles.
La Juan Blevins, South Huntsville

PURPLE COW

In tall glass put 1 or 2 scoops vanilla ice cream and finish filling with grape soda. Serve with straw. Variation: Use different-flavored soda pop, 1 tablespoon molasses, ½ cup cold milk, or 1 scoop vanilla ice cream and finish filling with chilled club soda.
Jeanie Marsh, Harvest

SMILING PANCAKES

Make pancakes according to directions on Bisquick box. Heat pan; pour small amounts into pan in form of a smiling face; let cook till bubbly then pour more batter over face. Cook until bubbly; turn; cook till browned.
Jeanie Marsh, Harvest

MICROWAVE

MAIN DISHES

BAKED CHICKEN PIECES

2 lbs. chicken pieces, skinned Paprika

Place chicken in baking dish and sprinkle with paprika. Cover and cook for 14 minutes, turn, and rearrange pieces. Cook for 12 minutes longer, until done. Let stand for 10 to 15 minutes before serving. To brown meat you can place under broiler in conventional oven for a few minutes.

Louise McGehee, Hurricane

BAKED HAM SLICE

1 ham slice, 1½-inch thick   1 tsp. prepared mustard
2 T. brown sugar

Place ham in shallow baking dish. Spread mustard on top and sprinkle with brown sugar. Cover, cook for 10 to 12 minutes. Rotate dish halfway through cooking time. Allow to stand for 5 minutes before serving.

Louise McGehee, Hurricane

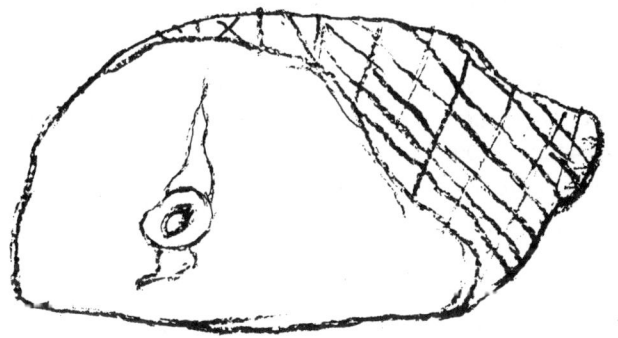

BEEF STROGANOFF

¼ cup butter
3 lg. onions, sliced
1 T. mustard
1 tsp. salt
Dash of black pepper

2 lbs. top round steak, cut into thin strips
2 4-oz. cans mushroom stems and pieces, drained
1 cup dairy sour cream

Hot buttered noodles or rice

Combine butter, onions, mustard, salt, and pepper in a 3-quart glass casserole. Cover and cook on *saute* for 5 minutes. Add beef. Cover and cook on *high* for 10 minutes; stir once. Add mushrooms, cover, and cook on *simmer* for 25 minutes or until meat is tender. Stir once or twice while cooking. Add sour cream, cover, and cook on *defrost* for 5 minutes. Serve with noodles or rice.

Dorothy Mellette, Central

CHICKEN DIVAN

2 whole chicken breasts, boned
1 cup water
⅛ tsp. dried rosemary leaves
¼ tsp. salt
⅛ tsp. pepper
2 10-oz. pkg. frozen chopped broccoli

2 can cream of chicken soup
¼ cup dry white wine
½ cup shredded processed Swiss cheese (2 ozs.)
¼ cup grated Parmesan cheese
Paprika

Cut chicken into ¼-inch cubes. Combine chicken, water, rosemary, salt, and pepper in a 1½-quart casserole. Cover with clear plastic wrap; microwave at medium high for 5 to 7 minutes or until done. Drain chicken, reserving ¼ cup broth; set aside. Pierce broccoli packages with a fork; place packages in a flat baking dish. Microwave on high for 7 to 9 minutes. Drain broccoli. Combine soup, wine, Swiss cheese, and reserved broth. Place chicken in a 12x8x2-inch baking dish; pour half of soup mixture over chicken. Top with broccoli then remaining soup mixture. Cover with wax paper; microwave at medium for 9 to 11 minutes. Sprinkle with Parmesan cheese and paparika. Cover and microwave at medium for 1½ to 2½ minutes. Yield: 6 to 8 servings.

Mary Anne Riley, South Parkway

CHICKEN LIVERS AND ONIONS

8 ozs. chicken livers, halved (about 10)

2 T. melted butter
1 med. onion, sliced

Melt butter in baking dish on high setting for 30 seconds. Put livers in dish and coat with butter. Slice onion over livers and cook uncovered for about 6 minutes on half power. Turn and rearrange livers halfway through cooking cycle.

Nancy Lackey, Piedmont

TURKEY, BACON, TOMATO SANDWICH

1 English muffin
Crisp bacon, crumbled
Mayonnaise

Turkey slices
1 slice of tomato
Cheese slices

Slightly toast English muffin. Combine crisp, crumbled bacon with mayonnaise and spread on muffin. Add sliced turkey and a thick slice of tomato and top with strips of cheese. Place in microwave on low heat until cheese melts, on 8 for about 1½ minutes.

Nita Gillespie, Piedmont

JAN'S MEATZA PIE

1 lb. ground beef	1 can mushrooms, drained
½ tsp. salt	½ tsp. garlic salt
Dash of pepper	1 tsp. oregano
⅔ cup evap. milk	½ tsp. onion salt
½ cup bread crumbs	2 T. Parmesan cheese
8 ozs. tomato sauce	½ cup grated mozzarella cheese

Mix first 5 ingredients. Put onto sides and bottom of a 10-inch pie plate. Bake for 4 minutes on high, turning once. Spread tomato sauce over mixture. Arrange mushrooms on top. Top with mixture of remaining ingredients. Bake for 4 minutes, turning once. Let stand for 4 minutes, covered.

Mary Ann Riley, South Parkway

PIZZA FRANKS

1 8-oz. can tomato sauce	8 frankfurters
½ tsp. dried oregano leaves	8 frankfurter buns, split
¼ tsp. dried basil leaves	6 ozs. shredded pizza cheese

Combine tomato sauce, oregano, and basil in bowl. Mix well. Place a frankfurter in each bun; top each with 2 tablespoonfuls tomato sauce mixture. Place prepared buns in glass baking dish; cover with pizza cheese. Cover with wax paper and cook in microwave oven on high setting for 3 minutes or until cheese is melted.

Alta Newman, Central

Don't say the thing is impossible;
The chances are you can do it.
Because some fool who doesn't know
Will come along and do it!

PORK LIVER STROGANOFF

2 T. butter or margarine
1 med. onion, sliced
¾ lb. pork livers
1 can Campbell's mushroom soup
½ tsp. salt
Dash of pepper
1 T. all-purpose flour
¾ cup dairy sour cream

Place butter and onions in 10-inch ceramic skillet or 2-quart utility dish. Cook in microwave oven on full power for 2 or 3 minutes until onions are tender. Cut pork livers in 1-inch pieces. Add livers and mushroom soup to onion mixture; sprinkle with salt and pepper. Cook covered on full power for 6 or 8 minutes or until livers are cooked. Stir halfway through cooking time. Stir flour into sour cream; spoon over livers; cook on full power for 1 minute until heated through. This may be served over cooked rice or noodles. Note: May substitute 1 14-ounce can of sliced mushrooms, drained, for mushroom soup.

Alta Newman, Central

SWEET AND SOUR PORK I

4 med. carrots, pared, sliced thin
¼ cup cooking oil
1 med. onion, sliced
2 green peppers, seeded, sliced
2 lb. lean pork cut in ¾-inch cubes
¼ cup cornstarch
1 16-oz. can pineapple chunks, drained (reserve ½ cup syrup)
½ cup soy sauce
½ cup brown sugar
¼ cup vinegar
1 T. Worcestershire sauce
¼ cup hot pepper sauce
½ tsp. pepper

Put carrots and oil in 3-quart microproof casserole; stir-cook, covered, on high (maximum power) for 4 minutes. Add onions, green peppers, and pork. Cover and cook on high (maximum power) for 5 minutes. In a bowl, mix cornstarch and reserved pineapple syrup. Blend in remaining ingredients. Add to pork, along with pineapple chunks. Stir. Cover and cook on high (maximum power) for 10 minutes or until sauce has thickened and pork is done. Serve with rice or chow mein noodles.

Pat Smith, South Huntsville

SWEET AND SOUR PORK II

1½ lbs. lean pork shoulder, cut in ½-inch cubes
1 sm. onion, chopped
1 tsp. salt
1 8-oz. can pineapple slices
1 2-oz. pkg. sweet and sour mix
2 green peppers, seeded and cut in squares

Place pork cubes, onions, and salt in a 2 to 3-quart baking dish. Cook, covered, on *high* for 20 minutes; stir once; drain off pork fat. Drain pineapple slices, reserving juice. Add enough water to pineapple juice to make 1¼ cups liquid. Add to pork mixture. Cook, covered, on *high* for 10 minutes, stirring once. Stir in sweet and sour mix, cover, and cook on *high* for 8 minutes, stirring once. Cut pineapple slices in small pieces. Add to pork mixture with green pepper squares. Cook, covered, on *high* for 4 minutes, stirring once. Remove from oven and let stand for 5 minutes. Serve with hot cooked rice or chow mein noodles. Note: This dish tastes better when it is made early in the day and then reheated at dinner time.

Dorothy Mellette, Central

SWISS STEAK

2 T. butter or margarine	1½-2 lbs. boneless beef round steak
2 T. all-purpose flour	
1 tsp. salt	1 med. onion, sliced
¼ tsp. pepper	¼ cup packed brown sugar
¼ tsp. dry mustard	½ cup catchup

Place butter in 2-quart (12x7-inch) glass baking dish. Microwave on roast for 1 minute or until melted. Combine flour, salt, pepper, and mustard in plate. Cut meat into serving pieces and coat in seasoned flour. Pound with wooden mallet. Arrange seasoned meat in melted butter. Cover with glass lid or plastic wrap. Microwave on high for about 5 minutes or until no longer pink. Turn meat over. Place onion rings on top. Combine catchup and brown sugar in 2-cup measure. Pour over meat. Cover with plastic wrap. Microwave on *simmer* for 15 minutes. Rearrange meat, recover, and continue cooking on simmer until fork tender. Let stand, covered, for 5 minutes before serving. Serves 4.

Madison County

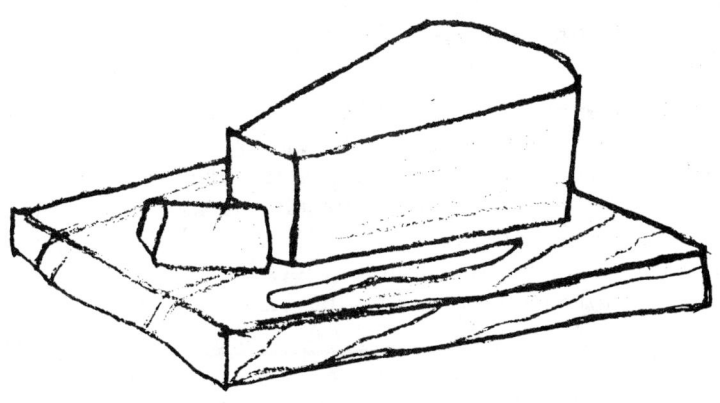

MICROWAVE YELLOW SQUASHEROLE

Power level: High (10) and Medium (5)
Microwave time: 16½ to 21 min., total

2 tbsp. butter
¼ cup buttery flavored cracker crumbs
¼ cup chopped pecans
¼ cup water
½ tsp. salt
1 lb. yellow squash, sliced
¼ cup mayonnaise
1 egg, beaten
½ cup shredded cheddar cheese
2 tbsp. butter, melted
2 tbsp. butter, melted
1½ tsp. sugar
¼ to ½ tsp. minced onion

In 1-qt. casserole place butter. Microwave at high ½ to 1 minute until melted. Add crumbs and pecans. Microwave at high 2 minutes, stirring after 1 minute. Pour crumbs onto waxed paper and set aside. In same casserole, place water, salt and squash. Cover. Microwave at high 8 to 10 minutes, stirring after 4 minutes until tender. Drain. Mix together mayonnaise, egg, cheese, butter, sugar and onion. Pour over squash, mixing well. Microwave at medium 4 minutes. Stir, then add crumb topping. Microwave at medium 2 to 4 minutes more until center is set. Let stand 5 minutes before serving. Makes about 4 servings.

Toni Duggar, South Parkway

MICROWAVE CHOCOLATE CHIP BARS

Power level: High (10)
Microwave time: 5 to 7 min., total

½ cup (¼ lb.) butter, softened
¾ cup brown sugar (packed)
1 egg
1 tbsp. milk
1 tsp. vanilla extract
1¼ cups unsifted all-purpose flour
½ tsp. baking powder
1/8 tsp. salt
1 cup (6 oz.) semi sweet chocolate pieces, divided
½ cup chopped nuts (optional)

In small mixer bowl cream together butter and sugar, until fluffy. Add egg, milk, and vanilla. Mix well. Stir together flour, baking powder and salt. Add to creamed mixture. Blend well. Stir in ½ cup chocolate pieces and nuts. Spread in greased 8-inch square dish. Sprinkle with remaining ½ cup chocolate pieces. Microwave at high 5 to 7 minutes, rotating dish ¼ turn ever 2 minutes, until done. Cool and cut into bars. Makes about 24 bars.

Toni Duggar, South Parkway

SIDE DISHES

ASPARAGUS CASSEROLE

1 can mushroom soup
1 stick margarine
1 can sm. peas (English)
1 can asparagus
2 cups cracker crumbs
1 cup Velveeta cheese, grated

Cook soup and margarine together for 2 minutes on full power. Put ½ the peas in a casserole. Add asparagus, then remaining peas followed by crumbs. Top with cheese and pour oleo-and-mushroom mixture over all. Cook on full power for 4 minutes.

Margaret Birchfield, Central

BAKED BEANS

2 cups cooked white beans
½ tsp. dry mustard
1 sm. onion, chopped fine
¼ cup catchup
2 T. brown sugar
4 slices bacon

Combine beans, mustard, onion, catchup, and brown sugar in 1-quart glass casserole. Top with bacon. Cover. Cook in microwave oven for 9 to 11 minutes or until bubbling throughout. Total cooking time about 10 minutes. (Optional: Pork and beans maybe used instead of white beans). Serves 4.

Louise McGehee, Hurricane

CHEESY BAKED POTATO

1 10¾-oz. can Cheddar cheese
  soup
½ cup milk
½ tsp. salt
½ tsp. pepper
Dash of red pepper
5 cups sliced potatoes
2½ cups sliced onions

Combine soup, milk, salt, and pepper. Place ½ of potatoes in 2-quart casserole. Top with ½ of onions and ½ of soup mixture. Repeat the process. Cook, covered, on cookmatic level 8 for 20 to 25 minutes or until potatoes are tender.

Alta Newman, Central

CREAMY SCALLOPED POTATOES

4 med. potatoes, peeled, sliced thin (3 cups)
1 med. onion, sliced thin
1 10½-oz. can condensed cream of celery soup
½ cup milk
Salt
Pepper
2 T. butter or oleo
¼ cup bread crumbs

Layer potatoes and onion in 1½-quart ovenware casserole. Set aside. Combine soup and milk in 2-cup glass measure and cook in microwave for 2½ to 3½ minutes or until mixture starts boiling. Add salt and pepper and dot potatoes with butter. Spread soup over top. Cover. Cook in microwave oven 12 minutes, stirring after 6 minutes and after 12 minutes of cooking. Add bread crumbs to top of casserole. Cook for 4 to 6 minutes or until potatoes are tender. Let stand for 5 minutes before serving. NOTE: When stirring, spoon potatoes from center of dish to outside. Total cooking time is about 20 minutes. Serves 6.

Louise McGehee, Hurricane

FROZEN CREAM-STYLE CORN

Bacon drippings or margarine
1 T. flour
1 pt. corn
½ cup sweet milk
Salt
Sugar

Mix bacon drippings and flour in 1⅓-quart casserole dish. Add corn and milk. Mix well and cover. Cook in microwave for 4 minutes. Stir corn, cover, and cook for 4 minutes longer. Add salt and a little sugar, stir, and let stand, covered, for 4 minutes before serving.

Louise McGehee, Hurricane

HERB CHEESE SPREAD

3 lbs. cream cheese
¾ cup milk
Chives
Garlic powder
Onion powder
Salt

Heat cream cheese in casserole in microwave for approximately 10 minutes, stirring and turning as necessary until softened. Add milk and blend ingredients. Start with 2 teaspoons of each seasoning and increase amount to your own taste. Return to microwave for another 10 minutes, stirring every 2 minutes to blend flavors. Test to see if flavor suits you. You may add other ingredients if you like for variety; pimientos, olives, bacon bits, etc. When taste is to you liking, transfer to airtight containers for the refrigerator. May be kept for 1 to 2 months.

Betty Cothran, Athens Pike

MIXED FRUIT SALAD

1 can mandarin oranges
1 can chunk pineapple
1 can peaches

1 box tapioca pudding
1 box vanilla pudding
3 bananas, sliced

Cherries (optional)

May vary size of recipe by using small, medium, or large-size cans. I use medium-size cans. Drain fruit and add enough water to juice to equal 3 cups liquid. Add 1 box of tapioca pudding mix to liquid; then add 1 box vanilla pudding. Place in deep dish, cover with Saran Wrap, and pierce with fork. Cook in microwave for 8 minutes on high. Cool and fold in fruit.

Nita Gillespie, Piedmont

SPAGHETTI SQUASH

Pierce squash with fork in several places. Place on paper towel and cook in microwave on high setting for 12 to 15 minutes or until shell is soft, turning squash 4 times. Let stand for a few minutes to complete cooking. Cut in half. Fluff pulp with fork, tossing lightly to separate spaghettilike strands.

Ham And Nut Topping

2 T. oil
1 tsp. garlic salt

¼ cup pecans
1 cup minced cooked ham

Heat oil, stir in garlic salt, add remaining ingredients, and continue stirring until hot. Spoon over fluffed up squash and serve from shell.

Alta Newman, Central

STEAMED CABBAGE

4 cups shredded cabbage

2-3 T. water

Butter (optional)

Put ingredients in casserole with water. Cook for 7 to 10 minutes on full power, stirring once. Remove and add butter if desired.

Nancy Lackey, Piedmont

TOMATO PARMESAN

2 med. tomatoes, sliced
1 T. Parmesan cheese
1 tsp. sesame seeds
1 tsp. minced onion
⅛ tsp. garlic salt
1 tsp. paprika

Arrange tomatoes in baking dish. Mix cheese and remaining ingredients; pour our tomatoes. Cover with Saran Wrap and cook for 10 minutes on about 7.

Nita Gillespie, Piedmont

DESSERTS AND CANDIES

CHOCOLATE PUDDING

⅔ cup sugar
¼ cup cocoa
3½ T. cornstarch
¼ tsp. salt
2 cups milk
3 T. butter
1 tsp. vanilla

Combine first 4 ingredients in medium-sized glass bowl; stir milk in gradually. Microwave on full power for 5 mintues, stirring once during cooking time. Put back in oven and cook for another 1 to 2 minutes or until thickened. Remove and add butter and vanilla. Pour into serving dishes and chill.

Betty Butcher, Athens Pike

FRESH APPLE BREAD PUDDING

½ cup dried currants
¼ cup apple juice, apple concentrate, or apple brandy
¼ cup butter or margarine
4 med. apples, peeled, cored, sliced
3 cups stale French bread, cut into ½-inch cubes
1½ cups milk
½ cup heavy cream
⅓ cup brown sugar
5 eggs

Soak currants in apple juice, concentrate, or brandy and set aside. Melt butter in cake pan, add apple slices, stir, and cook on high power for 2 minutes. Remove from oven and stir in bread cubes. Set aside. Measure milk and cream into 4-cup Pyrex bowl and heat for 3 to 4 minutes but do not allow to boil. Remove from oven, add sugar, and stir in beaten eggs. Add softened currants, pour this mixture over bread and apples slices and let stand for 5 minutes to absorb the liquid. Microwave on medium power for 10 to 12 minutes, turning pan and stirring pudding every 3 minutes. After last stirring, sprinkle topping over pudding.

Topping

½ cup chopped walnuts   2 T. brown sugar

Let stand for 10 minutes before serving. Serve warm with whipped cream, if desired.

Angie Pamfiles, Westbury

EASIEST EVER COCOA FUDGE

3⅔ cups powdered sugar (1 lb.)
½ cup Hershey's cocoa
¼ cup milk
½ cup butter
1 T. vanilla
½ cup chopped nuts (optional)

Microwave powdered sugar, cocoa, milk, and butter on high (full power) until butter is melted, about 2 or 3 minutes; stir until smooth. Blend in vanilla and nuts. Spread into buttered 8-inch square pan. Cool...cut into squares.

Pat Smith, South Huntsville
Nita Gillespie, Piedmont

FUDGE PIE

1 stick margarine
¾ cup flour
1 cup sugar
1 tsp. vanilla
Pinch of salt

2 whole eggs
¼ cup cocoa
¼ pecans or walnuts (optional)
Whipped or sour cream (optional)

Make margarine for 30 seconds in a pie plate. Combine flour and sugar. Rub margarine in pie plate and add margarine to the flour-and-sugar mixture. Add vanilla, salt, eggs, and cocoa. May also add nuts. Cook for 4 minutes on full power in microwave oven (700 watts). Top with whipped cream or sour cream, if desired.

Margaret Birchfield, Central

LAST-MINUTE SHORTCAKE

1 cup unsifted all-purpose flour
3 T. sugar
1 tsp. baking powder
¼ tsp. salt

¼ cup butter or margarine
⅓ cup milk
1 egg
Sweetened fruit
Whipped cream

Combine flour, sugar, baking powder, and salt in large mixing bowl. Cut in butter until crumbly. Measure milk in small bowl and beat in egg. Blend into flour mixture. Spoon into 4 or 5 individual glass custard cups. Microwave on simmer for 3 minutes. Microwave on high for 2 to 3 minutes or until cake is no longer doughy. Serve warm topped with sweetened fruit and whipped cream.

Anne Jones, Hurricane

MILKY WAY ICE CREAM

1 16-oz. pkg. Milky Way miniatures

1 can Eagle Brand milk
3 qts. milk
8 ozs. chocolate syrup

Melt Milky Way bars in microwave on high for almost 1½ minutes. In mixer blend melted Milky Way with Eagle Brand milk. Add 1 quart of milk and chocolate syrup. Pour into freezer can. Add 2 more quarts of milk. Freeze.

Rainbow Mountain

PEANUT BRITTLE

1 cup sugar
½ cup light Karo syrup
1 ½ cups raw peanuts

Pinch of salt
1 tsp. vanilla
1 T. butter
1 T. soda

Mix sugar, syrup, raw peanuts, and salt. Cook for 8 minutes, stirring every 2 minutes. Add vanilla and butter. Mix and cook for 2 minutes. Add soda, stir, and pour immediately onto greased sheet. Do not try to spread out as it breaks the foam. Cool and break. Roasted nuts may be used, but add after the vanilla and butter.

Irma Long, University

SOUTHERN PRALINES

1 ½ cups firmly packed light
   brown sugar
⅔ cups half-and-half

⅛ tsp. salt
2 T. butter or margarine
1 ½ cups pecan halves

Combine sugar, half-and-half, and salt in a deep 3-quart casserole; mix well. Stir in butter, microwave at high for 7 to 9½ minutes or until mixture reaches soft ball stage (235 degrees), stirring once. Stir in pecans and cool for about 1 minute. Beat by hand until mixture is creamy and begins to thicken (about 3 minutes). Drop by tablespoon onto wax paper; let stand until firm. Yields: about 2 dozen.

June Cope, Hurricane

PARTY FOODS

CANAPES AND APPETIZERS

CHICKEN CANAPES

1 cup finely ground chicken,
   cooked
1 T. mayonnaise or salad dressing
¼ cup chopped nuts

1 tsp. scraped onion
½ tsp. celery salt
1 T. sweet pickle relish
Ritz crackers

Combine chicken and mayonnaise; stir in nuts, onion, celery salt, and relish. Spread on Ritz crackers or any other crackers you wish.

Alta Newman, Central

CUCUMBER SANDWICHES

1 med. cucumber	½ tsp. salt
1 med. onion	Dash of Tabasco sauce
1 8-oz. pkg. cream cheese	Bread
Mayonnaise or butter	

Grate cucumber and onion. Mix with softened cream cheese or blend in blender with salt and Tabasco sauce. Freeze bread: this spreads and cuts better. Spread each side of bread with mayonnaise or butter and cucumber spread and serve.

Alta Newman, Central

NO-BAKE DATENUT ROLLS

1 lb. English walnuts, chopped	1 lg. bag miniature marshmallows
1 lb. pecans	1 jar maraschino cherries
1 lg. box pitted dates, chopped	1 can Eagle Brand milk
2 boxes raisins	2 boxes graham cracker crumbs

Mix all ingredients except milk and crumbs. Then add 1 box crumbs and milk; mix thoroughly. Shape by hand into desired shaped rolls, approximately 5 inches or 6 inches and roll in graham cracker crumbs. Wrap in Saran Wrap then foil. Refrigerate, freeze or tie a ribbon around them for a tasty Christmas gift.

Diane McFarland, Harvest

FRUIT CAKE LOGS

1 20-oz. box vanilla wafers	1 can coconut
2 cups pecans	½ cup candied cherries
1 cup seedless raisins	1 can Eagle Brand milk

Roll vanilla wafers into fine crumbs. Mix ingredients; shape into logs and refrigerate. Good for Christmas!

Ursula Bumpus, Central

HAM ROLLS

2 sticks melted margarine
1 tsp. Worcestershire sauce
3 T. table mustard
3 T. poppy seeds

1 onion, chopped
2 pkgs. twin dinner rolls
Swiss cheese
Ham, sliced thin

Mix margarine, Worcestershire sauce, mustard, poppy seeds, and onion for filling. Slice rolls and spread ½ of filling on both sides of rolls; place Swiss cheese and ham between layers. Spread remaining filling on top of rolls. Bake (in foil pans the rolls were in) at 400 degrees about 15 minutes. May be made ahead and baked just before serving.

Anne Weaver, Fleming Hills

HOT HAM BUNS

1 stick margarine, melted
1 med. onion, chopped
1 T. Worcestershire sauce
3 T. prepared mustard

2 tsp. poppy seed
1 pkg. Pepperidge Farm party rolls
6 slices ham, chopped
6 slices Swiss cheese, grated

Combine margarine with onions. Cook until partly tender. Mix with Worcestershire sauce, mustard, and poppy seed. Mix and spread on each side of opened rolls. Fill with ham and cheese; place in oven at 350 degrees for 25 minutes or in microwave oven for 30 seconds or until cheese partly melts.

Alta Newman, Central

MARINATED MUSHROOMS

1 8-oz. can button mushrooms
½ cup low-calorie Italian-style dressing

Tarragon
Pepper
1 garlic clove, halved (optional)

Put mushrooms and dressing in small saucepan; bring to boil and simmer for a few minutes. Pour into glass or plastic dish; add sprinkling of tarragon and pepper and garlic, if desired. Cool covered and refrigerate overnight or for a few hours. Serve at room temperature. (30 calories to 1 cup.)

Evelyn Hall, Athens Pike

MARINATED SHRIMP, MUSHROOMS, AND ARTICHOKE HEARTS

3 pkgs. Good Seasons salad dressing dry mix
Vinegar
Oil
3 onions, sliced thin
1 btl. drained capers
2½ lbs. shrimp, cooked, peeled
8 oz. whole mushrooms, drained
2 pkgs. frozen artichoke hearts, cooked (or 2 14-oz. cans, drained)
½ to 1 tsp. salt

Prepare salad dressings omitting water and replace with additional vinegar. Slightly less oil may be used. Recommended dressings are 1 blue cheese, 1 Italian, and 1 cheese and garlic. Combine all other ingredients and pour salad dressing over them. Marinate at least overnight before using.

Vicki Coffee, Extension Agent

PARTY CHICKEN SALAD

2 cups coarsely diced cooked chicken
2 T. lemon juice
½ tsp. salt
1 cup sliced celery
1 cup seedless white grapes
4 hard-cooked eggs
½ cup mayonnaise
¼ cup halved or slivered blanched almonds, toasted

Sprinkle chicken with lemon juice and salt. Chill several hours. Add celery, grapes, 2 chilled and chopped eggs, mayonnaise, and almonds; toss lightly. Season salad with salt to taste. Serve in lettuce-lined bowl.

Daisy Trim

Quarter 2 hard-cooked eggs lengthwise. Remove yolks; save. Arrange whites for petals; center with yolks. Serves 4 to 5.

Mrs. O. V. Mitchell, Central

PIG IN BLANKETS

1 lb. wieners
1 can biscuits

Take biscuits out of can. Take a wiener and wrap the biscuit around it, making sure the dough is together around the wiener. Bake at 325 degrees for 10 to 15 minutes or until golden brown. Serve hot with mustard and catchup.

Patsy Whitt, New Sharon

RUMAKI

1 lb. chicken livers
½ cup soy sauce
1 8-oz. can water chestnuts

Bacon
¾ cup brown sugar
1 btl. sweet and sour sauce

Marinate chicken livers, cut in bite-size pieces, in soy sauce for several hours. Put 1 piece of water chestnut in each piece of liver and roll in brown sugar. Wrap each piece in half strip of bacon. Secure with toothpick and roll in brown sugar again. Bake at 350 degrees for 20 to 30 minutes. May freeze before cooking. Serve with bottled sweet and sour sauce.

Mary Alice Clark, Westbury

SALMON BALL

1 5½-oz. can salmon
1 8-oz. pkg. cream cheese, softened
1 T. lemon juice

¼ tsp. salt
2 tsp. grated onion
1 tsp. horseradish
Parsley, chopped

Combine all ingredients, shape into a ball, and roll in parsley.

Mary Frances Mitchell, Madison Cross Roads

SHRIMP TREE

1 styrofoam cone
Aluminum foil
Lettuce
Toothpicks
2 lbs. cleaned, cooked shrimp

Cheese squares
Olives
2 carrots, cut in bite-size pieces
Radishes
Mushrooms buttons

Cocktail sauce or dip

Cover cone with foil, then with lettuce leaves, attaching them with toothpicks. Place shrimp, cheese, olives, carrots, radishes, and mushrooms on cone with toothpicks until cone is covered. Place cone on lettuce-covered tray; arrange more vegetables around cone. Serve with cocktail sauce or your favorite dip. May substitute ham squares for shrimp. I use Cheddar cheese for cheese squares.

Diane McFarland, Harvest

SOFT PRETZELS

1 pkg. dry yeast
1½ cups warm water
4 cups all-purpose flour
1½ tsp. sugar

¾ tsp. salt
1 egg white
Kosher salt (table salt may be substituted)

Mustard (optional)

Dissolve yeast in warm water (105 to 115 degrees). Combine flour, sugar, and salt; add yeast mixture and mix until well blended. Turn out onto a lightly floured surface and knead until smooth and elastic (about 5 minutes). Using kitchen shears dipped in flour, cut dough into 18 pieces; roll each into a ball. With floured hands, roll each ball between hands to form a rope about 14 to 16 inches long and about ½ inch in diameter; twist each into a pretzel shape, and place on a lightly greased baking sheet. Beat egg white until frothy and brush on each pretzel; sprinkle with salt. Bake at 400 degrees for 15 minutes or until lightly browned. Serve warm or cold with mustard, if desired. Yield: 1½ dozen.

Janice Coome, Hurricane

STUFFED DILL PICKLES

2 lg. dill pickles   1 sm. jar Old English cheese spread

Slice ends off of pickles and remove center with apple corer. Drain. Fill center with cheese and pack firmly. Wrap in Saran Wrap and refrigerate several hours. Slice just before serving. Serve on round crackers as hors d' oeuvres or T.V. snack.

Evelyn Hall, Athens Pike

SWEET SANDWICH FILLING

1 lemon (juice and grated rind)
1 cup sugar
1 cup mayonnaise

1 cup cut raisins
1 egg
Nuts

1-inch sq. margarine

Mix all ingredients except nuts and margarine together in saucepan and cook slowly, stirring constantly until the mixture begins to bubble. Add nuts, if desired. After mixture bubbles, remove from heat and add a 1-inch square of margarine. Will keep in refrigerator a long time. Nuts improve the flavor.

Sue Price, Westbury

TUNA ROLL-UPS

1 6½-7 oz. can chunk tuna
1 stalk celery, chopped
1 piece onion, chopped
1 egg
Salt
Pepper
Biscuit dough
Butter
1 can cream of mushroom soup
½ soup can milk

Mix tuna, celery, onion, egg, salt, and pepper. Make recipe for biscuits based on 2 cups flour. Roll out to rectangle approximately 10x15 inches and spread with butter; then spread with tuna mixture and roll like jelly roll from long edge. Cut in 12 pieces and put in a 12-cupcake pan, cut side down. Bake at 400 degrees until raised and brown (like biscuits). Serve with 1 can cream of mushroom soup diluted with ½ can milk and large piece of butter. Good served with green peas and cole slaw.

Irma Long, University

ZUCCHINI APPETIZER

3 cups grated zucchini
½ cup finely chopped onion
2 T. dried parsley
½ tsp. seasoned salt
½ tsp. oregano
½ cup vegetable oil
4 eggs, slightly beaten
1 cup Bisquick
½ cup Parmesan cheese
½ tsp. salt
½ tsp. marjoram
1 garlic clove, pressed

Mix all ingredients together. Bake in a greased 9x13 pan in a 350-degree oven for 30 minutes. Serve warm.

Sue David, South Parkway

CHEESE

APPETIZER CHEESE PIZZAS

1 lb. sharp Cheddar cheese
1 green pepper
1 sm. onion
3 or more slices raw bacon
1 tsp. Worcestershire sauce
Mayonnaise to spread
1 loaf party rye bread

Combine first 5 ingredients in meat grinder or food processor. Add enough mayonnaise to make spreadable. Spread on sliced party rye. Broil for 7 minutes.

Nancy Teasdale, South Huntsville

BILLY'S CHEESE CANAPES

Dill pickles   Crackers
                Cheese, sliced

Slice dill pickles thin and place on crackers. Cover with sliced cheese. Place in oven until cheese melts. Serve hot.

Margaret Birchfield, Central

CHEESE BALL I

2 8-oz. pkgs. cream cheese, softened
2 oz. bleu cheese, grated
½ lb. sharp Cheddar cheese, grated
Nuts, slivered

Cream thoroughly, form into balls, and roll in slivered nuts. Let set overnight.

Roberta Freidman, Harvest

CHEESE BALL II

2 lg. pkgs. cream cheese
4-6 green onions (tops and bottoms) chopped fine
½ tsp. Accent or garlic salt
1 tsp. Worcestershire sauce
1 sm. jar dried beef

Put beef in blender to chop. Mix all ingredients, saving ½ of beef. Form into ball and roll in remaining beef.

Charlene Byrd, South Parkway

CHEESE BALL III

1 jar Old English cheese
1 jar roka or bleu cheese or ½
½ cup bleu cheese
8 oz. cream cheese
1 garlic clove, minced, or ½ tsp. garlic powder
Pecans, chopped, or parsley, chopped
2 T. wine vinegar

Allow cheeses to soften; mix with vinegar then chill for easier handling. Form into ball. Roll in chopped pecans or chopped parsley.

Mary Anne Riley, South Parkway

Miscellaneous

CHEESE BALLS

1¼ cups flour
2 cups grated Cheddar cheese
½ cup butter
1 sm. jar pitted green olives

Work flour into cheese with pastry cutter or fingers until mealy. Add butter and work with hands until smooth. Take about 1 teaspoonful and flatten out in your hands and roll around olive. Chill at least an hour. Bake at 400 degrees for 15 to 20 minutes until pastry is set and lightly browned.

Donna Newton, South Parkway

CHEESE LOG

8 slices American cheese
8 slices pimiento cheese
8 ozs. cream cheese
½ tsp. garlic salt
1 cup finely chopped pecans
Paprika

Grate cheeses and mix with garlic salt and ½ cup pecans. Form into logs; sprinkle the logs with paprika, and roll in ½ cup nuts. Wrap in foil and refrigerate. Remove from refrigerator 30 minues before serving time. Serve with party crackers.

JoAnn Wester, Fleming Hills

CHEESE SPREAD

1 cup sweet milk
1¼ lb. sharp Cheddar cheese, grated
3 eggs
¼ tsp. salt
¼ tsp. mustard
1 sm. can pimientos

Put milk and cheese in top of double boiler; after cheese melts add beaten eggs, salt, and mustard. Cook 1 minute. Beat constantly while cooking on stove; remove from stove. Chop pimientos and add to mixture. Store in refrigerator. Will keep for weeks.

Alta Newman, Central

CHEESE STRAWBERRY RING

1 lb. colby cheese
1 sm. onion or 4 or 5 green onions
1 cup mayonnaise
1 cup pecans
Strawberry preserves

Grate cheese fine. Grate (or cut up) onion and mix with mayonnaise. Chop nuts and mix. Place in mold and chill. Unmold and fill center with strawberry preserves. Serve with crackers.

Evelyn Hall, Athens Pike

CREAM CHEESE TARTS

¾ cup graham cracker crumbs
2 T. sugar
2 T. melted butter
½ lb. cream cheese
½ tsp. vanilla
¼ cup sugar
1 egg
1 can fruit pie filling

Mix graham cracker crumbs, 2 tablespoons sugar, and melted butter together until the crumbs hold together. Put double liners in muffin tins. Spoon mixture evenly in paper cups and pat down. In second bowl put cream cheese, egg, vanilla, and ¼ cup sugar. Beat until creamy with an electric mixer. Put 2 tablespoons of mixture on top of crumbs in each cup. Bake for 12 minutes at 375 degrees. Cool. Fill each cup to the top with fruit pie filling. Serves 12.

Connie Kramer, Darwin Downs

DIANE'S CHEESE STRAWS

1 lb. New York sharp cheese
½ tsp. red pepper
1 stick margarine
2 cups flour

Grate cheese; add pepper to cheese. Use hands to work in margarine. Add flour; mix well; press out strips from cookie press. Cut before cooking into desired lengths. Cook 350 degrees for 15 to 20 minutes. Salt while hot so the salt will stick. Makes about 30 straws.

Mrs. Gustavus Brown (Eva), Monrovia

GARLIC CHEESE

1 lb. sharp cheese
2 3-oz. pkgs. cream cheese
Paprika
3 T. Worcestershire sauce
3 T. lemon juice
1 T. Tabasco sauce
Garlic salt to taste

Grate cheese and set aside to soften; add other ingredients. Sprinkle a strip of wax paper with paprika with a teaspoon. Mix cheese and remaining ingredients. Form in a long roll, sprinkle again with paprika, and roll up. Leave in refrigerator until firm. A good appetizer and will keep several days.

Maxie Wilbourn, Central

GARLIC CHEESE ROLL

1 lb. sharp Cheddar cheese, grated
1 8-oz. pkg. cream cheese
½ tsp. salt
2 garlic cloves, crushed
3 dashes of Tabasco (or more, to taste)
1 T. Worcestershire sauce
1 T. mayonnaise
¼ tsp. dry mustard
2 T. paprika
2 T. chili powder
½ cup very finely chopped pecans

In large bowl of mixer blend cheeses. Add all seasonings except paprika and chili powder; add pecans; mix until smooth. Dust hands with flour and shape into 2 rolls about diameter of a silver dollar. Mix paprika and chili powder; spread on sheet of wax paper. Roll cheese in this mixture until completely coated. Flatten ends and coat them too. Wrap in wax paper and refrigerate for 24 hours before using. Freezes well.

Martha R. Sparks, Rainbow Mountain

JEZEBEL SAUCE

8 oz. pineapple preserves
8 oz. apple jelly
Horseradish (up to ½ jar)
1 jar Bahama mustard (or ½ jar Poupon mustard)
8 ozs. cream cheese

Mix first 4 ingredients together. Better if mixed at least 1 day before serving. Pour over block of cream cheese. Serve with favorite party crackers. Also delicious served with ham or pork roast.

Mrs. Bettye T. Burns, Harvest

LAMBA CHI ALPHA

2 8-oz. pkgs. cream cheese, softened
1 med. onion, chopped
4 jalapeno peppers, chopped

Mix together and roll into log. Chill. Serve with crackers. Better if made day before using.

Nancy Lackey, Piedmont

MINI CHEESECAKES

3 8-oz. pkgs. cream cheese
1 cup sugar
5 eggs
1½ tsp. vanilla

Cream cream cheese and sugar. Add eggs 1 at a time. Add vanilla and pour into cupcake liners. Fill ¾ full. Bake for 30 minutes at 300 degrees. Cool slightly.

Topping

1-1½ cups sour cream
¼ cup sugar plus 2 T.
¼ tsp. vanilla
Jelly

Mix sour cream, sugar, and vanilla well. Spoon mixture on top of cream cheese in cups. Using a small spoon, put any flavor jelly in center. Bake 5 minutes at 300 degrees. Makes about 2 to 3 dozen. Freezes well. Thaws in 15 minutes. Keeps about 1 week in refrigerator.

Bonnie Nelson, Heritage

PARTY SANDWICH

8 ozs. cream cheese
1 sm. can crushed pineapple, drained

Mix together for spreading consistency; put on bread and trim crust off.

Estelle Pinion, Central

PARTY SANDWICH SPREAD

8 ozs. cream cheese, softened
¾ cup chopped nuts
¼ cup chopped green pepper
¼ cup chopped onion
1 T. catchup
3 hard-cooked eggs, chopped
¾ tsp. salt
Dash of pepper

Combine all ingredients and spread on crackers or party bread.

Dona Priest, Piedmont

WONDA'S PIMIENTO CHEESE SPREAD

1 cup milk
Dash of salt
½ tsp. powdered mustard
1 lb. Kraft cheese, grated
3 eggs
1 sm. can pimiento

Heat milk in double boiler; add salt, mustard, and cheese. Stir over heat until smooth; add well-beaten eggs gradually and cook until thickened; add mashed pimiento.

Mrs. Leo Wall (Lawsie), Monrovia

DIPS

ARTICHOKE DIP

2 cans artichokes
1 cup mayonnaise

Dash of Tabasco sauce or
cayenne pepper
1 cup Parmesan cheese, grated

Tear artichokes into small bits. Mix remaining ingredients. Put in Pyrex dish and bake at 350 degrees until bubbly. Use with variety of crackers.

Angie Pamfiles, Westbury
Debbie Hallisey, Piedmont

CHILI CON QUESO DIP

1 med. onion
1 T. butter
1 8-oz. can tomatoes

1 lb. Velveeta cheese
1 sm. can green chili peppers with
tomatoes
Fritos

Saute chopped onion in butter, add well-drained tomatoes, diced cheese, and chili peppers with tomatoes. Serve piping hot with Fritos.

Stella Miller, Fleming Hills

CRAB DIP

8 ozs. cream cheese
1 T. milk
2 T. minced onion

Horseradish to taste
⅓ cup slivered almonds
1 6-7-oz. can crabmeat

Soften cheese with milk. Add onion, horseradish, and crabmeat. Mix well. Top with almonds. Bake in 300-degree oven for 15 to 20 minutes. Especially good with tiny rounds of rye bread.

Doris B. Sells, South Parkway
Mrs. Frank Ernst, Pulaski Pike

CURRY DIP

1 cup mayonnaise
3 tsp. curry powder
3 T. Worcestershire sauce

1 tsp. grated onion
¼ tsp. salt
¼ tsp. pepper

Mix together and serve with fresh vegetables as a dip.

Martha Sparks, Rainbow Mountain

DEVILED HAM DIP

8 ozs. cream cheese, softened
2 T. milk
1 cup (4½ ozs.) deviled ham
1 tsp. Worcestershire sauce
1 onion, sliced thin

Place all ingredients in blender container. Cover and process to mix until smooth. Stop blender and scrape down sides of container with rubber spatula, if necessary. Chill before serving. Yield: 1 cup.

Evelyn Hall, Athens Pike

DILL DIP FOR RAW VEGETABLES

1 pt. sour cream
1 pt. mayonnaise
3 T. chopped parsley
3 T. minced onion
3 tsp. dill weed

Mix all ingredients and chill. Serve with any and all raw vegetables.

Elizabeth Nixon, Davis Hills

DIP FOR RAW VEGETABLES

1 T. & 1 tsp. of Good Seasons low-calorie Italian dressing
1 cup buttermilk
Several sprinkles garlic powder
Chives, fresh

Combine first 3 ingredients and shake immediately. Garnish with cut-up fresh chives.

Evelyn Hall, Athens Pike

FRESH FRUIT DIP

1 8-oz. pkg. Philadelphia Brand cream cheese
1 7-oz. jar Kraft marshmallow creme

Combine softened cream cheese and marshmallow creme; mix until well blended. Serve with fresh fruit and cookies as dippers. Yield: 2 cups. Variation: Add 1 tablespoon orange juice and 1 teaspoon grated orange rind to mixture. May also be served as a sauce over fresh fruit or shortcake.

Peggy Wallace, Poplar Ridge

HOT CHEESE DIP

1 lb. Velveeta cheese
1 can Campbell's Cheddar cheese soup
1 can El Paso tomatoes & Jalepino peppers
¼-½ chili powder

Pour ingredients into pan and heat at low temperature until thoroughly melted.

Evelyn Hall, Athens Pike

HOT MEXICANA DIP

1 can bean-bacon soup
1 6-oz. pkg. garlic-flavored cheese, diced
1 cup sour cream
¼ cup minced onion
¼ tsp. hot pepper sauce
Dash of chili powder

Combine soup and cheese, heating and stirring until cheese melts. Stir in sour cream, onion, and hot sauce. Heat through. Sprinkle with chili powder. Serve hot with corn chips or crackers.

Mrs. Lyle Needham, South Huntsville

HOT SHRIMP DIP

1 lb. cream cheese
1 6-oz. pkg. frozen shrimp
1½ garlic cloves
½ med. onion, minced
½ med. tomato, chopped
2½ banana peppers
2 Torrido chili peppers (Troppers')

Mix all together in double boiler and serve with Fritos.

Yvonne Whitman, Heritage

LEMON FONDUE FOR FRUIT

1 cup milk
1 cup sour cream
1 T. grated lemon peel
2 T. lemon juice
1 pkg. lemon instant pudding mix
½ cup whipping cream

In a medium mixing bowl blend together milk, sour cream, lemon peel, and lemon juice. Add pudding mix; beat on low speed for 2 minutes. Cover and chill. Whip the cream until stiff and fold into pudding mixture. Pour into serving bowl and place in center of serving tray. **Prepare fresh and canned (drained) fruit in bite-size pieces (banana, pineapple, strawberries, apples, grapes, etc.). Bits of angel food cake or ladyfingers are good dippers, too.**

Dixie Nixon, Davis Hills

MEXICAN DIP

1 4-oz. can Old El Paso green chilies
1 can cream of mushroom soup
1 lb. block Velveeta cheese

Chop chilies. Mix with soup in blender. Melt cheese in double boiler or microwave. Add to chili-soup mixture. Place in chafing dish over flame. Serve hot with plain Dorito chips. Note: If you prefer a hotter dip (with pepper) use the whole green chilies instead.

Mrs. Frank Ernst, Pulaski Pike

MOCK SOUR CREAM DIP

½-1 tsp. Knox gelatin, unflavored
1 oz. cold water
7 ozs. buttermilk
½ tsp. McCormick Season-All
½ tsp. dried onion flakes
Sprinkle of garlic powder
Sprinkle of pepper
1-2 pinches sweetener

Soften the gelatin in cold water; then bring to a boil. Allow to cool. Add all of the other ingredients and refrigerate.

Evelyn Hall, Athens Pike

OLIVE DIP

1 8-oz. pkg. cream cheese, at room temperature
1 cup chipped olives
½ cup chopped nuts
½ cup mayonnaise
2 T. olive juice
Dash of pepper

Mix together and serve immediately or refrigerate until needed.

Wilma Drake, Monrovia

PIMIENTO CHEESE DIP

½ cup mayonnaise
1 2-oz. jar pimiento with liquid
2 tsp. Worcestershire sauce
1 tsp. prepared mustard
1 cup Cheddar cheese, cubed

Put first 4 ingredients and ½ the cheese into the blender container, cover, and process at blend until smooth. Remove feeder cap and add remaining cheese. Process at blend until smooth and creamy, using spatula if necessary to keep mixture flowing into processing blender. Yield: 1½ cups.

Evelyn Hall, Athens Pike

SOUR CREAM VEGETABLE DIP

1 cup sour cream
1 cup mayonnaise
½ T. garlic powder
½ tsp. salt
1 T. parsley flakes
1 T. Worcestershire sauce
Dash of Tabasco sauce
1 sm. onion, grated

Mix together above ingredients. Serve with fresh raw vegetables.

Mrs. Tom Baker, Hurricane Club

SPINACH DIP

1 10-oz. pkg. frozen chopped spinach
1 8-oz. pkg. cream cheese
3 T. milk
2 T. butter
⅛ tsp. ground nutmeg
6 slices bacon, cooked, and crumbled
1 T. lemon juice
Dash of salt

Cook spinach according to package directions, drain well. In saucepan, over low heat, cook and stir together cream cheese, milk, butter, and nutmeg until cheese is melted. Add spinach, bacon, salt, and lemon juice. Turn into serving dish and garnish with bacon. Serve warm or cold with crackers or raw vegetables. Especially good served warm with raw zucchini slices.

Jeanne Peters, South Parkway

VEGETABLE DIP I

1 pt. Hellmann's mayonnaise
3 T. Heinz chili sauce
½ tsp. curry powder
1 tsp. Worcestershire sauce
½ tsp. onion salt

Blend all ingredients well. This keeps indefinitely in refrigerator.

Winnie Linney, South Huntsville

VEGETABLE DIP II

8 ozs. cream cheese	¼ tsp. thyme
1 cup sour cream	¼ tsp. marjoram
1 T. sherry	¼ tsp. savory
2 tsp. Lawry seasoning salt	1 tsp. onion powder

Mix well with mixer. Serve as a dip with raw vegetables.

Shirley Milam, Pulaski Pike

POPCORN AND NUTS

CARAMEL POPCORN

1 cup margarine	1 tsp. salt
2 cups firmly packed brown sugar	½ tsp. soda
½ cup light or dark corn syrup	1 tsp. vanilla
6-8 qts. popped popcorn	

Melt margarine in large saucepan. Stir in brown sugar, corn syrup, and salt. Bring to a boil, stirring constantly. Boil without stirring for 5 minutes. Remove from heat; stir in soda and vanilla. Gradually pour over popped corn in 2 large shallow baking pans. Mix well. Bake at 250 degrees for 1 hour, stirring every 15 minutes. Remove from oven. Cool completely. Break apart and store in containers.

Faye C. Gwin, Madison Cross Roads
Patsy Whitt, New Sharon

CHEESE CORN

2 qts. freshly popped popcorn, unsalted	1 cup grated Parmesan or Cheddar cheese
¼ cup butter	1 tsp. salt

Place popcorn in an ovenproof bowl; dot with butter; sprinkle with cheese and salt. Heat in 300-degree oven for 12 to 15 minutes. Toss well. Serves 4 to 6.

Diane McFarland, Harvest

KARO CRAZY CRUNCH

2 qts. popped popcorn
1⅓ cups pecans
⅔ cup almonds or other nuts
1⅓ cups sugar
1 cup margarine
½ cup Karo syrup
1 tsp. vanilla

Mix popcorn and nuts on a cookie sheet. Combine sugar, margarine, and Karo in a 1½-quart saucepan. Bring to boil over medium heat, stirring constantly; boil, stirring occasionally, 10 to 15 minutes or until mixture turns a light caramel color. Remove from heat, stir in vanilla, and pour over popcorn and nuts to coat well. Spread to dry. Break apart; store in tightly covered container. Yield: About 2 pounds.

Polly Hay, New Sharon

STRAWBERRY BALLS

3 boxes strawberry Jello
1 cup coconut
2 cups finely chopped pecans
1 can Eagle Brand milk

Mix ingredients, reserving 1 box of Jello. Roll into balls and roll in Jello from third box. Refrigerate.

Mildred Kuykendall, Darwin Downs

STRAWBERRIES

1 cup crushed pecans
1 cup angel flake coconut
¾ cup Eagle Brand milk
2 3-oz. pkgs. strawberry Jello
½ tsp. vanilla
Red sugar crystals
Almonds, slivered
Green food coloring

Combine first 5 ingredients, and refrigerate for about 1 hour. Roll into balls and shape like strawberries, then roll in red sugar crystals. Place stems made from slivered almonds that have been colored with green food coloring.

Patsy Brazelton, Owens Cross Roads

PECAN PASTRIES

1 stick margarine
3-oz. pkg. cream cheese
1 cup plain flour
¾ cup brown sugar
2 T. margarine
1 tsp. vanilla
1 whole egg
⅔ cup chopped nuts

Soften and mix margarine and cream cheese. Add flour and mix unti smooth. Place in refrigerator until firm (about 30 minutes.) Roll into 24 small balls. Flatten and press into very small ungreased muffin tins. Return to refrigerator while preparing filling. Combine brown sugar with 2 tablespoons margarine, vanilla, and egg. Mix and add nuts. Fill pastry shell. Bake for 30 minutes at 350 degrees. Yield: 2 dozen.

Patsy Biazelton, Owens Cross Road

HOLIDAY NUTS

1 cup light brown sugar
½ cup white sugar
½ cup sour cream
1 tsp. vanilla
2½ cups pecan halves

Over low heat in saucepan stir sugars with sour cream until dissolved; cover and boil; coat pecan halves.

Winnie Linney, South Huntsville

SPICED NUTS

1 T. Egg Beaters
2 cups peanuts
¼ cup sugar
1 T. ground cinnamon

Pour Egg Beaters over nuts; stir until nuts are coated. Combine sugar and cinnamon and sprinkle over nuts. Spread evenly in large shallow baking pan. Let dry for 10 minutes. Roast at 300 degrees for 20 to 30 minutes. Store in tightly covered container. Yield: 2 cups.

Sue Kachelhofer, University

NUTS AND BOLTS SUPREME

1 box Cherrios
1 box Rice Chex
1 box Wheat Chex
1 cup pecans
2 cups peanuts
1 box pretzels (thin)
1 lb. margarine
1 scant tsp. garlic salt
1 tsp. celery salt
4 tsp. Worcestershire sauce

Place cereal, nuts, and pretzels in the bottom of a large roasting pan. Stir. Melt margarine and add garlic and celery salts and Worcestershire sauce. Pour margarine mixture over the cereal-and-nut mixture and stir. Bake in the open pan for 3½ hours at 200 degrees. Stir from bottom of pan every hour. Store in 1-gallon jars. This is nice at Christmas to share with friends.

Sue Price, Westbury

CANDIED PEANUTS

1 cup raw peanuts
1 cup sugar
½ cup water

Cook together until water evaporates. Pour onto cookie sheet and bake for about 10 to 15 minutes at 300 degrees.

Patsy Brazelton, Owens Cross Roads

SAUSAGE TREATS
GLAZED SAUSAGE BITES

1 lb. bulk pork sausage
1 egg, slightly beaten
½ cup fine cracker crumbs
⅓ cup milk
½ tsp. sage
½ cup water
¼ cup catchup
2 T. brown sugar
1 T. vinegar
1 T. soy sauce

Combine sausage, egg, cracker crumbs, milk, and sage. Beat at high speed in mixer for 5 minutes. Shape into 3 dozen 1¼-inch balls. (Mixture will be soft. For easier shaping wet hands occasionally.) In ungreased skillet, brown meat slowly on all sides for about 10 minutes. Pour off excess fat. Combine remaining ingredients: pour over all the meat balls. Cover and simmer 15 minutes, stirring occasionally.

Mrs. Claude Bridges (Laura), Monrovia

SAUSAGE BALLS

1 lb. mild sausage
1 lb. hot sausage
1 lg. jar apple butter

Mix sausage. Make into small balls. Cook on cookie sheet in oven at 350 degrees for about 20 to 25 minutes. Heat apple butter and drop in sausage balls. Great prepared in slow cooker.

Evelyn Hall, Athens Pike

SAUSAGE CHEESE BALLS

1 lb. hot sausage
1 lb. cheese
3 cups Bisquick

Crumble sausage, grate cheese, and mix; add Bisquick and mix well. Roll into small balls and bake in oven at 275 degrees for 5 to 10 minutes. If serving immediately, brown well on cookie sheet. If planning to serve later, just brown lightly; refrigerate for the day or store in container and put in freezer. Take out and reheat to serve.

Mrs. O. V. Mitchell, Central
Vivian Lee, University

SAUSAGE PINWHEELS

2 cups flour
1 T. baking powder
1 tsp. salt

¼ cup shortening
⅔ cup milk
1 lb. sausage

Mix dry ingredients with shortening and add milk. Make dough. Roll dough and pat sausage over dough. Roll like jelly roll and refrigerate 1 hour. Cut and bake at 350 degrees for 20 minutes. Yield: 3½ dozen.

Reba K. Cornell, Hazel Green
JoAnn Webster, Fleming Hills

SAUSAGE ROLLS

1 batch Bisquick biscuit dough   1 sausage roll

Let dough chill. Roll into thin crust, spread with soft sausage roll, and chill. Slice thin, place in pan, and cook at 400 degrees until light brown. (Good and looks pretty for parties.)

Alta Newman, Central

SUN CITY PARTY SANDWICHES

2 lbs. hot sausage
2 lbs. hamburger
1 lb. Velveeta cheese

1 tsp. oregano
½ tsp. garlic salt
1 T. Worcestershire sauce
1½ loaves party rye

Brown sausage and hamburger and drain off fat. Add cheese, oregano, garlic salt, and Worcestershire sauce. Mix well and spread on party rye.

Mabel Albright, Darwin Downs

FRUIT SIDE DISHES

CRANBERRY CASSEROLE

3 cups chopped apples, some unpeeled
2 cups raw cranberries
1¼ cups granulated sugar

1½ cups quick-cooking oats
½ cup brown sugar
⅓ cup chopped pecans
½ cup margarine, melted

In 2 or 3-quart casserole combine apples, cranberries, and 1¼ cups sugar. Top with mixture of remaining ingredients. Bake at 350 degrees for 1 hour. Serve hot. Good with turkey or chicken.

Bettye Richardson, South Parkway

CURRIED FRUIT

1 No. 2 can pear halves
1 No. 2 can peach halves
1 No. 2 can pineapple chunks
1 can fruit cocktail

1 can apricots
¼ cup melted butter
⅓ cup brown sugar
2 T. curry powder

Pour fruit in colander and drain. Pour into a large baking dish. Add melted butter, brown sugar, and curry powder mixed together; pour over fruit and bake at 350 degrees for 45 minutes.

Margaret Mann, Owens Cross Roads
Dixie Nixon, Davis Hills

CURRIED HARVEST FRUIT

1 12-oz. pkg. mixed dried fruit
1 13-oz. can pineapple chunks
1 21-oz. can cherry pie filling

½ cup dry sherry
¼ cup water
1-2 tsp. curry powder

Cut large pieces of dried fruit in half in 2-quart casserole. Combine dried fruit and undrained pineapple chunks. Combine pie filling, sherry, water, and curry powder. Pour over fruits. Cover and bake in 350-degree oven for 1 hour. Serve warm with pork or ham. Serve in your prettiest glass serving bowl for a shower dish.

Mrs. Erle Douglass (Evelyn), Monrovia

DOUBLE BATCH GRANOLA

1 cup oil
1 cup honey
1 tsp. vanilla
8 cups rolled oats
3 cups coconut
2 cups wheat germ

2 cups chopped nuts
2 cups hulled sunflower seeds
1 cup sesame seeds
1 cup flax seed
2 cups ground roasted soybeans (soygrits)
1 cup bran

Heat oil, honey, and vanilla. Pour over other ingredients in a large shallow pan and mix well. Bake at 325 degrees for 15 minutes, stirring occasionally.

Diane McFarland, Harvest

FRIED APPLES
(A 100-Year-Old Recipe)

6 apples
2 T. butter

2 T. sugar
2 T. molasses
1 T. water

Cut apples into eighths; peel 1 strip of skin from each piece. Melt butter in skillet. Add sugar, molasses, and water. Mix well. Add apples; cover and cook until tender. Remove cover; cook until juice is boiled away and apples are brown. Serve with country pork sausage, scrambled eggs, and hot buttermilk biscuits.

Madison County

HOT FRUIT

1 lg. can peach halves
1 lg. can pear halves
1 lg. can chunk pineapple

1 lg. can purple plums
3 bananas, sliced
Brown sugar
Pecans, chopped

Drain fruit well. Place in deep dish or pan and layer fruit with sliced banana between each layer. On top add brown sugar and chopped pecans. Cook at 350 degrees for 30 minutes. Serve hot. Good with meats—especially ham.

Barbara Keller, Westbury

LEONA'S CANDIED APPLES

6-8 apples
Sugar

Margarine
Red cinnamon

Peel and core apples and put them in pan with margarine. Fill each core opening with plenty of sugar. Dissolve red cinnamon candies in enough water to fill pan about ¼-inch deep. Pour over apples and cook slowly until done, 30 to 40 minutes. They will be light cherry red. They make a real nice dessert with any dinner.

Leona Mills, Big Cove

SAUCES AND SEASONINGS

BAR-BE-CUE SAUCE

¾ cup chopped onion
⅓ cup oil
¾ cup catchup
¾ cup water
⅓ cup lemon juice or vinegar

3 T. sugar
3 T. Worcestershire sauce
3 T. prepared mustard
½ tsp. pepper, hot sauce, or red pepper to taste
2 T. salt

Cook onions in oil till tender; add other ingredients. Simmer for 15 minutes. Pour over meat. Cover with foil. Bake for 1 hour at 350 degrees. Uncover and cook for 30 minutes longer.

Opaline West, Madison Cross Roads

BBQ SAUCE

¼ cup butter
¼ tsp. pepper
¼ cup vinegar
¼ cup lemon juice

½ tsp. Tabasco sauce
1½ tsp. salt
¼ cup catchup
¼ cup Worcestershire sauce

Melt butter; add remaining ingredients. Bring to boil.

Susie Hoffmeyer, Hillwood

QUICK BARBECUE SAUCE

1 onion, chopped
¼ cup Wesson oil
1 8-oz. can tomato sauce
½ cup water
¼ cup lemon juice

¼ cup brown sugar
3 T. Worcestershire sauce
2 T. prepared mustard
2 tsp. salt
¼ tsp. pepper

Cook onion in oil until tender. Add remaining ingredients. Simmer for 15 minutes. Use for skillet barbecued chicken or broiled chicken. Yield: 3 cups.

Lila M. Brown, Harvest

WHITE BBQ SAUCE FOR CHICKEN

6 T. mayonnaise
1 T. black pepper
1 T. salt

3 T. lemon juice
3 T. vinegar
2 T. sugar

Mix all together and use for basting chicken in oven or on grill. Yield: Enough for 1 chicken.

Barbara Webster, Owens Cross Roads

EASY, EASY BLENDER MAYONNAISE

1 whole egg
2 tsp. wine vinegar

½ tsp. salt
1 tsp. dry mustard
1 cup oil

Place egg, wine vinegar, salt, and mustard in the blender container. Turn blender to high and dribble oil through the top until mixture emulsifies and thickens. Takes about 1 minute.

Jeanette Kromis, Westbury

GRANDMOTHER'S HOMEMADE MAYONNAISE

1 whole egg
1 pt. Wesson oil
1 tsp. salt

1 tsp. dry mustard
1 tsp. paprika
Juice of 1 lemon

Beat egg well; add oil gradually, drop by drop until thick, then by spoonful until pint is used. Beat well and add salt, dry mustard, and paprika. Add lemon juice. Beat well and put in jar. Refrigerate.

Susie Hoffmeyer, Hillwood

MEXICAN SAUCE

1 med. onion, chopped
2 T. butter
1 red, pepper, chopped
1 green pepper, chopped
1 garlic clove, minced

2 tomatoes, chopped
1 tsp. chili powder
1 tsp. Worcestershire sauce
½ tsp. celery salt
Salt to taste

Cook onion in butter for 5 minutes. Add other ingredients and cook for 15 minutes.

Mrs. Jessie Little, Harvest

RESTAURANT DRESSING

4 cups oil
2 cups vinegar
3 cups sugar
¼ cup celery seed
1 tsp. salt
1 lg. onion, grated
3 T. dry mustard

Beat 2 cups oil, 1 cup vinegar, and sugar well, then mix with beater and add remaining 1 cup vinegar and 2 cups oil, celery seed, salt, onion, and mustard. Mix well and store in refrigerator.

Estelle Pinion, Central

SEASON SALT

1 cup salt
1½ tsp. oregano
2½ tsp. paprika
2 tsp. dry mustard
¼ tsp. dill seed
1½ tsp. thyme
1 tsp. garlic salt
1 tsp. curry powder
½ tsp. onion powder

Mix all ingredients together and store as you would salt.

Dottie Hess, Pulaski Pike

SOUR CREAM AND RELISH SAUCE

1 cup sour cream
⅓ cup sweet pickle relish
½ tsp. celery salt
⅛ tsp. pepper

Combine all ingredients in a bowl and mix well. Serve with hamburgers.

Naomi Hicks, New Sharon

SPEEDY-DO CHERRY SAUCE

1 No. 2·can cherry pie filling
2 tsp. vinegar
1½ tsp. horseradish
¼ tsp. dry mustard

Combine the pie filling, vinegar, horseradish, and mustard in a saucepan and mix well. Heat through. Serve with ham or lamb.

Jane Clark, New Sharon

SWEETENED CONDENSED MILK

1 cup dry milk
⅔ cup sugar
½ cup boiling water
3 T. melted margarine

Process all ingredients in blender until smooth in texture. May be stored in refrigerator, covered tightly, for several weeks. Yield: 1¼ cups.

Mrs. N. Ray Rohland, Big Cove

STEWS, SOUPS, AND NOODLES

BIRDIE'S HAM DUMPLINGS

2 cups cornmeal
¼ cup flour
1 tsp. salt
½-1 tsp. sage
2 T. melted bacon drippings
1 cup boiling liquid from ham

Mix all ingredients, using more liquid if necessary for good consistency. Dough should be rather thick. Shape into small pones and place in boiling ham liquid. Cover and simmer until done, 15 or 20 minutes.

Opaline West, Madison Cross Roads

BREAD STUFFING RECIPE

½ cup finely chopped onion
½ cup finely chopped celery
¾ cup melted butter
3 cups crumbled bread cubes or biscuits
4 cups crumbled cornbread
2 tsp. salt
½ tsp. pepper
1 tsp. poultry seasoning
2 cups broth plus 2 chicken bouillon cubes

Brown onion and celery in butter in heavy skillet; combine with bread cubes, cornbread, and seasonings. Pour on broth and stir lightly to blend; stuff in fowl and bake in oven at 350 degrees. Cover and bake for 20 minutes; uncover and bake for 10 minutes.

Dorothy Mellette, Central

BRUNSWICK STEW

2½ or 3 lb. chicken
1 pt. tomatoes (canned)
1 pt. corn
1 pt. butterbeans
1 stick butter
1 scant tsp. sugar
1 lg. onion
2 lg. potatoes, boiled in water, mashed
Sm. piece country ham or lean salt pork, cooked
Salt
Pepper
Pinch of hot pepper

Cut up chicken and cook in 1½ quarts of water. Remove bones and skin and cut chicken into small pieces; put in large kettle along with broth; add other ingredients and simmer for about 1 hour. (I put tomatoes and cooked ham or salt pork through the blender.)

Mrs. Leo Wall (Lawsie), Monrovia

CREAMY POTATO SOUP

1 med. onion, sliced
4 T. butter
4 T. flour
1 tsp. salt
Pepper to taste

2 cups water (for cauliflower use chicken broth)
2 cups milk
1½ cups potatoes, cooked (2 med. potatoes) or cauliflower or broccoli

If using potatoes, cook then mash while still hot. Cook onion in butter till tender and lightly browned. Stir in flour and salt and pepper until smooth. Slowly stir in water. Cook and stir till slightly thickened. Remove from heat; add milk. Stir in vegetables. Heat till hot but not boiling.

Margie Brooks, Vestavia

Are you trying to make something for yourself or something of yourself?

EASY GOURMET SOUP

2 lbs. stew meat
2 T. margarine
2 lg. potatoes, pared, cubed
2 lg. onions, chopped
2 cups sliced celery

2 cups chopped cabbage
1 46-oz. can cocktail vegetable juice
1 tsp. seasoned pepper
1 tsp. salt

1 4-oz. can sliced mushrooms

Cut meat in bite-size pieces; brown on all sides in margarine in large kettle or Dutch oven. Add remaining ingredients, except mushrooms. Cover and simmer about 4 hours. About ½ hour before serving, add drained mushrooms and heat through. Soup is thick. Add additional juice, tomato juice, or water is desired. Yield: 3 quarts.

Cathy Gilbert, Davis Hills

No man's opinion is entirely worthless; even a watch that will not run is right twice a day.

FIVE-HOUR STEW

1 tsp. sugar	1 cup carrots
3 T. Minute tapioca	½ cup celery
1 12-oz. can V-8 juice	3 med. potatoes
1 lb. stew meat, cut up	1 med. onion

Mix sugar, tapioca, and juice; pour over remaining ingredients. Mix well, cover, and bake for 5 hours at 250 degrees. Salt when ready to serve.

Nora Drake, Big Cove

FRENCH ONION SOUP

3 med. onions, chopped	Salt to taste
2 cans Campbell's beef broth	Pepper to taste
1 can water	Hard rolls or croutons
1 env. Lipton soup mix	Mozzarella cheese, sliced

Boil onions in small amount of water. Add to beef broth, water, dry soup mix, and seasoning. Bring to boil. Put in individual dishes. Top with hard rolls or croutons. Put sliced mozzarella cheese on top and bake at 350 degrees for 30 minutes or until cheese is melted and browned.

Patsy Brazelton, Owens Cross Roads

GREEK "EGG" LEMON SOUP

1 qt. water	¼ cup uncooked rice
4 pkgs. instant chicken broth	2 T. lemon juice

¾ cup Egg Beaters or 2 eggs

Bring water to a boil; add instant broth. Add rice and cook until tender. Beat lemon juice into eggs; pour into broth. Cook until thickened. Do not boil. Serves 4.

Sue Kachelhofer, University

Miscellaneous

GRANDMA'S NOODLES

2½ cups flour
3 eggs

½ cup water
Dash of salt

Mix—will have to use hands. It is very stiff dough. Roll out thin, ½ of dough at a time. Cut into thin noodles. Let noodles dry overnight. May be stored in jars when fully dried. Add to chicken stock and let simmer till big and fat. Yummy!

Pat Zurasky, Rainbow Mountain-South Parkway

HOMEMADE NOODLES

4 cups all-purpose flour
6 egg yolks

1 tsp. salt
¼ cup or less water

Sift flour; make a well in flour; add rest of ingredients and work until you have a stiff dough. Roll dough very thin, sprinkle with flour, and roll up. Slice with sharp knife, unroll, and drop into boiling broth, chicken, ham, or whatever kind of broth you have. Cook slowly for about 15 minutes.

Mrs. Allen Drake (Wilma), Monrovia

NOODLES

2 or 3 whole eggs
Plain flour

Dash of salt

Beat eggs with fork. Should measure ½ to ⅔ cup. May use some water if necessary. Mix eggs and salt; add flour until all liquid is absorbed; then add more flour until dough is stiff. Divide dough into baseball-size sections and roll each into a sheet as thin as possible, not letting each sheet get more than 15 inches long. Lay out on towel or paper towel to dry for about 1 to 1½ hours, turning them occasionally and changing the towel if it is wet. If sheets stick together when stacked, they are too wet; allow to dry a while longer. Cut sheets into about 2-inch strips. Stack 8 or 10 strips and slice as narrow or wide as you like. Cook in chicken broth like regular noodles. Freeze well; spread on cookie sheets and freeze. Place in plastic bags and store in freezer until needed.

Mabel Albright, Darwin Downs

KUGEL

½-lb. box noodles
4 eggs
1 lb. cottage cheese

1 cup sour cream
Salt and pepper
Fruit (optional)

Boil noodles and drain; add other ingredients. Place in buttered casserole. Bake for 45 minutes at 375 degrees.

Kathy Albers, Fleming Hills

HOLIDAY OYSTER STEW

2 12-oz. cans oysters
2 slices bacon, chopped
⅓ cup chopped onion
4 cups oyster liquid and milk

1 10½-oz. can frozen condensed
   cream of potato soup
1¼ tsp. salt
Dash of white pepper

Parsley, chopped

Drain oysters, reserving liquid. Fry bacon until crisp. Remove bacon from fat. Cook onions in bacon fat until tender. Add oyster liquid, milk, soup, and seasonings. Heat, stirring occasionally. Add bacon and oysters, heat for 3 to 5 minutes longer, or until edges of oysters begin to curl. Sprinkle with parsley; serve at once. Serves 6.

Madison County

NEW ENGLAND CORN CHOWDER

6 slices bacon
1 med. onion, thinly sliced
2 cups water
2 cups diced potatoes

Salt
Pepper
1 1-lb. can cream-style corn
2 cups milk

2 T. butter

Cook bacon in saucepan until crisp; remove. Lightly brown onions. Put water and potatoes in pan with salt and pepper to taste. Simmer covered for about 20 minutes; add corn and milk and simmer for another 5 minutes. Just before serving, crumble bacon and add with butter. Serves 6.

Estelle Pinion, Central

SENATE BEAN SOUP

2 cups navy beans
3 qts. water
1 meaty ham bone
½ cup cooked mashed potatoes
3 minced onions

4-5 stalks celery
1 garlic clove
¼ cup minced parsley
Salt to taste
Pepper to taste

Soak beans overnight in the water. Add ham bone, cover, and simmer for 1 hour or until beans are tender. Add mashed potatoes and mix until smooth. Add onion, celery, garlic, and parsley. Simmer for 1 hour longer or until beans are soft. Remove ham bone, dice meat, and return to soup. Thin with hot water if needed (soup should be thick). Season to taste; garnish with lemon slice if desired. Serves 10 to 12.

Mrs. D. T. Thomas (Mary Lee), Monrovia

Remember the steam kettle;
Though up to its neck in hot water, it continues to sing.

TEXAS BEEF SOUP

2 lbs. beef brisket
1 beef bone
2 qt. water
2 tsp. salt
Few grains pepper
1 cup chopped onions
1 cup chopped green pepper

1 cup sliced carrot
1 cup diced celery
1 cup diced potatoes
1 16-oz. can tomatoes
1½ tsp. chili powder
⅛ tsp. ground cumin
1 cup uncooked elbow macaroni

Place meat and bone in water with salt and pepper in Dutch oven. Cover and bring to boil; skim off the scum that will form on surface of the soup. Simmer for 2 hours or until tender. Cool and chill in refrigerator several hours or overnight to allow fat to harden. Remove and discard fat. Add onions, green pepper, carrot, celery, potatoes, tomatoes, chili powder, and cumin; simmer for 1 hour. Remove from heat. Remove bone and meat from stock. Trim fat and cut meat into bite-size pieces. Place meat and macaroni in stock; bring to boil and simmer for ½ hour. Serves 9 to 10.

Jeannette Broad, Big Cove

V-8 SOUP

1 lb. hamburger
1 cup chopped onion
1 stick oleo

2 cups chopped or grated carrots
1 can celery soup
1 lg. can V-8 juice

Brown meat and onions with oleo, add other ingredients, and cook over medium heat. Yield: 6 bowls.

Mrs. Claude Bridges (Laura), Monrovia

HOGHEAD CHEESE

Have butcher cut hoghead in ½ and remove eyes, ears, and brain. Clean well. Add 4 cleaned feet to each head. Place in cold water in large pot. Bring to a boil. Cook on medium heat until all meat comes loose from bones. When done, drain off all liquid and set aside. Remove *all* bones from meat with fingers. Put meat through coarse blade of food chopper. Put ground meat into clean pot and add enough liquid to stir well. Add salt, red pepper, and small amount of sage. Heat until it is simmering. Let simmer for about 10 minutes stirring all the time. Have a thin muslin bag ready (as for sausage); hold bag over a pan and dip hot meat into it. Tie bag and place where it can drip. Let it drip overnight or till the bag feels firm. Slice as you would *Bologna*.

Mrs. O. V. Mitchell, Central

GREEN GODDESS SOUP

1 cup sliced potatoes, unpeeled
½ medium onion, sliced
1 tbsp. butter
2 cups chopped watercress
2 cups chopped parsley
1 can (4 oz.) water packed artichoke hearts, chopped
1 can chicken broth
1 tsp. tarragon
2 cups low fat milk
small cooked shrimp

Cook potatoes and onions till limp. Add watercress, parsley, artichokes, chicken broth and tarragon. Cover and simmer 15 minutes. Add milk and simmer 1 minute. Blend soup and put through food mill. Add salt and pepper to taste. Serve hot or chilled, garnish with watercress and small cooked shrimp. Makes 4 servings.

Sue Kachelhofer, University

CHICKEN CORN SOUP (PA. DUTCH)

1 qt. chicken stock
2 stalks celery
2 hard cooked eggs (diced)
1 med. onion (diced)
1 #2 can corn
2 med. potatoes (diced)
Diced cooked chicken

Heat chicken stock, add salt and season to taste. Add celery, onions, and potatoes. Cook until soft. Add chicken, eggs, corn and salt if desired. 8 servings.

Dottie Catts, Westbury

DONNA'S CHICKEN NOODLE SOUP

2 pkgs. chicken flavor chinese noodles
1 whole chicken (remove meat from the bones)
garlic to taste
1 tsp. salt
1 tsp. pepper

Stew chicken. Remove chicken from the stock and remove bones. Refrigerate stock until grease comes to the top, skim off. Put stock in pan to boil. Add noodles and seasoning packages, then add chicken. Cook 30 minutes. (may add any vegetables, I like mushrooms.)

Donna McCrary, South Parkway

PINEAPPLE CASSEROLE

1 medium can chunk pineapple, drained
½ cup butter
1 roll of Ritz crackers, crushed
1½ cups grated cheese
⅓ cup pineapple juice

Spread pineapple chunks over bottom of 2 qt. casserole dish. Put butter in a skillet and melt. Add crushed Ritz crackers and lightly brown. Put this over the pineapple chunks. Sprinkle grated cheese over cracker crumbs. Pour pineapple juice over entire mixture. Place in 350° oven until cheese has melted.

Wilma Drake, Monrovia

HOT SPICED FRUIT

4 cans (16 oz.) fruit cocktail
1 can bing cherries
1 can marachino cherries
1 cup light brown sugar
½ cup slivered almonds
¾ stick butter
4 tsp. curry powder

Drain all Fruit. Make syrup of butter, sugar, and curry. Layer fruit, (except for cherries) almonds, and syrup. Top with marachino cherries. Bake 35 minutes at 350°.

Jeanne Peters, South Parkway

JESSE'S PINEAPPLE CASSEROLE

1 large can crushed pineapple
1 cup sugar
2 tbsp. flour
3 tbsp. melted margarine
¼ tsp. salt
¼ lb. grated cheddar cheese
10 Ritz crackers (crushed)

Mix sugar, flour and salt well, add to pineapple. Cook in sauce pan over medium heat until bubbling or clear—stir often. Stir in cheese and place in buttered casserole dish. Top with crackers, pour 3 tbsp. melted margarine over top. Bake in 350° oven for 20 minutes or until topping is brown. Good with baked ham. Serves 6 to 8.

Mrs. Marskoee (Mabel) Byrd, Jr., Madison Cross Roads

GLAZED FRUIT
("APPLE PIE TEA ROOM" KNOXVILLE, TENN.)

1 (16 oz.) can unsweetened sliced peaches, drained
1 (15 oz.) can unsweetened pineapple chunks, drained
1 (11 oz.) can unsweetened mandarin oranges, drained
1 cup seedless green grapes, halved
2 tbsp. cornstarch
¼ to ½ tsp. grated orange rind
1 (12 oz.) can peach nectar
2 tbsp. orange juice

Combine first four (4) ingredients and spoon into 6 individual dessert dishes, set aside. Combine cornstarch and peach nectar in small saucepan. Cook over medium heat stirring constantly until thickened. Add orange juice and lemon rind and cook a couple minutes more. Spoon sauce over fruit. Chill thoroughly. 6 servings.

Virginia Cornelison, Hurrican Club

VEGETABLES

Vegetables 423

ASPARAGUS AND PEAS CASSEROLE

1 can cut asparagus, drained
1 can green peas, drained
2 hard-boiled eggs, chopped
1 cup grated cheese
1 can cream of chicken soup
Salt and pepper to taste
Crushed potato chips or 1 can onion rings

Mix all ingredients together except potato chips. Pour into greased casserole. Top with crushed potato chips or onion rings. Bake at 350 degrees for 30 minutes.

Billie Creel, Big Cove

ASPARAGUS CASSEROLE I

2 cans asparagus, drained
1 can mushroom soup
1½ cups buttered bread crumbs

Alternate layers of asparagus, soup, and crumbs in a buttered casserole dish. Bake at 350 degrees for 20 to 25 minutes until done. To change flavor, cream of chicken or celery soup may be substituted.

Mrs. William B. Whitt, Heritage

ASPARAGUS CASSEROLE II

Place in casserole: layer of asparagus, layer of sliced boiled eggs, layer of sliced almonds, layer of grated medium Cheddar cheese. Pour White Sauce (see below) over top. Repeat layers. Cover with remaining White Sauce. Top with crumbled Ritz crackers (soaked in melted margarine). Bake at 350 degrees until crackers are browned.

White Sauce

4 T. butter
4 T. flour
2 cups milk
½ tsp. salt
¼ tsp. pepper

Melt butter and blend in flour. Add milk gradually stirring constantly. Reduce heat and cook 3 minutes longer. Add seasonings.

Earlene Britt, Rainbow Mountain
Patsy Kennedy, Hazel Green

ASPARAGUS-KOOWERUP

1 oz. bread crumbs
2 T. clarified butter
2 T. butter
2 T. arrowroot
½ cup asparagus juice
12-18 oz. milk

Salt
White pepper
Nutmeg
1 oz. Cheddar cheese, or ½ cup
6 slices ham
12 spears asparagus, canned

Saute bread crumbs in clarified butter until crisp and golden. Melt butter in saucepan. Mix arrowroot with asparagus juice then add 12 to 18 ounces milk. Cook on low heat until it boils. Whisk until smooth. Season with salt, pepper, and nutmeg. Add cheese. On each slice of ham lay 2 spears asparagus; roll up and place on greased oven-proof dish. Spoon sauce over roll-ups, sprinkle with buttered crumbs, and place under hot broiler for 1 minute. Serves 4.

Mary Ann Riley, South Parkway

BAKED BEANS AND CORNBREAD

1 lg. can of pork and beans
1 sm. bell pepper, chopped
1 sm. onion, chopped

½ cup grated cheese
Dash of Worcestershire sauce
Cornbread, crumbled

1 stick margarine, melted

Mix beans, pepper, onion, cheese, and Worcestershire sauce. Pour into casserole bowl. Mix cornbread and oleo. Top beans with cornbread mixture. Bake at 350 degrees for 30 minutes or until bubbly. Delicious!

Gracie McCurdy, Madison Cross Roads

BEAN CALYPOL

1 can baby lima beans
1 can French-style green beans
1 can English peas

Heat and drain.

Sauce

1½ cups mayonnaise
1 med. onion, chopped
1 tsp. prepared mustard

4 tsp. salad oil
1 tsp. Worcestershire sauce
Dash of Tabasco

3 hard-boiled eggs, chopped

Mix sauce ingredients together the night before. Mix cold sauce with hot vegetables and serve.

Charlene Byrd, South Parkway

BEAN COMBO

4 strips bacon
1 lg. can cut green beans
1 No. 2 can kidney beans
2 or 3 T. margarine

Fry bacon until crisp. Remove bacon and crumble. Drain green beans and add to hot grease. Add kidney beans and margarine. When heated thoroughly serve with crumbled bacon over top. A good camping "fill up."

Connie Kramer, Darwin Downs

CALICO BEANS

8 slices bacon
4 med. onions, chopped, sauteed in bacon fat
1 No. 303 can green beans, drained
1 can white lima beans
1 can pork and beans
1 can kidney beans
¾ cups dark brown sugar
½ cup vinegar
½ tsp. garlic salt
1 tsp. dry mustard

Brown bacon; saute onion in fat. Put beans and bacon in 2½ or 3-quart casserole. Cover with sauce made by combining remaining ingredients. Bake for 1 hour at 350 degrees.

Oheita Craighead, Fleming Hills

GREEN BEAN CASSEROLE

2 12-oz. pkgs. frozen French-style green beans *or* 2 cans
1 ⅝-oz. pkg. creamy mushroom sauce mix *or* 1 can mushroom soup
1 cup evap. milk
½ can water chestnuts, sliced
1 cup canned French-fried onion rings *or* fry 2 whole onions

Cook beans according to package directions. Drain; stir sauce mix into beans; then carefully stir in evaporated milk. Add water chestnuts, and cook and stir over medium heat until thickened. Turn beans into 1-quart casserole. Top with onion rings. Bake in preheated hot oven at 400 degrees until bubbly, about 10 minutes. Serves 4 to 6.

Margaret Birchfield, Central

OLD-FASHIONED STRING BEANS

½-1 gal. fresh string beans 1 piece salt pork
Potatoes and onions (optional)

Wash string beans and snap in 1-inch pieces. Place in just enough cold water to cover beans; add salt pork and extra salt if needed. Bring to rolling boil. Then turn to low and cook 2 hours. Thirty minutes before they are done add potatoes and onions if you like. After 2 hours, remove lid, turn heat up; and dry all liquid out.

Mrs. O. V. Mitchell, Central

PLANTATION GREEN BEANS

2 9-oz. pkgs. frozen French-style green beans, thawed
4 slices bacon, diced
½ cup green onion, chopped
¼ tsp. pepper

About 20 minutes before serving, prepare beans, but cook only 5 minutes. In medium skillet over medium heat, fry bacon until crisp. With slotted spoon, drain and place on paper towel. Cook green onions in bacon drippings until tender. Add pepper and beans and cook until tender. Stir in bacon pieces. Serves 6. Calories: 50 per serving.

Evelyn Hall, Athens Pike

MARINATED BEETS

1 can beets
½ cup vinegar
1½ cups water
6 cloves sticks

Onion powder
Dill
Sugar
Chives

Drain beets. Combine vinegar, water, and cloves in saucepan on stove. Add remaining ingredients to taste. Bring to boil. Add beets and bring to second boil. Chill.

Sylvia Elsner, South Huntsville

PICKLED BEETS

2 16-oz. cans beets
½ cup sugar
1 cup white vinegar

Use juice of 1 can of beets; drain the other. Bring ingredients to a boil, put in jar, cool, and refrigerate. An easy and cool accompaniment for several meals to come.

Linda Warren, South Huntsville

BROCCOLI AND RICE CASSEROLE

1 sm. onion, chopped
3 tsp. butter
1 pkg. frozen broccoli
1 can mushroom soup
1½ cup cooked rice, salted
1 cup grated Cheddar cheese
Almost ½ cup milk

Saute onion in butter. Add broccoli and mushroom soup. Cook 10 minutes on medium heat. Add rice, cheese, and milk. Pour into buttered casserole and bake 25 to 30 minutes at 350 degrees.

Mrs. Lewis Vaughn (Frances), Monrovia

BROCCOLI BAKE

1 cup boiling water
½ med. onion, chopped
½ cup Cheez Whiz
1 pkg. frozen chopped broccoli
1 can cream of chicken soup
½ cup milk
1 cup Minute Rice
Salt
Pepper

Mix all ingredients with cooked rice; salt and pepper to taste. Bake at 350 degrees for 30 minutes or until bubbly.

Dean Hill, University
Ruth Whitt, Madison Cross Roads

BROCCOLI CASSEROLE I

3 pkgs. broccoli, cooked, drained
2 eggs, slightly beaten
1 can mushroom soup
½ cup grated Cheddar cheese
½ cup mayonnaise
1 T. grated onion
1 stick margarine
1 stack pack Ritz crackers

Mix together all but margarine and crackers, and put in a greased deep baking dish. Top with margarine and crushed crackers. Bake at 375 degrees for 30 to 45 minutes until set.

Linda DeHaye, Vestavia
Estelle Pinion, Central

BROCCOLI CASSEROLE II

2 pkgs. chopped broccoli or
   broccoli cuts
1 can mushroom soup
1 3-oz. pkg. cream cheese
2 T. mayonnaise
Cheese Nips Tidbits or buttered
   bread crumbs

Cook broccoli as directed. Heat soup; add chopped cheese and mayonnaise. Pour over drained broccoli and mix. Put crushed Cheese Nips Tidbits *or* buttered bread crumbs over top and bake at 350 for 25 minutes.

Margaret Strickland, Westbury

BROCCOLI CASSEROLE III

2 10-oz. pkgs. chopped frozen
   broccoli
1 cup mayonnaise (not salad
   dressing)
1 can mushroom soup or celery
   soup
1 cup grated med. Cheddar cheese
1 tsp. onion (optional)
1 egg, slightly beaten
Salt and pepper to taste
Bread crumbs

Cook broccoli; drain. Mix remaining ingredients reserving bread crumbs to put over top of casserole, just enough to cover. Bake for 30 minutes at 350 degrees or until bubbling. Serves 6 to 8.

Lucille Mitchell, Madison Cross Roads
Gina Guess, Hazel Green

CHEESE, BROCCOLI, AND RICE CASSEROLE

1 10-oz. pkg. frozen chopped
   broccoli
1 cup minced onion
1 T. oleo
1 8-oz. jar process cheese spread,
   warm
1 10¾-oz. can condensed cream
   of mushroom soup
½ tsp. dry mustard
3 cups cooked rice
4 hard-boiled eggs, quartered
1 3-oz. can French-fried onion rings

Cook broccoli according to package directions; drain. Cook onions in butter until softened but not brown; stir in cheese spread then gradually the soup; stir in mustard and rice; fold in eggs, then broccoli. Turn into a buttered shallow 2-quart baking dish. Sprinkle with onion rings. Bake in preheated 350-degree oven until hot through—about 20 minutes. You can also add Chinese water chestnuts.

Barbara Keller, Westbury

SAUCE FOR BRUSSELS SPROUTS

½ cup butter or margarine
2 T. minced onion
2 cups cooked Brussels sprouts, drained
1 T. prepared mustard
½ tsp. salt
1 tsp. Worcestershire sauce
Dash of cayenne pepper

Melt butter and cook onion until soft. Blend in remaining ingredients. Place Brussels sprouts in hot vegetable dish. Pour sauce over and serve at once.

Josie Asquith, South Parkway

CABBAGE CASSEROLE

1 sm. or med. onion
3 T. butter
1 lb. ground beef
1 tsp. salt
⅛ tsp. pepper
6 cups coarsely shredded cabbage
1 10½-oz. can condensed tomato soup

Saute onion in butter. Add, heating through but not browning, ground beef, salt, and pepper. Spread 3 cups of cabbage in 2-quart baking dish. Cover with meat mixture. Spread a small amount of soup on top (about ⅓ of can. You may add a little tomato catchup to it at this time so you will have a thin layer of tomato sauce. Top with remaining cabbage. Pour rest of soup over top and spread evenly. Bake covered 1 hour at 350 degrees.

Mrs. William B. Whitt, Heritage
Florence Moore, Central

GERMAN CABBAGE SOUP

2 10½-oz. cans beef broth
2½ cups water
1 8-oz. can tomato sauce
2 tsp. lemon juice
3 cups shredded cabbage
2 cups diced apples
1 sm. onion, minced
1 T. caraway seed
1 tsp. sugar
1 sm. clove garlic, minced
Salt and pepper to taste

Combine broth, water, tomato sauce, and lemon juice and bring to boil. Add remaining ingredients and cover. Simmer 20 minutes and serve with rye bread. Serves 6 to 8.

Gisa Hall, Westbury

RED CABBAGE

1 sm. head red cabbage, chopped
1 tsp. salt
3 strips bacon, crumbled
1 cinnamon stick
6 whole cloves
1 sm. onion, chopped
1 to 2 ripe apples or pears
2 T. wine vinegar
2 T. sugar

Cook first seven ingredients about 30 minutes in bacon grease. Add wine vinegar and sugar. Refrigerate 6 hours. Can be made days ahead. Remove from refrigerator and add more vinegar to bring back red color.

Marianne Mullen, Westbury

RUSSIAN PIE
(A Delightful Vegetarian Meal)
Pastry

1¼ cups flour
1 tsp. sugar
1 tsp. salt
4 ozs. cream cheese, softened
3 T. butter
Water to mix to pie consistency

Mix pastry; divide in two sections. Roll out one section and put in 9-inch pie pan. Reserve other section for top crust.

Filling

3 T. butter
1 sm. onion, chopped
½ cup green pepper
1 sm. head cabbage, shredded (3 cups)
Spices: basil, tarragon, marjoram, salt, pepper
½ lb. fresh mushrooms, sliced
4 ozs. cream cheese, softened
3 hard-boiled eggs
1 cup grated sharp cheese

Melt butter; saute onion, green pepper, and cabbage, stirring constantly; add ¼ tsp. basil, tarragon, marjoram, salt, and pepper to taste. Cook mixture until cabbage wilts and onions and green pepper are soft. Saute mushrooms in butter 5 to 6 minutes. Spread softened cream cheese in bottom of pie shell, then layer sliced boiled eggs, cabbage, and a final layer of mushrooms. Sprinkle 1 cup grated sharp cheese on top and cover with top crust. Prick top and bake at 400 degrees for 15 minutes; reduce heat to 350 degrees and bake for 20 minutes or until crust is golden brown.

Margaret Strickland, Westbury

SAUERKRAUT

1 can Bush's or Stokley's chopped kraut
½ cup chopped celery
1 lg. sweet onion, chopped
1 green pepper
1 2-oz. can pimiento, chopped
Carrot, grated (optional)
Hot pepper (optional)
½ cup sugar
4 T. vinegar

Drain kraut. Add celery, onion, pepper, and pimientos. Mix sugar and vinegar and pour over kraut mixture. Let stand in refrigerator overnight. Drain in mesh strainer and serve with outdoor cookouts. (Good.)

Rachel Sturdivant, University

CARROT CASSEROLE

1 lb. carrots
1 can cream of celery soup
¼ lb. Velveeta cheese
Bread crumbs, buttered

Cook carrots until tender. Place half of the carrots, soup, and cheese in casserole dish; finish with remaining carrots, soup, and cheese. Top with buttered bread crumbs. Bake at 350 degrees (covered) for 30 minutes or until cheese melts.

Jo Ann Quiggle, Fleming Hills

CARROTS
(Marinated)

5 cups sliced carrots
1 med. sweet onion
1 sm. green pepper
½ cup salad oil
1 10¾-oz. can cream of tomato soup
¾ cup vinegar
1 tsp. prepared mustard
1 tsp. Worcestershire sauce

Cook carrots; drain and cool. Cut onion and green pepper in round slices and mix with cooled carrots. Mix other ingredients together and pour over vegetables. Cover and marinate for 12 hours. Drain to serve. This will keep for 2 weeks in refrigerator.

Pearl Franklin, Madison Cross Roads

CARROT SOUFFLE

1 stick butter, melted
3 eggs, well beaten
3 cups cooked, mashed carrots
2 T. flour
1 tsp. baking powder
1 cup sugar
Dash of cinnamon

Add butter and eggs to carrots. Blend in dry ingredients. Pour into greased baking dish. Bake at 400 degrees for 15 minutes; reduce heat to 300 degrees and bake for 45 minutes.

Evelyn Hall, Athens Pike

GLAZED CARROTS WITH ORANGE SLICES

½ stick butter
½ cup sugar
1 orange, unpeeled, thinly sliced
1 No. 303 can sliced carrots (or 1 pkg. frozen carrots, cooked) or 2 cups cooked carrots

Melt butter and sugar; cook on low for 5 minutes. Remove seeds from orange slices and simmer with butter and sugar. Add drained carrots; simmer for 15 minutes. Serves 3 to 4.

Peggy Bliss, Blossomwood
Laura Mae Wilbourn, Hurricane

RICE AND CARROT RING

3 cups cooked regular rice
2 cups grated carrots
¼ cup grated onion
2 T. all-purpose flour
1 11-oz. can Cheddar cheese soup, undiluted
1 egg, slightly beaten
1 tsp. salt
¼ tsp. pepper
1 tsp. Worcestershire sauce
Dash of hot sauce
1 10-oz. pkg. frozen English peas

Combine rice, carrots, onion, and flour in large bowl. Add next 6 ingredients, mix well. Pack mixture into a greased 8-inch ring mold. Allow to cool 10 minutes. Cook peas according to package directions; drain. Invert rice ring onto platter and fill center with English peas (broccoli spears may be substituted for English peas). Serves 6.

Gracie McCurdy, Madison Cross Roads

Vegetables

SWEET AND SOUR CARROTS

1 pkg. carrots, cut up
1 green pepper, cut up
1 8-oz. can pineapple chunks, save juice
⅓ cup sugar
1 T. cornstarch
½ tsp. salt
2 T. vinegar
2 T. soy sauce

Cook carrots and peppers. Mix sugar, salt, cornstarch, vinegar, and soy sauce. Take juice from pineapple and add enough water to make ⅓ cup. Combine all these ingredients and cook until bubbly and thick. Add vegetables and pineapple and heat. Serves 5.

Mrs. W. L. Kennedy, Hazel Green

CELERY CASSEROLE

5 cups sliced outside celery stalks
1 can condensed mushroom soup
⅓ cup milk
¾ cub grated Cheddar cheese
¼ cup bread crumbs, buttered

Cook celery in salted water until just tender. Drain; add soup and milk; turn into 1-quart casserole. Top with cheese and bread crumbs. Bake at 350 degrees for 30 minutes.

Laura Mae Wilbourn, Hurricane

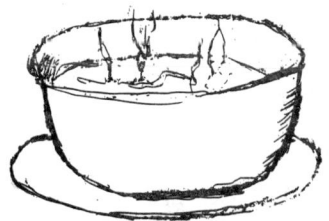

CORN CASSEROLE I

2 cups cream-style corn
¼ cup evap. milk
1 egg
1 sm. can mushrooms
1 T. chopped onion
½ cup chopped celery
¼ cup bell pepper (optional)
½ tsp. salt
Pinch of black pepper

Mix together and bake at 325 degrees until brown (30 minutes)

Mrs. Eugene Smith (Nina), Monrovia

CORN CASSEROLE II

1 med. onion, chopped
1 green pepper, chopped
1 stick margarine
2 cups cooked rice
1 can tomatoes, mashed

1 can cream-style corn
1 tsp. Worcestershire sauce
½ tsp. Tabasco
Salt and pepper
1 cup grated cheese

Brown onion and pepper in margarine; add other ingredients except cheese and mix well. Pour into greased casserole. Heat at 325 degrees until bubbly. Cover with grated cheese and return to oven until cheese melts. Can be frozen.

Mrs. Jo Ann Daniels, Heritage

CORN PUDDING

2 cups fresh corn, cut from cob
  or frozen
1 cup milk
2 T. margarine

2 T. flour
2 tsp. salt
1 T. sugar
3 eggs
Pepper to taste

Combine corn, milk, margarine, flour, and seasonings. Beat eggs together until light; add to corn mixture. Pour into greased casserole and bake at 350 degrees for 1 hour or until firm like custard. Serves 4 to 5.

Donna Butler, Poplar Ridge

HOMINY CASSEROLE

1 sm. onion, chopped
½ bell pepper, chopped
½ stick margarine
1 sm. can mushrooms
1 lg. can hominy

3 T. flour
1½ cups milk
½ tsp. dry mustard
½ cup olives
Bread crumbs, buttered

Saute onions and pepper in margarine. Add mushrooms; add remaining ingredients, except crumbs, and pour into casserole and sprinkle with buttered bread crumbs. Bake at 350 degrees for 45 minutes.

Florence Moore, Central

HOMINY-GREEN CHILI CASSEROLE

1 No. 2 can hominy, drained
1 T. chopped onion
1 sm. can chopped green chilies
Dash of garlic powder
1 cup sour cream
¼ lb. grated Cheddar cheese

Mix together all ingredients. Reserve some cheese for top of casserole. Bake at 350 degrees for 30 minutes.

Beth Sidnam, Hurricane

SCALLOPED CORN

1 No. 2 can whole corn (2½ cups) or cream-style corn
½ to ¾ cup milk
1 cup dry cracker crumbs
½ sm. onion
3 T. chopped green pepper
Salt
Pepper
2 T. butter

Combine whole corn and ¾ cup milk or cream-style with ½ cup milk. Add crumbs, onion, green pepper, and seasonings. Pour into greased 1-quart casserole. Dot with butter. Bake at 350 degrees for 30 minutes. Serves 6.

Cynthia Blanchard, Athens Pike

EGGPLANT CASSEROLE I

4 slices bacon
1 med. onion
1 green pepper
1 med. eggplant
2 tsp. salt
¼ tsp. pepper
1 6 to 10-oz. can Hunt's tomato sauce
1 cup water
Crumbs
Butter
1 cup or less Parmesan cheese

Fry bacon until crisp. Remove from pan. Brown onion and green pepper; add cubed eggplant, salt, pepper, tomato sauce, and water. Simmer 15 to 20 minutes. Put in 1½-quart baking dish. Put crumbs, butter, and cheese on top. Crumble bacon and sprinkle on top. Bake at 350 degrees for 25 minutes.

Mrs. Bob Freeman, Poplar Ridge

EGGPLANT CASSEROLE II

1 lg. eggplant
1 egg
1 T. milk
1 cup bread crumbs
⅓ cup shortening

1 lg. onion, chopped
½ cup green pepper, chopped
1 can cream of chicken soup
½ cup milk
1 cup grated cheese
½ tsp. salt

Peel and slice eggplant. Mix egg and 1 tablespoon milk. Dip eggplant in milk-and-egg mixture, roll in ⅔ cup of bread crumbs. Fry until crisp and brown in shortening. Cook onions and pepper until soft. Add soup, ½ cup milk, ⅔ cup cheese, and salt; cook until bubbly. Place eggplant in bottom of casserole dish and pour cheese mixture over this. Top with remaining cheese and bread crumbs. Bake 45 minutes at 350 degrees.

Mary Moore, Central

EGGPLANT SOUFFLE

1 lg. eggplant
½ stick butter
Salt and pepper to taste
2 eggs, beaten

¾ cup milk
8 to 10 saltines, crumbled
¼ cup chopped onion
1 cup grated cheese

Preheat oven to 350 degrees. Peel and boil eggplant until done. Mash with potato masher. Stir in butter while hot. Season with salt and pepper. Stir in eggs, milk, saltines, and onions. Put into casserole and top with cheese. Bake at 350 degrees for 40 minutes. Serves 6 to 8.

Earlene Britt, Rainbow Mountain

FRIED EGGPLANT

Peel eggplant and cut into 1-inch cubes. Cube directly into a bowl containing buttermilk. When all eggplant is cubed, drain and coat with a mixture of 5 parts cornmeal to 1 part flour. Season with salt and pepper to taste. Fry in hot vegetable oil until golden brown. Remove and drain on paper towels.

Linda Clark, Owens Cross Roads

CREOLE OKRA

1 med. onion, sliced
1 med. green pepper, diced
1 sm. garlic clove, crushed
¼ cup bacon drippings
2 lbs. okra, cut in ½-inch slices

4 med. tomatoes, peeled, chopped
1 tsp. Worcestershire sauce
¼ tsp. sugar
Salt and pepper
1 tsp. file powder

Hot cooked rice

Saute onion, pepper, and garlic in bacon drippings in a Dutch oven until onion is tender. Add next four ingredients; salt and pepper to taste. Cover and cook over medium heat about 20 minutes. Remove from heat; stir in file powder. Serve over rice. Serves 8. (Note: file powder is ground sassafras used in New Orleans in jambalaya.)

Betty Johnson, Hurricane

FRITTER-FRIED OKRA

1 cup all-purpose flour
1 T. baking powder
½ tsp. salt

2 eggs, well beaten
⅓ cup milk
5 cups thinly sliced okra

Hot oil

Combine flour, baking powder, and salt in a medium mixing bowl; add eggs and milk, beating until smooth. Add okra, stirring until coated. Spoon okra into hot oil in a large skillet; cook, stirring occasionally, until golden brown. Serves 6.

Betty Johnson, Hurricane

PEA CASSEROLE

1 can peas, drained
1 cup grated cheese
½ cup chopped onion

½ cup chopped celery
1 bell pepper, chopped
1 can tomato soup

Mix first 5 ingredients. Pour soup on top. Bake at 350 degrees for 40 minutes or at 325 degrees for 50 minutes. Serves 8.

Reba K. Cornell, Hazel Green

QUICK GREEN PEA CASSEROLE

1 can English peas, drained
1 can cream of mushroom soup, undiluted
2 or more boiled eggs, chopped
1 tsp. minced onion
Pimiento, chopped (optional)
Cornflakes
Cheese

Mix first 5 ingredients. Put in casserole. Top with crushed cornflakes and cheese. Bake at 325 degrees until hot and cheese melts. Instead of English peas, green beans, asparagus, or mixed vegetables may be used. May add bits of bacon, tuna, ham, or any luncheon meat to give meaty flavor.

Madison County

EASY-TO-DO SCALLOPED POTATOES

Wash, peel, and slice potatoes. Boil in salted water until tender. Drain and put into a baking dish. Alternate layers of potatoes with grated cheese until the pan is nearly full. Onions may be added if desired. Season to taste with salt and pepper. Dot with butter and add enough white sauce (milk thickened with flour) to cover the potatoes; sprinkle with paprika for added color. Bake in a 350-degree oven until the cheese has melted (about 30 minutes).

Dorothy Mellette, Central

HASH BROWN CASSEROLE

2 lbs. frozen hash browns (big bag)
½ cup melted margarine
1 cup sour cream
2 cups shredded Cheddar cheese
1 can cream of chicken soup
1 sm. onion, chopped
Salt and pepper
2 cups crushed cornflakes or crackers
¼ cup melted oleo

Dump all but cornflakes and ¼ cup margarine in big casserole dish. Mix and top with crushed cornflakes or crackers. Pour ¼ cup melted margarine over that. Bake at 350 degrees for 45 minutes.

Marcy Jones, South Huntsville

ORANGE MASHED POTATOES

2 lbs. potatoes
¼ cup orange juice
¼ cup skim milk
3 T. margarine
¼ tsp. salt
2 T. grated orange peel

Scrub potatoes; cook until tender. Drain and peel. Mash potatoes with orange juice, skim milk, 1 tablespoon margarine, and salt. Whip till light. Pile into 1½-quart casserole. Sprinkle with orange peel and dot with margarine. Broil till lightly browned and bubbling. Serves 4.

Sue Kachelhofer, University

POOR MAN'S HASH

In a deep skillet with small amount of grease, place layer of peeled, sliced potatoes, then onions. Sprinkle 3 tablespoons flour, salt, and pepper over top. Continue layering until you have amount desired then add enough water to almost cover. Use tight-fitting lid and cook on medium until potatoes are done. You may add leftover ham bits or 1 can corned beef or sliced Spam.

Winnie Beck, Davis Hills

POTATOES AU GRATIN

8 med. potatoes
1 can cream of mushroom soup
1 tsp. salt
1 tall can evap. milk

¼ cup melted butter
1 lg. grated onion
½ tsp. black pepper
8 oz. Velveeta cheese

½ tsp. curry powder

Peel potatoes and dice into small squares. Steam in tightly covered pan with salted water to level of potatoes. Do not overcook. Drain water and place potatoes in casserole or baking dish. Mix and heat other ingredients; pour over potatoes. Sprinkle with paprika and bake in 350-degree oven until sauce bubbles through potatoes.

Sue Carter, Hazel Green

POTATO CASSEROLE

3 cups thinly sliced potatoes
2 lg. onions, sliced thin
1 stick margarine or butter

2 T. flour
2 cups milk
3 Cheddar cheese slices

Melt the margarine in a heavy saucepan; add flour until it looks like a paste; then add milk, a little salt, and black pepper to taste. Cook for a few minutes until thickened. Grease a 2-quart casserole dish. First place a layer of potatoes, then a layer of onions. Add cheese to sauce, stir until it melts, then pour over potatoes and onions. Repeat until you use all of the ingredients. Cook at 350 degrees in oven for 45 minutes.

Mrs. Paul Bledsoe, Hurricane

SOUR CREAM POTATOES

Bake potatoes (1 for each serving) until well done. Cut off a portion of the top and scoop out. Mash potatoes, add salt, white pepper, butter, cream, Parmesan cheese, sour cream, and chopped onions to taste. Put back into shells and bake in a 350 degree oven until onions are done and potatoes are lightly browned.

Carolyn Underwood, Hazel Green

TATER TOT CASSEROLE

1 lg. bag frozen Tater Tots
2 cans cream of mushroom soup
1 cup of sour cream
1 lg. can sliced mushrooms, drained
1 sm. jar pimiento, drained
2 cups Cheddar Cheese

Mix first 5 ingredients together. Bake in 9x13-inch pan at 350 degrees for 50 minutes. Top with cheese and continue to bake for 10 more minutes.

Gina Guess, Hazel Green

ARKANSAS CUMIN RICE

⅓ cup chopped onions
¼ cup chopped green pepper
1 cup uncooked rice
2 T. oil
2 cups boiling beef broth or consomme
1 T. Worcestershire sauce
¾ tsp. salt
¾ tsp. cumin seed

Saute onion, green pepper, and rice in oil. Use low heat and do not overbrown. Put into shallow 2-quart casserole. Add remaining ingredients. Cover tightly and bake at 350 degrees for 30 minutes or until rice is tender and liquid absorbed.

Pat Zurasky, Rainbow Mountain-South Parkway

BAKED RICE

1 cup uncooked rice
1 tsp. salt
2 T. margarine
2¼ cups water

Combine all ingredients and cover tightly. Bake at 350 degrees for 1 hour or until rice is tender and liquid is absorbed.

Diane McFarland, Harvest

CALAS

Calas are really sweet rice fritters, made famous in New Orleans. They were made and sold by the Negro women of an earlier time, who used to carry the hot calas on their heads, and wind their way through the streets of New Orleans singing, "Calas, calas, calas, tout chaud." Sprinkle the calas while hot with powdered sugar and serve as you would any hot doughnut.

2 egg yolks
1 cup boiled rice
1 cup sugar
2 cups flour

½ tsp. cinnamon or nutmeg, or
  1 tsp. grated lemon rind
2 tsp. baking powder
2 egg whites

Beat together the egg yolks, rice, and sugar. Stir in the flour, spice or lemon rind, and baking powder until well blended. Then fold the stiffly beaten egg whites through the mixture. Drop by spoonfuls into hot deep fat.

Lila M. Brown, Harvest

CHINESE FRIED RICE

2 cups cold cooked rice
Salt and pepper

2 T. peanut oil
2 eggs

Season rice well with salt and pepper. Heat oil in pan and fry rice gently over medium heat until all oil is absorbed. Beat eggs until smooth and pour onto rice in a thin stream until all eggs are gone, stirring all the time. Heat gently stirring until egg is evenly distributed and set. Serve immediately. (Chopped ham or peas may be added to this recipe.)

Sue David, South Parkway

COMPANY RICE

2 cups rice
1 can consomme
1 can onion soup

1 can beef broth
1 can chicken broth
6-oz. can mushrooms

½-1 stick margarine or butter

Combine all ingredients together in saucepan. Cover and simmer about 20 minutes.

Angie Pamfiles, Westbury

EASY PILAF RICE

1 cup uncooked rice
1 can consomme
1 can water
1 stick butter
1 beef bouillon cube

Mix, cover, and bake for 50 to 60 mintues at 350 degrees. Stir after 30 minutes. Serves 6.

Cynthia Rich, Heritage

RICE CASSEROLE

1 stick margarine
1 cup Uncle Ben's long-grain rice
1 can beef consomme
1 can onion soup
1 sm. can mushroom pieces, drained

Melt margarine in 1½-quart casserole. Add raw rice, consomme, soup, and mushrooms. Bake covered at 350 degrees for 1 hour. Add ½ teaspoon oregano if you like. Serves 6.

Peggy Bliss, Blossomwood
Thelma Freeman, Poplar Ridge

RICE FOR FOWL

1 cup uncooked rice
2 cans beef consomme
1 med. onion, chopped
1 stick margarine, melted

Mix all ingredients together; add salt and pepper. Cook in oven at 350 degrees 1½ hours, sometimes less in uncovered dish.

Mrs. Jo Ann Daniels, Heritage

SPANISH RICE

¾ cup rice
1 med. onion
1 med. red pepper
1 med. green pepper
1 T. sugar
½ tsp. salt
1½ cups canned tomatoes
½ cup grated cheese
1 tsp. monosodium glutamate

Cover rice with water and steam in double boiler for about 20 minutes. Saute onion and peppers in oil until done. Add all ingredients to rice and cook together for ten minutes, stirring often.

Maxie Wilbourn, Central

SPINACH BALLS

6 eggs
1½ sticks butter, softened
1 cup Parmesan cheese
2 cups seasoned croutons
2 pkgs. frozen spinach, chopped

Mix eggs, butter, and cheese. Add remaining ingredients. Roll into small balls. Freeze until needed, then bake at 350 degrees for 15 minutes or until done.

Marcy Jones, South Huntsville

Only those who have the patience to do simple things perfectly will acquire the skill to do difficult things easily.

SPINACH AND POTATO PIE

1 lb. spinach
6 med. potatoes
1 med. onion
3 eggs, beaten
Dash of pepper
¼ cup melted butter or margarine
1 tsp. salt

Wash spinach. Chop fine and set aside. Shred potatoes and onion into eggs. Add remaining ingredients and mix. Spread half of potatoes in shallow baking dish. Spread spinach to make second layer and top with remaining potatoes. Bake in preheated moderate oven (350 degrees) for 30 minutes or until potatoes are browned. Serves 6.

Dorothy Gillespie, Fleming Hills

SPINACH CASSEROLE
(for those who do not like spinach)

1 10-oz. pkg. chopped spinach, cooked, drained
1 sm. onion, chopped
2 eggs
4 American cheese slices, chopped
½ can cream of mushroom soup

Cook and drain spinach. Mix all ingredients. Bake in a casserole dish at 325 degrees for 45 minutes. Top with buttered croutons.

Connie Wagner, Rainbow Mountain

CANDIED SUMMER SQUASH

2 med. yellow squash
1 cup dark corn syrup

2 T. butter or margarine
Ground cinnamon

Wash squash; cut in pieces. (If yellow summer squash are used, slice crosswise ½-inch thick.) Arrange squash slices in oiled 1½-quart baking dish. Pour corn syrup over squash. Bake at 325 degrees for 35 to 40 minutes. Uncover; dot with butter or margarine. Sprinkle with cinnamon. Bake 5 to 10 minutes longer. Serves 6.

Nell Long, Big Cove

FRESH SQUASH

2 cups sliced yellow squash
½ cup water

3 slices American cheese
Salt and pepper to taste

Boil water. Add squash, salt, pepper, and cheese. Cook over very low heat, covered, no longer than 5 minutes.

Connie Wagner, Rainbow Mountain

RATATOUILLE
(Squash Stew)

2 lg. onions, sliced thin
2 garlic cloves, mashed
1 med. eggplant, peeled, cut in
  ½-inch cubes
6 zucchini or yellow squash (or
  both), sliced thick

2 lg. bell peppers, cut in strips
4 lg. tomatoes, chopped
Salt
Pepper
2 tsp. dried basil
Parsley
6 T. olive oil

Layer onions, garlic, eggplant, squash, peppers, and tomatoes in 5 or 6-quart casserole. Press vegetables down and pour olive oil over all. Cover tightly and bake at 350 degrees for 2 hours. Baste during cooking, uncover for last ½ hour. Mix gently with fork before serving. Freezes well. Serves 6.

Beth Sidnam, Hurricane

SCALLOPED SQUASH

1 lb. yellow squash
1 onion, diced
1 tsp. sugar
½ lb. grated Cheddar cheese

2 T. butter
1 egg
1 cup bread crumbs
Salt and pepper to taste

Cook squash and onion until tender in salted water. Drain well. Put squash in large mixing bowl; add remaining ingredients, saving ¼ cup crumbs. Beat with rotary beater until light. Put in buttered casserole. Top with bread crumbs. Bake in 350-degree oven until cheese is melted and egg set. About 30 minutes. Serves 6 to 8.

Mrs. Burns Drake, Big Cove

SQUASH BALLS

2 cups cooked squash
1 onion (cooked with squash)

1 pkg. Mexican cornbread mix
1 egg
Fat

Drain squash and onion. Mix with cornbread mix and egg; roll into balls. Fry in deep fat.

Madison County

SQUASH CASSEROLE I

2 lbs. yellow squash, cut up
1 med. onion, chopped
3 T. butter
1 egg, beaten

1 T. Worcestershire sauce
1 tsp. salt
1 tsp. pepper
5 soda crackers, crushed
½ cup grated, sharp cheese

Combine squash and onion. Cook in boiling, salted water until tender. Drain and mash. Preheat oven to 350 degrees; lightly grease a 2-quart casserole. Combine squash and onions, butter, egg, Worcestershire sauce, salt, pepper, and cracker crumbs. Put in casserole. Top with cheese. Bake 30 minutes. Serves 4 to 6.

Donna Brannan, Owens Cross Roads

SQUASH CASSEROLE II

3 lbs. yellow squash
3 med. onions
3 med. carrots
½ tsp. salt

8 oz. sour cream
2 cans cream of chicken soup
¼ lb. margarine
1 pkg. herb dressing mix

Cut up squash, onions, and peeled carrots. Add salt and cover with water. Cook until tender. Drain well and mash; add sour cream and soup. Melt margarine and combine with dressing mix. Into buttered casserole put layer of crumbs then squash mixture. Continue alternating layers, topping with crumbs. Bake at 350 degrees for 25 minutes. Serves 12. This can be made into 2 smaller casseroles—one to eat and one to freeze.

Mrs. Peggy Barber, Fleming Hills
Anne Jones, Hurricane
Clydia M. Reynolds, Madison Cross Roads
Dean Hill, University

SQUASH CASSEROLE III

4 cups cooked summer squash
1 lg. white sweet onion
1 sm. jar pimientos
2 eggs, beaten

1 cup grated Cheddar cheese
2 T. sugar
2 T. butter
Salt to taste

Crackers for topping

Simmer squash and onion in small amount of water until tender. Drain. Mix all other ingredients at once and blend well. Sprinkle club crispy or cheesy crisp crackers (crumbled) over and bake at 350 degrees for 25 minutes in a buttered casserole.

Rachel Sturdivant, Darwin Downs

SQUASH CASSEROLE IV

3 cups squash, sliced
½ cup milk
2 eggs, beaten
½ tsp. salt

½ tsp. garlic powder
¼ tsp. pepper
6 soda crackers
½ cup grated aged Cheddar cheese

½ cup chopped onion

May use various kinds of squash. Cook squash until tender, but firm. Add above ingredients, reserving enough cheese to sprinkle on top. Bake in 325-degree oven for 20 to 25 minutes until liquid is absorbed and eggs are cooked.

Marjorie Jones, Athens Pike

SQUASH CASSEROLE V

4 to 5 med. squash	Cheese
2 slices white bread	1 egg
1 cup milk	Cracker crumbs
Ham	Cheese slices
Minced onion	

Cook squash until tender. Mash. Soften bread in milk. Cut ham and cheese into chunks. Beat egg then mix all ingredients together. Place in casserole dish and cover with cracker crumbs and cheese slices. Bake in oven for 20 to 30 minutes at 350 degrees.

Betty Butcher, Athens Pike

SQUASH CROQUETTES

1-pt. pkg. frozen squash	1 whole egg
1 med. onion	Salt and pepper to taste
3 or 4 cornbread muffins	Accent to taste
Cracker crumbs or bread crumbs	

Cook squash until done; drain well; mash fine. Saute cut-up onion in oleo or oil until done; add to squash. Add all other ingredients, except crumbs. Chill until cold, form into croquettes and roll in crumbs. Cook in deep fat until brown. For variety I sometimes add grated cheese and ¼ teaspoon ginger root before chilling.

Maxie Wilborn, Central
Mrs. Carlos Cole (Lillian), Monrovia

SQUASH HUSHPUPPIES

4 cups sliced or diced squash	½ cup flour
1 onion	½ T. baking powder
1 green pepper	Dash of Worcestershire sauce
Dash of black pepper	1 egg, beaten
1 T. sugar	1 cup meal
Salad oil	

Combine squash, onion, green pepper, black pepper, and sugar; cook in small amount of water until tender. Drain and add all other ingredients; add enough meal and flour to make thick enough to drop from a teaspoon into hot deep oil. Brown and lift out on paper towel.

Mrs. C. W. Fanning (Mildred), Monrovia

SQUASH PIE

4 cups chopped zucchini or yellow squash
1 cup chopped onion
1 cup Bisquick
½ cup oil
½ cup Parmesan cheese

4 eggs
1 T. parsley
½ tsp. oregano
1 tsp. salt
½ tsp. pepper
Dash of garlic powder

Toss and mix well. Bake in a greased pan for 60 minutes at 350 degrees.

Ila Wilkinson, Central

YELLOW SQUASH CASSEROLE

Squash and onion
1 sm. jar pimiento

½ cup mayonnaise
Bread or cracker crumbs

Use enough squash and onion for your family. Steam squash until done. Drain. Add pimiento, mayonnaise (I use less than ½ cup), and crumbs. Mix well. Bake for 20 minutes at 350 degrees. Place crumbs on top of casserole.

Leta Sims, Vestavia

ZUCCHINI CASSEROLE

4 med. zucchini, grated
1 can Cheddar cheese soup
¾ cup sour cream
2 eggs

1 cup cracker crumbs
1½ cups chopped ham
½ med. onion, chopped
Italian seasoning to taste

⅛ tsp. pepper

Bake in a covered casserole for 45 minutes at 350 degrees then uncover for 15 minutes and bake at 375 degrees.

Linda Clark, Owens Cross Roads

ZUCCHINI SQUASH

3 sm. zucchini, sliced
⅓ cup chopped onion
1 can tomatoes (approx. 10½ ozs.)
1 T. butter

1 sm. can mushrooms (approx. 4 ozs.)
1 sm. can tomato sauce (approx. 8 ozs.)
Salt and pepper to taste

Place all ingredients into medium saucepan; simmer until zucchini is done, about 45 minutes to 1 hour, stirring occasionally.

Jeanie Marsh, Harvest

ZUCCHINI SQUASH CASSEROLE

1 lb. ground beef
2 med. onions, chopped
2 T. salad oil
16 ozs. canned tomatoes (2 cups fresh)
1 8-oz. can tomato sauce
1 6-oz. can tomato paste (optional)
1 green pepper, chopped (optional)
1 cup grated Cheddar cheese
½ tsp. oregano
1 tsp. salt
4 med. zucchini
¼ tsp. garlic powder
½ cup Parmesan cheese

Brown meat and onions in oil. Add tomatoes, sauce, paste, and green pepper; simmer 10 minutes. Blend cheese, oregano, salt, zucchini squash cut in ¼-inch cubes, and garlic. Simmer 10 minutes more. Use 3-quart casserole; cover with Parmesan cheese and bake for 45 minutes at 350 degrees. Serves 6.

Jennie Bowen, Piedmont

ZUCCHINI-TOMATO CASSEROLE

2½ cups sliced zucchini
3 med. onions, sliced (about 1½ cups)
1 garlic clove
2 T. salad oil
1 can tomatoes (about 3½ cups)
1 tsp. oregano
2 tsp. salt
⅛ tsp. pepper
1 T. wine vinegar
3 T. grated cheese

Arrange zucchini in greased 3-quart casserole. Saute onion and garlic in oil (use small glass dish with cover) in microwave for 3 minutes on high. Remove from microwave. Add tomatoes, seasonings, and vinegar. Pour over zucchini in casserole dish, cover, and cook in microwave for 20 minutes on high. Remove from microwave and add cheese. Let set until cheese has melted then stir.

Dot Atwell, Athens Pike

Do not tell me that worry does not do any good. I know better. The things I worry about do not happen.

BUMPUS SWEET POTATOES

3 cups mashed sweet potatoes 2 eggs
1 cup sugar 1 T. vanilla
½ cup margarine

Mix above ingredients and put in buttered casserole big enough for pie to rise.

Topping

1 cup brown sugar ⅓ cup margarine
⅓ cup flour 1 cup chopped pecans

Mix and sprinkle over casserole. Bake 30 minutes at 350 degrees.

Ursula Bumpus, Central
Regna Howard, Madison Cross Roads

CANDIED SWEET POTATOES

6 med. sweet potatoes or equivalent canned ¼ cup margarine
1 cup hot water or liquid from can 1 T. lemon juice
½ cup brown sugar and ½ cup white sugar ½ tsp. salt
Cinnamon to taste
Dash of cloves
Dash of nutmeg
1 tsp. vanilla

If using raw potatoes, cook in boiling water until almost done, cool, and peel. Boil liquid and sugar for 5 minutes. Slice potatoes into ½-inch pieces, placing in baking dish. Add remaining ingredients to liquid and sugar; pour over potatoes. Bake at 350 degrees until potatoes are clear and syrup is thick. Serves 10.

Cora Bodie, Blossomwood

GRATED SWEET POTATO PUDDING

3 cups sweet potatoes 1 cup butter
2 eggs 1 tsp. cinnamon
1 cup sweet milk 1 tsp. nutmeg
1 tsp. salt

Grate sweet potatoes fine. Mix ingredients. Bake in iron skillet at 350 degrees until well done.

Vernie Mae Holt, New Sharon

HAWAIIAN YAMS

2 cups mashed sweet potatoes
2 eggs
2 cups sweet milk
1 cup sugar
1 tsp. vanilla
½ tsp. salt
1 cup Angel Flake Coconut
1 7-oz. jar red cherries
1 lg. can pineapple
1 cup sugar
3 T. cornstarch

Mix first 7 ingredients together and bake 20 minutes at 350 degrees or until firm. Mix cherries, pineapple, sugar, and cornstarch together for topping and cook slowly until thick, stirring constantly. Pour over potatoes and bake for 10 minutes.

Myrtle Breithaupt, Westbury

SWEET POTATO BAKE

3 cups mashed sweet potatoes
1 cup milk
1 egg
½ cup sugar
¼ tsp nutmeg
¼ tsp. cinnamon
1 stick margarine
1 cup cornflakes
1 cup nuts
½ cup packed brown sugar

Place first 6 ingredients in square baking dish. Top with melted margarine, cornflakes, nuts, and brown sugar. Bake 350 degrees for 10 or 12 minutes.

Barbara Stluka, Davis Hills

SWEET POTATO CASSEROLE I

3 cups cooked, mashed sweet potatoes
1 cup sugar
2 eggs
¼ cup milk
1 tsp. vanilla
1 stick margarine, melted
1 sm. can coconut
Juice, grated rind of 1 orange
1 cup brown sugar
½ cup flour
1 stick butter
1 cup chopped nuts

Mix first 8 ingredients and place in large casserole. Combine brown sugar and flour then cut butter into this. Add nuts. Sprinkle on potato mixture. Bake for 20 to 30 minutes at 350 degrees.

Opaline West, Madison Cross Roads
Mrs. Kathleen Vaughn, Monrovia
Rachel Koger, Hurricane

SWEET POTATO CASSEROLE II

3 cups cooked, mashed sweet potatoes	1½ cups sugar
¾ stick margarine	2 eggs
1 cup canned milk	½ tsp. nutmeg
	½ tsp. cinnamon
1 tsp. vanilla	

Mix all ingredients and pour into baking dish. Bake at 425 degrees for 15 minutes.

Topping

¾ stick margarine	½ cup nuts
½ cup light brown sugar	1 cup crushed cornflakes

Melt margarine, add sugar, nuts, and cornflakes. Mix well with spoon and spread over potatoes. Bake 15 minutes at 400 degrees.

Mary Ward, Fleming Hills

SWEET POTATO PUDDING

4 cups grated raw sweet potatoes	1⅓ cups milk
2 cups sugar	4 eggs, beaten
½ cup molasses	½ tsp. allspice
½ heaping tsp. cinnamon	

Peel and grate sweet potatoes. Mix with other ingredients. Bake in a shallow greased dish for 1 hour (or until milk is absorbed) in a 350-degree oven. (Molasses may be omitted, may reduce sugar if molasses used.)

Virginia Laux, Madison Cross Roads

BAKED TOMATOES

4 lg. tomatoes	2 T. chopped basil
Salt	2 T. chopped dill
Pepper	1 tsp. celery seed
1 T. minced onion	½ cup bread crumbs
4 tsp. butter	

Remove stem end from tomatoes—without cutting the meat. Cut tomatoes in half horizontally. Set cut side up in a shallow dish. Sprinkle with salt and pepper, onion, herbs, and toasted bread crumbs—dot with butter. Bake at 400 degrees for 15 minutes. Serves 4.

Mrs. Grinell Vaughn (Kathleen), Monrovia

TOMATOES AU GRATIN

4 med. tomatoes	2 T. minced parsley
1 sm. garlic clove, minced	¼ tsp. salt or to taste
2 T. fine dry bread crumbs	⅛ tsp. peppers or to taste
2 T. grated Parmesan cheese	2 T. margarine

Peel tomatoes and cut in half crosswise. Place tomatoes cut side up in greased shallow baking dish. Mix garlic, bread crumbs, cheese, parsley, salt, and pepper. Sprinkle over tomatoes. Dot with margarine. Bake in a preheated 400 degree oven until tomatoes are tender but still keep their shape and tops are golden brown (10 to 15 minutes).

Jeanne Peters, South Parkway

MIXED VEGETABLES

EASY GARDEN VEGETABLE PIE

2 cups chopped fresh broccoli or sliced fresh cauliflower florets	½ cup chopped green pepper
	1½ cups milk
1 cup shredded Cheddar cheese (about 4 ozs.)	¾ cup Bisquick baking mix
	3 eggs
½ cup chopped onion	1 tsp. salt
	¼ tsp. pepper

Heat oven to 400 degrees. Lightly grease pie plate, 10x1½ inch. Heat 1 inch of salted water (½ teaspoon salt to 1 cup water) to boiling. Add broccoli. Cover and heat to boiling. Cook until almost tender, about 5 minutes; drain thoroughly. Mix broccoli, cheese, onion, and green pepper in pie plate. Beat remaining ingredients until smooth, 15 seconds in blender on high speed or 1 minute with hand beater. Pour into pie plate. Bake until golden brown and knife inserted halfway between center and edge comes out clean, 35 to 40 minutes. Let stand 5 minutes before cutting. Garnish as desired. Refrigerate any remaining pie. Serves 6. One 10-ounce package frozen chopped broccoli or cauliflower, thawed and drained, may be substituted for the fresh broccoli or cauliflower. Do not cook.

Lucille Mitchell, Madison Cross Roads
Margie Spencer, Vestavia

MARINATED VEGETABLES

2 lbs. carrots
1 onion, sliced
1 green pepper, cut in rings
1 can tomato soup
Salt and pepper to taste

½ cup salad oil
1 cup sugar
¾ cup vinegar
1 tsp. prepared mustard
1 tsp. Worcestershire sauce

Cut and boil carrots in salted water until tender. Drain and cool. Alternate vegetables in bowl. Make marinade and pour over vegetables and refrigerate 2 or 3 days in covered dish. Drain and serve.

Ursula Bumpus, Central

MIXED VEGETABLE CASSEROLE

1 lg. pkg. frozen mixed vegetables
1 med. onion, chopped
1 cup chopped celery

1 cup grated cheese
1 cup mayonnaise
1 stick margarine

1 tube of crackers, crumbled

Cook vegetables according to directions on package until just tender. Put in greased casserole. Next mix onion, celery, cheese, and mayonnaise and spread over vegetables. Melt oleo and mix with cracker crumbs and sprinkle on top. Bake about 30 minutes at 350 degrees.

Mary Ward, Fleming Hills

STIR-FRY VEGETABLES

4 cups shredded cabbage
1 green pepper, sliced thin
2 lg. onions, sliced thin
2 lg. tomatoes cut in thin wedges

3 T. salad oil
2 tsp. sugar
¾ tsp. salt
¼ tsp. pepper

Combine vegetables and toss lightly. Heat oil in skillet; add vegetables and sprinkle with sugar, salt, and pepper. Cover and cook 10 minutes over medium heat, stirring twice during cooking period. Serves 4 to 6.

Evelyn Hall, Athens Pike

VEG-ALL CASSEROLE

2 cans Veg-All, drained
1 med. onion, diced
1 cup cheese, diced

1 cup mayonnaise
1 long pkg. Ritz crackers
1 stick margarine

SQUASH CASSEROLE

1½ lb. squash
1 small jar pimentos
1 cup sour cream
1 stick margarine
1 can cream of chicken soup
1 pkg. Pepperidge Farm dressing mix

Cook squash in salted water. Drain and mash. Add remaining ingredients, reserving half of dressing. Mix well. Line a casserole with reserved dressing which has been mixed with a stick of softened margarine reserving enough to sprinkle on top. Fill with squash mixture and cover with dressing mix. Bake at 350° for 30 minutes.
May be prepared day before and baked when needed.

Dottie Cutts, Westbury

VEGETABLE CASSEROLE

Mix Veg-All, cheese, onion, and mayonnaise. Place in large casserole. Crush crackers and sprinkle over vegetables. Pour melted margarine over crackers. Bake for 30 to 45 minutes at 350 degrees.

Opaline West, Madison Cross Roads
Rachel Koger, Hurricane
Mildred Kuykendall, Darwin Downs

CORN AND RICE CASSEROLE

2 cans Green Giant mexicorn
1 pkg. Mahatma yellow rice (5 oz.)
1 stick margarine
1 cup cream of celery soup
1 cup sharp cheddar cheese, grated
1 cup cheese (save for topping)

Prepare rice according to instructions. Add margarine until melted. Add corn and soup and grated cheese. Drain just one can of corn. Bake 30 min. at 350°. Remove, sprinkle with remaining cup of cheese and heat to melt cheese. Sprinkle with paprika.

Laura Hall, from Kaye Askew, Westbury

MY MAMA TONEY'S POTATO NESTS

To 2 cups of hot riced potatoes add 2 tbsp. butter, ½ tsp. of salt, the beaten yolks of 2 eggs and enough hot milk to make a mixture that can be shaped as nests, brush over a little beaten yolk of egg diluted with 1 tbsp. of water, brown in a hot oven. Serve filled with cubes of boiled Puritan Ham, that have been reheated.

Beverly Brown, Monrovia II

AUNT JO'S BAKED BEANS

1 lb. ground beef, browned & drained
3 cans Navy beans (14-15 oz.)
½ cup brown sugar
1 cup ketchup
1 medium onion, chopped
2 tbsp. Worcestershire sauce
3 tbsp. prepared mustard (not dry)
4 tbsp. bacon drippings
½ medium green pepper, chopped

Brown beef and drain. Mix all ingredients in a casserole dish (3 quart or larger), cover and bake at 375°, 1 hour.

Annie Brasseale, Rainbow Mountain

CARROTS WITH CHEESE

2 lb. carrots
1 stick margarine or butter
½ lb. Velveeta cheese

Scrape and slice carrots, cook until tender, drain. Melt cheese and margarine together stirring until thoroughly mixed. Pour over drained carrots. Serves 8 to 10.

Mrs. Leo (Lawsie) Wall, Monrovia

RICE VERDE

3/4 to 1 lb. Monterey Jack Cheese
1 pint sour cream
8 oz. green chilies, chopped
3 cups cooked rice (salt & pepper to taste)
¼ cup grated cheese

Cut Jack cheese in strips. Combine sour cream and chilies. Layer rice with sour cream mixture and cheese strips, in that order, ending with rice on top. Bake at 350° for 30 minutes. Sprinkle top with grated cheese about 10 minutes before done. Good with any meat or poultry.

Judy Case, Rainbow Mountain

CELERY CASSEROLE

1 cup celery
1 small jar pimentos
¼ cup almonds
1 can water chestnuts
1 can cream of chicken soup

Cook 1 cup celery (cut approximately ¾ or 1-inch long) until tender. Drain and mix with water chestnuts, drained and chopped, pimentos and cream of chicken or cream of celery soup. Put into a buttered casserole. Top with 1 cup soft bread mixed with 1 stick margarine or butter and ¼ cup almonds. Bake about 20 minutes in a 250° oven or bake until bubbly. Serves 8.

Mrs. Leo (Lawsie) Wall, Monrovia

GREEN PEA CASSEROLE

½ stick margarine
⅔ cup chopped onion
½ cup chopped bell pepper
⅔ cup chopped celery
1 can undiluted cream of mushroom soup
1 can chopped water chestnuts
1 large can drained english peas
Bread or cracker crumbs

Melt margarine in a large skillet. Add onion, bell pepper, and celery and saute until tender. Pour into 2 qt. casserole dish. Add cream of mushroom soup, water chestnuts and english peas. Mix and top with either cracker or bread crumbs, and ½ stick margarine, melted. Bake at 350° for approximately 30 minutes.

Vivian Lee, University

LIMA BEANS IN SOUR CREAM

2 10 oz. pkg. of frozen lima beans
2 tbsp. chopped onions
2 tbsp. pimento-chopped & drained
2 tbsp. margarine melted
1 cup sour cream
1/8 tsp. white pepper

Cook beans according to package directions, drain and set aside. Saute onions and pimento in margarine until onions are tender; remove from heat, and add sour cream and pepper, stirring well. Add sour cream mixture to lima beans, stir until blended. Cook over low heat until thoroughly heated. Serve immediately. About 6 servings.

Margaret Hornsby, Hurricane

VEGETABLE CASSEROLE

1 24 oz. pkg. frozen mixed vegetables
1 8 oz. can water chestnuts (chopped)
1 cup mayonnaise
1 cup chopped celery
1 med. onion chopped (optional)
1 cup shredded cheese
1 stick margarine
1 stick (¼ lb.) crackers

Cook vegetables according to directions on package. Drain slightly, and add drained water chestnuts. Put into greased 2-quart casserole. Mix mayonnaise, celery, onion and cheese, spread over vegetables, mix by stirring through several times. Melt margarine and mix with crushed crackers and put on top. Bake 30 min. at 350°. Serves 8 or 10.

Mrs. Leo (Lawsie) Wall, Monrovia

SPINACH CASSEROLE

3 pkgs. frozen chopped spinach
1 stick margarine
1 8 oz. block of cream cheese
3/8 tsp. salt (optional)
1/8 tsp. allspice (optional)

Cook spinach according to directions. Drain well. While still hot, put in margarine and cream cheese, salt and allspice. Mash out lumps. Put into casserole dish.

Topping:
Toss together:
1-2 tbsp. margarine
1 tbsp. rubbed sage
¾ cup Progresso Italian Bread Crumbs

Put on top of spinach mixture. Bake at 375° for 15-20 minutes. Serves 6-8.

Jeanne Peters, South Parkway

48 HOUR POTATOES

6 or 8 medium potatoes
8 oz. cheese (cubed)
1 stick margarine
1 tsp. salt
1 pt. Half and Half

Boil potatoes in plan water until tender. Leave potatoes in water and sit in refrigerator for 48 hours. Drain potatoes and grate (skin can be included). Add cheese, cubed, melt margarine and add salt and Half and Half. Pour over cheese and potatoes. Mix and bake at 325° for 1 hour. This is good to make ahead. Mix together and refrigerate until ready to bake. Serves 8.

Catherine Mitchell, Hurricane

VEGETABLE CASSEROLE

1 box frozen French-style green beans	½ pt. whipping cream
1 box frozen peas	½ pt. Hellmann's mayonnaise
1 box frozen limas	2 T. Parmesan Cheese
	Additional Parmesan cheese

Butter 13x9-inch casserole. Cook each vegetable separately in salt water and drain well. Place green beans in bottom of casserole, peas next, then limas. Whip cream and combine with ½ pint of Hellman's mayonnaise and Parmesan cheese. Pour over vegetables and work down with a knife. Sprinkle with Parmesan cheese and bake at 350 degrees for 30 minutes.

Sue Kachelhofer, University

HELPFUL HINTS

SPECIAL TIPS

As homemakers, we are conditioned by Madison Avenue to buy its products, attracted by its jingles and fancy packaging. We tend to forget that the basic ingredients are about the same and the "flavors" and "models" are what change.

It is possible to concoct inexpensive and quite adequate substitutes if you have the time and interest to do so.

Charlotte Shearer, Harvest

ANTIPERSPIRANT LIQUID

½ cup isopropyl alcohol
2½ cups water
1 T. powdered alum
1 T. powdered zinc oxide

Keep in plastic squeeze bottle.

CHIMNEY SOOT REMOVER

1 cup salt
1 cup zinc oxide

Add smaller amount to hot fire. As with any cleaners, take special care to store away from small children.

DEODORANT CREAM

3½ cups water
¼ cup stearic acid
2 T. triethanolamine
2 T. powdered alum

Heat 2 cups water and stearic acid. Separately, mix 1½ cups water and triethanolamine. Add second mixture to first. Cool to lukewarm and stir in 2 tablespoons powdered alum. Pour immediately into jars.

DRAIN CLEANER

1 cup soda
1 cup salt
¼ cup cream of tartar

Add ¼ cup of cleaner mixture to 1 cup boiling water. Flush with cold water.

FABRIC SOFTENER

4 cups lauryl pyridinium chloride

1 cup isoprophyl alcohol
⅓ cup water

Use 2 tablespoons per load.

GLASS SPRAY CLEANER

1 cup isopropyl alcohol

2 cups water
5 drops lactic acid

HAND CLEANER

1 cup mineral oil

¼ cup diglycol laurate

Keep in squeeze bottle.

LIQUID HAND SOAP

1 cup water
2½ tsp. triethanolamine

1 cup kerosene
5 tsp. oleic acid

Mix first 2 ingredients; then last 2; then mix together.

MOUTHWASH

4 cups water

$1/16$ tsp. borax
1½ tsp. boric acid

Add red food coloring and few drops of oil of cloves. Cost: 1 cent per ounce!

PERSPIRATION STAIN REMOVER

3 T. sodium perborate

2 cups water

Pre-test fabric. Saturate and rinse before adding clothes to washer.

SEPTIC TANK CLEANER

1 qt. water   1 lb. brown sugar
                 1 env. yeast

Note: Septic tank owners should *not* use Clorox. It kills the beneficial bacteria.

SHAMPOO

1 ¼ cups oleic acid   1 cup coconut oil
         1 ½ cups triethanolamine

WINDOW CLEANER

                 3 cups water
  2 T. ethylene glycol (which is permanent antifreeze)

Use like Windex.

One of the hardest things to teach our children about money matters is that it does.

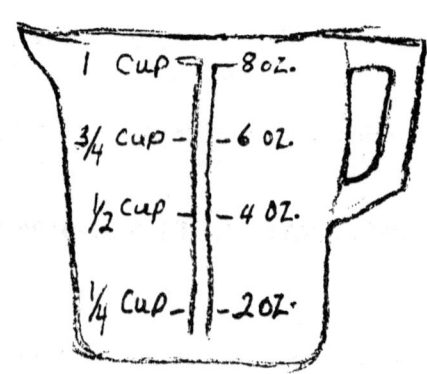

FOOD EQUIVALENTS

FOOD	AMOUNT	APPROXIMATE MEASURE
Butter or other shortening	1 lb.	2 cups
Cheese		
Cheddar or American	4 ozs.	1 cup shredded
cottage	1 lb.	2 cups
cream	3-oz. pkg.	6 T.
	8-oz. pkg.	1 cup (16 T.)
Chocolate		
chips	6-oz. pkg.	1 cup
unsweetened	8-oz. pkg.	8 sqs. (1 oz. each)
Coconut	4-oz. can	about 1⅓ cups
Coffee, ground	1 lb.	80 T.
Cream		
whipping	½ pt.	1 cup (2 cups whipped)
sour	8 oz.	1 cup
Eggs		
whites	1 cup	8-11 whole eggs
yolks	1 cup	11-12 whole eggs
whole	1 cup	4-6 whole eggs
Flour		
all-purpose	1 lb.	about 3½ cups
cake	1 lb.	about 4 cups
Lemon		
juice	1 med.	2-3 T.
peel, lightly grated	1 med.	1½-3 tsp.
Marshmallows	1 lg.	10 miniatures
	about 11 lg. or 110 miniatures	1 cup
Nuts		
almonds	1 lb., in shell	1-1¾ cups nutmeats
	1 lb., shelled	3½ cups
pecans	1 lb., in shell	2¼ cups nutmeats
	1 lb., shelled	4 cups
peanuts	1 lb., in shell	2¼ cups nutmeats
	1 lb., shelled	3 cups
walnuts	1 lb., in shell	1⅔ cups nutmeats
	1 lb.; shelled	4 cups
Orange		
juice	1 med.	⅓-½ cup
peel, lightly grated	1 med.	1-2 T.
Salt	1 dash	less than ⅛ teaspoon

Sugar
  brown   1 lb.   2¼ cups (firmly packed)
  powdered   1 lb.   about 4 cups
  granulated   1 lb.   2 cups

EQUIVALENT MEASURES

3 tsp.	=	1 T.	=	.015 l. ~ 15 ml.
16 tsp.	=	1 cup	=	.236 l. ~ 250 ml.
2 cups	=	1 pt.	=	.473 l. ~ 500 ml.
2 pt.	=	1 qt.	=	.946 l. ~ 1 l.
4 qt.	=	1 gal.	=	3.785 l. ~ 4 l.
4 T.	=	¼ cup	=	.059 l. ~ 50 ml.
5⅓ T.	=	⅓ cup	=	.080 l. ~ 80 ml.
2 T.	=	1 fluid oz.	=	.030 l. ~ 30 ml.
1 cup	=	8 fluid oz.	=	.237 l. ~ 250 ml.
16 oz.	=	1 lb.	=	454. g.

~ = approximately
l. = liter
ml. = milliliter
g. = gram

OVEN TEMPERATURES

Degrees Fahrenheit

Slow 250-325
Moderate 325-400
Hot or quick 400-450
Very hot 450-500

SIZE OF CANS

Size	Cups
8 ozs.	1
No. 1	2
No. 2	2½
No. 2½	3½
No. 3	4
No. 10	13

EMERGENCY SUBSTITUTIONS

Remember recipe results will vary when substitutions are made. This can be done to achieve desired changes in recipes or, of course, when you are out of a required ingredient.

For	Use
1 cup fresh whole milk	½ cup evap. milk plus ½ cup water or 1 cup reconstituted nonfat dry milk plus 2 T. butter
1 cup light cream	½ cup milk plus ½ cup heavy cream
1 cup buttermilk	1 cup milk plus 1 T. vinegar, let set 10-15 minutes
sour cream, whipped cream, or buttermilk	yogurt, approximately the same amounts
white flour	whole wheat flour
1 oz. unsweetened chocolate	3 T. cocoa plus 2 T. fat
1 cup shortening	½ cup butter or ⅓ cup oil
broth	wine, cooking sherry, in equal amounts
1 cup brown sugar	½ cup molasses
1 cup white sugar	½ cup honey (use extra flour to absorb excess liquid)
1 egg	2 egg yolks plus 1 T. water
1½ cups all-purpose flour	2 cups whole wheat flour (whole wheat does not absorb as much liquid as white flour)
1 tsp. flour, as thickener	½ tsp. cornstarch
grated lemon or orange peel	lemon or orange extract
currants	raisins
walnuts	pecans
yeast, 1 pkg. granular	6/10 oz. cake yeast or slightly more than ¼ of a 2-oz. cake

Amount Of Meat Per Serving

1 lb. boneless meat	4 average people
1 lb. bone-in meat	1 average person
1 lb. whole fish	1 average person
1 lb. fish fillets	2-3 people
each pound ready-to-cook chicken or duck with bone	2 people

When using salt remember: salt rice for Western cooking but no salt for Oriental cookery.

INDEX

A

Afternoon Festive Dessert 108
Almond, Jellied Chicken 300
American Lasagna 229
Angel
   Bavarian Cake 109
   Biscuits 28
   Food Lemon Fluff 109
Appetizers, See Party Foods 385
Appetizer Cheese Pizza 391
Appetizer, Zucchini 391
Apples
   Cake I And II 67
   Cheese Dessert 115
   Crisp 115
   Date Cake 68
   Dumplings 115
   Fried Apple Pies 170
   Hot Apple Cider Punch 16
   Hot Cider Punch I And II 16, 18
   Muffins 33
   Pie I And II 156
   Pie Filling 353
   Pie
      Golden Delicious 157
      Shredded Apple Pie 173
      Sour Cream 157
   Fried 396
   Salad 305
   Red Apple Salad 209
   Spiced, Granny's 123
Applesauce Beef Loaf 229
Applewich I And II 366
Apricot(s)
   Cake
      Nectar 86
      Nut 86
   Cornish Hens 281
   Milk Drink 14
   Salad 305
   Jello 305
Arkansas Cumin Rice 440
Armenian Cookies 181
Arroz Con Pollo 281
Artichokes
   Dip 397
   Evelyn's 321
   Hearts, Marinated Shrimp,
      And Mushrooms 388
Asparagus
   Casserole 379
   Casserole I And II 423
   Casserole With Peas 423
   Koowerup 424
Aunt Ann's Wacky Cake 69
Aunt Lottie's Lane Cake 86
Avocado, Guacamole Salad 322

B

Bacon
   Bacon-Egg Casserole 259
   Bacon-English Muffins 367
   Bean-Bacon Salad 319
   Bacon Omelet 367
   Bacon, Turkey And Tomato
      Sandwich 374
Baked Beans 379
Baked Beans And Cornbread 424
Baked Chicken 282
Baked Chicken Pieces 372
Baked Ham Slice 373
Baked Rice 440
Baked Tomatoes 452
Bakeless Pudding 116
Banana
   Banana Bread 38
   Banana Butter 352
   Banana Muffins 33
   Banana Nut Bread I And II 39
   Banana Nut Cake 87
   Banana Pudding 116
   Banana Slush Fruit Punch 14
Barbecue
   Beans And Hamburger Meat 230
   Beef Dinner 250
   Burgers 230
   Chicken 282
   Ground Beef Cups 230
   Pork 268
   Sauce 409
   Sauce, White 410
   Spareribs 268
   Wieners 367
Shingles or Bark Candy 199
Beans
   Bean And Bacon Salad 319
   Bean Calypol 424
   Bean Combo 425
   Bean Salad, Extra 321
   Bean Salad, 24-hour 326
   Green Bean Casserole 425
   Old-Fashioned String Beans 426
   Pinto Bean Pie 167
   Plantation Green Beans 426

Pork Chop And Navy Bean
  Casserole 269
Senate Bean Soup 417
Beef
  American Lasagna 229
  Applesauce Beef Loaf 229
  Bar-B-Q Beef Dinner 250
  Bar-B-Q Ground Beef Cups 230
  Barbecued Beans And Hamburger
    Meat 230
  Barbecue Burgers 230
  Beef Pot Roast And Vegetable
    Dinner 250
  Beef Stroganoff 373
  Beef Stroganoff I And II 249
  Bruno Special 230
  Cheeseburger Loaf 231
  Cherokee Casserole 231
  Chili I And II 232
  Chili Cheese Festivity 232
  Easy Chili 233
  Fritos Chili Casserole 233
  Chinese Beef 233
  Chinese Casserole 234
  Chopped Suey, American Style . 234
  Cold Fillet Of Beef 250
  Corn Beef Casserole 251
  Dinner In A Pocket 234
  Dried Beef Supreme 251
  Easy Stroganoff Casserole 235
  Flank Steak Roll-ups 252
  Fazline 235
  Fried Beef Slices With Onions .. 252
  Ghost-Town Burgers 236
  Greco 236
  Ground Beef Casserole 236
  Hamburger Favorite 237
  Hamburger Pie I And II 237, 238
  Hamburger Stroganoff 238
  Holiday Spaghetti 238
  Hot Tamale Balls 239
  Hunter's Stew 239
  Italian Beef 252
  Julie's Beef Rounds 240
  Macaroni And Beef Casserole ... 240
  Man-Sized Steak Salad 253
  Meal In One 240
  Meatballs I And II 241
  Porcupine Meatballs 241
  Saucepot Meatballs 242
  Meat Loaf I And II 242
  Prize-Winning Meat Loaf 242
  Meat-Rice Casserole 253

  Meat Salad 254
  Mexican Meat Cups 243
  Onion-Smothered Steak 254
  Oriental Beef Skillet 254
  Pepper Steak I And II 255
  Pizza 243
  Planked T-Bone Steak 255
  Ragu Beef Casserole 244
  Rolled Steaks 256
  Rushing Stew 244
  Sauerbraten 256
  Shepherd's Pie 244
  Sherried Beef 256
  Southern Beef Roll 245
  Spaghetti Sauce 245
  Spanish Delight Casserole 246
  Spanish Rice Pronto 246
  Steak Casserole 256
  Stuffed Beef Rolls 246
  Sukiyaki 257
  Super Supper 247
  Texas Beef Loaf 247
  Texas Hash 248
  Two-Bean/Beef Bake 248
  Western Mac Casserole 248
Beignets, Glenda's 59
Believe-It-Or-Not Cookies 367
Beets
  Beetcups, Sparkling 314
  Beet Jelly, Red 360
  Beets, Jerrie's 359
  Beets, Marinated 426
  Beets, Pickled 426
Best Deviled Eggs 223
Beverages
  Apricot Milk Drink 14
  Blender Drink 14
  Coffee Mixes, Instant 25
  Dr Pepper, Hot 18
  Egg Nog 15
  Fruit Crush 16
  Grape Wine 16
  Milkshake 20
  Mixes
    Hot Chocolate Mix I And II 17
    Hot Chocolate Mix II 17
    Hot Mocha Mix 18
    Instant Russian Tea I And II ... 19
    Hot Tea Mix 19
  Punch
    Banana Slush Fruit 14
    Chocolate Mocha 14
    Economy 15

Frosty Golden 15
Hot 18
Hot Apple Cider 16
Hot Cider I And II 17
Lime Ice 18
Lime Jello 20
Mary Katherine's Punch 25
Milk 20
Orange Pineapple 21
Party I And II 21
Pink Party 22
Punch 22
"Recital" 22
Rosy 23
Ruby Fruit 23
Russian Tea 24
Seven-Up Surprise 24
Tea
  Hot Spice 19
  Instant Russian Tea I And II ...19
  Russian Tea I And II 23
  Summertime Iced 24
Tomato Juice Cocktail 26
Billy's Cheese Canapes 392
Birdie's Ham Dumplings 412
Biscuit Ring Cake 88
Blackberry Jam Cake 80
Blueberry
  Blueberry Cheese Pie 157
  Blueberry Muffins 63
  Blueberry Tart, Five-Layer 120
  Blueberry Tea Bread 39
Blue Cheese Salad Dressing 335
Boiled Candy Cookies 181
Boiled Custard 116
Boiled Oatmeal Cookies 189
Boiled Shrimp 346
Bourbon Balls 182
Boyfriend Cookies 189
Bran-Nut Bread 63
Breads
Biscuits 28
  Angel Biscuits 28
  Leona's Hot Biscuits 28
  Mayonnaise Biscuits 28
  Sourdough Biscuits 28
Bread Sticks 29
Chili Corn Bread 31
Fruit And Quick Breads
  Cheese Breads 63
  Banana Bread 38
  Banana Nut Bread I And II 39
  Blueberry Tea Bread 39

Bran-Nut Bread 63
Boston Brown Bread 40
Corn and Sour Cream
  Cornbread 60
Cranberry Bread 41
Cranberry-Nut Bread 41
Easy Cheese Bread 64
Fruit Bread For Diabetics 180
Good Date Loaf 41
Heloise Waffles 62
Honey Nut Bread 64
Hot Herb Bread Italian Style ...30
Hushpuppies 30
Lemon Bread 42
Pineapple Bread 42
Plain Corn Bread 65
Poppy Seed Bread 43
Pumpkin Bread I, II,
  And III 43-44
Raisin Bread 44
Raisin Spice Roll 61
Spiced Zucchini Bread 44
Spoon Bread 45
Strawberry Bread 45
Zucchini Bread I And II 45, 46
Muffins
  Apple 33
  Banana 33
  Blueberry Muffins 63
  Bran Muffins I And II 34
  Brer Rabbit Muffins 34
  Cream Of Wheat Muffins 35
  Country Sausage Muffins ...35
  Master's Muffins 63
  Yeast Muffins 35
Pancakes
  Pancake Hawaiian 36
  Pancakes 37
  Peanut-Butter Hotcakes 37
  Potato Pancakes 37
  Puffy German Pancakes 38
Rolls
  Batter Buns 46
  Beer Rolls I And II 47
  Buttermilk Rolls 47
  Cinnamon Rolls 62
  Clover Tea Rolls 47
  Icebox Yeast Rolls 48
  No-Knead Refrigerator Rolls ...49
  Refrigerator Rolls 49
  Rolls 49
  Pauline's Rolls 64
  Spoon Rolls 50

Susan's Refrigerator Rolls 50
Whole Wheat Yeast Rolls I
 And II 50, 51
Yeast Roll 51
Sweet Rolls And Doughnuts
 Cindy's Sally Lunns 57
 Cream Cheese Danish 57
 English (Harlequin) Scones 58
 French Toast 59
 Glenda's Beignets 59
 Quickie Doughnuts 59
 Yeast Rolls 60
Yeast Bread
 Brown Yeast Bread 51
 Cheese Bread 52
 Cracked Wheat Bread 52
 Dilly Bread 53
 Irish Bread 53
 Raisin Casserole Bread 53
 Soy Nut Bread 54
 Staff Of Life Bread 55
 Two-Tone Rye Twist 55
 Whole Wheat Bread I
  And II 56, 57
Bread And Butter Pickles I And II ..355
Bread Pudding I And II 117
Bread Pudding, Mama's
 Chocolate 127
Bread Stuffing 412
Breakfast Before 368
Breakfast Pizza 266
Bride's Chicken Salad 283
Broccoli
 Broccoli Bake 427
 Broccoli Casserole I, II,
  And III 427, 428
 Broccoli And Rice 427
 Broccoli Salad I And II 319, 320
Brownies 182
Brownies, Hilma's 182
Brownies, Kim's 370
Bruno Special 230
Brunswick Stew 412
Buckey's Candy 180
Bumpus Sweet Potatoes 450
Busy Day Cake 88
Butter Brickle Dessert 117
Buttermilk
 Buttermilk Coconut Pie 146
 Buttermilk Pie 145
 Buttermilk Rolls 47
 Buttermilk Salad 306
 Buttermilk Tea Cakes 198

Butterscotch Pie 146
Butternut Squash Cake 88

C

Cabbage
 Casserole 429
 Red 430
 Salad, Dainty Winter 316
 Slaw 315
  Chinese 317
  Cole 316
  Lula's Freezer 318
 Soup, German 429
 Steamed 381
Cakes
 Apple Cakes
  Cakes I And II 67
  Date 68
  Fresh 68
  Vermont 69
 Chocolate Cakes
  Angel Cake 110
  Aunt Ann's Wacky 69
  Cheesecake 112
  Choco-Dot Pumpkin 70
  Eclair 70
  Four Layer 111
  Fudge 71
  Mississippi Mud 72
  Mocha 73
  Nut Zucchini 71
  Peter Paul Mound 73
  Quick Syrup 74
  Randy's Cookie Sheet 74
  Tunnel-Of-Fudge 75
  Yeast 72
 Coconut Cakes
  Cake I And II 75, 76
  Easy Refrigerator 76
  Fresh 75
 Fruit Cakes
  Fruit Cake 114
  Christmas 76
  Dark 76
  Golden 78
  Mrs. Bryant's 79
  Small 79
  White 79
 Jam Cakes
  Blackberry 80
  Quick And Easy 80
 Pound Cakes
  Chocolate 80

Coconut 81
Cream Cheese 81
Five-Flavor 82
Grandmother's 82
Granny's Old-Fashioned 83
Kentucky Wonder 83
Orange 83
Pound I And II 84
Red Velvet 84
Sour Cream 85
Sugerless For Diabetics 210
White 85
General Cakes
Apricot Nectar 86
Apricot Nut 86
Aunt Lottie's Lane 86
Banana Nut 87
Biscuit Ring 88
Busy Day 88
Butternut Squash 88
Carrot 88
Carrot Pineapple 89
Cheesecake I And II 90
Cherry Jubilee 91
Chess 91
Cranberry Coffee 470
Cream Cheese Bars 92
Crunch 92
Cleo's Orange Date 92
Date Coffee 93
Dela's Pumpkin Roll 111
Diabetic Date-Nut 179
Dump 93
Fast Fixin's Fruit And Cake ... 93
Fig Preserve and Honey 94
Georgia 94
Gingerbread 95
Gold And Silver 95
Golden Cake—For Diabetics . 204
Golden Shell 369
Gooey Butter 96
Hermit 96
Honey 96
Hummingbird 97
Jessie Sanderson's Royal
  Sponge 97
Italian Cream 98
Lemon Cheese 98
Lemon Sponge Cups 110
Neapolitan 98
No Name Cake 112
1-2-3-4 (Yellow) 99
Orange Date 99

Plum Good 100
Poppy Seed Refrigerator
  Torte 100
Prune 101
Ribbon Icebox 101
Pineapple I And II 102
Pineapple Upside-Down 103
Rotten 103
Self-Filling Cupcakes 104
Seven-Up 104
Snippy Doodle Coffee 104
Sour Cream Walnut 105
Strawberry 106
Strawberry Soda Pop 110
Watergate 106
White 106
Yellow Angel Food 107, 111
Toppings, Cakes—See Icings/
  Frostings 107
Calas 441
Calico Beans 425
Candied
Leona's Apples 408
Peanuts 405
Summer Squash 444
Sweet Potatoes 450
Candy
Aunt Annie's Elephant
  Drop 199
Buckey's 180
Chocolate Nut Balls 175
Date Balls 175
Divinity 176
  No-Cook 176
Fudge
  Coconut 176
  Easiest Ever Cocoa 383, 385
  Five-Minute 177
  Old-Fashioned Chocolate 177
  Peanut Butter 208
  Quick, Sure 177
Good-For-You 178
Hand-dipped Chocolates 178
Health Balls 178
Hickory Nut, Old-Fashioned ... 179
Mary Ball 179
Peanut Brittle 179
  No-Fail 179
Pralines
  Chris's Butterscotch 175
  Southern 385
  White 181

Index

Reese Cup
  Balls 180
  Peanut Butter 180
  Shingles or Bark 199
Caramel
  Frosting 107
  Pie 146, 172
  Popcorn 402
Carrots
  Cake 88, 89
  Casserole 431
  Glazed With Orange Slices 432
  Lemon-Nutmeg 205
  Marinated 431
  Marshmallow Salad 330
  Rice Ring 432
  Souffle 432
  Sweet And Sour 433
  Celery Casserole 433
  Cherokee Casserole 231
Cheese
  Balls 393
  Ball I, II, And III 392
  Baked Eggs 223
  Bread 52
  Broccoli, Rice Casserole 428
  Burger, Loaf 231
  Cake 90, 113
  Cakes, Mini 395
  Canapes, Billy's 392
  Corn 402
  Easy Cheese Bread 64
  Cottage Cheese Spinach Cups ... 12
  Cream
    Party Sandwich 396
    Party Sandwich Spread ... 396
    Tarts 394
    Pastry Shell 12
  Dip
    Hot 399
    Pimiento 401
  Garlic 394
  Roll 395
  Herb Spread 380
  Log 393
  Pizzas, Appetizer 391
  Rice Krispie Cheese Ball ... 10
  Wadi's Cheese Ball 11
  Sauce
    Jezebel 395
    Lambda Chi Alpha 395
  Sausage Balls 405
  Spreads 333, 393, 396

Pimiento, Wonda's 396
Strawberry Ring 393
Straws, Diane's 394
Cheesy
  Baked Potato 379
  Sausage Quiche 265
Cherry
  Cake 91
  Congealed Salad 306
  Ice Cream 136
  Jessie Cherry Dessert 133
  Pie, Party 158
  Salad 330
    Frozen 330
    Supreme 306
  Tortonis 201
  Cherry Yum Yum 134
Chess
  Cake 91
  Pie
    I, II, And III 147
    Chewy 147
    Lemon 151
  Squares 183
Chicken
  Arroz Con Pollo 281
  Baked 282
  Barbecue 282
  BBQ 282
  Breasts
    Easy Cann Hawaiian 299
    Wellington 285
    With Dried Beef 286
    With Orange Sauce 287
  Cacciatore 287
  Canapes 385
  Casseroles
    I, II, III, IV, And V 288, 290
    Almond 290
    Asparagus 285
    Chopped 298
    Dressing 284
    Easy Broccoli 299
    Kraut 284
  Chinese 297
  Chow Mein 290
  Crunch 290
  Crunch 290
  Divan 291, 374
  Dressing 283
  Dumplings 284
  Fantastic 299
  Fried 300
  How-So 291

Index

In Cola 291
Italiano 292
Jellied, Almond 300
Livers 258, 374
   Rumaki 389
   Mayonnaise With Walnuts 292
   Mother Hen Pie 301
   'N Rice Bake 292
   Oriental 293
   Parmesan 293
   Pie 293, 294
   Pronto 294
   Salad 201, 327
      Bride's 283
      Hot I And II 328
      Party 388
   Saltimbocca 295
   Sauterne 295
   Spaghetti 285, 295
   Supreme 296
   Teresa's In Sour Cream Sauce .. 301
   Tetrazzini, Double 298
   With
      Cashews 296
      Dried Beef 297
      Rice 297
   Yogurt Bake 201
Chili
   Chili Cheese Dip 10
   I And II 232
   Cheese Festivity 232
   Cornbread 26
   Easy 233
   Fritos, Casserole 233
   Sauce 360
Chinese
   Beef 233
   Casserole 234
   Fried Rice 441
   Slaw 316
Chocolate
   Beverages 14, 17, 18
   Cakes 69-72
   Candy 173
   Chip Cookie Crust 139
   Cookies 182, 184, 185, 198
   Pies
      I, II, And III 143-144
      Chess I And II 142
      Cream 142
      Frozen 144
      Fudge 145
      Satin 145

Yogurt 143
Pudding 382
   Bread, Mama's 127
   Four-Layer 121
Chopped Suey, American Style ... 234
Chow Mein, Chicken 290
Chowder, New England Corn 416
Christmas Cake 76
Cinnamon Roll 62
Cleo's Orange Date Cake 92
Cobblers
   Jeffy 161
   Peach 163
   Sweet Potato 168
Cindy's Sally Lunns 57
Coca-Cola Salad 307
Cocoa, Easiest Ever Fudge 383
Coconut
   Cakes 75, 76
   Cookies 185
   Fudge 176
   Pies 148-150, 172
Coffee
   Instant Coffee Mixes 25
   Cake—Also See Sweet Rolls And
      Doughnuts 57, 60
   Date 93
Coleslaw—See Cabbage
Congealed Salads
   Apple 305
   Apricot 305
   Buttermilk 305
   Cherry 306
      Supreme 306
   Coca-Cola 307
   Cool Gelatin 307
   Cranberry I And II 307
   Cucumber Supreme 308
   Fresca 308
   Fruit Fluff 309
   Jello 310
      Dry 308
      Ice Cream 309
      With Topping 310
      Orange 311
      Strawberry 314
   Mint, Frozen Lime 309
   Molded Cranberry, Orange, And
      Pineapple 311
   1-2-3-4 311
   Orange, Cottage Cheese 208
   Pear 312

Pineapple
  Cheddar 312
  Cranberry 313
Pretzel 313
Sea Foam 313
Sparkling Beetcups 314
Spiced Peach 314
Viola Marshmallow Delight 315
Yum Yum 315
Cookies
Armenian 181
Boiled Candy 181
Boiled Oatmeal 189
Bourbon Ball 182
Boyfriend 189
Brownies 182
Cathedral Window 183
Chess Squares 183
Chewy Peanut Butter Bars 190
Chip Pan 184
Chocolate, Boiled 184
Chocolate-Covered Peanut
  Butter Balls 191
Chocolate Fudge Boiled
  Cookies 198
Cinnaomn Crispies 190
Cinnamon Squares 183
Clara, From Texas 195
Cookie Monsters 184
Cookies For A Diabetic 208
Corn Flake 184
Cream Cheese 186
Date Balls 186
Easy Peanut Butter 191
Forgotten 186
Fruit 187
Fruit Cake 187
Granola 188
Hilma's Brownies 182
Icebox 188
Italian Chocolate 184
Lizzies 188
Lori's Orange Ball 186
Macaroons, Coconut 185
Magic Bars 185
No-Bake Three Layer 185
Oatmeal Crisps 190
Peanut Blossoms 192
Peanut Butter 192
Pecan Butterballs 193
Pecan Crunch 193
Pecan Pie Surprise Bars 194
Potato Chip 194

Prize-Winning 199
Rice Krispies 194
Rich Peanut Butter Bars 192
Salted Peanut 193
Skillet 195
Spry Sugar 196
Snickerdoodles 195
Sugar 196
Tea Cakes
  Buttermilk 198
  Mother's I And II 197
  Old-Fashioned 197
  Russian 198
  The Best 196
Corn Beef Salad 328
Corn Bread
  Mexican I And II 32, 33
  Supreme 32
  Casserole I And II 432, 433
  Corn and Sour Cream 60
  Chowder 416
  Frozen Cream-Style 380
  Ham Casserole 261
  Meal Dumplings 32
  Pudding 433
  Salad I And II 320
  Scalloped 435
Cornish Hens 281, 298
Cottage Cheese
Low-Calorie Cottage
  Cheese Dip 205
Orange Salad 208
Salad 208
Crab
Dip 397
Deviled 342
New Jersey Seafood 342
Robbie's Crab And Shrimp
  Casserole 344
Seafood Quiche 347
Crackers
Great Crackers 11
Pecan Pie 165
Graham Crackers 30
Graham Cracker Pudding 123
2-Grain Wafers 3
Cranberry
Cake 113
Bread 41
Frozen Salad 331
Nut Bread 41
Casserole 407
Salad I And II 307, 308

Index

Cream Cheese
- Bars 92
- Danish 57
- Pound Cake 81
- Cream Of Wheat Muffins 35
- Creole Okra 437
- Crepes, Dinner 260
- Crisco Pie Crust Mix 139
- Crunch Cake 92

Cucumber
- Crisp Cucumber Sticks 356
- 14-Day Cucumber Pickles 356
- Salad Supreme 308
- Sandwiches 386
- Sliced For Freezer 362
- Cupcakes, Self-Filling 104

Curry
- Dip 397
- Fruit 407
- Fruit Casserole 330
- Harvest Fruit 407

Custard, Chess, Lemon Pies/Tarts
- Eagle Brand Custard 120
- Lazy Pie 151
- Mama's Egg 152
- Mock Boiled 127
- Old-Fashioned Egg Custard I And II 153
- Rachel's Egg 153

D

- Dainty Winter Salad 317
- Danny's Italian Dressing........335
- Dark Fruit Cake 76

Dates
- Cleo's Orange Date Cake 92
- Date Balls 175
- Date Balls 186
- Date Coffee Cake 93
- Date-Nut Cake, Diabetic 202
- Date, Orange Cake 99
- Date-Pecan Pie 166
- Date Rolls 119
- Datenut Rolls, No-Bake 386
- Good Date Loaf 41
- Dela's Pumpkin Roll 111
- Delicious Sweet Potato Pie 169
- Deluxe Pecan Pie 166

Desserts
- Afternoon Festive Dessert 108
- Angel Bavarian Cake 109
- Angel Food Lemon Fluff 109
- Apple Cheese Dessert 115
- Apple Crisp 115
- Apple Dumplings 115
- Bakeless Pudding 116
- Banana Pudding 116
- Boiled Custard 116
- Bread Pudding I And II 117
- Butter Brickle Dessert 117
- Cherry Delight 118
- Cherry Yum Yum 134
- Chocolate Float 118
- Chocolate Mouse 118
- Chocolate Pecan Torte 119
- Date Roll 119
- Eagle Brand Custard 120
- Five-Layer Blueberry Tart 120
- Four-Layer Chocolate Pudding ..121
- Fresh Strawberry Frost 121
- Frosty Strawberry Dessert 122
- Frozen Date Delight 122
- Frozen Dessert 123
- Fruit Crush 123
- Fruit Dessert 135
- Graham Cracker Pudding 123
- Granny's Spiced Apples 123
- Grape-Nut Pudding 124
- Heavenly Hash 124
- Jesse's Cherry Dessert 133
- Icebox Dessert 125
- Icebox Pudding 125
- Lemon Fruit Freeze 125
- Lemon Snow-Freeze 126
- Lemon Squares 126
- Macaroon Whip 127
- Mock Boiled Custard 127
- Mama's Chocolate Bread Pudding 127
- My Mama Toney's Carrot Pudding 134
- Nut Torte 132
- Old Fashion Bread Pudding with Rum Sauce 133
- Orange Cream Trifle 128
- Peaches With Bourbon 128
- Pink Arctic Freeze 128
- Plum Pudding 129
- Sugar Plum Pudding 129
- Strawberry Delight 129
- Super Peach Crisp 130
- Texas Delight 131
- Tropical Freeze 131
- War Tack 136
- Ice Cream And Sherbet 136
- Cherry Ice Cream 136

Index

Gelatin Ice Cream 136
Homemade Peach Ice Cream . . . 137
Ice Cream 137
Lemon Ice Cream 137
Orange Sherbet 137
Strawberry Ice Cream 138, 134
Vanilla Ice Cream I And II 138
Yummy Ice Cream Dessert 139
Deviled Crab 342
Diane's Cheese Straws 394
Dietetics
   Cherry Tortonis 201
   Chicken Salad 201
   Chicken/Yogurt Bake 201
   Deviled Ham Dip 201
   Diabetic Date-Nut Cake 202
   Diet Salad 202
   Five-Cup Salad 202
   Fresh Vegetable Omelet 203
   Fruit Bread For Diabetics 203
   Golden Cake For Diabetics 204
   Ladyfingers 204
   Lean And Light Pancakes 205
   Lemon-Nutmeg Carrots 205
   Lo-Cal Baked Chicken 205
   Low-Calorie Cottage Cheese Dip 205
   Low-Calorie Onion Soup Dip . . . 206
   Low-Calorie Waldorf Salad 206
   Low-Fat Orange Salad 206
   Low-Sodium Mayonnaise 207
   Oatmeal Drops 207
   Old-Fashioned Ginger Squares . . 207
   Orange Cottage Cheese Salad . . . 208
   Peanut Butter Fudge 208
   Cookies For A Diabetic 208
   Pudding Cookies 209
   Red Apple Salad 209
   Sauerkraut Salad 209
   Skillet Cabbage 210
   Strawberry Pie 210
   Sugarless Pound Cake For
      Diabetics 210
   Sunshine Salad 211
   Surprise Chocolate Cake 211
   Diet Salad 202
Dill Pickles 356
Dill Pickles, Stuffed 390
Dilly Bread 53
Dinner Crepes 260
Dinner In A Pocket 234
Dips
   Deviled Ham Dip 201
   Deviled Ham Dip 398

Dill Dip For Raw Vegetables 398
Dip For Raw Vegetables 398
Fresh Fruit Dip 398
Hot Cheese Dip 399
Hot Mexicana Dip 399
Hot Shrimp Dip 399
Low-Calorie Cottage Cheese Dip 205
Low-Calorie Onion Soup Dip . . . 206
Mexican Dip 400
Mock Sour Cream Dip 400
Olive Dip 400
Pimiento Cheese Dip 401
Sour Cream Vegetable Dip 401
Spinach Dip 401
Taco Dip 401
Vegetable Dip I And II 401
Divinity Candy 176
Divinity, No-Cook 176
Do-It-Yourself Peanut Butter 352
Double Batch Granola 408
Double Chicken Tetrazzini 288
Doughnuts, Quickie 59
Dove 302
Dressing, Chicken And 283
Dried Beef, Chicken With 297
Dried Beef Supreme 251
Dr Pepper, Hot 18
Dry Jello Salad 308
Duck, Roast Wild 302
Dump Cake 93
Dumplings
   Apple 115
   Birdie's Ham Dumplings 412
   Cornmeal Dumplings 32
   Dropped Ham Dumplings 261

E

Easy Cheese Bread 64
Eggs
   And Bacon Souffle 259
   Casserole, Bacon 259
   Cheese Baked 223
   Confetti-Filled 224
   Custard, Mama's 152
      Old-Fashioned I And II 153
      Rachel's 153
   Deviled, Best 223
   French Country Omelet 223
   Garlic Grits 224
   Gertrude's Cheese Casserole . . . 227
   Hot Holiday Deviled 226

… 476 …

Pie, Mother's 152
  Old-Fashioned 153
  Quiche 225
  Quiche Lorrane 225
  Quiche Supreme 225
  Soup, Greek Lemon 414
  Supreme, Spanish 226
Eggplant
  Casserole I And II 435
  Fried 436
  Souffle 436
  Squash, Ratatouille 444
Emergency Substitutions 464
English Muffins, Bacon 367
Equivalent Measures 463

F

Fast Fixin Fruit and Cake 93
Fazline 235
Fig
  Jam 353
  Preserve And Honey Cake 94
  Strawberry Preserves 353
Fish, Also See Seafood
  Puffs 342
  Oceanburgers 343
Five-Flavor Pound Cake 82
Fondue, For Fruit, Lemon 399
Food Equivalents 462
Frankfurter-Noodle Casserole 368
Franks, Pizza 375
French Toast 59
French Country Omelet 223
Fresca Salad 308
Fried
  Apples 408
  Beef Slices With Onion 252
  Chicken 300
  Eggplant 436
  Ham Patties 261
  Okra, Fritter 437
  Peaches, For Pies 355
  Potted Peaches, For Pies 355
Frostings/Icings
  Caramel Frosting 107
  Caramel Icing 107
  Fluffy White Not Too Sweet 108
  Icing, Chocolate 108
  Mama Nell's Cake Frosting 108
Frozen
  Cherry Salad 331
  Cranberry Salad 331

Fruit Salad Cups 332
Lime Mint Salad 309
Pink Salad 332
Salad 332
Fruit
  Bread For Diabetics 203
  Cakes, Also See Cakes 76-80
  Cake Cookies 187
  Cake Logs 386
  Casserole, Curried 330
  Cookies 187
  Fluff Salad 309
  Crush 16
  Curried 407
  Curried Harvest 407
  Dessert 135
  Dip, Fresh 398
  Hot 408
  Pies. Also See Pies 156
  Salad I And II 333
    Fast And Easy 332
    Frozen 333
    Frozen, Cups 333
    Mixed 381
    Poppy Seed 334
    With Sauce 333
Fudge
  Coconut 176
  Easiest Ever Cocoa 383
  Five-Minute 177
  Old-Fashioned Chocolate 177
  Peanut Butter 208
  Pie 145, 384
  Quick, Sure 177

G

Garlic Cheese 394
Garlic Cheese Roll 395
Garlic Grits 224
Garlic Toast 29
Gelatin Ice Cream 136
Georgia Cake 94
German Cabbage Soup 429
Gertrude's Cheese Casserole 227
Ghost-Town Burgers 236
Gibson's Coconut Pie 172
Gingerbread 95
Glazed Carrots With Orange Slices 432
Glazed Sausage Bites 405
Glazed Strawberry Pie 168
Glenda's Beignets 59
Gold And Silver Cake 95

Golden Cake For Diabetics 204
Golden Fruit Cake 78
Golden Shell Cake 369
Good Date Loaf 41
Good For You Candy 178
Good Stuff 369
Gooey Butter Cake 96
Graham Crackers 30
Graham Cracker Pudding 123
Grandmother's Pound Cake 82
Grandmother's Homemade
  Mayonnaise 410
Grandmother's Pound Cake 82
Grandma's Noodles 415
Granny's Old-Fashioned Pound
  Cake 83
Granny's Spiced Apples 123
Granola 370
Granola Cookies 188
Grape Juice Pie 159
Grape Wine 16
Grasshopper Pie 159
Grated Sweet Potato Pudding 450
Great Crackers 11
Greco 236
Greek Egg Lemon Soup 414
Green Bean Casserole 425
Green Chili-Hominy Casserole ...434
Ground Beef Casserole 236
Ground Beef, See Beef-Ground
Guacamole Salad 321

H

Ham
  Ham Breakfast Pizza 266
  Ham Cones 256
  Corn And Ham Casserole 261
  Dinner Crepes 260
  Dropped Ham Dumplings 261
  Ham And Egg Casserole 256
  Ham Loaf 262
  Ham Kabob 262
  Ham Omelet 263
  Ham Patties 263
  Ham Patties, Fried 261
  Ham Rolls 387
  Plantation Style Ham Slices 264
Hamburger, See Beef-Ground
  Hamburger Favorite 237
  Hamburger Pie I And II 237, 238
  Hamburger Stroganoff 239

Hash Brown Casserole 438
Hash, Poor Man's 439
Hash, Texas 248
Hawaiian Pie 159
Hawaiian Yams 451
Health Bars 178
Hearty Tuna Salad 328
Heavenly Hash 124
Heavenly Fruit Pie 160
Heavenly Salad 333
Heloise Waffle 62
Herb Cheese Spread 380
Hermit Cake 96
Hickory Nut Candy, Old-
  Fashioned 179
Hilma's Brownies 182
Hoghead Cheese 418
Hog's Head Stew 363
Holiday Nuts 404
Holiday Oyster Stew 416
Holiday Spaghetti 238
Homemade Hominy 363
Homemade Catchup 360
Homemade Noodles 415
Homemade Peach Ice Cream 137
Hominy Casserole 434
Hominy-Green Chili Casserole ...435
Honey Cakes 96
Honey Cake And Fig Preserve 94
Honey Nut Bread 64
Hot Apple Cider Punch 16
Hot Cheese Dip 399
Hot Chicken Salad I And II ...328, 329
Hot Chocolate Mix I And II 17
Hot Cider Punch I And II 17, 18
Hot Crab Salad, Tasty 329
Hot Dogs 367, 368, 370, 375, 388
Hot Dog Relish 361
Hot Dr Pepper 18
Hot Fruit 408
Hot Ham 12
Hot Ham Buns 387
Hot Herb Bread Italian Style 30
Hot Holiday Deviled Eggs 226
Hot Link Sausage Casserole 267
Hot Mexicana Dip 399
Hot Mocha Mix 18
Hot Pepper Jelly 361
Hot Punch 18
Hot Shrimp Dip 399
Hot Spice Tea 19
Hot Tamale Balls 239
How To Freeze Irish Potatoes 366

I

Ice Cream And Sherbet
   Ice Cream And Sherbet 136
   Cherry Ice Cream 136
   Gelatin Ice Cream 136
   Homemade Peach Ice Cream ... 137
   Ice Cream 137
   Lemon Ice Cream 137
   Orange Sherbet 137
   Strawberry Ice Cream 134, 138
   Vanilla Ice Cream I And II 138
   Yummy Ice Cream Dessert 139

Hummingbird Cake 97
Hunter's Stew 239
Hushpuppies 31
Hushpuppies, Squash 447

Ice Cream Jello Salad 309
Ice Punch, Lime 20
Icebox Cake, Ribbon 101
Icebox Cookies 188
Icebox Dessert 125
Icebox Pie I And II 160
Icebox Pudding 125
Icebox Yeast Rolls 48

Icings And Frostings
   Caramel Frosting 107
   Caramel Icing 107
   Fluffy White Not Too KSweet .. 108
   Icing, Chocolate 108
   Mama Nell's Cake Frosting ... 108

Impossible Pie 149
In Cola, Chicken 291
Incredible Coconut Pie 150
Instant Russian Tea I And II 19
Irish Bread 53
Irish Potatoes, How To Freeze ... 366
Italian Beef 252
Italian Cream Cake 98
Italian Style, Hot Herb Bread 30
Italiano, Chicken 292

J

Jam Cake, Quick And Easy 80
Jam, Fig 353
Jam, Strawberry I And II 354, 355
Jan's Meatza Pie 375
Jean's Spinach Salad 325
Jellied Chicken Almond 300
Jello Pie 150
Jello Punch, Lime 20
Jello Salad 310
Jello Salad, Apricot 305
Jello Salad, Dry 308
Jello Salad, Ice Cream 309
Jello Salad, Orange 311
Jello Salad, Strawberry 314
Jello With Topping 310
Jelly, Hot Pepper 361
Jelly, Pepper 362
Jelly, Red Beet 360
Jerrie's Beets 359
Jessie Sanderson's Royal Sponge
   Cake 97
Jezebel Sauce 395
Jiffy Cobbler 161
Jubilee Cake, Cherry 91
Juice Pie, Grape 159
Julie's Beef Rounds 240

K

Karo Crazy Crunch 403
Kentucky Wonder Pound Cake 83
Kim's Brownies 370
Kraut 361
Kraut Salad 317
Kraut, Spareribs And 271
Kugel 416

L

Ladyfingers 204
Lamb, Butterfly Leg Of 257
Lamb Stew 258
Lamba Chi Alpha, Cheese Roll ... 395
Lasagna I And II 264, 265
Lasagna, American 229
Last-Minute Shortcake 384
Lazy Pie 151
Lean And Light Pancakes 205
Lemon Bread 42
Lemon Cheesecake 98
Lemon Chess Pie 151
Lemon Fondue For Fruit 399
Lemon Fruit Freeze 125
Lemon Ice Cream 137
Lemon-Nutmeg Carrots 205
Lemon Snow Freeze 126
Lemon Soup, Greek "Egg" 414
Lemon Sponge Cups 110
Lemon Squares 126
Lemon Tarts, Velvety 155
Lemonade Pie 151

Index

Leona's Candied Apples 408
Leona's Hot Biscuits 28
Lettuce Salad 317
Lime Ice Punch 20
Lime Jello Punch 20
Liver Casserole 258
Liver, Chicken 258
Liver, Chicken Rumaki 389
Liver Surprise 259
Lori's Orange Ball Cookies 186
Lo-Cal Baked Chicken 205
Low-Calorie Cottage Cheese Dip .205
Low-Calorie Onion Soup Dip 206
Low-Calorie Waldorf Salad 206
Low-Fat Orange Salad 206
Low-Sodium Mayonnaise 207
Lula's Freezer Slaw 318

M

Macaroni And Beef Casserole 240
Macaroon Whip 127
Mac's Sour Cream Raisin Pie 161
Magic Cookie Bars 185
Mandarin Stuffed Pork Chops 269
Man-Sized Steak Salad 253
Maple Syrup 366
Marinated
    Beets 426
    Mushrooms 387
    And Artichoke Hearts,
        Shrimp 388
    Tomatoes 322
    Vegetable Salad 322
    Vegetables 454
Marshmallow Torte Pie 161
Mary Katherine's Punch 25
Masters Muffins 63
Mayonnaise
    Biscuits 28
    Easy, Easy, Blender 410
    Grandmother's Homemade 410
    Low-Sodium 207
Meal In One 240
Meats
    Bacon 259, 367, 374
    Beef 229-257, 265, 373, 377,
        413, 414, 417, 418
        Corn 251
        Dried 251,286
        Ground .229-248, 370, 375, 406
    Chicken 281-301, 371, 374,
        385, 388, 412

Cornish Hens 281, 298
Dove 302
Duck 302
Ham 260-264, 266, 373, 387, 398, 412
Hot Dogs ...367,368, 370, 375, 388
Lamb 257-258
Liver 258-259, 374, 376, 389
Pork 268-272, 376
Quail 302
Sausage 264-267, 368, 405, 406
Turkey 293, 301, 302, 374
Veal 272-274
Venison 303
Meringue 152
Mexican
    Corn Bread I And II 32, 33
    Dip 400
    Meat Cups 243
    Sauce 410-411
Mile-High Pie 162
Milk
    Apricot Drink 14
    Punch 20
    Shake 20
Milky Way Ice Cream 384
Million-Dollar Pie 162
Millionaire Pie 162
Mincemeat And Oatmeal Pie 163
Mint
    Frozen Lime Mint Salad 309
    Grasshopper Pie 159
    Mississippi Mud Cake 72
    Mixed Fruit Salad 381
    Vegetable Casserole 454
    Vegetable Pickles 357
Mocha
    Cake 73
    Mix, Hot 18
    Punch, Chocolate 14
Mock Boiled Custard 127
Mock Sour Cream Dip 400
Molded Salads, See Congealed Salads
Mama's Chocolate Bread Pudding .127
Mama's Egg Custard 152
Mother Hen Pie 301
Mother's Tea Cakes I And II 197
Mousse, Chocolate 118
Mrs. Bryant's Fruit Cake 79
Muffins
    Apple 33
    Banana 33
    Bran I And II 34
    Brer Rabbit 34

Country Sausage 35
Cream of Wheat 35
Yeast 35
Mushrooms, Pickled 358
Mustard Pickles By Arte 357

N

Neapolitan Cake 98
New England Corn Chowder 416
New Jersey Seafood 342
No-Bake Datenut Rolls 386
No-Bake Three Layer Cookies ... 185
No-Cook Divinity 176
No-Fail Peanut Brittle 179
No-Knead Refrigerator Rolls 49
No Name Cake 112
Nuts Also See Specific Kind
  Breads
    Banana I And II 39
    Cranberry 41
    Soy 54
  Cakes
    Apricot 86
    Banana 87
    Chocolate-Nut Zucchini 71
  Grape-Nut Pudding 124
  Hickory Nut Candy,
    Old-Fashioned 179
  Holiday 404
  Nuts And Bolts Supreme 404
  Nut Torte 132
  Peanuts 154, 179, 193, 385,
  Walnut, Sour Cream Cake 105

O

Oatmeal
  Cookies
    Boiled Oatmeal 189
    Boyfriend 189
    Drops 207
  Meat Loaf 370
  Mincemeat Pie 163
Oceanburgers 343
Okra
  Creole 437
  Pickles I And II 358
Old-Fashioned
  Chocolate Fudge 177
  Egg Custard I And II 153
  Egg Pie 153
  Ginger Squares 207

Hickory Nut Candy 179
Potato Salad 323
String Beans 426
Tea Cakes 197
Old-Time
  Popcorn Balls 371
  Sweet Potato Cobbler 168
Olive Dip 400
Omelet
  French Country 223
  Fresh Vegetable 203
  Ham 263
1-2-3-4
  Cake 99
  Congealed Salad 311
Onion
  Chicken Livers And 374
  Fried Beef Slices With 252
  Smothered Steak 254
  Soup Dip, Low-Calorie 206
  Soup, French 414
Orange
  Cream Trifle 128
  Cakes
    Date 99
    Date, Cleo's 92
    Pound 83
  Mashed Potatoes 437
  Pineapple Punch 21
  Salads
    Cottage Cheese 208
    Jello 311
    Low-Fat 206

P

Pancakes
  Hawaiian 37
  Lean And Light 205
  Peanut-Butter Hotcakes 37
  Potato 37
  Puffy German 38
  Smiling 372
Parmesan
  Chicken 293
  Tomato 382
Party Foods
  Canapes And Appetizers ... 385, 391
  Cheese 391, 396
  Chicken Canapes 385, 386
  Cucumber Sandwiches 386
  Datenut Rolls, No-Bake 386
  Dips 397, 402

Fruit Cake Logs	386	Chocolate-Covered	191
Ham Rolls	387	Rich	192
Hot Ham Buns	387	Cookies	192
Marinated Mushrooms	387	Easy	191
Marinated Shrimp, Mushrooms, And Artichoke Hearts	388	Do-It-Yourself	352
		Fudge	208
Party Chicken Salad	388	Hotcakes	37
Pig In Blankets	388	Reese Cups	180
Popcorn And Nuts	402, 405	Reese Cup Balls	180

Pear

Relish	354
Salad	312
Stuffed	334

Rumaki 389
Party Rye Squares 9
Salmon Ball 389
Sausage 358, 359
Shrimp Tree 389
Soft Pretzels 390
Stuffed Dill Pickles 390
Sweet Sandwich Filling 390
Tuna Roll-Ups 391
Zucchini Appetizer 391

Pastry, Pie Crust
Chocolate Chip Cookie Crust .. 139
Crisco Pie Crust Mix 139
Miniature Cream Cheese Pastry Shell 12
Flaky Pastry 140
Pat-In-The-Pan Pie Crust 140
Perfect Pie Crust 141
Pie Crust 141
Pie Pastry 141

Patio Salad 329
Pauline's Rolls 64

Peas
Casserole 437
Asparagus 423
Quick Green 438

Peaches
For Fried Pies 354
Homemade Ice Cream 137
Potted For Fried Pies 354
Spiced Salad 314
Super Crisp 130
With Bourbon 128

Peanuts
Blossoms 192
Brittle 179, 358
No-Fail 179
Candied 405
Cookies, Salted 193
Pie 154
Spiced Nuts 404

Peanut Butter
Bars
Chewy 190

Pecan
Butterballs 193
Chocolate Torte 119
Crunch 193
Pastries 403
Pie I, II, III And IV 164-165, 170
Cracker 165
Date 166
Deluxe 166
Mystery 171
Surprise Bars 194
Slices 166

Pepper
Jelly 362
Hot 363
Steak I And II 255

Peppermint—See Mint
Perch 'N Taters Bake 343
Peter Paul Mound Cake 73

Pickled
Beets 426
Mushrooms 358
Okra I And II 358

Pickles
Bread And Butter I And II 355
Crisp Cucumber Sticks 356
14-Day Cucumber 356
Dill 356
Mixed Vegetable 357
Mustard By Arte 357
Squash 359
Stuffed Dill 390
Um-m-m 359

Pie
Chocolate
Chess I And II 142
Cream 142
Frozen Cho- 144
Fudge 145, 384
Pie I, II, And III 143

Satin 145
Yogurt 144
Custard, Chess, Lemon Pies/Tarts
  Buttermilk 145
  Buttermilk Coconut 146
  Butterscotch 146
  Caramel 146
  Chess
    I, II, And III 147
    Chewy 147
    Lemon 151
  Coconut 148
    Estelle 149
    French I And II 149
    Gibson's 172
    Impossible 149
    Incredible 150
    Supreme 148
  Custard
    Granny B's Old-Fashioned . 151
    Mama's Egg 152
    Mother's Egg 152
    Old-Fashioned Egg I
      And II 153
    Rachel's Egg 153
    Velvety Lemon Tarts 155
  Egg, Old-Fashioned 153
  Jello 150
  Lazy 151
  Lemonade 151
  My Mama Toney's
    Nut Pie 171
  My Mama Toney's
    Caramel Pie 172
  Peanut 154
  Saratoga Tart 154
  Spice 155
  Toffee Ice Cream 155
  Fruit
    Apple I And II 156
      Fried Apple Pie 170
      Golden Delicious 157
      Sour Cream 157
      Shredded 173
    Blueberry Cheese 157
    Cherry Party 158
    Cobblers
      Jiffy 161
      Peach 163
      Sweet Potato 168
    Company 158
    Grape Juice 159
    Hawaiian 159

Heavenly Fruit 160
Icebox I And II 160
Mac's Sour Cream Raisin ... 161
Marshmallow Torte 161
Mile-High Pie 162
Million-Dollar 162
Millionaire 162
Oatmeal And Mincemeat 163
Pineapple Cream 167
Peach
  Fresh 163
  Quick 164
  Supreme 164
Pecan
  I, II, III, And IV ... 164-165, 170
  Cracker 165
  Date 166
  Deluxe 166
  Slices 166
  Mystery 171
Pinto Bean 167
Pumpkin 167
Strawberry
  Diet 210
  Glazed 168
  Icebox I 160
  Mile-High 162
Sweet Potato
  I And II 169
  Delicious 169
  Thousand Islands 169
Meat
  Chicken 294
    Mother Hen 301
  Hamburger I And II 237-238
Vegetable
  Easy Garden 453
  Squash 448
Pie Crust, See Pastry
Pie Filling
  Apple 353
  Peach 354
Pig-In-Blankets 388
Pimiento
Cheese
  Dip 401
  Spread, Wonda's 396
Pineapple
  Bread 42
  Cake I And II 102
  Cheddar Salad 312
  Cream Pie 167
  Cranberry Squares 313

Index

Upside-Down Cake 103
Pink Arctic Freeze 128
Pistachio
  Cake, Watergate 106
  Salad, Watergate 334
Pizza
  Appetizer Cheese 391
  Breakfast 266
  Easy Sausage 266
  Pizza 243
Plain Corn Bread 65
Planked T-Bone Steak 255
Plantation Green Beans 426
Plum
  Good Cake 100
  Pudding 129
Popcorn
  Balls, Old-Time 371
  Caramel 402
  Cheese 402
  Karo Crazy Crunch 403
Poppy Seed
  Bread 43
  Fruit Salad 333
  Refrigerator Torte 100
Popsicle 372
Porcupine Meatballs 241
Pork
  Bacon 259, 367, 374
  Bar-B-Q 268
  Chops
    Casserole 269
    Mandarin Stuffed 269
    Navy Bean Casserole, And ...269
    Rice, And I And II 270
    Rice, With Amber 270
    Saucey Baked 270
    Spareribs And Kraut 271
    Stuffed 271
    Sweet And Sour 272
  Ham 260-264, 266, 373, 387,
    351, 400
  Hot Dogs ...367, 368, 369, 375, 388
  Liver Stroganoff 376
  Sausage 264-267, 368, 405-406
  Sweet And Sour I And II ...272, 376
Potatoes
  Au Gratin 439
  Casserole 439
  Cheesy Baked 379
  Chip Cookies 194
  Creamy Scalloped 380
  Easy-To-Do Scalloped 438

Poor Man's Hash 439
Orange Mashed 438
Pie, Spinach And 443
Salad
  I And II 323, 324
  Creamy 322
  Old-Fashioned 323
Soup 413
Sour Cream 440
Sweet 385
Tater Tot Casserole 444
Potted Peaches For Pies 354
Poultry
  Chicken, Also See
  Chicken 281, 302
  Cornish Hens 298
  Apricot 281
  Dove 302
  Duck 302
  Quail 302
  Turkey
    Curry 301
    Hot Salad Souffle 302
Pound Cake, See Cakes, Pound
Praline
  Chris's Butterscotch 173
  Southern 385
  White 181
Preserves, Also See Jelly
  Beet Jelly, Red 360
  Fig
    Jam 353
    Honey Cake 94
    Strawberry Preserves 353
  Jam Cakes 80
  Pear Relish 354
  Pepper Jelly 362
  Strawberry I And II 354, 355
Pretzels
  Chocolate Coated 10
  Salad 313
  Soft 390
Prize-Winning Cookies 199
Prize-Winning Meat Loaf 242
Prune Cake 101
Pudding
  Bakeless 116
  Banana 116
  Bread
    I And II 117
    Chocolate, Mama's 127
    Fresh Apple 383
    Chocolate 382

Index

Cookies 209
Corn 434
Graham Cracker 123
Grape-Nut 124
Icebox 125
My Mama Toney's
   Carrot Pudding 134
Old Fashioned Bread Pudding
   With Rum Sauce 133
Texas Delight 131
Pumpkin
Bread I, II, And III 43, 44
Cake 111
Pie 167
Punch
Party I And II 21
Pink 372
Pink Party 22
Purple Cow 372

Q

Quiche
Cheesy Sausage 265
Lorraine 225
Quiche 225
Sausage 266
Supreme 225
Quick Breads, See Breads, Quick
Quick
Chocolate Syrup Cake 74
Easy Jam Cake, And 80
'N Easy Salmon Patties 343
Peach Pie 164
Sure Fudge 177
Quickie Doughnuts 59

R

Rachel's Egg Custard 153
Ragu Beef Casserole 244
Raisin Bread 44
Raisin Casserole Bread 53
Randy's Chocolate Cookie
   Sheet Cake 74
Ratatouille 444
"Recital Punch" 22
Red Apple Salad 209
Red Beet Jelly 360
Red Cabbage 430
Red Velvet Pound Cake 84
Reese Cup Balls 180

Reese Peanut Butter Cups 180
Refrigerator Coconut Cake, Easy ... 76
Refrigerator Torte, Poppy Seed ... 100
Restaurant Dressing 411
Rice
Carrot Ring, And 432
Casserole 441
For Fowl 441
Rice Krispie Cheese Ball 10
Salad 324
Spanish 442
Rich Peanut Butter Bars 192
Robbie's Crab And Shrimp
   Casserole 344
Rolled Steaks 256
Rolls 62, 61, 46-51
Roquefort Dressing 335
Rosy Punch 23
Ruby Fruit Punch 23
Rumaki 389
Rushing Stew 244
Russian
Pie 430
Tea I And II 23
Tea Cookies 198
Tea Punch 24
Rye Sandwich 9

S

Salads
Congealed 305, 315
Diet 202
   Chicken 201
   Low-Calorie Waldorf 206
   Low-Fat Orange 206
   Red Apple 209
   Sauerkraut 209
Fruit
   Carrot Marshmallow 330
   Curried Casserole 330
   Cherry 330
   Fast And Easy 331
   Five Cup 202
   Frozen 332
      Cherry 331
      Cranberry 331
      Cups 332
      Pink 332
   Fruit I And II 332, 333
   Heavenly 333
   Poppy Seed 333

Index

Stuffed Pears 334
Watergate 334
White 334
With Sauce 333
Green
  Dainty Winter 317
  Kraut 317
  Lettuce 317
  Santa Maria 318
  Sauerkraut 318
  Seven-Layer 319
  Slaw
    Cabbage 315
    Chinese 316
    Cole 316
    Lula's Freezer 318
Meat And Seafood
  Chicken 327
    Bride's 283
    Hot I And II 328, 329
  Corn Beef 328
  Crab, Tasty Hot 329
  Hot Turkey Souffle 302
  Man-Sized Steak 253
  Meat 254
  Patio 329
  Tuna 329
    Hearty 328
Vegetable
  I And II 327
  Bean And Bacon 319
  Broccoli I And II 319, 320
  Carrot Marshmallow 330
  Corn I And II 320
  Evelyn's Artichokes 321
  Extra Bean 321
  Guacamole 322
  Marinated 322
  Overnight 323
  Potato
    I And II 323, 324
    Creamy 321
    Old-Fashioned 323
  Rice 324
  Scandanavian 325
  Spinach 325
    Jean'a 325
  Tabouli 326
  Tomato 326
    Marinated 322
  24-Hour Bean 326
Salad Dressings
  Blue Cheese 335

Danny's Italian 335
  Restaurant 411
Roquefort 335
Salad 335
Salmon—See Seafood
Salted Peanut Cookies 193
Saratoga Tart 154
Sauce
  Barbeque 409
    White, For Chicken 410
  For Brussels Sprouts 429
  Mexican 410
  Sour Cream And Relish 411
  Spaghetti 245
  Speedy-Do Cherry 411
  Tomato 362
Sauerbraten 256
Sauerkraut 431
Sausage
  Ball 9
  Balls 405
    Cheese 405
  Bites, Glazed 405
  Breakfast Before 368
  Casserole
    Hot Link 267
    Rice 267
  Lasagna I And II 264, 265
  Pinwheels 406
  Pizza 266
  Quiche 266
    Cheesy 265
  Rolls 406
  Sandwiches, Sun City Party 406
Scalloped Corn 435
Seafood
  Combinations
    New Jersey Seafood 342
    Robbie's Crab And Shrimp
      Casserole 344
    Seafood Quiche 347
  Crab
    Deviled 342
    Dip 397
    Salad, Tasty Hot 329
  Fish
    Oceanburgers 343
    Perch 'N Tater Bake 343
    Puffs 342
    Salmon
      Ball 389
      Casserole, Flake 344
      Loaf 344

Index

Patties, Quick N' Easy 343
Tuna
   Log 349
   Roll 349
   Salad 328, 329
   Spoonlets 349
Oysters
   Escalloped I And II 345
   Stew, Holiday 416
Shrimp
   Boiled 346
   Creole 347
   De Jonghe 348
   French-Fried 346
   Hot Dip 399
   Mosca 348
   Sandwiches 9
   Tree 389
   Wriggle 348
Season Salt 411
Self-Filling Cupcakes 104
Seven-Up
   Cake 104
   Surprise Punch 24
Shepherd's Pie 244
Sherried Beef 256
Shingles or Bark Candy 198
Shrimp Tree 389
Sliced Cucumbers For Freezer 362
Skillet Cabbage 210
Skillet Cookies 195
Small Fruit Cake 79
Smiling Pancakes 372
Snickerdoodles 195
Snippy Doodle Coffee Cake 104
Soup
   Creamy Potato 413
   Easy Gourmet 413
   French Onion 414
   Greek "Egg" Lemon 414
   Senate Bean 417
   Texas Beef 417
   V-8 418
Sour Cream
   Apple Pie 157
   Potatoes 440
   Pound Cake 85
   Relish Sauce, And 411
   Vegetable Dip 401
   Walnut Cake 105
Sourdough Biscuits 28
   Starter 29
Southern Beef Roll 245

Southern Pralines 385
Soy Nut Bread 54
Spaghetti
   Chicken 295
   Sauce 245
   Squash 381
Spanish
   Delight Casserole 246
   Egg Supreme 226
   Rice 442
   Pronto 246
Speedy-Do Cherry Sauce 411
Spice Pie 155
Spiced
   Nuts 404
   Zucchini Bread 44
Spinach
   Balls 443
   Cottage Cheese Cup 12
   Casserole 443
   Dip 401
   Potato Pie 443
   Spoon Bread 45
   Rolls 50
Spry Sugar Cookies 196
Squash
   Yellow
      Balls 445
      Butternut Cake 88
      Candied Summer 444
      Casserole 445, 449
      Croquettes 447
      Fresh 444
      Hushpuppies 447
      Pickles 359
      Scalloped 445
   Zucchini
      Casserole 448, 449
      Tomato 449
      Pie 448
      Ratatouille 444
Staff Of Life Bread 55
Steak
   Casserole 256
   Onion-Smothered 254
   Pepper I And II 255
   Planked 255
   Roll-Up, Flank 252
   Rolled 256
   Salad, Man-Sized 253
   Swiss 377
Steamed Cabbage 381

Index

Stew
  Brunswick 412
  Five-Hour 414
  Hog's Head 363
  Holiday Oyster 416
  Hunter's 239
Strawberry
  Balls 403
  Bread 45
  Cake 106
  Delight 129
  Fig Preserves 353
  Frost 121
  Ice Cream 138
  Jam I And II 354, 355
  Pie 210
Soda Pop Cake 110
Stroganoff, Beef 373
  I And II 249
  Casserole, Easy 235
Stuffed Beef Rolls 246
Stuffed Dill Pickles 390
Stuffing, Bread 412
Substitutions And Special Tips ... 464
Sugar Cookies 196
Sugar Plum Pudding 129
Sugarless Pound Cake 210
Summertime Ice Tea 24
Sunshine Salad 211
Sukiyaki 257
Super Peach Crisp 130
Super Supper 247
Surprise Chocolate Cake 211
Susan's Refrigerator Rolls .. 50
Sweet Potatoes
  Bake 451
  Bumpus 450
  Candied 450
  Casserole I And II ... 451, 452
  Hawaiian Yams 451
  Pie I And II 169
  Pudding 450, 452
Sweet Rolls And Doughnuts ... 57-60
Sweet Sandwich Filling 390
Sweet And Sour
  Carrots 433
  Pork I And II 272, 376
Sweetened Condensed Milk 412
Swiss Steak 377

T

Tabouli 326
Taco Dip 11
Tamale Balls, Hot 239
Tasty Hot Crab Salad 329
Tea
  Hot Mix 19
  Hot Spice 19
  Instant Russian I And II .. 19
  Russian Punch 24
Tea Cakes, Cookies 196-198
Teresa's Chicken I Sour
  Cream Sauce 301
Texas
  Beef Loaf 247
  Delight Dessert 131
  Hash 248
Thousand Islands Pie 169
Toast, Garlic 29
Toffee, Ice Cream Pie 155
Tomato(es)
  Au Gratin 453
  Baked 450
  Juice Cocktail 25
  Parmesan 382
  Relish 362
  Salad 326
  Sauce 362
Tuna
  Fish Salad 329
  Log 349
  Roll 349
  Roll-Ups 391
  Spoonlets 349
Tunnel-Of-Fudge Cake 75
Turkey
  Curry 301
  Salad Souffle 302
Two-Bean Bake 248
Two-Tone Rye Twist 55

U

Un-m-m Pickles 359

V

V-8 Soup 418
Vanilla Ice Cream I And II .. 138
Veal
  Cutlets 272
  Parmesan 273
  Scallapini Alla Cacciatorie ... 274
Veg-All Casserole 454

Index

Vegetable
  Casserole 454, 455
  Dip 398
    I And II 401, 402
    Dill 398
  Marinated 454
  Omelet, Fresh 203
  Pickles, Mixed 357
  Pie, Easy Garden 453
  Salad
    I And II 327
    Overnight 323
    Stir-Fry 454
Velvety Lemon Tarts 155
Venison
  Hog's Head Stew 363
  Roast 303
  Swiss Steak 303
Vermont Apple Cake 69
Vodka Punch 22

W

Wadis Cheese Ball 11
Wafers, 2-Grain 31
Waffles, Heloise 62
Waldorf Salad, Low-Calorie ... 206
Walnut, Sour Cream Cake 105
War Tack 136
Watergate Cake 106
Watergate Salad 334
Wieners, Also See Hot Dogs
  Barbecued 367
Western Mac Casserole 248
Wheat
  Cracked
    Bread 52
  Whole
    Bread I And II 56, 57
    Yeast Rolls I And II .. 50, 51
White BBQ Sauce For Chicken .. 410
White Cake 106
White Fruit Cake 79, 114
White Pound Cake 85
White Pralines 181
White Salad 334
Wonda's Pimiento Cheese
  Spread 396

Y

Yeast
  Breads
    Brown Yeast Bread 51
    Cheese Bread 52
    Cracked Wheat Bread 52
    Dilly Bread 53
    Irish Bread 53
    Raisin Casserole Bread 53
    Soy Nut Bread 54
    Staff-Of-Life Bread 54
    Two-Tone Rye Twist 55
    Whole Wheat Bread I
      And II 56, 57
  Chocolate Yeast Cake 72
  Muffins 35
  Rolls 48, 51
    Sweet 60
    Whole Wheat I And II ... 50, 51
Yellow Angel Food Cake ... 107, 111
Yogurt Pie, Chocolate 144
Yummy Ice Cream Dessert 139
Yum Yum Salad 315

Z

Zucchini
  Appetizer 391
  Bread I And II 45, 46
  Bread, Spiced 44
  Cake, Chocolate-Nut 71
  Casserole 448
  Squash 448
  Squash Casserole 449
  Tomato Casserole 449